GCSE
Business Studies
Third Edition
Edexcel

Alain Anderton
with Rob Jones

Cover design by Tim Button
Cover illustration provided by Getty Images
Graphics by Kevin O'Brien
Cartoons by Alan Fraser
Photography by Andrew Allen
Page design by Caroline Waring-Collins
Edited by Dave Gray
Proof reading by Mike Kidson, Heather Doyle, Sue Oliver and
Sheila Evans-Pritchard

British Library Cataloguing in Publication Data
A catalogue record for this book is available from the British
Library.

ISBN 978-1-4058-6449-7

Pearson Education
Edinburgh Gate, Harlow, Essex, CM20 2JE
Contribution © Alain Anderton, Rob Jones
First edition 1995 (reprinted 3 times)
Second edition 1998 (reprinted 7 times)
Third edition 2007

Design, page origination and production by Caroline Waring-
Collins, Tim Button and Derek Baker.
Printed and bound by Scotprint, Haddington, Scotland.

Acknowledgements
The publishers and the author would like to thank the
following for materials and photographs used in the production of
this book.

Amazon, Argos, AstraZeneca, BBC, Betfair, BP, Cadbury
Schweppes, Countrywide Signs, Co-operative Union Limited,
Crown Cork & Seal, Direct Line, Enamore, Europe by Net,
Fitzgerald Lighting, GallifordTry, GSM Group, Hanson, Henderson
Group, innocent, iPrint, IPT Group, JVC, Lara Nichols, Levis
Strauss & Co, McBride, Melrose Resources, Nichols plc, Nokia,
Office Angels, Power Technology Solutions, Prontaprint, Rover
Group, Royal Dutch Shell, Scotsman Beverage Systems,
Smallbone plc, Sports Direct, Stagecoach plc, Sytner Group,
Tate & Lyle, Total Jobs, T&G, Ugo Foods Group, Vodafone
Group, Wensleydale Foods, Young's Bluecrest.
All other sources are acknowledged where information appears
in the book.

Photographs provided by:
Corel pp 40, 109, **Digitalvision** pp 25, 45, 57, 80, 82, 83, 93, 97,
101, 107, 110, 112, 115, 118, 119, 123, 128, 132, 134, 138, 157,
176, 193, 221, **Digital Stock** pp 13, 92, 98, 130, 132, 142, **Image
100** pp 96, 100, 114, 119, 122, 134, 148, **Rex Features** pp 9, 12,
24, 26, 51, 95, 215, **Photodisc** pp 8, 13, 18, 30, 45, 54, 77, 94,
104, 117, 121, 131, 132, 133, 143, 150, 154, 156, 179, 193,
Shutterstock pp 13, 14, 33, 37, 38, 39, 42, 45, 56, 60, 85, 142,
156, 164, 165, 174, 188, 190, 193, 200, 208, 209, 217, 219, 223,
226, **Stockbyte** pp 93, 94, 179, **Stockdisc** pp 6, 88, 93, 141,
Topfoto pp 12, 14, 46, 48, 54.

A source is given at the end of each unit. This shows the source
of the information on which the unit is based **or** that a business
has approved the material in the unit relating to its activities.
Units that do not contain a source have been based on real
business operations.

PREFACE

GCSE Business Studies (third edition) is
designed to be used as a core textbook for GCSE
Business Studies courses. It has been designed in
full colour to give candidates a distinctive and unique
resource for use in the classroom.

The book has a number of key features

Comprehensive The Edexcel version of **GCSE
Business Studies (third edition)** provides
comprehensive coverage of the Edexcel GCSE
Business Studies specification.

Unit structure The material has been organised
into two or four page units. Each unit contains text, a
section which outlines some of the key decisions
which businesses have to make, data questions and
case studies, research exercises, short answer
questions and definitions of key terms.

Case study based Each unit uses a business or an
industry to illustrate the text. This case study
approach is followed through with a large number of
other case studies in the unit with questions attached.

ActiveBook An ActiveBook version of
GCSE Business Studies (third edition) is
enclosed. This provides the book on CD and includes
features such as zoom areas and accessing key terms.

I would like thank Dave Gray, who as usual has done
a superb job editing the book. Peter Chapman and
Diane Wallace gave invaluable feedback in the
planning of the book. The page origination of the
book was sensitively accomplished by Caroline
Waring-Collins. Not least I would like to thank my wife
for all her help with the project.
The author and Causeway Press would welcome any
comments you have to make about the book, whether
critical or otherwise. We hope it will greatly help you
in your teaching or learning of Business Studies.

Alain Anderton

CONTENTS

Making decisions

People in business constantly have to make decisions. Businesses produce goods and services to satisfy the needs and wants of consumers. They have to decide:

- what goods and services will be produced;
- what resources, like raw materials and workers, are needed for production.

Do you eat sugar? Do you buy magazines? Are your clothes washed? Do you travel in a car? Do you brush your teeth? One company, Tate & Lyle, makes ingredients which go into the making of all of these products. So what makes a business?

What is a business?

A BUSINESS is an organisation which produces GOODS or SERVICES. Tate & Lyle makes a wide range of PRODUCTS. Other businesses make products too. For instance, Coca Cola makes drinks. BT provides telephone services. McDonald's produces fast food. Barnados provides child care services.

Some businesses like Tate & Lyle are large. Tate & Lyle, although UK based, owns companies across the world. It sells its products worldwide too. In the financial year 2006, its sales were worth over £3.7bn. It employed thousands of workers across the globe. Most businesses, however, are small, like the local butcher or hairdresser. Their sales might be measured in tens of thousands of pounds rather than billions. They might employ just a few workers, or the owner of the business might be its only worker.

Tate & Lyle is a **private sector** business. This means that it is not owned by government. Charities

1 What goods and services do each of the businesses shown here produce? Write down as many as you can.

Workers
(LABOUR)

A factory
(CAPITAL)

Machinery (CAPITAL)

Raw materials (LAND)

Figure 1 *Factors of production used by Tate & Lyle*

Services are non-physical products like hairdressing.

Goods are physical products like sugar.

like Barnados are private sector businesses too. The business organisations owned and run by government, like the National Health Service or the Royal Navy, are in the **public sector** of the economy.

Most private sector businesses, like Tate & Lyle, aim to make a **profit**. Other business organisations, like Barnados or the National Health Service Trusts, aim only to cover their costs and have other **objectives**, such as providing high quality care for people.

Production

To produce anything, a business has to use resources. Tate & Lyle granulated sugar, for instance, is made from sugar cane, a RAW MATERIAL (all raw materials are sometimes called LAND in Business Studies). Most of what Tate & Lyle produces is sold to other manufacturers for use in their products. For example, Tate &

Lyle sells natural and artificial sweeteners to companies like Cadbury Schweppes for use in a wide variety of food and drinks products. Products made by one business and sold to another are called PRODUCER GOODS. Tate & Lyle workers (or LABOUR) make products in over 65 production facilities throughout the world. These production facilities and the machinery in them (called CAPITAL or CAPITAL GOODS) are also essential to the production process.

Land, labour and capital are called the FACTORS OF PRODUCTION. They are the resources used in the production process.

Selling the product

Simply making products isn't enough for Tate & Lyle. It will only survive as a business if it can find CUSTOMERS for these products. Most of Tate & Lyle's 6 000 customers are other manufacturing

Mobile phones

Nokia is the world's largest manufacturer of mobile phones. In 2006, it sold almost twice as many phones as its nearest rival, Motorola. Nokia sells its phones mainly to mobile phone network companies such as Vodafone or Orange, distributors and retailers like Carphone Warehouse and large business customers. It is constantly changing its product range. This is because new technology is making mobile phones more and more powerful and adaptable. It also has to keep pace with changes in fashion in mobile phones. In 2006, Nokia manufactured one in every three mobile phones sold worldwide. It wants to increase this to 40 per cent, or four in ten manufactured worldwide.

Source: adapted from www.nokia.com; news.bbc.co.uk 28 February 2006.

1 Who are the customers of Nokia for mobile phones?
2 Consumers buy products to satisfy their 'wants'. What 'wants' do you think a mobile phone will satisfy?
3 Suggest THREE ways in which Nokia could increase its sales relative to all other producers.

companies. They use Tate & Lyle products as raw materials to make their own products.

However, some customers are other businesses like supermarket chains Sainsbury's or Tesco which buy finished products from Tate & Lyle like Lyle's Golden Syrup. This is an example of a CONSUMER GOOD, a product which is bought by CONSUMERS, ordinary people who use the product.

Why consume?

Why do people buy sugar or any of the other products that Tate & Lyle makes? Consumers have NEEDS. These are the things people must consume to survive.

People need food, drink, shelter, warmth and clothes. Eating sugar could satisfy people's need for food.

Needs are part of people's broader WANTS. Wants are people's desires to consume all goods and services, not just those products needed for basic survival. There seems to be no limit to how much people want to consume. In the rich countries of the world, such as the UK, people are not just buying more but also increasing the quality of what they are buying. Tate & Lyle has to cope with this changing demand. For instance, people in Britain are eating less sugar than before but using more artificial sweeteners.

The business environment

Businesses have to operate in a harsh environment. If their products don't sell, they are likely to go out of business. Even if they have successful products at the moment, their competitors might launch better products onto the market in future. The government might affect businesses too by passing laws which restrict what they can do. For instance, there might be restrictions on the ingredients a food business like Tate & Lyle uses in its products.

Successful long term businesses, like Tate & Lyle, are businesses which find solutions to these problems. Over a period of time they continue to provide products which appeal to their customers. They adapt how they operate to conform to government regulations and laws. They motivate their workers to produce as high quality goods as possible within cost budgets.

Source: information from Tate & Lyle.

You have organised yourself into a mini-company. EITHER answer the following questions for the business idea which you have chosen OR assume you have decided to make washing cars your business activity.
1 Make a list of all the resources your business will have to use to provide this service.
2 Find out how: (a) a local garage; and (b) a local valeting service cleans cars. How do they differ from you in the resources they use?
3 How would you decide whether your business has been a success?

Assume that each member of your class or teaching group could spend up to £30 on one item. It could be a computer game, a trip to the bowling alley, or a new pair of jeans, for instance.

1 Survey ten or more people in your class and find out what they would spend the money on.

Name of product	Hit Hat
Name of producer	Nestlé
Good or service	Good
Want satisfied	Hunger
Where bought	Tesco
Name of product	////////
Name of producer	////////
Good or service	////////
Want satisfied	////////
Where bought	////////
Name of product	////////
Name of producer	////////
Good or service	////////
Want satisfied	////////
Where bought	////////

Figure 2

Database

2 Produce a database from your findings. The diagram will help you. The database should include:
(a) the name of the product bought;
(b) the name of the business which produced the product;
(c) whether it was a good or a service;
(d) the want which you think the product satisfies (e.g. food, transport, entertainment);
(e) a business where the product might be bought (e.g. a DVD produced by Sony might be bought at HMV. In the case of a service, like a trip to a bowling alley, the business both produces the service and sells it.)

3 Describe your findings, using graphs where appropriate. For instance, were people buying very similar products or were they very different? Were they buying similar products but from different businesses?

key terms

Business - an organisation which produces goods and services.

Capital goods - physical goods used to produce other producer and consumer goods and services.

Consumer - the person who ultimately uses (or consumes) a product.

Consumer goods - goods and services which are sold to people (consumers) rather than other businesses.

Customer - any person or organisation which buys or is supplied with a product by a business.

Factors of production - land (natural resources), labour (workers) and capital (defined above in capital goods) used in the production process.

Goods - physical products, like a car or a cabbage.

Labour - workers used in the production process.

Land - natural resources used in production process.

Needs - the basic products that people need in order to survive: food, drink, shelter, warmth and clothing.

Producer goods - goods which are sold by one business to another and which are then used to produce other goods and services.

Products - goods made or services provided by businesses.

Raw materials - natural resources, like copper or coffee beans, used to make products.

Services - non-physical products, like a haircut or a train journey.

Wants - the desire to consume goods and services. Wants are unlimited because there is no limit to the amount of goods and services people would like to consume.

SUMMARY CASE STUDY

STAGECOACH PLC

Stagecoach is an international company with operations in the UK and North America. It runs 12 000 buses, coaches, trains and trams and employs 27 000 workers.

Source: adapted from www.stagecoach.com.

1 What business activity operated by Stagecoach is shown in the photographs?
2 Who are the customers of the business?
3 What factors of production are used in the business?
4 Suggest THREE ways in which Stagecoach could make the business more successful.

Checklist ✓

1 What is a business?
2 'British Gas is a private sector business.' What does this mean?
3 What resources do you think are needed to make a McDonald's hamburger?
4 What are the THREE factors of production?
5 What is the difference between a customer and a consumer?
6 Here is a list of products: a tin of baked beans, a shop counter, a washing machine, a pair of jeans, a factory, an industrial sewing machine, a cup and saucer, a fork lift truck.
Explain which of these are: (a) consumer goods; and (b) producer goods.
7 What are a person's basic needs?
8 What is the difference between a need and a want?

Making decisions

Businesses operate in markets. They have to decide what they are going to sell to their customers and how they are going to organise production. The market then gives its verdict. If the business is providing a product that customers want, it may make sales and, more importantly, make a profit if the price is right. If customers don't buy enough or pay enough, the business will make a loss. Profits and losses are the sign for businesses to expand or cut back production. Businesses which fail to respond to the market and don't provide what their customers want in the long term are likely to go out of business. Businesses have to respond to the market if they are to survive.

Royal Dutch Shell plc is one of the world's largest companies. It operates in over 140 countries and employs approximately 109 000 people. Shell is an energy company, best known for selling oil and petrol. But it also sells other forms of energy such as gas, biofuels from plants and electricity from wind farms, and is major manufacturer of chemicals made from oil.

Markets

Shell has to operate in the **market place**. When the word MARKET is used, most people think of a street market where there are numerous stalls with traders selling everything from food to clothes to furniture. Consumers wander round the market buying the products. In business studies, the word 'market' is used more widely. It exists in any situation where buyers and sellers exchange goods and services.

1 What is being bought and sold in each of the markets shown in the photographs?
2 Who are the likely buyers and who are the likely sellers in each market?
3 Is the market shown in each photograph a local market, a national market or an international market?

DTP
4 With a small group of friends, you decide to set up a business.
(a) What market could you realistically enter? (e.g. you could sell stationery to other people in your school or college but you couldn't set up as an international car manufacturer).
(b) Design an advertising poster about your business, showing the product that you are selling and who are the potential customers for your product. You could use a desktop publishing package to do this.

1 Explain how prices will be fixed in each of the three cases shown in the illustrations.

Mobile phones
OFFERED

Lobster 585 *pink camera phone, good condition, boxed with new sim card,* **£30 ovno.**

Motorola V220 *colour screen, photo messaging, camera, games, personal hands free kit, charger, user guides, all boxed, perfect working order and condition, easy to use, ideal camera phone, Orange network,* **£75 ovno.**

Nokia 6600, *great phone and lots of functions, all networks,* **£50.**

Samsung D900, *2 of, good as new, open to all networks, come with all accessories,* **£300 ono.**

Samsung D600, *excellent condition, including all accessories sim free and open to all networks, black, in its original box,* **£90 no offers.**

Sony Ericsson W810i, *black with 512mb memory duo stick, mint condition, good for present,* **£150.**

Different types of markets

There is a wide variety of markets. The local street market is one. Another is the local market for fuel, where local garages, such as those owned by Shell, sell fuel to local customers. There is a national market for fuel where producers, such as Shell, sell fuel to other companies who in turn supply garages up and down the country. There is also an international market for crude oil. Oil producing companies, like Shell, refine oil and sell products directly to consumers. They also sell oil to other oil companies for transport, refining and processing. Oil is then refined and sold on as fuel to consumers in national markets.

In some markets, buyers and sellers meet face to face. This is true on a garage forecourt for instance. In other markets, buying and selling might be done over the telephone. Shell, for instance, might sell a tanker of crude oil to another oil company in a telephone deal. Buying and selling might also be done through the post, by fax or over the internet. Buying by mail order is an example of this.

Fixing the price

In some markets, the price of a product is determined by the seller. For instance, a Shell garage sets a price for a litre of petrol. Motorists either accept the price and buy or go elsewhere for their petrol.

In other markets, buyers and sellers might haggle over or negotiate a price. In the international market for crude oil, companies will negotiate the price of each deal made. The eventual price agreed is usually somewhere between the seller's original price and what the buyer first offered.

In an auction, buyers compete amongst themselves, bidding up the price until one buyer is left. However, the seller is not legally bound to accept the bid if it is less than the reserve price - a minimum price that the seller has decided upon before the auction starts. If the bid price doesn't reach the reserve price, the sale does not go through.

Opportunity cost

Prices provide an easy way for a business like Shell to calculate OPPORTUNITY COST. This is the benefit lost when making a decision about how best to allocate resources. For instance, Shell

At shell petrol stations buyers and sellers meet face to face.

Wensleydale Foods

Elizabeth Guy set up her company, Wensleydale Foods, a year ago. Based in North Yorkshire, it sells mashed potato-topped pies and a range of puddings, such as lemon curd and sticky toffee. Only the best, local produce is used to produce these frozen ready meals. For £2.95, a customer can buy a Squeaky Lamb Pie which would serve two children containing locally reared lamb, carrots, onions, cabbage and mashed potato. The target market is parents buying pre-prepared food for their children but the company has found that adults too are eating the meals.

Elizabeth Guy didn't have the money or time initially to market her products both at the trade and at consumers. She chose to spend the first six months targeting speciality food fairs, retailers and the trade press. As a result, her products began to be stocked by independent food shops. Budgens, the supermarket chain, also agreed to sell her products. The next six months were spent targeting consumers, by going to fairs and contacting the consumer press. A web site has also been set up which allows consumers to order products online.

Source: adapted from *The Sunday Times*, 10.9.2006; www.wensleydalefoods.co.uk

1 (a) Explain what is meant by opportunity cost. (b) 'In the first six months, the opportunity cost for Elizabeth Guy of marketing to the trade was marketing to consumers.' Explain what this means.

2 Suggest why customers are prepared to pay £2.95 for a Squeaky Lamb Pie when they could buy 4 economy sausages, a tin of baked beans and two portions of oven ready chips for 95p.

might decide to buy a new petrol station. The opportunity cost is then the benefit lost from not being able to buy the same priced petrol station on a different site.

Businesses are constantly having to make opportunity cost decisions. They have to decide how to allocate their scarce resources between different uses. For the same price, what would have to be given up if a computer was bought, or certain offices were rented, or a particular worker was employed?

Market forces

The market is very powerful. This is because it allocates so many resources in the world today. The market is like a vast voting machine with buyers and sellers being the MARKET FORCES which determine what is bought and what is produced.

Buyers Buyers have money to spend. They choose which products they want to buy from the millions on offer from sellers. For

instance, an ordinary family will perhaps buy 500 different items per week. Each time the family buys one of these products, it is casting a spending vote. Each week, the number of spending votes cast by buyers in the UK runs into billions.

Sellers Producers need those votes in order to survive. Shell would go out of business if nobody bought its products. On the other hand, if motorists bought 20 per cent more fuel from Shell petrol stations this year, then Shell would almost certainly receive a large reward - an increase in profits.

Profit is essential to the working of the market system. A business will tend to stop making a product if it can't make a profit. Big profits will encourage more production. Profit is what makes a petroleum company decide whether or not to develop a new oil field or buy a new tanker.

The market for fuel is a **competitive market**. This is where there is a number of businesses,

such as BP, Texaco and Shell, which compete for supplies or customers. In a competitive market, businesses have to find ways of attracting customers who might otherwise buy from other businesses. They can do this by offering low prices, or a better product, or a better service for example. Ways in which businesses compete are explained in more detail in the section of this book on marketing and the '4Ps'.

Many markets are not so competitive. At one extreme, some businesses are **monopolists**, the only sellers of a product to a group of customers. In the UK, for instance, households have no choice about where to buy their water. The local water company, like Thames or Severn Trent, is a monopoly seller. The more a business can control a market, the less power its customers will have. This gives the business more of an opportunity to make profits.

Source: information from Royal Dutch Shell.

Beautiful Vending

Women sometimes spend a long time in the toilets of pubs and night clubs. Two Scottish entrepreneurs saw a business opportunity here and set up a company, Beautiful Vending. They came up with the idea of a wall-mounted vending machine that rented the use of a pair of ceramic styling tongs. These tongs can be used to straighten hair, which is all the fashion at the moment.

The company installs the machines and charges customers £1 for 90 seconds of use of the tongs. Club and bar owners are paid a percentage of this in return for allowing the machines to be located on their premises.

Neil McKay, one of the owners of the company, says he was 'amazed' at the uptake among women on nights out.

Source: adapted from *The Financial Times*, 23.9.2006.

1 Who are Beautiful Vending's customers?
2 (a) What is meant by a 'monopoly'? (b) 'For women in a night club toilet, Beautiful Vending is a monopoly supplier of tongs.' Explain what this means.
3 Discuss whether charging £1 for 90 seconds use of tongs is too high or too low a price.

key terms

Market - where buyers and sellers meet to exchange goods and services.
Market forces - the forces of buying (or demand) and selling (or supply) which determine price and quantity bought and sold in a market.
Opportunity cost - the benefit lost from the next best alternative when making a choice.

SUMMARY CASE STUDY

SCOTSMAN BEVERAGE SYSTEMS

Scotsman Beverage Systems manufactures drink cooling and dispensing equipment. If you go into a pub, there is a good chance that the equipment used to pull your pint of beer will have been made by the company. The equipment to cool lager or soft drinks to just the right temperature could also have been made by Scotsman Beverage Systems.

Based in Halesowen in the West Midlands, the company supplies local companies like Wolverhampton & Dudley Breweries, as well as national and international brewery chains like Scottish Courage and Carlsberg. One recent major contract has been to supply a new font for the world famous Czech beer, Pilsner Urquell. The font, which forms part of the bar display in a pub, features a slender, gold coloured, satin finish, condensating body with a floating Pilsner Urquell brand flag above. 2 000 fonts were initially ordered and installed in a range of export markets including Hungary, Poland, Italy, Germany, Russia, the Canary Islands and South Africa as well as in the UK.

Scotsman Beverage Systems faces strong competition from other suppliers of equipment in Europe. To maintain a competitive edge, it has been investing heavily. Over the past few years, £5 million has been ploughed into the company, most of that to upgrade the factory and equipment in Halesowen. The investment seems to be paying off. Sales are growing strongly and the company is optimistic about the future.

Source: adapted from the *Express & Star*, 26.9.2005; www.scot-bev.com.

1 'Scotsman Beverage Systems sells in local markets, national markets and international markets.' Explain what this means.
2 What might be the opportunity cost for Scotsman Beverage Systems of spending millions of pounds upgrading its factory facility in Halesowen ?
3 How might Scotsman Beverage Systems compete in its market?

Checklist ✓

1 In any market there are two groups. (a) Who are they and (b) what do they do in the market place?
2 The oil market is a market. Give FIVE other examples of markets.
3 Give an example of a business which operates: (a) in your local market selling bread; (b) in the national market selling cars; (c) in the international market buying coffee beans.
4 Who decides what price is fixed: (a) in a supermarket; (b) when a house is bought; (c) at a cattle auction; (d) when a car is serviced; (e) when a car is bought second hand?
5 A business spends £10 000 on Xerox photocopiers. What might be the opportunity cost of this decision for the business? In your answer, give THREE possible examples.
6 How are producers rewarded in a market system when they sell products which consumers want to buy?
7 Explain what happens to businesses which fail to supply goods that consumers want to buy.

Making decisions

Businesses choose to make a particular range of products. Some businesses are involved in primary production, but most businesses either make manufactured products or supply services. The changing structure of the economy provides businesses with opportunities and threats. The growth in demand for services, for instance, may allow new businesses to set up.

Yum! is a US company which specialises in quick-service restaurants. Among the brands that it owns are Pizza Hut and KFC. These brands can be found across the world including the UK. Pizza Hut is a restaurant chain which specialises in selling pizzas, either for consumption in one of its restaurants, or for takeaway. There are over 650 Pizza Hut restaurants just in the UK.

A *Diamond mining*

B *Polishing diamonds*

C *Selling jewellery*

1 Describe what is being produced in each of the photographs.
2 What industry (primary, secondary or tertiary) is shown in: (a) photograph A; (b) photograph B; (c) photograph C?
3 How might the following affect businesses in the diamond industry: (a) a rise in the world price of diamonds; (b) an increase in the UK in VAT (a tax) on jewellery; (c) the discovery of large new diamond reserves; (d) an increase in the wages of diamond mining workers in South Africa?

Primary, secondary and tertiary industry

The food ingredients used by Pizza Hut and KFC in their products are first grown or reared on farms. These include wheat, tomatoes and milk for cheese used to make pizzas or chicken used in KFC products. Farming is part of PRIMARY INDUSTRY, where raw materials are extracted, grown or cut down. Fishing, mining and oil extraction are also examples of primary production.

These raw materials are then processed by SECONDARY or MANUFACTURING INDUSTRY. In secondary industry raw materials are turned into manufactured goods. The products that Pizza Hut sells are made by secondary industry. They include food such as desserts and drinks sold in restaurants. Pizza Hut will also buy tables, plates and cash tills for its restaurants. Cars that deliver takeaway pizzas are also produced in the secondary sector.

Ingredients   **Production of pizzas**   **Sales to consumers**

Figure 1 *A chain of production of a pizza.*

Primary industry

Agriculture
Forestry & fishing   Mining & quarrying
Oil & natural gas extraction

Secondary industry

Energy & water   Construction
Manufacturing

Tertiary industry

Repairs   Distribution
Other services   Hotels & catering
Transport & communication
Tourism

Figure 2 *Types of production.*

Pizza Hut and KFC are part of the TERTIARY or SERVICE industry. This is where services are provided. It includes retailing (mainly shops), hairdressing, education, health, financial services and hotel accommodation. Pizza Hut and KFC offer services to their customers. These include dining facilities and takeaway meals.

The chain of production

Primary, secondary and tertiary industries are linked together in a CHAIN OF PRODUCTION. Farmers rearing pigs are part of primary industry. They also grow vegetables and wheat and collect milk from cows. These businesses are part of primary industry. Meat is bought by manufacturers such as a food processing factory, which turns it into pepperoni sausage, for example. The meat processing business is part of secondary industry. The sausages are then delivered to Pizza Hut to be put onto pizzas in its restaurants. The eating out service provided in a Pizza Hut restaurant is part of tertiary industry.

Businesses add value at each stage of production, as the ingredients are transformed into

1 Draw and label a chain of production for a woollen top. Start with primary industry and finish with tertiary industry.

a product sold to the final customer, the business paying for the buffet.

Interdependence

The chain of production shows that businesses and their customers are highly INTERDEPENDENT. Farmers depend on firms Pizza Hut and KFC for sales of their products. Pizza Hut and KFC depend on firms which make ovens for their equipment. Cooker manufacturers depend on transport to deliver their products. The transport industry depends on oil companies which make petrol for vans and lorries. Oil companies depend on workers all round the world who are employed in the oil industry. Workers depend on farmers for food.

Specialisation and the division of labour

Interdependence leads to SPECIALISATION. This means that businesses, as well as individuals and whole economies, concentrate on making just a few products. For instance, Pizza Hut and KFC specialise in providing food dining services. Microsoft specialises in producing software for computers. Boeing specialises in manufacturing aeroplanes.

Specialisation explains why businesses today are so efficient.

- It allows knowledge and skills to be built up. Pizza Hut and KFC are expert at providing dining services, but know little about producing computers. If they want computers, they buy them from a specialist manufacturer.
- It means that specialist machinery and equipment can be used. For instance, Pizza Hut and KFC have specialist cooking equipment.
- It permits businesses to employ specialised workers. They can do different jobs, such as cooking, serving or ordering supplies, building up their expertise through training and experience. This specialisation of workers is known as the DIVISION OF LABOUR.

Production in the UK

What businesses produce in the UK changes over time. Figure 3 shows production since 1960 has gone up. Businesses are now producing more than before. However, there has been a faster growth in the provision of services than in the production of manufactured goods. Service businesses, like Pizza Hut and KFC, have prospered. The relative growth of tertiary businesses has occurred for three reasons.

- Wages are going up over time. Consumers are spending much of the extra money they earn on services rather than on goods. This has attracted new businesses to service industry.
- Many of the manufactured goods we buy are imported from abroad. 50 years ago, they would have been made in Britain. UK businesses which export have had to fight hard to survive and many have gone out of business. However, UK businesses are now selling more services abroad.
- The prices of services have gone up much faster on average than the prices of manufactured goods. It costs more today to buy the same amount of services than the same amount of goods. Manufacturing businesses have had to cut costs to survive the competition from low cost imports from abroad.

The labour force

Changes in what is being produced in the economy are bound to lead to changes in where and how people work. There has been a growth in jobs in service industries and a fall in those in primary and manufacturing industries. What is more, the rate of decline of jobs in manufacturing has been even greater than the relative fall in manufacturing output.

One reason for this is new technology. Manufacturing industry

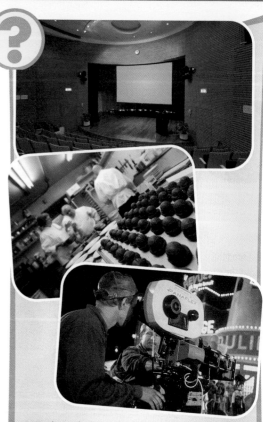

1 Explain what each business shown in the photographs specialises in producing.
2 How are the three businesses shown in the photographs interdependent?

has been revolutionised over the past fifty years. Machines have replaced workers. New, ever more productive, machines have been replacing older ones. A few factories today employ almost no labour at all. In fifty years time, it could be usual for factories to employ no workers and just a few supervisors.

Service industry may not have had the same scope for automation. In some service industries, like restaurants, better service means more workers, such as waiters, rather than less. In others, however, automation and changes in ICT have led to reductions in the labour force. For example, in the late 1990s and early 2000s workers in the communications industry may have lost their jobs as technology allowed automatic answering.

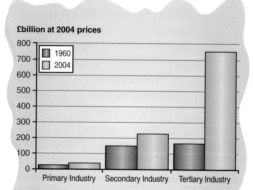

£billion at 2004 prices

| | 1960 |
| | 2004 |

800
700
600
500
400
300
200
100
0

Primary Industry   Secondary Industry   Tertiary Industry

Figure 3 *How production has changed*

Source: information from www.yum.com.

Table 1 shows changes in how consumers spent their money between 1996 and 2005. For instance, the first column shows spending on food and non-alcoholic drinks such as baked beans, beef and soft drinks.

Table 1 *Changing consumer spending in the UK*

	Food & non-alcoholic drink	Alcohol & tobacco	Clothing & footwear	Restaurants & hotels
	£billion (at 2003 prices)			
1996	56.3	26.8	24.8	71.2
1997	57.3	27.1	25.7	71.2
1998	58.1	26.8	26.7	73.8
1999	59.9	27.6	28.7	74.2
2000	61.9	26.7	31.7	76.3
2001	61.0	26.5	34.5	76.4
2002	62.1	26.9	38.5	78.3
2003	63.2	27.3	41.2	78.9
2004	65.2	27.4	44.1	81.8
2005	65.8	27.2	46.1	83.8

Source: adapted from *Monthly Digest of Statistics*, Office for National Statistics.

DTP/Graphics

You work for a food manufacturing company. It produces beverages such as instant coffee, canned foods such as baked beans and chilled and frozen foods. You have been asked to produce a report on trends in spending in the economy. In particular, the company is thinking of expanding into new markets. It thinks there might be opportunities in expanding into the alcoholic drinks market, or into clothing or hotel and restaurants.

Your report should include the following terms: 'manufacturing industry', 'service industry', 'chain of production', 'specialisation'. The report could be produced using a desktop publishing package. It should be structured as follows.

1 An introduction explaining the purpose of the report.
2 A section on trends in consumer spending in the four industries shown in Table 1. Give a detailed account of how spending has changed. This should include a line graph constructed from the figures in the table. Put years across the bottom of the graph and £ million on the vertical axis. There should be four lines on the one graph corresponding to the four types of spending.
3 A concluding section which explains which of the three markets looks most promising for the company. You will need to consider which markets have grown the fastest. You should also think about whether the company has any expertise it could offer in the production or sale of alcoholic drinks, clothing or catering services.

SYTNER GROUP

SUMMARY CASE STUDY

The Sytner Group was established over 30 years ago. It sells prestige and specialist cars such as Rolls-Royce and Porsche. Currently it has 90 sites or dealerships in the UK and has just purchased another 9 dealerships from another company, the Ryland Group.

BMW Alpina is one of the range of cars that Sytner Groups sells. Alpina is a company which buys BMW cars and then customises them, adding a variety of luxury features. BMW Alpina cars are then sold on to customers through dealerships like the Sytner Group.

Cars offered for sale by the Sytner Group before the Ryland purchase - Audi, BMW, BMW ALPINA, Bentley, Chrysler, Ferrari, Honda, Jaguar, Jeep, Land Rover, Lexus, Maserati, Mercedes-Benz, Porsche, Rolls-Royce, Saab, Toyota and Volvo.
Cars offered for sale at the recently purchased Ryland dealerships - Daimler Chrysler, BMW.

Source: adapted from www.sytner.co.uk, 2007.

1 Explain in what industries (a) BMW and (b) Sytner Group operate.
2 In what ways are (a) BMW and the Sytner Group and (b) the Sytner Group and ALPINA interdependent?
3 Discuss THREE factors that might influence the success of the Sytner Group's purchase of the Ryland Group's businesses.

Checklist ✓

1 Explain the difference between primary, secondary and tertiary industry.
2 Are the following workers part of primary, secondary or tertiary industry? (a) A coal miner; (b) a car production worker; (c) a shop assistant; (d) a hairdresser; (e) a teacher; (f) a secretary in an engineering company; (g) a farmworker; (h) a North Sea oil diver; (i) an estate agent; (j) a furniture maker; (k) a banker.
3 What is the chain of production?
4 Construct a chain of production for: (a) a bed; (b) a lesson in a school or college; (c) a packet of oven chips.
5 Why does the chain of production lead to interdependence in the economy?
6 Why does specialisation mean that more can be produced?
7 Specialisation by workers is given a special name. What is it?
8 What has happened in the UK since 1960 to: (a) the volume of total production; and (b) the monetary value of the output of the service sector compared to the manufacturing sector?
9 Why has automation led to a loss of jobs in the economy?

Making decisions

A business has to operate in a local environment. The business will affect that environment. It will have to decide how many local people to employ and whether to sell its products locally. It may also have to consider its impact on the local landscape. In turn, the business will be affected by the local environment. It will have to respond to changes in orders from local businesses. The availability of local labour may affect its ability to recruit new workers. The quality of the local roads, railways and airports may affect its costs.

United Utilities was created from the merger of North West Water and Norweb in 1995. It provides water services and distributes electricity to around 7 million customers in the North West of England. It employs around 17 000 people in its main business. It buys products from over 500 key suppliers. In 2006, its sales were £1.229 billion.

Producing for the local community

Many businesses, like United Utilities, operate at a local level. Their market is a local community. For instance, United Utilities supplies water and electricity to cities, towns and villages in the North West of England. It also provides sewage and waste disposal services. United Utilities doesn't just supply water and electricity to households, it also supplies thousands of businesses. These include everything from hair salons to car factories to hospitals.

Equally, United Utilities buys from businesses in its local area. It uses over 500 key suppliers to provide resources such as equipment, telecommunications, computer services and materials such as pipes. Some of these are supplied by local firms.

Creating jobs in the community

Businesses provide jobs for local people. United Utilities employs around 17 000 people in its main business. Even more workers, such as those employed by businesses supplying goods and services to United Utilities, are dependent for jobs on the success of United Utilities.

So United Utilities is directly and indirectly responsible for the creation of thousands of jobs. It is also responsible for training workers. It gives them skills which they can use for the company or for other businesses if they choose to change jobs. More skills tend to lead to higher pay. Training creates prosperity in the local community.

United Utilities is a **utility**, providing essential products and services to households. Households and businesses will always want water and electricity. However, some industries suffer declines because demand for their product falls. For instance, demand for shipbuilding, steel and coal has fallen in the UK over the past 40 years. Some areas of the country, like the North East and Scotland, were heavily dependent for jobs on these industries. When businesses shrink or close, unemployment rises. Job creation goes into reverse and the local area becomes less prosperous.

Your teacher will give you a map of your local area.
1 Mark on it TEN businesses located in the area. Each business should produce a different product or service.
2 On a separate sheet of paper or in your books, write down what each business produces for the local community.

Demography

DEMOGRAPHY is the study of population. Business is affected by the size and distribution of the population in a local area and how it is changing. Equally, changes in the business environment could well affect the size of the population. In the North West, United Utilities has had to respond to demographic changes. For example, it has had to provide water, sewerage services and electricity to areas where there has been a boom in new housing development as a result of growing population. Places such as Tarleton, central Manchester and parts of Merseyside have seen an increase in the number of residents.

The water and electricity distribution businesses are relatively mature businesses. In the North West United Utilities is unlikely to find large numbers of new customers. To improve its profitability the company is working hard to cut costs and improve quality. It is trying to make better use of its resources. For example, it is trying to reduce the number of leaking pipes in the system. To expand its current activities it might have to look for more customers abroad in the future. United Utilities already has operations in Australia for example.

Not all industries are mature or are expanding. The contraction of the steel, coal and shipbuilding industries had very damaging effects on some areas of the UK. Some people responded to very high unemployment in a local area by moving out. This then created a downward spiral in the area. If people move out, they stop spending money on local services, like shops and restaurants. Some of these firms will then go out of business, creating more unemployment.

Industrial tradition

Particular local areas tend to attract certain types of business. For instance, London is a major centre for financial businesses, attracted by the concentration of other similar businesses in the City of London. Stoke-on-Trent has a heavy concentration of pottery companies like Wedgwood. This happens because pottery companies gain by being close together. There is a long history of pottery businesses in Stoke. The local workforce is trained in the skills required for the industry. Individuals also have specialised

A static market

The population of Southport, Merseyside has remained at around 100 000 for many years now. This is a problem for many small businesses supplying personal services such as hair dressing, beauticians and dental care. Dave Merryman, who runs a traditional barbers shop in the centre of the town, has seen his sales stuck at around £47 000 for the last seven years. However, in an effort to boost sales he made some changes to his business. He changed the name of the business to make it more appealing to younger clients. He also modernised the salon and employed two much younger assistants to help improve the image. Finally, he provided a different range of magazines for waiting clients to read, provided free fresh coffee and installed two computers to provide Internet access.

1 Why is a static population a problem for businesses like Dave Merryman's?
2 How has Dave got round this problem?
3 A local college is constructing a new building with rooms for 400 students around the corner from Dave's salon. (a) What effect is this likely to have on his trade? (b) To what extent will the changes made to the business affect the numbers of students he is likely to attract?

knowledge to allow them to set up new businesses in the industry. Finally, there are many local firms which supply the pottery industry and so it is easy to get raw materials and components locally.

Businesses also tend to be sited in particular areas in a town. United Utilities sewage treatment plants are not located in town centres. Sewage treatment avoids residential areas. Land prices are too high and land is scarce. Locating downstream from a town allows waste water to flow under gravity, avoiding pumping costs. Businesses that need to be in town centres and can afford the rents tend to be shops and financial services like banks. Near the town centre are likely to be office blocks for a wide variety of workers, from local authority employees to headquarters staff for a construction company. Out on the main roads from the town will be shops like Toys 'R' Us or motor repair centres like Kwik-Fit where rents are cheaper and parking is easy.

Manufacturing industry is often

found on industrial sites separate from local housing. Land prices are lower than in the town centre. Also, keeping industry separate from housing means that there are fewer social costs of production.

Infrastructure

United Utilities provides part of the local INFRASTRUCTURE because it builds and maintains electricity lines, water pipes, pumping stations, reservoirs and water treatment works. Infrastructure is the built environment of an area. Other examples of infrastructure are roads, bridges, buildings, schools, houses, telephone networks and gas pipes.

The size and quality of the local infrastructure is important to businesses. For instance, a restaurant would find it difficult to operate if its water supplies were polluted, or it were without water for part of the day. United Utilities would find it difficult to operate if telecommunications were unreliable. United Utilities also relies on local schools and universities to provide it with skilled workers. It needs local hospitals to treat its workers when they fall ill and get them back to work quickly. A supermarket store would find it more difficult to get supplies in and attract customers if local roads were severely congested.

The environment

United Utilities has a major impact on the local environment. When it makes decisions about how to operate, it looks at its PRIVATE COSTS and PRIVATE BENEFITS. These are the costs and benefits to the company. For example, when it bids for an overseas contract to supply water management services, it will have to compare the costs and revenues from the contract. It will bid if it thinks that the revenues will be larger than the costs, so that it can make a profit.

But the activities of United Utilities don't just affect the company. For instance, United Utilities is involved in a number of local and regional schemes designed to support environmental initiatives. With Groundwork, United Utilities is investing in public open spaces and local community environmental schemes. With the Wildlife Trusts, it works jointly on operating nature reserves on its own land. With the RSPB, it is working jointly to conserve rare species and sensitive habitats, often on its own land. With the Peak District National Park, it is investing to restore upland moorland. Improvements which bring no private benefits to the company are known as EXTERNALITIES. The private benefits to United Utilities added to the positive externalities to the community equal the SOCIAL BENEFITS of the activity. The social benefits are all the benefits to society of an economic activity.

Businesses can sometimes impose costs on society which are not included in their own private costs. Any pollution that results from business activity is an example of an externality. The private costs added to the negative externalities equal the SOCIAL COSTS of business activity. The social costs are all the costs to society of an activity.

A company like United Utilities is very environmentally conscious. It knows that it is being judged on its environmental record. So, it attempts to eliminate environmental costs and works towards increasing social benefits.

Local government

Government affects a business like United Utilities in many ways. At a local level, United Utilities has to work with local authorities to get planning permission for new works. These local authorities provide the roads which United Utilities' vehicles travel along. The local police and fire service protect United Utilities' property. Local schools provide schooling for future employees of the company. The local authority is responsible for enforcing consumer protection laws, some of which cover water and electricity supply. The European Union also imposes regulations which affect United Utilities' construction plans, such as the building of sewage treatment works.

Source: adapted from United Utilities website, www.unitedutilities.com.

Wind Farm Protest

In January 2007, Shetland Islands Council-owned company Viking Energy signed an agreement with energy giant Scottish & Southern Energy to build around 200 wind turbines in the islands' central mainland. Construction work is not expected to get under way before 2011, and will cost more than £1 billion. During construction the local economy is likely to be boosted as employment rises in the area.

However, a group of islanders is planning to oppose the massive 600 megawatt wind farm in Shetland. A spokesman for the newly-formed Shetland Against Windfarms Group (SAWG) said the proposed development was ecologically and financially 'unsustainable' and would send the isles on the 'wrong route'. SAWG organiser Stuart Dobson said it was time that somebody started to question the plan, as it was a difficult one for local environmentalists to tackle. Ecologists are obviously keen to promote green energy. On the other hand, hundreds of wind turbines are likely to ruin the environment and the wildlife as well. The Shetland Bird Club has also expressed unease about the scale of the plans.

Source: adapted from *The Shetland News*, 26.1.2007.

1 What might be the private benefits to Viking Energy if the wind farm is built?
2 Suggest ONE example of a positive externality, one which will benefit the local community, of the wind farm.
3 Explain why damage to the environment would be a negative externality for Viking Energy.
4 Discuss whether it would be possible to reduce the negative externalities caused by the construction of the wind farm.

Wind turbines like these could appear on the Shetland Islands.

National Waterfront Museum

In October 2005, the National Waterfront Museum was opened in Swansea. This £30.8m project celebrates Wales' heritage and achievements and tells the story of Welsh industry and innovation, and its role in shaping today's economy. The money for the project was provided jointly by the private sector and the government. The Museum forms the centerpiece of the regeneration of Swansea's waterfront.

With the creation of many new jobs and offering free entry to an estimated 250 000 visitors per year, the city will reap huge rewards. Experts predict that visitors will inject around £17m each year into the local economy. This will help the area to recover further from the decline in mining and steel on which the economy depended so heavily in the past.

The building itself combines old and new architecture. The Grade II listed warehouse, former home of the Swansea Maritime and Industrial Museum, has new stylish galleries of slate and glass designed by award winning architects Wilkinson Eyre. The objective of this project is to create a major attraction in Wales for 21st century audiences, supporting wider economic regeneration and national pride. Visitors will leave with an understanding as to how Wales came to be the powerhouse of the Industrial Revolution.

Source: adapted from the Visit Wales website.

1 How did the government help the local Swansea economy?
2 Why did Swansea need government funds?
3 What effect do you think the National Waterfront Museum will have on: (a) local businesses; (b) local jobs; and (c) the local environment?

key terms

Demography - the study of population.
Externalities - the cost or benefit of an activity. which is not paid for or received by the individual, business or government engaged in that activity.
Infrastructure - the built environment, like roads, factories, schools and hospitals.
Private costs and benefits - the costs and benefits to individuals, businesses or governments of an economic or business activity.
Social costs and benefits - the costs and benefits to society as a whole of the activities of individuals, businesses and governments. Social costs and benefits = private costs and benefits plus externalities.

Checklist ✓

1 A building society is opening a new branch in the near future. At the moment, work is being done on the building before the opening. What jobs are going to be created in the local community: (a) in the short term; and (b) in the longer term?
2 Give FOUR social costs created by a local coal mine.
3 Give FOUR social benefits created by a local hairdressing salon.
4 Give THREE examples of industries where negative externalities might be quite large.
5 There is a large increase in the number of old people aged 80 and over in your local area. What effect might this have on local businesses?
6 A tyre manufacturer, the largest employer in an area, closes down. What effect will this have on: (a) workers; and (b) other businesses in the area?
7 (a) Stoke-on-Trent is famous for what industry? (b) Why do firms in that industry concentrate together in the same locality?
8 Give FIVE examples of the infrastructure in your local area.
9 Why is infrastructure important to a local business?
10 How can local government affect a business?

SUMMARY CASE STUDY

BIRKDALE STATION REVAMP

In March 2007 it was announced that Birkdale railway station in Merseyside was to receive a £100,000 revamp. The refurbishment will involve improved facilities, including a new electronic information system telling passengers when the next train is due. The waiting room will have automatic doors fitted, more heating and lighting and there will be extra seating provided on both platforms. More CCTV will be installed to improve personal security in and around the station.

The cost of the development is likely to exceed £100,000 and will be met jointly by Merseytravel, the private train operator, and the government's Department of Transport. Gary Jenkins of Merseytravel said: 'The work will be finished by the end of March, and we are being sympathetic to the overall look of the station when implementing the improvements'.

The announcement was welcomed by local groups. Ralph Gregson, Chairman of the Birkdale Civic Society, said: 'This is fantastic news, and we are delighted the work is taking place.' 'We are also pushing for toilet facilities at the station and an indoor waiting area on the Liverpool to Southport side of the platform'. Susan Cairns, who lives opposite the station, said: 'It's about time. The station looks a mess at the moment. It's a hundred years old'.

Source: adapted from the Southport Champion, 7.3.2007.

1 State one private benefit to Merseytravel of its contribution to the investment.
2 Explain why Birkdale Station is part of the local infrastructure.
3 What might be the positive externalities of the revamp?
4 The rail industry is booming at the moment. Explain what this means to: (a) a company like Merseytravel; (b) the local community.

Making decisions

Businesses operate in a difficult national economy. Although the UK economy is growing slowly over time, it keeps on moving from boom to recession. Businesses need to decide how to cope with these changes in demand for their products. They also need to know how best to cope with changing patterns of demand coming from increased consumer incomes or changing population patterns. Inflation too can cause difficulties for businesses. Alongside this, businesses must meet government rules and regulations which set out how they can operate.

Hanson is one of the world's largest suppliers of heavy building materials to the construction industry. It employs 26,000 people, operating primarily in North America, the UK and Australia. In the UK, the company is split into two divisions. Hanson Aggregate UK produces aggregates and asphalt used, for example, to build roads. Hanson Aggregate UK also produces ready mixed concrete. Hanson Building Products UK supplies a wide range of heavy building products such as bricks, clay roofing and bagged cement. Both divisions are affected by what happens in the UK economy.

Growth, boom and recession

Economies tend to grow in size over time. Over the past forty years, for instance, production in the UK has more than doubled. So people can buy and consume more.

Some businesses benefited more than others from this growth. Many service industries, such as health or catering, grew faster than the average for the rest of the economy. Other industries grew less quickly. Jam makers, for instance, suffered. Consumers bought less jam as their incomes increased. They switched to convenience foods or to healthier food like fresh fruit. The construction industry, which is supplied by materials from Hanson, grew by 66 per cent between 1997-2004 when output of the whole economy grew by 44 per cent.

The overall growth in the economy is uneven. When the economy is in BOOM, it is growing very fast. Spending is high and

Table 1 *Output of the whole economy, engineering industry and Bodycote plc*

			at 2001 prices[1]
	Output of the whole economy £ bn	Output of engineering industry £ bn	Output of Bodycote plc £m
2001	1 132	123	469
2002	1 155	116	415
2003	1 186	118	408
2004	1 225	124	389
2005	1 249	128	421
2006	1 283	142	487

[1] i.e. adjusted for inflation
Source: adapted from *Monthly Digest of Statistics*, Office for National Statistics; Bodycote plc, *Annual Report and Accounts.*

Bodycote plc is a UK engineering company. It specialises in supplying specialist testing and thermal processing services both in the UK and in overseas markets.

1 Look at Table 1. Give the output of the whole economy in (a) 2001 and (b) 2006.
2 'Between 2004 and 2006 the economy was in a boom.' (a) What does this mean? (b) Explain what effect this might have had on the output of the UK engineering industry and Bodycote plc.
3 'Between 2001 and 2004, the international economy experienced a recession.' (a) What does this mean? (b) Explain what effect this might have had on the output of Bodycote plc.
4 Discuss whether Bodycote should be increasing its spending on investment in new plant and machinery in 2007.

In boom periods new homes may be built, benefiting construction businesses.

In his 2006 Budget the Chancellor announced a number of measures. These included and increase in air passenger duty and a rise in fuel duty-free insulation and central heating for 300,000 households and higher penalties for failing to pay the minimum wage to rise. His theme was a green Budget and he announced that stamp duty was to be cut on experimental carbon zero homes which are constructed from renewable materials and use environmentally friendly means of power generation.

Source: adapted from news.bbc.co.uk.

1 Explain how (a) an increase in taxes on flights and (b) tougher legislation on minimum wages could affect businesses.
2 How might his green measures benefit certain businesses?
Wordprocessing
3 You work in the public relations department of a large petrol company. Write a letter (preferably wordprocessed) to the Chancellor complaining about the latest rise in tax on petrol and explaining why it may be bad for customers and businesses in the UK.

unemployment falls. Businesses tend to do well in a boom because it is easier to sell products. In the boom of 1986-88, output of the construction industry increased by one quarter. This was over twice the average increase in output in the rest of the economy.

In a RECESSION, the economy doesn't grow or even shrinks, as was the case in the period 1990-92 in the UK. Less is spent and produced than before and unemployment rises. Businesses tend to do badly because consumers are buying fewer of their products. The construction industry was badly affected by the recession of 1990-92. Output fell by 10 per cent. Even worse, when the rest of the economy began to recover from 1993, construction industry output barely changed. By 1997, construction output was little more than it had been in 1990.

Between1992-2006 there were only minor booms and recessions over the period. Lower growth took place in 1996, 2001-02 and 2005-06, but there were higher growth rates in 1994, 2000 and 2004.

Inflation

INFLATION is a general rise in prices in the economy. Businesses lose and gain from inflation. They lose because their costs go up. For instance, Hanson will lose out if has to pay more for its materials and equipment. It will also lose out if it has to pay its workers more. They are likely to want higher wages to pay the higher prices in the shops.

Businesses can also gain. If prices are rising, Hanson may be able to put up the prices of the products it sells to construction businesses. Higher prices could mean less sales. But if all businesses are putting up their prices, and workers are getting higher wages, then sales for a business should stay the same.

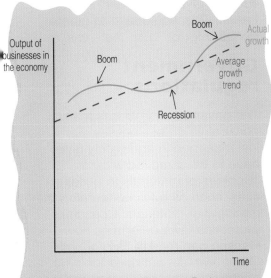

Figure 1 Booms and slumps. Businesses are producing more and more over time. However, sometimes in a boom, growth in business is particularly fast. At other times, in a recession, output can sometimes fall.

Taxes and government spending

Decisions that government makes about its spending and taxes (called fiscal policy) affect all businesses.

For instance, the government might lower taxes on people's income (income tax or National Insurance contributions) or business profits. As a result, people and businesses will have more money left to spend. People might spend more at the supermarket, or on holidays, benefiting supermarket and tourist companies. But they might decide that they can now afford a larger home or make improvements to their existing home. Construction businesses may be able to build more houses. Hanson will benefit if it supplies more materials for house building.

The government might also change tax rates on goods and services. Value added tax (VAT) has to be paid on most products at 17.5 per cent. New homes, though, are exempt. An increase in VAT would hit sales of products like televisions or clothes. Hanson could be affected if the government raised corporation tax, the tax on company profits.

A general increase in

Kingfisher is a large company which sells DIY (do-it-yourself) products. In the UK, it owns B&Q, the UKs largest DIY retailer. 2005-06 has been a challenging period for Kingfisher. There was a good performance in overseas markets. But the UK market was weak.

There has been significant cost inflation this year. Prices paid to suppliers have increased and this has helped reduce profits.

UK sales of DIY products have been disappointing. Consumers have been hit by rising prices of oil, gas and electricity and higher taxes. There is also less confidence in the housing market with fewer houses being sold and so less spending on DIY when people move.

Source: adapted from Kingfisher plc, *Annual Report and Accounts*, 2006.

1 What does Kingfisher sell.
2 Explain why sales at Kingfisher might have fallen because of changes in: (a) energy prices; (b) taxes; (c) the housing market.
3 How might inflation hit profits at B&Q?
4 What would be an ideal national economic environment for a DIY retailer like Kingfisher?

government spending will mean more spending in the whole economy. This should benefit a business supplying construction materials because some of that extra spending will be on new homes or roads. Increases in government spending on particular programmes can also benefit businesses. For instance, increased government spending on housing for rent might increase orders for Hanson's products. A decrease in defence spending, in contrast, might hit manufacturers of weapons.

Interest rates

Most businesses borrow money. Hanson, for instance, in 2006 had £1.4 billion in borrowings. Rises in interest rates usually add to the costs of a business because it will have to pay more in interest on its loans. A fall in interest rates, on the other hand, means lower interest payments.

Rising interest rates also affect the customers of a business. The mortgage rate is the rate of interest on money borrowed to buy a home. If it goes up, then repayments on the loan to buy a house will increase. This will discourage people from buying

new houses. Construction companies could be faced with falling sales and buy fewer bricks and other products from Hanson. A fall in interest rates will have the opposite effect. It will make the repayments on buying a new car, some new furniture or a new home fall. So car and furniture manufacturers, construction companies and suppliers of construction materials should benefit.

Population

The population of the UK only increases slowly. This might seem like bad news for a business like Hanson. But people are always buying new homes. One reason for this is that the structure of the population is changing. There are more old people than before living on their own. The number of single parent families has increased. Increased divorce rates have split up families. People are choosing to live on their own. So the number of households has increased as the numbers in each household has tended to fall. Each household needs a home. This could lead to more demand for the construction materials of Hanson.

Changes in the structure of the

population can have effects on other businesses. In the 1980s, for instance, a fall in the number of school aged children meant that many schools closed. Rising numbers of those over 75, on the other hand, increased the business opportunities for retirement homes.

Hanson may also benefit from changes in where people live. For instance, since 2000 there has been an increase in demand by people to live in inner city areas and a growth in flats built in cities such as Liverpool, Manchester and Leeds. This would lead to greater demand for building materials.

Government regulations

The government imposes many constraints on businesses. For instance, health and safety laws have to be complied with for suppliers of materials to building sites, such as rules concerning the handling of materials. Consumer protection laws determine how Hanson can market its products. Other laws set out rules for contracts between buyers and sellers.

Source: information from Hanson.

Population

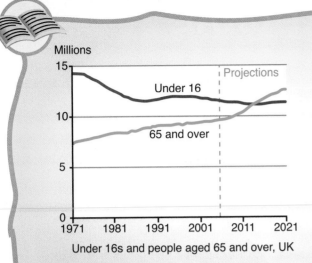

Figure 2 *Under 16s and people aged 65 and over*
Source: adapted from *Social Trends*, Office for National
Statistics, 2006.

1 What is predicted will happen to the number of people (a) under 16 and (b) over 65 in the population to the year 2021?
2 What opportunities will this create for businesses in terms of selling products aimed at those aged 65 and over?
3 Discuss TWO problems for businesses that may result from these trends.

Checklist ✓

1 What is the difference between a boom and a recession?
2 What is the likely effect of a recession on a business?
3 What happens to unemployment in a recession and how might this affect businesses?
4 How does inflation affect a business?
5 Explain how the following tax changes might benefit or harm businesses:
(a) a rise in income tax; (b) a fall in VAT; (c) a fall in corporation tax.
6 Which businesses might benefit most from an increase in spending on road building?
7 'Rocketing interest rates have hit my costs and my orders.' Explain why this could be true for a business.
8 Explain which businesses might be affected by a rise in the number of births in the population: (a) now; (b) in 20 years time; (c) in 75 years time.
9 Find and list FIVE examples of government regulations which affect businesses.

SUMMARY CASE STUDY

THE HUMPTY DUMPTY PLAYGROUP

The Humpty Dumpty playgroup operates on a large new estate of owner-occupied houses in a Sussex town. The estate is yet to be finished, with another 300 houses planned. It has attracted mainly families, many with children, or young couples hoping to have children. New houses are currently selling very fast because the local economy is booming.

Sarah Milford set up the playgroup from scratch. The initial advertising, purchase of equipment and the first year's loss came to around £3 000 which she borrowed from the bank. The playgroup's current running costs are about £30 000 per year. That includes hire of a hall, staff costs including a wage for herself, and materials. She charges £4 a session (morning, afternoon or after school) and last year the fees came to £31 000.

All playgroups today are strictly regulated. They have to conform to the requirements of the Childrens Act, which, for instance, lays down how many staff there have to be per child.

1 The Humpty Dumpty playgroup is a success. Explain why:
(a) population changes in the local area; and (b) the state of the economy are helping it to be successful.
2 At the moment, interest rates are low. Why is this an advantage to Sarah?
3 How do government regulations affect Sarah's business?
4 Discuss THREE factors which in the future could cause the playgroup to turn from being in profit to suffering losses.

Making decisions

All businesses are likely to be affected by the world economy. Some businesses decide to export their goods and services abroad. They have to make decisions about which foreign customers to sell to and where to focus their export efforts. Even if businesses don't export products, they are likely to buy products from abroad. They have to decide whether to buy British products or foreign products.

Richard Branson is a high profile business person. He has set up a chain of companies under the Virgin brand name. These operate in sectors such as travel and tourism, leisure, finance and money, shopping and media and telecommunications. One of his companies is Virgin Atlantic, an airline which operate flights to the USA and many other world destinations. The airline carried 4.49 million passengers in 2005.

Exports

Virgin Atlantic is a well known airline in the UK. But it also relies on sales to foreign passengers.

Sony

Sony is a large Japanese company which produces electronic goods such as televisions and computers, games such as PlayStation, entertainment such as motion pictures and music, and financial services such as insurance and banking.

1 Sony has manufacturing plants all around the world. For instance, it sells microchips made in Japan to UK manufacturers. For Japan, these are exports. What are they for the UK?
2 Sony has to bring its products to Europe by ship or aeroplane. If it uses a UK shipping company, why would this be an export of a service for the UK?
3 If Sony used the banking services of a British bank, what would this be classified as for the UK?
4 Suggest THREE ways in which Sony could increase the amount it sells into its UK markets.

Goods (sometimes called visibles) and services (sometimes called invisibles) which are sold to foreigners are called EXPORTS.

Virgin Atlantic sells a service to foreigners. This could be a flight for which passengers pay. Virgin Atlantic, a British company, receives the money from the sale of the ticket. So the flight is an exported service because it is a service sold to foreigners.

Imports

Virgin Atlantic is always looking to get the best value for money. When it buys supplies from other businesses, it wants to buy at the lowest price. It also wants goods of the 'right' quality, which can be delivered on time and which, if necessary, offer an after sales service. Sometimes, a British company can offer this package. But equally, the best value might be offered by a foreign company. For instance, Virgin Atlantic buys many of its new aeroplanes from Boeing, a US company.

When Virgin Atlantic takes

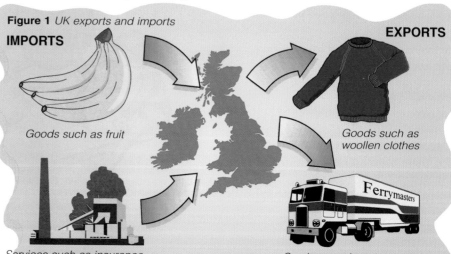

Figure 1 *UK exports and imports*

IMPORTS

Goods such as fruit

Services such as insurance

EXPORTS

Goods such as woollen clothes

Services such as transport

delivery of a new Boeing aeroplane, it has to pay Boeing, a foreign company. This becomes an IMPORT for the UK. It is an imported good because a British company is buying a physical product from a foreign company.

Threats and opportunities

Working in an international environment leads to both threats and opportunities for British businesses. One threat is that competition from foreign businesses may take away sales from UK businesses.

Virgin Atlantic, for instance, is in direct competition with other airlines like Emirates, Delta and TWA. Virgin Atlantic needs to provide a high quality service, to the right airports in the world and at a competitive price to keep its share of the market.

On the other hand, without its foreign customers Virgin Atlantic would be a much smaller business.

It also has the chance to take away sales from its foreign competitors. Providing greater comfort in its Business Class seating, or offering cheaper fares on various flights at different times of the year, could increase the numbers travelling with Virgin Atlantic.

Being able to buy from abroad also means that Virgin Atlantic can get the most competitive supplies for its operations rather than just having to rely on British suppliers.

Exchange rates

A British traveller is likely to pay for a Virgin Atlantic service in pounds sterling. A USA tourist, however, is likely to pay in dollars. But the price of dollars for pounds, the EXCHANGE RATE, is constantly changing. These changes can have an important effect on Virgin Atlantic. Assume that the exchange rate is $2=£1. This means that $2 can be exchanged for £1. A £300 Virgin Atlantic flight from New York to London will therefore cost an American $600 (£300 x $2).

What if the exchange rate changed? The value of the pound might fall to $1.50=£1. Virgin Atlantic has to decide whether to change its prices. If it chooses to keep the price at £300, the price in dollars will fall. The price of the same flight in dollars will now be $450 (£300 x $1.50). This new lower price should encourage Americans to use Virgin Atlantic's services more. In general, a fall in the value of the pound means that foreigners can buy British goods more cheaply and should buy more.

If instead the value of the pound rises, so that $2.50=£1, then the flight would be more expensive for Americans. It would cost $750 (£300 x $2.50) and Americans should buy fewer Virgin Atlantic services. A rise in the value of the pound will tend to make British goods and services more expensive to foreigners and they should buy less.

The opposite will be true for imports of goods and services into the UK. A fall in the value of the pound will make imports more expensive to British buyers. A fall from £1=$2 to £1=$1.50 could increase the price of a $1 000 American holiday to a British tourist from £500 ($1 000÷$2) to £667 ($1 000÷$1.50). So imports should fall.

Relocation of call centres

Some businesses need to operate call centres. These are usually large office blocks where hundreds of staff deal with customers over the telephone. Companies offering financial services such as Natwest, Norwich Union and Skandia employ thousands of staff in call centres.

In recent years many companies have moved their call centre business overseas. Mumbai in India has been a popular choice. For example, the telecommunications company, 3, said in January 2007 it would transfer more calls to its Mumbai office at the expense of jobs in Glasgow. Prudential also moved many of its call centre jobs to Mumbai in 2002.

However, there are examples of companies moving back from India. Powergen, the energy company, has moved all call centre jobs back to the UK to places such as Bedford, Bolton, Leicester and Nottingham. A company spokesman said that customer service had improved dramatically since the change. 'The move back to the UK had proved popular with customers' he said.

Source: adapted from USB Prices and Earnings, 2006.

Figure 2 *Gross hourly wage*

Source: adapted from USB Prices and Earnings, 2006.

1 Why do you think many British companies locate their call centres in Mumbai?
2 What might be a disadvantage of locating call centres in places such as Mumbai?
3 How might businesses in countries like India threaten British businesses in the future?

A rise in the value of the pound from £1=$2 to £1=$2.50 makes imports cheaper to the British. The price of a $1 000 American holiday could fall from £500 to £400 ($1 000÷$2.50). Imports should rise as a result.

The government helping business

A government can help businesses deal with foreign competitors. For instance, it could:

- subsidise exports - this means giving a grant for each export sold, allowing businesses to charge lower prices and win more orders;
- impose tariffs on imports - tariffs (sometimes called customs duties) are a tax on imported goods, making them more expensive;
- impose quotas on imports - a quota is a limit on the number of goods coming into the country over a year;
- try to push down the value of the pound which will make the price of imports more expensive and the price of exports to foreigners cheaper.

However, the British government is limited in what it can do. The UK is a member of the European Union which doesn't allow tariffs and quotas on trade between European countries. The UK is also a member of the World Trade Organisation which limits tariffs and quotas.

Many British companies don't want restrictions on trade. If the UK keeps out foreign goods through tariffs and quotas, there is more chance that other countries will do the same to UK exports.

The government and managing the economy

The UK has to pay its way in the world. Exports have roughly to equal imports over time. If imports were greater than exports, the difference would have to be borrowed from foreigners. To repay it, exports would have to be greater than imports.

The values of UK exports and imports are shown on the BALANCE OF PAYMENTS. The balance of payments is a record of all the money coming into and going out of the UK. Sometimes, on the news, you may hear about the BALANCE OF TRADE. This is the difference between values of exports and imports of goods only. The difference between the value of exports and imports of both goods and services is called the CURRENT BALANCE.

What if there is a current account deficit (i.e. where imports are greater than exports)? The government may try to correct this.

- It could try to force down the value of the pound, making it easier for UK businesses to export and making imports more expensive.
- It could push up interest rates. This should lead to a fall in spending in the UK and so lead to a fall in imports. However, a fall in spending could lead to a recession in the economy which would be bad for UK businesses.
- It could increase tariffs and quotas, although this would be difficult because of membership of the European Union.

Source: adapted in part from information on the Virgin Atlantic website, www.virgin-atlantic.com

The Australian Dollar

In 2002, John Nolan and his son James went to Australia to watch England in the Ashes series. Mr Nolan spent a lot of time working out a budget for the trip. For the six weeks out in Australia they felt that he would need 24 000 Australian dollars to pay for travel, tickets, accommodation and other expenses.

1 How much would the trip cost in sterling if the exchange rate was £1 = $3?
2 In 2006, Mr Nolan wanted to make exactly the same trip again. He reckoned that with one or two cut backs it would cost 24 000 Australian dollars again. However, the exchange rate was now £1 = $2.40. Explain the effect of the change in the exchange rate on the cost of the trip.
3 Discuss how hotels in Australia might be affected by this change in the exchange rate.

The US government has put tariffs on imports of wooden furniture from China. The new tax range varies from item to item, but on bedroom furniture the tax will treble the cost of importing from China. In recent years, US companies have been hit hard by increased imports. In bedroom furniture, Chinese made goods have increased their market share in the USA from 10 per cent in 2000 to over a quarter today. Meanwhile, the workforce of US-based wood furniture makers has fallen by a quarter to 29 500 workers in the same period.

US furniture manufacturers and trade unions representing US furniture workers have lobbied the US government hard to impose the tariffs. However, US furniture retailers have opposed the new tariffs because they will raise the selling price of made-in-China furniture in their shops.

Source: adapted from http://news.bbc.co.uk, 18.6.2004

1 What is meant by a 'tariff'?
2 A Chinese-made table is sold to a US importer for $50. A tariff of 100 per cent is now put on the table. How much will the table cost after the tariff has been paid?
3 How might the tariff help US furniture manufacturing businesses?
4 Why might US consumers lose out from the tariff?

GLENFIDDICH

Glenfiddich is the best-selling single malt whisky in the world. It is the only Highland Scotch Whisky to be distilled, matured and bottled at its own distillery. The company is a family business and was set up in 1886 by William Grant. The same family still owns the business today.

Glenfiddich is well known for the quality of its product. It uses soft, clear spring water from the Robbie Dhu spring which is situated in the Conval Hills, Banffshire. Glenfiddich owns 1,200 acres of the land surrounding the spring in order to protect its purity. The quality of the product has been recognized internationally. In 2006 Glenfiddich won a record 10 medals at the International Wines and Spirits competition.

The Glenfiddich name is so famous that it was voted one of the top 10 Superbrands in the UK last year. Competition was stiff, and fellow contenders included Coca-Cola, Chelsea Football Club, Nokia and Virgin Atlantic. Glenfiddich is the only single malt whisky to have won this award in 2006. However, at least 75% of Glenfiddich's sales are overseas. A good proportion of this 75% goes to customers in America.

Source: adapted from the Glenfiddich website.

A graph showing the rise of the dollar in recent years

1 Suggest why Glenfiddich is so popular with overseas customers.
2 What impact does Glenfiddich have (a) on UK exports; and (b) on the UK balance of payments?
3 Explain why a rise in the value of the pound is bad for Glenfiddich.
4 Discuss TWO measures that the government could take to help companies like Glenfiddich when the exchange rate rises.

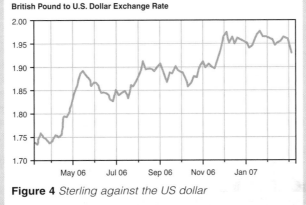

British Pound to U.S. Dollar Exchange Rate

Figure 4 *Sterling against the US dollar*

Checklist ✓

1 What is the difference between an export and an import?
2 Explain whether each of the following is an export of a good, an export of a service, an import of a good or an import of a service: (a) a Nissan car made in the UK sold to Germany; (b) a Japanese made DVD player bought by a British consumer; (c) medicines made in the UK and sold to France; (d) a British tourist taking a holiday in Austria; (e) a Japanese company insuring its company with a British insurer; (f) a French company buying steel from the UK.
3 What are the advantages of being able to export for a UK business?
4 What are: (a) the disadvantages; and (b) the advantages of being able to import for a UK business?
5 What is an exchange rate?
6 Explain whether a fall in the value of the pound would be good for: (a) a UK business exporting cars to France; (b) a French business exporting clothes to the UK; (c) a UK engineering business buying steel from Germany.
7 Why do fluctuating exchange rates pose a problem for businesses?
8 How can government help UK businesses to export and compete against imports?
9 (a) What is the current account on the balance of payments? (b) How might government measures to correct a deficit on the current account affect UK businesses?

Making decisions

The European Union (EU) is increasingly important for businesses in Europe. Today European businesses have to comply with EU regulations. More importantly, though, the Single European Market is opening up Europe to competition, making it easier for UK firms to sell products in Europe and for Continental firms to sell into the UK. European businesses have to face up to these challenges and make decisions about how to meet the competition.

McBride plc is Europe's leading manufacturer of own label household cleaning and personal care products. This includes fabric conditioners, dishwasher tablets, soap and shampoo. It manufactures products for leading retailers like Tesco and Sainsbury in the UK and for other supermarket chains in Europe. It has 18 manufacturing plants across the European Union including the UK, Spain, Italy, France, Belguim, Luxembourg and Poland. The existence of the European Union provides the company with opportunities to trade and grow which would be more difficult outside the EU.

A common market

The UK is a member of the European Union or EU. With 27 countries and a combined population of 500 million, it is a powerful economic force in the world today. The European Union is a **common market** or **customs union**. This means that goods can be traded freely between member countries. Within a common market, there are no taxes (taxes on imported goods are called **tariffs**) to be paid when goods are exported or imported between member countries. McBride, for instance, doesn't have to pay taxes on its cleaning products from its plant in Burnley in Lancashire when it sends them to a customer in France. Equally, countries cannot impose **quotas** which restrict the amount of imports coming from other member countries.

When Britain joined the EU in 1973, this was a great opportunity for British companies. Before 1973, some countries had imposed tariffs on products made in the UK. After Britain joined, UK businesses could compete on the same terms as other European companies and win orders throughout the EU. On the other hand, European businesses could also compete with British businesses on the same terms in the UK. **Competition** within the UK increased. As more and more countries, like Poland and Romania have joined the EU, the opportunities for UK businesses like McBride have increased. Equally, competitive pressures on a company like McBride have increased over time because of the expansion of the EU.

Baxi

Baxi is a UK manufacturer of central heating boilers. In 2005 it bought Roca, a leading Spanish boiler maker. Mark Edwards, Baxi's chief executive, says the move would strengthen the company in Spain and Portugal, where Roca has most of its sales. 'We will use the acquisition to sell more of our existing products in Spain, which is one of Europe's fastest growing countries for boilers' says Mr Edwards. About half of Baxi's sales come from the UK, with the rest mainly in continental Europe. In Britain, Baxi claims the number one position in the boiler business in volume.

They are also keen to switch more households, particularly in countries such as Turkey or in eastern Europe, away from solid fuels and towards 'cleaner' natural gas. Mr Edwards foresees steady growth in the next few years across most of the countries that Baxi sells to. But he reckoned that in 2005 there would be a downturn in the UK owing to government regulations requiring plumbers to install new energy-saving boilers. 'We could be in for a period of uncertainty in the UK boiler business' says Mr Edwards. 'The overall UK market for boilers, which has been pretty strong in the past few years, could fall 3 to 5 per cent this year and this would have an impact on us.'

1 What does Baxi produce?
2 Why might Baxi have chosen to buy Roca, the Spanish company?
3 Discuss whether Baxi should try to expand its operations in the UK **or** in other European countries in future.

	Country	Population (millions)	National Income (€bn)*	Income as % of EU average	Date Joined
1.	Germany	82.4	2076	117	1958
2.	France	63.4	1529	112	1958
3.	United Kingdom	60.2	1530	118	1973
4.	Italy	58.8	1378	109	1958
5.	Spain	45.0	895	103	1986
6.	Poland	38.1	428	52	2004
7.	Romania	22.3	168	36	2007
8.	Netherlands	16.4	422	119	1958
9.	Greece	11.2	211	89	1981
10.	Portugal	10.6	167	74	1986
11.	Belgium	10.5	272	122	1958
12.	Czech Republic	10.3	162	74	2004
13.	Hungary	10.0	146	68	2004
14.	Sweden	9.0	228	117	1995
15.	Austria	8.2	229	130	1995
16.	Bulgaria	7.8	63	39	2007
17.	Slovakia	5.4	78	67	2004
18.	Denmark	5.4	156	134	1973
19.	Finland	5.3	138	122	1995
20.	Ireland	4.2	147	162	1973
21.	Lithuania	3.5	43	60	2004
22.	Latvia	2.2	26	54	2004
23.	Slovenia	2.0	38	88	2004
24.	Estonia	1.3	19	69	2004
25.	Cyprus	0.8	15	84	2004
26.	Luxembourg	0.5	27	273	1958
27.	Malta	0.4	6	76	2004

*Calculated at 1 Euro = $1.3

Figure 1 *The European Union: population and income, 2007*

Source: adapted from http://wikipedia.org

1 How many member countries of the European Union were there in 2007?

2 Which country had the largest population and which had the smallest?

3 Which country had the highest income as a percentage of the EU average and which had the smallest?

4 What are the (i) opportunities and (ii) threats, if any, of the UK's membership of the EU for: (a) a UK manufacturer of car parts; (b) a supermarket chain like Sainsbury's or Tesco; (c) a local hairdresser in Bristol?

Location

McBride has manufacturing plants across the EU from the UK to Poland and Italy. There is a number of reasons why businesses might be located in a number of different countries.

Cost Different countries have different costs of production. Eastern European countries, like Poland, tend to have lower wages and lower land costs than Western European countries like the UK. This provides an incentive for companies to be located in low cost countries and export products to the rest of the EU.

The customer For some businesses, it is important to be near the customer. Transport costs of finished products might be so high that production has to take place locally. For many service industries, like hairdressers, shops or private hospitals, customers are not prepared to travel far to buy the service.

Markets Many businesses like McBride grow through buying other companies. It is often more successful for a UK company wanting to expand into the Polish market to buy a Polish company than to try and launch UK products into Polish markets.

Economic and Monetary Union (EMU)

There are still barriers to trade between EU countries. One is the fact that different countries use different currencies. The pound goes up and down in value every second of the day against the euro or the US dollar. When McBride exports products from its UK plants, it does not exactly know how much it will receive in pounds for those sales. Equally, it does not know how much in pounds it will pay for any products it imports.

What is more, McBride has to pay banks a commission to exchange foreign currency. Even if this is only 0.1 per cent, it still means a cost of £10 000 on a £1 million order.

There are ways in which businesses can minimise the risk of large changes in the value of the currency. For instance, it can agree a price at which to buy or sell currency for delivery in three months' time. This is known as **hedging**. However, it costs money to do this. For a company like McBride with plants in a number of different EU locations, its purchases from Europe in euros can be paid from the euros it earns from sales in Europe.

To get round the costs of having different currencies, a number of EU countries have created the Economic and Monetary Union (EMU). Member countries, such as France, Germany, Italy and Spain, use the same currency called the euro. This gives businesses in these countries a competitive advantage when they trade with other euro countries compared to businesses outside the euro area (or euro zone). This is because they don't have to pay commission on exchanging currencies and they have certainty about the price they pay or receive for products.

Regulations

Membership of the EU affects UK businesses in other ways. The EU has its own laws and regulations which British businesses and British courts have to conform to. For instance, McBride has to comply with EU health and safety regulations. Its workers have rights under European law on issues such as **equal opportunities** and **working time**. Its production is affected by EU directives on the environment and pollution. It also has to comply with product standards and **copyright** and **patent** laws of the EU.

Regional policy

Some regions of the EU, like the South of England, or the North of Italy, are very prosperous. Average wages are high, unemployment is low and citizens tend to enjoy a high standard of living. Other regions of the EU, like Poland or parts of Wales have below average wages and unemployment is relatively high. To help even out the differences between the regions, the EU has a **regional policy**. The EU allocates money to poorer regions to be spent on a variety of projects, from road building to training of workers. The cash spent results directly in job creation. But it is also designed to create resources which will encourage businesses to invest and so create more jobs and higher incomes.

A company like McBride benefits from regional policy. It will transport goods along roads that have been financed by EU monies. It may employ workers in Poland that have received EU funded training. It can also sell more goods to poorer regions of the EU because their incomes are higher than they would have been without EU regional policy.

Barriers to trade

Barriers to trade between European countries still exist though.

Language is a problem. Selling to Germany means that McBride have to communicate in German with their customers or their customers have to speak a language used by McBride

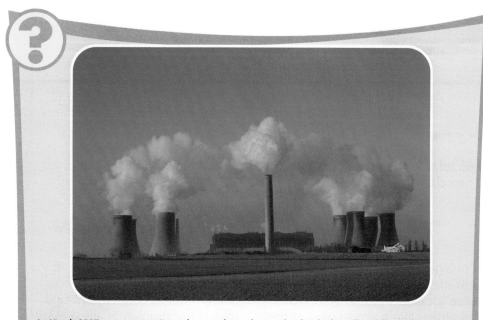

In March 2007 a meeting in Brussels was taking place to decide whether all coal-fired power stations built in the European Union after 2020 could be forced to capture their carbon dioxide (CO2) emissions. A British official speaking before the meeting was 'confident that a target for carbon capture and storage for all new plants would be agreed'. The restrictions were also likely to be extended to gas-fired power plants, to avoid distorting fuel choice. That would mean the entire EU electricity industry would switch to low-carbon generation. Some argued that the technology to separate CO2 and store it beneath the sea bed or in underground caverns is expensive and has not yet been shown to work on a commercial scale.

Source: adapted from the Financial Times, 4.3.2007.

1 What regulations were being proposed at the meeting in 2007?
2 How might the regulations affect (a) the businesses that own power stations and (b) consumers of electricity?

employees. Language barriers are coming down as more people speak two languages. However, continental companies are more likely to have English speakers than British companies have, say, French or German speakers. This can put British companies at a competitive disadvantage.

Different market characteristics

McBride has to adapt its products both to the needs of each of its customers, but also to the country into which it sells. Something as simple as washing detergent could need a different formulation, different packaging and different sizes of packet depending on the market.

Distance can also be a problem. It is easier to communicate with a business half a mile away than one in another country. Transporting goods can also be very costly for low value high bulk products like cement or bricks.

Source: information from McBride plc.

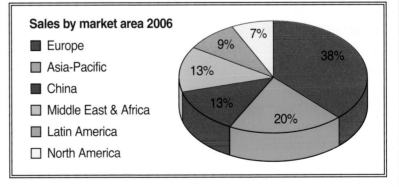

Checklist ✓

1 Explain THREE reasons why McBride may have found it easier to export to Europe after 1973.
2 Why was Britain joining the EU both a threat and an opportunity for UK businesses?
3 (a) Why might you find several languages on the wrapping of a food packet?
   (b) Why do you think businesses don't simply use different wrapping for each country?
4 How would Economic and Monetary Union help a business like McBride?

NOKIA

Nokia is a Finnish mobile communications company. Nokia phones are famous worldwide. The company sells its products throughout the world as well as having manufacturing facilities round the globe. In the European Union, it has manufacturing plants in Finland, Germany, the UK and Hungary.

Operating internationally means that Nokia buys and sells large amounts of different currencies, like the UK pound, the US dollar and the Japanese yen. Within the euro area, life is simpler though because 13 countries now share the same currency, the euro. It doesn't have to hedge transactions when sales are made in Germany from a factory in Hungary, or when products are supplied from Finland to the French market. Nokia has estimated that it saves at least £3 million a year from not having to exchange currencies on trade within the euro area. That also doesn't count the savings made by suppliers on not having to exchange currencies that ultimately benefit Nokia. 'It makes the whole supply chain more efficient', says Nokia Chief Financial Officer Rick Simonson.

Source: adapted from www.businessweek.com, www.nokia.com.

1 What does Nokia produce?
2 (a) What is meant by hedging? (b) Why does being a member of a country that is part of the euro area mean that Nokia does not have to hedge.
3 Explain the benefits to Nokia of operating in a country which is part of the euro area.
4 Discuss whether Nokia should try to increase its sales to North America in future.

Nokia flagship store in Helsinki

Sales by market area 2006

- ■ Europe
- ▨ Asia-Pacific
- ■ China
- ☐ Middle East & Africa
- ▨ Latin America
- ☐ North America

38%
20%
13%
13%
9%
7%

Figure 2 *Nokia, sales by market area*

Making decisions

Businesses have to make decisions which involve issues about what is right and what is wrong. These ethical decisions occur, for instance, when a business decides what to produce, who to sell to, who to buy from, how to treat its workers, how to care for the local environment and whether or not to get involved in the local community. The law provides some guidelines on ethical issues, but many people believe that businesses should often do more than the legal minimum.

Marks & Spencer is one of the UK's largest retailers. In 2006, it sold over £8 billion worth of products. In 2007, it launched 'Plan A', a five year programme costing £200 million, to take forward its environmental and ethical business practices. The detailed 100-point plan covers climate change, waste, raw materials, fair trade and healthy living. Chief Executive, Stuart Rose, said: 'We think this is the right thing to do because our customers, employees and, increasingly, shareholders are asking us to. We believe those people will embrace a responsible business.'

The ethical business

Businesses, like people, have to make ethical choices. They have to decide whether an activity is morally right or wrong. BUSINESS ETHICS are becoming more important to businesses today. Many large businesses want to show that they are ethically responsible. So they produce Corporate Responsibility Reports (CRR) each year. The *Annual Report and Accounts* of a company explains its financial position. The Corporate Responsibility Report explains how the company is performing on a range of measures to do with the ethics of a business. They cover issues such as production, suppliers, workers, customers, competitors, products, the environment, local communities and corporate governance.

Production

Marks & Spencer is a retailer. It produces a service, buying goods in bulk from suppliers and selling them individually to customers from its stores. Like any business, it has choices about how to produce. One choice is about the amount of waste it produces and what it does with its waste. Financially, it should choose the cheapest option, but this might not be the most environmentally friendly option. Marks & Spencer has chosen, as part of 'Plan A', to aim to stop sending any waste from its stores to landfill sites. It hopes to achieve this through a combination of recycling and reducing waste It also wants the company to be carbon neutral. This means that its net carbon dioxide emissions, one type of greenhouse gas, will be zero. It aims to do this, for example, by cutting energy use in its stores, buying electricity from renewable energy sources and increasing the amount of bio-fuels used in its lorries to 50 per cent.

Suppliers

A business like Marks & Spencer has ethical choices about how it treats its suppliers and what it will buy from suppliers. Financially, to maximise profit, a business should pay its suppliers the lowest prices possible. However, these prices may not be 'fair'. In the UK, supermarket chains have been accused of paying farmers too little for the produce they supply. The supermarkets have exploited their big buying power against small farmers who have very little market power. In response, Marks & Spencer introduced a 'Milk Price Pledge' in 2003. This promised UK farmers who supplied milk to Marks & Spencer that prices would be kept constant over a 12 month period. Marks & Spencer also promised to pay a price which reflected not just market prices but also changes in costs to farmers. The result has been that Marks & Spencer has paid farmers more for their milk than most, if not all, other food companies.

Marks & Spencer also buys Fair Trade products from developing countries. Fair Trade products pay producers higher prices. Marks & Spencer is aiming to increase both the range of Fair Trade products it offers and the amount sold under its 'Plan A' programme.

Marks & Spencer works closely with suppliers on a variety of ethical issues. For example, it has banned its farming suppliers from using 60 types of pesticide, with another 19 more to be banned within three years. In Scotland, it has worked on a scheme with fishermen to reduce the number of other fish caught accidentally when they are fishing for haddock to be supplied to Marks & Spencer. This helps increase fish stocks of other fish such as cod. Animal welfare is another important issue. Marks & Spencer now only sells free-range eggs.

Workers

Different businesses treat their workers in different ways. Some pay their workers as little as possible and only give them their minimum legal rights in the workplace. Other businesses, like Marks & Spencer, have a different attitude to workers. They see workers as important stakeholders in the business to whom they have a moral responsibility. Marks & Spencer has set targets for training and career development, to allow its employees to realise their work potential. There are targets for diversity which relates to gender, ethnic origin and age. For example, it has training programmes in discrimination for human resources managers. These managers are responsible for recruiting staff and it is important that they do not discriminate against any applicants for jobs. Marks & Spencer is committed to reducing accidents in the workplace. It has a variety of occupational health schemes designed to help employees with physical and mental health problems.

Customers

Businesses need customers to survive. If there are no customers, there are no sales. However, different businesses have different attitudes to customers. A company like Marks & Spencer attempts to listen to its customers and give them what they want. 'Plan A', Marks & Spencer's five year plan on corporate responsibility, partly came out of market research conducted on its customers.

Some businesses won't sell to certain customers on ethical grounds. For example, the Co-operative Bank won't offer any services to arms manufacturers and dealers. Many businesses won't export to countries like Burma which have governments that don't give their people basic human rights.

Competitors

Businesses have to decide how far they can go in trying to win customers from their competitors. Marks & Spencer has always set itself high standards in this area. Some other businesses, though, are faced with more difficult ethical problems. Arms manufacturers, for example, have in the past commonly given bribes to secure contracts with overseas governments. Today, giving bribes is illegal for any UK company, but bribery still takes place. Is this ethical? Another example is pricing. Some companies deliberately lower their prices when a new business comes into the market in an attempt to force the new business out. When the new competitor withdraws, prices are put back up. Is this unfair competition? In 2007,

ethiscore.org

www.ethiscore.org was set up by the Ethical Consumer Research Association (ECRA). ECRA provides information on the companies behind the brand names and promotes the ethical use of consumer power. It has published *Ethical Consumer* magazine since 1989, and now offers a range of other products designed to encourage purchasers to take environmental and social issues into account when buying products.

Brand	Rating (out of 20)
Green People toothpaste [A,S]	16
Kingfisher toothpaste [S]	16
Weleda toothpaste [S]	15.5
Bioforce toothpaste [S]	15
Sarakan toothpaste [A,S]	13.5
JASON toothpaste [S]	12.5
Clinomyn toothpaste	12
Tom's of Maine toothpaste [S]	11.5
Arm & Hammer toothpaste	11
Mentadent toothpaste	11
Pearl Drops toothpaste	11
Colgate toothpaste	7.5
Theramed toothpaste	6.5
Aquafresh toothpaste	5
Macleans toothpaste	5
Sensodyne toothpaste	5
Crest Tartar Control toothpaste	0
Crest toothpaste	0

[A] = Animal Welfare
[S] = Other Sustainability

Source: adapted from www.ethiscore.org.

The ethiscore website is designed to help users quickly and easily identify the best products to support and the worst companies to avoid. It does this by calculating an 'ethical score' out of 20 for a wide range of consumer products and services. Roughly speaking:
• 15 to 20 is good;
• 10 to 14 is average;
• 5 to 9 is poor;
• 0 to 4 is very poor.
The score is a calculation based on a company's rating in each of Ethical Consumer's 23 main ethical categories. The table below gives the score for a range of toothpastes.

Source: adapted from www.ethiscore.org.

1 Which toothpaste would you buy if you were an 'ethical consumer'?
2 How does ethiscore.org help 'ethical consumers'?
3 How might ethiscore.org pose a threat to some businesses?

Kenyan flower pickers

Workers picking and packaging flowers in Kenya, so shoppers in the UK have colourful bouquets for every occasion, are no longer forced into overtime and casual contracts. This is a result of companies signing up to ethical codes of conduct. Pay slips are now available to staff on Kenyan flower farms, as are employment contracts, better medical facilities, improved housing and increased maternity leave. Better training on the use of pesticides and stricter controls on the spraying of pesticides have been introduced. More women have been promoted to supervisory roles and staff welfare committees have been established. Workers are taking up membership of trade unions in increasing numbers. These changes were carried out after an investigation by an Ethical Trading Initiative (ETI) member, the Women Working Worldwide Group, showed that workers' rights in the African flower industry were being violated.

Source: adapted from www.eti2.org.uk.

1 What is an ethical code of conduct?
2 How have the Kenyan flower pickers benefited from an ethical code of conduct?
3 Why was an ethical code of conduct introduced for Kenyan flower pickers?
4 How might businesses growing flowers in Kenya benefit from adopting ethical codes of practice?

supermarkets were being investigated for holding large 'land banks'. These are plots of land on which a supermarket might or might not build a new store. Some were accusing supermarkets of holding onto land to prevent another supermarket from buying it and building a new store would compete with one of their existing stores.

The product

A business like Marks & Spencer has to decide which products to make. Marks & Spencer has adopted a strong ethical stance towards its products. For example, on animal welfare grounds, it only sells free-range eggs. Because it believes that GM (genetically modified) crops could damage the environment, it doesn't sell any products containing GM ingredients. It is committed to reducing the amount of salt in its products because eating too much salt can damage your health. 85 per cent of all clothes sold at Marks & Spencer can be washed at low temperatures. This saves on energy bills for customers and on dry cleaning, which is less environmentally friendly than washing clothes at home. Many businesses have to make choices about what to sell. For example, should a shop sell replica guns? Should adult magazines be sold in a newsagent where children will also shop?

The environment

All businesses have an impact on the environment. Some businesses, like coal mining companies or companies operating landfill sites, have a major impact on the local environment. Owners of coal, gas and oil fired power stations making electricity are major contributors to greenhouse gases. Service industry businesses like Marks & Spencer have less direct impact on the environment but it is still likely to be negative. Businesses therefore have to decide whether to put caring for the environment as a major objective. Most businesses, for example, can cut the amount of waste they generate, or increase the amount of waste recycled. They can cut energy use and reduce the number of miles travelled by suppliers, workers and customers. Marks & Spencer, for example, is committed to buying more food locally in order to cut down the number of miles travelled by their products.

Local communities

Many businesses have little or nothing to do with their local communities apart from providing jobs, and perhaps selling goods. Some argue, however, that businesses should do more than this. Some businesses support local charities. Other businesses are prepared to pay more to put up a beautiful building, or landscape the area when building new premises. They might build a car park so that local residents are not annoyed by workers or customers parking in front of their houses. Marks & Spencer is a large company and it supports charities in the developing world. When the coast of Sri Lanka was hit by a tsunami (a large wave) in 2005, which caused widespread destruction, it gave £250 000 to help rebuild homes in the country.

Corporate governance

Businesses are faced with a variety of ethical choices in how they are run or governed. There are a variety of corporate governance issues. For example, should the top managers and directors of a company seek to maximise their wages even if this hits the profits and performance of a company? Should directors get a 50 per cent pay rise when workers get 1 per cent? Should managers and directors be open and honest in how they are dealing with an issue such as making workers redundant or the quality of a product? Or should they be secretive and not worry too much about honesty so long as what they are doing is legal?

Source: adapted from Marks & Spencer, *Annual Report and Accounts*, www.marksandspencer.com.

BP

BP is aware that its oil drilling and exploration activities can have an impact on the environment. The company monitors its impact on the environment by keeping records in relation to such things as greenhouse gas (GHG) emissions and oil spillages. In 2006 BP's operational GHG emissions of 64.4 million tonnes of carbon dioxide were lower than in 2005. The growth of the business and reporting changes generated an extra 1.3 million tonnes of emissions, but these were offset by several factors. Continuing efficiency projects provided 1.2 million tonnes of reductions, while divestments and temporary operational variations accounted for a 2.5 decrease. In November, BP also launched the Environmental Requirements for New Projects, a new group practice covering all aspects of environmental management.

The total number of oil spills of one barrel or more from all BP operations during 2006 was 417, compared with 541 in 2005 and 1 098 in 1999. In 2006, two incidents occurred in Prudhoe Bay, Alaska. In March, an undetected leak led to a spill of some 4 800 barrels of oil. In August, the eastern part of the field was shut down as a precaution after the discovery of isolated pitting corrosion, which resulted in a small spill from an oil transit pipeline. Following a comprehensive inspection of the transit lines, the eastern part of the field was restarted 44 days later.

Source: adapted from BP, Annual Report & Accounts, 2006.

1 Comment on BP's 'environmental performance' in 2006.
2 How does BP monitor its environmental impact?
3 What measures is BP taking to reduce its environmental impact?

key terms

Business ethics - ideas about what is morally correct or not, applied in a business situation.

Checklist ✓

1 Explain whether you think a business should make and sell: (a) products which have first been tested on animals; (b) toy guns; (c) cigarettes; (d) landmines.
2 Is Marks & Spencer right to promote Fair Trade products?
3 Give THREE examples of unfair competitive practices.
4 Why might treating workers well benefit a business even though it might seem more costly?
5 Explain what responsibility a business might have to the local environment in which it operates.

GAP AND NIKE

SUMMARY CASE STUDY

Gap and Nike are two major global brands. Gap is a clothing retailer, whilst Nike is a supplier of trainers. In the past, both companies have been heavily criticised for buying supplies from factories in developing countries where workers have been exploited. Workers in places like Indonesia and Thailand have been found to be poorly paid with no job security and working long hours in dangerous conditions. Sometimes, products have been made using child labour.

This criticism has forced the two companies to change their policies. Today, Gap is a member of the Ethical Trading Initiative (ETI). This is a body made up of companies, charities (or non-governmental organisations) and trade unions. The ETI promotes and improves corporate codes of practice which cover working conditions of suppliers. Nike is in discussions to join ETI. Nike has also for several years published a corporate responsibility report outlining how it is achieving sustainable growth. It is almost unique amongst businesses in publishing a list of all its suppliers in developing countries. This means that any organisation can check to see whether suppliers are using child labour or abusing their workers.

Companies such as GA and Nike believe that their customers and their shareholders are becoming increasingly concerned about ethical standards. Their businesses can no longer afford to ignore the issue. Hannah Jones, the vice-president of corporate responsibility at Nike, said her company learned the hard way. 'It has taken a long time to get to this point at Nike and we have made many mistakes. For many years, we were defensive about it and saw it as just a PR problem. Now we see it as part of the way we run our business'. The report and the list of our suppliers was so that everyone can see where our goods come from. Nike is also convinced about the commercial rewards of treating workers in its supply chain humanely, giving them decent wages and basic labour rights, and wants to play a part in 'systemic change' on these issues across the clothes industry.

Source: adapted from www.eti2.org.uk.

1 What is the role of the ETI?
2 Why do you think Nike denied claims of worker exploitation?
3 Why did Nike have to disclose a comprehensive list of its suppliers?
4. Discuss whether it was in the best interests of Nike and Gap to adopt more ethical policies.

Making decisions

Businesses operate in a world where society and technology are constantly changing. They have to decide how to respond to these changes. If they fail to change, businesses risk losing sales and even being forced to leave the market. Embracing change could lead to higher sales and higher profits. Businesses also have to make decisions about environmental issues. Will they do the absolute minimum required by law or will they become much 'greener' in terms of what they make and how they produce.

Amazon is the world's largest e-commerce seller of books. Sales of other products by Amazon, such as DVDs, electronic equipment and furniture, are growing rapidly. The company is also offering download services for television programmes and films in a bid to take a large share of this growing market. Amazon was founded in 1994 in the USA by Jeff Bezos. Today, it operates in many countries including the UK.

Society

Businesses like Amazon have to operate within the laws of a country. But they are affected by the wider rules and conventions of society. These rules, conventions and expectations of society are constantly changing. There are many examples.

- Amazon operates today in a culture where women expect to be treated as men's equals. 50 years ago, the relationships between men and women in the workplace were likely to have been different. A bookselling business, for example, may have appointed men to senior positions of responsibility. Legislation today prevents this type of discrimination. Women employees expect businesses to take steps to ensure that they act legally in areas such as recruitment and promotion.
- Amazon's business model assumes that customers are prepared to pay for goods using credit cards. Over the past 50

years, there have been large changes in cultural attitudes in the Western world towards debt. When credit cards were first introduced in the 1960s, a lot of people were reluctant to use them because they were a type of borrowing.

- Amazon is an e-retailer. Over the past 10 years, there has been a revolution in society's attitude towards computers and the Internet. In the 1990s, they were still mostly used either exclusively in the workplace or by small numbers of enthusiasts at home. Today, many people at home use computers and the Internet for leisure and for shopping. Most households in the UK have a computer, many with broadband access.
- Amazon has to work within the religious framework of society. So it cannot expect an Orthodox Jewish employee to work on Saturdays. If it operates a canteen in one of its workplaces and has a number of Muslim employees, then it cannot offer

pork as the only main meal.

Changes in society create both threats and opportunities for businesses. In 1910, for example, most women in the UK wore a corset. By 1980, the corset was something only worn by some senior citizens. The result was that between 1910 and 1980, almost all UK corset manufacturers went out of business. Since the 1990s, however, corsets have started to come back into fashion for women. This has provided opportunities for a number of small businesses to set up and fill a gap in the market.

Amazon has benefited from changes in society. It has been able to exploit the growth of understanding and the use of information technology to create a multi-billion dollar business.

Technology

The rate of technological change has never been faster. New technologies are being developed and adopted all the time across almost all businesses. Amazon could not have existed without the rapid development and adoption of information and communication technology (ICT). Technology has impacted on Amazon's business model in a variety of ways.

Sales Amazon was a pioneer in developing a website that could easily be used by customers to order products. However, only a few per cent of all spending today is done via the Internet. Traditional sales channels, like shops, or visiting sales representatives, are likely to remain the main ways in which sales are made. But even these traditional sales channels are changing due to technology. For example, a visiting sales representative may well carry around a laptop computer. Many shops now use bar coding technology (EPOS - Electronic Point of Sale) to scan items through tills.

Products Many products are changing fast due to changes in technology. Personal computers (PCs), which customers use to buy from Amazon, didn't exist before the mid-1970s. DVDs, a main sales product for Amazon, didn't exist before the 1990s. Motorised vans, used to transport Amazon orders from the warehouse (called 'fulfilment centres' by Amazon) to the customer, didn't exist before the twentieth century. Changes in product technology pose both an opportunity and a threat to businesses. It is an opportunity for businesses like Amazon because they can move into new markets. It is a threat because it can make existing products obsolete. The makers of horse drawn carriages, for example, had to adapt or die when petrol driven vehicles entered the market.

Production methods Amazon provides a service. Its production methods use the latest technology, from computers to the Internet to automated purchasing and the latest in warehouse technology. Over time, production methods

Marriages

The pattern of relationship formation has changed a lot since the 1970s. The numbers of people getting married has dropped quite sharply. In the late 1960s the number of marriages per year peaked at 480 300. In 2003 this had dropped to 308,600. The age at which people get married for the first time has continued to rise during the same period. In 1971 the average age at first marriage was 25 for men and 23 for women in England and Wales; this increased to 31 for men and 29 for women in 2003.

Another change in society has been the growing acceptance of gay relationships. For example, in 2005 the Civil Partnership Act in the UK gave same-sex couples nearly all the rights enjoyed by heterosexual married couples. In the first six weeks after the law came into force, 3 648 civil partnerships were registered.

Source: adapted from *Social Trends*, Office for National Statistics, 2006.

1 How do changes in society, like those described above, affect businesses in general?
2 How might: (a) a house-builder; (b) a wedding organiser; (c) a car manufacturer be affected by the changes?
3 How might a business running a dating agency respond to the changes in society described above?

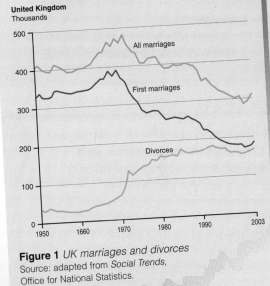

Figure 1 *UK marriages and divorces*
Source: adapted from *Social Trends*, Office for National Statistics.

have become more capital intensive. This means that more capital is used compared to the other factors of production, land and labour. The use of capital, such as machines, plant and infrastructure, allows production methods to be far more efficient. There is far less wastage and so fewer raw materials need to be used in production. Equally, the use of more capital means that less labour is used. Changes in technology have particularly benefited the manufacturing industry. But service industries too have been transformed by new technologies. Banks and other financial companies are now completely dependent upon

information technology to produce their services. In health care, machines have transformed diagnosis and treatment. In education, there is ever-increasing use of IT in lessons.

The environment

Businesses are increasingly aware of the environmental impact of their activities. The fuel used to deliver books from Amazon to the customer creates greenhouse gas emissions. The process of making paper for books creates some environmental pollution. The building of an Amazon warehouse facility has an impact on the local environment. Businesses are

I-play

I-play owns a franchise to mobile phone games based on 'The Fast and the Furious' and '24'. You can star in your own version of the television hit show '24' thanks to I-play, which develops and distributes mobile-phone games based on sports and movies.

Venture capitalists Apax Partners and Argo Global Capital have invested £26.4 million in the London company, run by David Gosen. The company is based in central London and employs 155 staff, many of whom are software engineers.

Last year, I-play added an office in San Francisco to bases in Europe and Singapore. Sales have grown 77 per cent a year from £3.8 million in 2003 to £11.9 million in 2005, when the company made a significant loss. With over 1.7 billion mobile phone users worldwide, mobile gaming will be the first truly mass-market form of video-gaming.

Source: adapted from www.fasttrack.co.uk.

1 What does I-play do?
2 I-play was set up in 1998. Could it have existed in 1978? Explain your answer.
3 What might be the future prospects for I-play?

---

affected by environmental issues in a number of ways.

Legislation, regulations and taxes Governments are forcing businesses to reduce their environmental impact through laws and taxes. Laws about issues such as planning permission for building or limits on pollution restrict the activities of business. Environmental or 'green' taxes are also used to change the behaviour of businesses. Putting a tax on petrol, for example, discourages businesses from using petrol. Amazon's activities are restricted throughout the world by different government's environmental regulations and taxes.

Customer demands Customers are putting pressure on some businesses to be more environmentally friendly. For example, supermarkets are increasingly looking at environmental issues when deciding which products to put on their shelves. Some consumers, when buying food, are choosing to buy environmentally friendly products like organic food. Businesses which can persuade customers that they are more environmentally friendly than their competitors can gain a competitive edge. They can use their environmentally friendly reputation

Greenhouse gas emissions and the aircraft industry

The airline industry is coming under increasing fire from environmental groups. Air travel contributes at least 3 per cent of global emissions, according to the UN. Although this is tiny compared with transport as a whole, which contributes 21 per cent, it is growing fast. However, the airline industry says that air travel is good for the global economy and that there is no alternative, particularly to long-haul flights. It says improving efficiency is the best way to reduce pollution. Newer aircraft use less fuel while towing planes to runways. Making a reduction in the time spent circling airports and other operational changes would cut aviation fuel consumption by nearly 18 per cent. One of the measures being considered by European governments to reduce emissions made by aircraft is to impose a 'green tax' on aviation fuel.

Source: adapted from the *Financial Times* 31.10.2006

1 Do you think the airline industry makes a significant contribution to global greenhouse gas emissions?
2 What is likely to happen to air fares if governments impose 'green taxes' on aviation fuel?
3 How might airlines respond to a 'green tax' on aviation fuel:
(a) in the short term;
(b) in the long term?

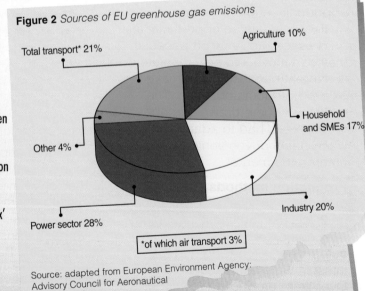

Figure 2 *Sources of EU greenhouse gas emissions*

- Agriculture 10%
- Total transport* 21%
- Household and SMEs 17%
- Other 4%
- Industry 20%
- Power sector 28%

*of which air transport 3%

Source: adapted from European Environment Agency; Advisory Council for Aeronautical Research.

as part of their public relations campaigns.

Business opportunities

Environmental concerns can represent a business opportunity. There are many new businesses which have been created to make energy-saving or renewable energy products. Solar panel producers and wind farm electricity companies are examples. Other businesses create products which reduce pollution.

Source: adapted from www.amazon.com.

SUMMARY CASE STUDY

FOOTBALL AND NEW TECHNOLOGY

Football clubs are increasingly making use of new technology. Many have their own websites on the Internet. They provide a variety of information about the clubs and their history for fans. They advertise when tickets are on sale and give ticket prices. They sell tickets online and have online competitions. They have online shops where fans can buy club merchandise.

Clubs are also making use of new technology in grounds. Many have CCTV cameras to monitor fans and the flow of people into and out of the ground. Clubs may make use of bar codes on tickets that can be read at turnstiles to prevent hold ups. Flat screen televisions show replays of matches at half time. Some clubs, such as Chelsea, Manchester United and Celtic, have their own television stations.

Today large sums are available to football from television stations such as Sky and Setanta to show matches, although successful clubs tend to get more of the television money. A report in 2006, Football and Its Communities, examined the make-up of supporters. It 'mapped' where clubs' supporters live. The research showed that football clubs draw their support not from the poorer or deprived areas around them, but mostly from the better-off suburbs several miles away. Given the huge rises in the cost of tickets over the past ten years, this is, perhaps, is not a huge shock. But it is surprising to see that a sport that was regarded as appealing to the traditional 'working-class' should now have such as different support make-up.

Source adapted in part from the *Guardian*, 9.8.2006.

1 How has new technology provided opportunities for football clubs to increase turnover?

2 (a) How has the make-up of supporters changed? (b) How might this affect football clubs?

3 What possible threats might clubs face in future?

Checklist ✓

1 Describe THREE ways in which changes in the attitudes of society might affect a business.

2 Explain TWO ways in which changes in the attitudes of society might create opportunities and be a threat for a clothing business.

3 Explain TWO ways in which changes in technology in the last 5 years have improved the ordering of goods.

4 List FIVE products that have appeared on the market in the last 10 years as a result of new technology.

5 Suggest ONE change in IT that has affected: (a) banking, (b) health care and (c) education in the last 5 years.

6 How might a food manufacturer's packaging be affected by the views of government and consumers about the environment?

7 State THREE business opportunities that might have been created as a result of concerns about the environment.

Making decisions

Every business has to be located somewhere. A sole trader who works as a freelance cartoonist may operate from home. A multinational chemical company will have sites in several countries and probably several continents. So where is the best place to locate a business? The choice is likely to be affected by:

* cost - where is the cheapest place to locate?
* the market - which location will enable the business to exploit its market best?
* labour - where is labour available?
* government - what opportunities will government offer and what restrictions will it place on location?

n 2007 there were over 160 Taiwanese firms with an operation in the UK. This accounted for about 70 per cent of Taiwanese investment in Europe. The investments cover a variety of activities, including corporate HQs, sales and marketing, R&D, manufacturing and distribution.

Cost of land and premises

The UK has become a popular choice for overseas companies wanting to set up in Europe. Manufacturers may locate in GREENFIELD sites. One of the reasons for choosing to locate here is that the cost of the land may be low.

A greenfield site is an area of rural land where businesses have not previously built. Buying land in a town or city which has already been built on a, BROWNFIELD SITE, is likely to be far more expensive. It is also much cheaper to build an electronics complex from scratch than to buy an existing factory and try to convert it.

Retailers need to consider the cost of their sites as well. For example, some computer retailers are sited on the high street. But others have gone for cheaper locations out of the town centre. They can build larger stores and offer free parking for less cost than if they were in the high street.

Cost of transport

Some businesses are affected by costs of transport when deciding where to locate.

Costs of transporting raw materials and other inputs In some industries, like the steel industry, costs of transporting raw materials are high. Large quantities of bulky raw materials, such as coal and iron ore, are needed to make steel. So steel producers need to be sited where the cost of transport of raw materials is lowest.

In the past in the UK, this has

The cost of moving

Hiring office space in London is expensive. An office, for instance, might cost £425 per square metre per annum. Move to Hull or Middlesbrough and the same space would cost only a fraction of that price. Yet Hull, at £80 per sq metre or Middlesbrough at £75 per square metre are not being besieged by bargain hunters. This is because moving offices is a costly business. £30 000 per worker should be built into any calculation for a move. What's more, many offices are tied to a local area. Trying to run an accountancy firm serving clients mainly located in London from an office in Hull is a guaranteed route to failure. That is why most businesses only move a few miles.

An insurance company is considering moving its 2 000 sq metres office in the City area of central London with a rent of £400 per square metre **either** to the Euston area of central London with rents of £300 per square metre **or** to Hull with rents of £80 per square metre. It currently has 200 employees.

1 Calculate: (a) the rent cost per year of staying in its present offices; (b) the new rent cost per year if it moved to the same sized offices in the Euston area; (c) the yearly rent cost of the same sized offices in Hull.

2 Would it be financially worthwhile to move: (a) within London; and (b) from London to Hull if moving costs of £30 000 per worker were taken into account?

3 There would be non-monetary benefits for the company if it stayed in London rather than moving to Hull. For instance, a move to Hull could mean that a lot of existing workers might resign because they were not prepared to move. This would be disruptive for the company. Suggest TWO other non-monetary benefits to the company of staying in London.

Siting a convenience store

S&R is a business which runs convenience stores throughout the UK. The exact mix of products sold varies from location to location. However, in a city centre, it would be confectionery, soft drinks, tobacco products, magazines and possibly greetings cards and/or snacks such as sandwiches and/or selected groceries.

The business is considering opening a store in the centre of Balsford.

1 Consider the five possible sites on the map (A-E). Which do you think would give the highest level of sales turnover? Explain your answer carefully.
2 Which do you think would be the most expensive and the least expensive to rent per sq ft? In your answer, rank in order the five sites in terms of likely cost and explain your reasons.
3 What other factors would you have to take into account when making a final decision about where to site the store?

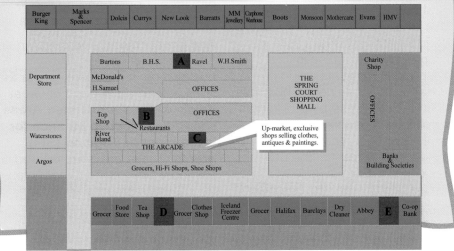

meant that steel works have been built next to coal mines and iron mines. However, the UK's iron ore deposits are now exhausted. So a steel producer like British Steel today buys its iron ore from abroad. Its plants are now sited on the coast, where the iron ore is delivered in large ships to reduce transport costs.

Transport costs of raw materials and components are not particularly high relative to final cost for certain industries. Some, such as Taiwanese business Delta Electronics (Scotland), which specialises in manufacturing power supply units for PCs and monitors for the European market, are not really affected by this when they decide where to locate.

Costs of transporting the finished goods Some industries need to be sited near to their customers because the cost of transporting the finished product is very high in relation to the value of the product. Bricks, for instance, may come from a local brick plant because the cost of transport is so high in relation to the value of a single brick.

The transport costs of finished electronic products are not high in relation to the value. Microtest Corporation, a Taiwanese business that manufactures automatic test and measurement equipment, bought a UK business in Bognor in July 2001. It could have set up anywhere. But it argued that setting up in the UK gave it greater access to European and worldwide markets for its products.

Microtest Corporation is typical of many businesses which are FOOTLOOSE. They are free to locate anywhere because transport costs are not very important.

The market

Being close to the market is vital for a number of industries. A retailer, for example, sited on the high street or in a retail shopping park is likely to sell more than a shop in a small town. There are many other industries apart from retailing where being near to the market is vital. For instance, in personal services, such as hairdressing or the restaurant trade, location is important. Banks and building societies also need convenient locations for the customer.

Being close to the market influenced the Akoko Bicycle Group to locate in Birmigham. It started its UK operation when it bought Reece Bicycle plc in 2002. It argued that having its designs near to its customers was crucial. Each European customer, country and region in the UK had its own preferences for style, colour and performance specifications of cycles.

Many industries don't need to be near their markets. Some manufacturers can transport their product anywhere around the world to their customers. Even in retailing, many products are now sold via the Internet. So businesses don't always need to be near to their customers.

Labour

The availability of workers, their skills and the wages they need to be paid can be important in influencing a Taiwanese business to locate in the UK. For example, parts of the UK have higher unemployment rates than the national average. There is likely to be an available pool of labour here.

Workers in the UK may also have the skills needed by businesses. Acer Inc of Taiwan, a computer manufacturer, chose to set up a multi-lingual marketing and technical customer support centre in Belfast, Northern Ireland, costing £1.9 million. The centre deals with customers in Belgium, Denmark, Sweden, Norway, Finland and the UK, for example. It needs well-educated and literate people, fluent in Northern European languages who can communicate well by telephone.

The cost of employing labour in the UK may also be low compared to other countries. Wages paid to workers in the UK are low in comparison with many European Union countries like Germany or France. They are also lower than in some Far Eastern countries like Japan. Also, the taxes on employing workers in the UK are low by international standards. In Germany, employers have to pay taxes worth around half the wage of a worker. These taxes on employment pay for health care, pensions and welfare benefits.

Import restrictions

All countries impose restrictions on imports to some extent. The European Union (EU) imposes common restrictions on all imports coming into Europe. A non-European manufacturer may find that the only way to sell into Europe is to locate a factory within the EU. For instance, one of the reasons why Japanese car manufacturers Nissan and Toyota set up car plants in the UK was because there were restrictions on imports of Japanese cars into the EU.

Regional aid

Businesses create jobs and prosperity in a **local economy**. Attracting a business to set up in an area can therefore be very important to a local council or a government.

In the UK, businesses may get help with locating from the local council, a regional body, the UK government or the European Union.

Local councils Many local councils in the UK have a department which tries to attract new businesses into the area. They advertise in newspapers, magazines and on television. They can help a business thinking of setting up by providing it with all the information it needs about how to get grants or other aid from the government or the EU. They can suggest where land or premises can be bought or rented locally. They can also help the business with any regulations for new buildings.

Regional development agencies A number of regions in the UK have development agencies. They are responsible for attracting businesses to set up in their region or expand their existing operations. For example, Taiwanese business Teco Electric, which manufactures electric motors, set up its European HQ in 1993 in Manchester. It has worked continuously with the Northwest Development Agency. This is an organisation that aims to develop the north west area and provides support and advice to businesses working in the area.

The government The government offers a variety of help to businesses. It may give grants to firms setting up in parts of Great Britain which are **Assisted Areas**, known as **Selective Finance for Investment in England (SFI) grants**. These are administered by Regional Development agencies for business creating or saving jobs.

Businesses willing to set up in run down urban areas may be able to get financial help from the **City Challenge** scheme. Various areas in the country have won grants from the government to help transform run down areas through a mixture of new housing, industrial development and training for the local workforce.

English Partnerships is a government-sponsored agency that also helps industry to regenerate run down urban areas. It gives help and advice. It is prepared to take an equity stake (i.e. put up money to buy shares) in a business that locates in a deprived area. It also offers loans to businesses.

Businesses in rural areas can get financial help from the **Rural Development Commission for England**. If a business creates new jobs, for instance, it may be able to get a grant from the commission. There are many other forms of assistance that the government offers through a variety of other schemes.

Most businesses seeking help might approach their local

Roberts Metal Packaging

Roberts Metal Packaging makes aluminium and tinplate screw caps and small containers for use in the cosmetic and hair care industry. For 80 years, it was sited in Peckham, SE London. But in 2007 it relocated to a new building in Birchmere Business Park, East Thamesmead. It had found the Peckham Site too small. Manufacturing over two storeys was difficult. There was no shift working due to its nearness to local homes. Also, delivery and staff parking were problems.

After investigating and choosing a new site, the business applied for a Selective Finance for Investment (SFI) grant from the London Development Agency in 2005. In September it was awarded £200 000. Gateway to London, an inward investment agency for the Thames Gateway area in London, offered advice throughout the negotiation phase of Robert's move. It introduced them to other business support organisations, such as the Department for Trade & Industry's Manufacturing Advisory Service and UK Trade & Investment. It also helped the company to get advice on training to meet their new larger requirements.

Source: adapted from www.gtlon.co.uk.

1 What type of financial help did Roberts Metal Packaging receive to help in its relocation ?
2 Why might Roberts Metal Packaging have needed the help of Gateway to London in its relocation?
3 Discuss why moving to a business park might help the company.

Business Link. These give help and advice to businesses. This means that they inform the business of the assistance it might be able to get and then help it to apply for the grant.

The European Union The EU gives a wide variety of loans and grants, mostly linked to high unemployment and factory closures. Certain areas of the UK have been particularly targeted because their income is below the EU average. The EU has been a major supporter of agriculture, through the Common Agricultural Policy (CAP). Businesses benefit from the funding that the EU gives to local authorities on infrastructure schemes, such as the building of new roads. The EU also funds training for workers.

Source: adapted from www.britishembassy.gov.uk, www.startinbusiness.co.uk.

key terms

Brownfield site - location available for building which has been built on in the past.
Footloose industries - industries where costs of transport of raw materials and finished goods are relatively low, so that they can be situated in a wide variety of locations.
Greenfield site - location available for industrial building that is currently agricultural land.

Checklist ✓

1 Why might a business choose to locate on a greenfield site?
2 Why might a shoe manufacturer choose not to locate in a city centre site whilst a shoe retailer would be attracted to the area?
3 It costs more to transport clay to make bricks than do the bricks themselves. Where should a plant making bricks be located?
4 'Computer manufacturers are footloose.' What does this mean?
5 Give FIVE examples of businesses which need to be located near to their markets and explain why this is the case.
6 A business wants to employ workers who are as highly skilled and motivated as possible. It also wants to keep costs to a minimum. Wages are higher and unemployment lower in East Anglia than in Scotland. Which region should prove the most attractive to businesses and why?
7 Why does government offer incentives to businesses coming to a particular area of the country?

SUMMARY CASE STUDY

PODMORES

The business - Podmore's is a fast expanding company which makes electrical components. Its customers are mainly in the south of England. However, it has a growing trade with Europe, particularly Holland, Germany and Scandinavia. It is currently based in Newham in London. Its factory is now too small and the company is looking for new premises. It could stay in Newham. There is a suitable site just ¼ of a mile away. It could also move elsewhere in the country. A variety of costs, including the cost of transporting goods to buyers and the cost of employing staff, would be different depending upon the location. These are shown in Table 1.

Marketing - The marketing department is concerned about rumours that the company is thinking of moving away from the London area. It feels that being near its customers is essential if sales are to continue to grow and current customers kept satisfied. If the company did move from the south of England, the marketing department feels that it may be necessary to open a new office in the south. This would add considerable cost to the marketing effort and lead to communication problems with a factory based hundreds of miles away.

Staff - Staff are concerned by reports that the company might move out of London. Very few shop floor workers would be prepared to go with the company to a new location hundreds of miles away. Some senior staff have also expressed reservations about moving. It would take time to build up an effective new team of workers if key workers failed to relocate with the company.

1 As a director of the company, study the information provided about the four sites. Write a short report explaining which of the four sites the board should choose.

Hull An existing factory near the port, with good motorway connections to the A1 south and the west coast via the M62. The factory is ideally suited to present capacity needs.

Edinburgh New factory shell premises on an industrial estate with good road access to Glasgow and the south. Land included on the site could allow up to 30 per cent expansion of the building.

Liverpool Renovated 19th century building of great historical interest near to the city centre. The inside has been completely gutted to make it suitable for 21st century manufacturing. The building is about 20 per cent larger than is currently needed for production.

Table 1 Estimated costs (+) and savings (-) of the move.

	£ million estimated			
	Edinburgh	Liverpool	Hull	Newham
Annual change in labour costs	– 2.0	– 2.5	– 1.7	0
Annual change in transport costs	+ 1.2	+ 1.0	0	0
Annual change in other costs	– 0.3	– 0.3	– 0.3	0
Cost of new factory with equipment (including any regional aid)	+ 9.0	+ 7.0	+ 7.5	+ 11.5
Cost of moving	+ 2.0	+ 2.0	+ 2.0	+ 0.5

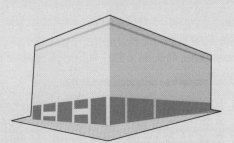

Newham An existing factory with about 10 per cent more space than is currently needed. Office accommodation is cramped and poor quality.

Making decisions

Businesses have a number of different stakeholders. These include owners, workers, customers and suppliers. Each set of stakeholders must decide what are its objectives and how it will try to influence how the business operates. Owners, for example, may decide that they want the business to maximise profits whatever the cost to other stakeholders. Workers may decide they want to get the highest wages possible even if the business makes a loss as a result.

Kellogg's is a US company with worldwide sales of over $11 billion. It is the world's largest producer of breakfast cereals and is also a major producer of foods such as biscuits, cereal bars and meat alternatives. In the UK, its brands include Kellogg's Corn Flakes, Frosties, Rice Krispies, All Bran, Special K and Kellogg's Raisin Bran. Many people and businesses which have an interest in what happens to the company and how it behaves.

Stakeholders

Kellogg's as a company has an impact on many groups. For example, the customers of Kellogg's want high quality food products at competitive prices. Workers employed by the company want satisfying jobs. Businesses which supply products to Kellogg's want to continue to sell to the company at a profit. Any individual or group affected by the activities of a business is known as a STAKEHOLDER in that business.

Owners

One group with an interest in a business is the owners of the business. For example, the owner of a local corner grocery shop selling Kellogg's products could well be a **sole trader** working for himself. He depends on the money he makes from the business for his livelihood. A large company like Kellogg's has **shareholders**. They have bought shares in the business to make a return on their investments. They can receive money from the business by being paid a **dividend**, a share of the profits made by the business. So profit is important for shareholders. The owners of a company can also make a return on their investments if the value of the company goes up. The value is reflected in the

Asda dividend

Asda, owned by US company Wal-Mart, cut its dividend payment to zero despite increased sales, as it prepared for a difficult trading period in 2005. Sainsbury's and Tesco were putting pressure on Asda. At the same time there was a slowdown in high street spending. The money remained within the UK, where it was to be used to fund investments. 'We are investing substantially. All of the profit we make we reinvest in new stores and distribution centres,' a spokesperson said. Asda hoped to have opened 40 stores in 2005, including 8 non-food stores.

Source: adapted from the *Independent*, 9.11.2005.

1 (a) Which stakeholders might have been interested in Asda's decision to declare no dividend in 2005? (b) How were they affected?
2 Why did Asda take the decision to declare no dividend?
3 Discuss whether Asda should declare no dividend in each of the next three years.

Figure 1 *Stakeholders in Kellogg's*

price of shares in the company. If the company grows in size and becomes more profitable, the share price tends to rise. So shareholders of a company like Kellogg's want the company to be successful financially.

Customers

The customers of a business are another important group of stakeholders. For Kellogg's, the immediate customers are mostly the wholesalers and large supermarket chains that buy products directly from the company. Ultimately, however, the customers are ordinary consumers who buy Kellogg's products from retailers.

Wholesalers and supermarket chains want a range of products from Kellogg's that sell well and from which they can make a profit. They want reliability of supply, which means that they can have Kellogg's products on their shelves whenever their customers want to buy them. Quality of products is also important because quality matters to their customers.

Consumers are looking for food that is nutritious and tastes good. It must be presented and packaged in ways that are convenient for the consumer. Prices must be competitive with alternative products from other companies. Food must also be

safe to eat, which is why Kellogg's must be so stringent in its manufacturing processes.

Suppliers

Suppliers are businesses which sell products to other businesses. For example, the suppliers of Kellogg's include farming businesses from which it buys raw food ingredients, such as wheat and rice. Food refining and processing companies, such as sugar manufacturers, are also suppliers. Electricity companies, transport companies and office equipment companies also sell to Kellogg's. Suppliers want to keep their contracts with the company and, if possible, expand sales. They want to be paid a fair price so that they can make a profit.

Employees

The employees and workers of a business like Kellogg's are important stakeholders. They depend on the company for their jobs. Employees want the company to give them job security, opportunities for promotion and fair pay and benefits. Safety at work is also important as are issues to do with equal opportunities. Some of Kellogg's employees are represented by trade unions. For example, at Kellogg's manufacturing plant in Wrexham in

ReTyre

Darragh McIlroy runs a business that makes recycled tyres for industrial vehicles such as tractors. He and his partner rely on materials from existing vehicles for recycling. This may come from scrap yards or from other recycling businesses that have excess stock of materials.

Recently he has faced problems in obtaining enough materials. Improvements in tyre manufacturing and an increasing awareness of the impact on the environment of recycling have cut supply. In the last six months he has lost three major orders because he was unable to guarantee delivery.

1 (a) Why are scrap yards and recyling businesses stakeholders of ReTyre?
   (b) How have their actions affected (i) ReTyre and (ii) ReTyre's customers?
2 Explain why (a) improvements in manufacturing and (b) an increasing awareness of the impact on the environment of recycling might have cut supply to Darragh's business.
3 What action could Darragh and his partner take to deal with the problems it faces?

Customers can be businesses that sell Kellogg's products or consumers

Employees who work for Kellogg's have an interest in the business.

Powergen

Powergen is part of E.ON UK. It is one of the biggest gas and electricity producers in the UK. The company provides gas and electricity for around 6 million household customers and businesses. It has schemes in place for elderly customers in conjunction with Age Concern and the company sponsors both national and community events such as the Powergen Cup.

In 2007 Powergen Energy UK guaranteed not to raise fuel prices until March 2010. Powergen Energy UK also removed standing charges from standard electricity and gas schemes, so customers only pay for what they use.

Powergen Energy's UK operation is committed to green energy. It runs 20 wind farms in the UK as well as hydro electric power (HEP) stations. It was also been developing a huge biomass power station in Scotland to improve the UK's contribution to renewable gas and electricity.

Source: adapted from www.freeindex.co.uk.

1 Which stakeholders of Powergen are customers of the business?
2 How might customers be affected by Powergen's pricing policies?
3 Explain how Powergen's operations could (a) benefit and (b) be a problem for the local community.

---

the North West of England, some workers are represented by USDAW, the food and retail trade union. Where employees are represented by trade unions in a business, they too become stakeholders.

Managers and directors

Managers and directors in a company like Kellogg's are employees too. However, directors are elected at the Annual General Meeting of a company by its shareholders. Directors are legally responsible for looking after the interests of the owners, the shareholders, in directing the company. Managers are appointed by directors to carry out their strategies. So managers and directors are more likely to focus on the financial success of a business than, for example, other workers.

The local community and government

The local community is another

example of an important group of stakeholders. A company like Kellogg's has a direct impact on the local communities where they have manufacturing plants and offices. A decision to expand a plant and take on more workers will provide extra job opportunities. Reducing the size of a plant or

Government is a stakeholder of businesses. Government receives taxes from Kellogg's and makes laws which affect its operations .

closing it down will create unemployment, at least in the short term. There will be knock-on effects in terms of making employment decisions. Creating new jobs, for example, could benefit local shops because spending power in the local community will increase.

Decisions about the location, expansion or contraction of plants will also have an environmental impact. Local communities will have an opinion about whether the environmental impact is acceptable or not.

Local and national governments often represent the views of local communities. A decision to expand a plant, for example, would have to be approved by the local authority planning department and committee. Where industries are of national importance, like railways or gas, then national governments might monitor companies in the industry.

Kellogg's also donates money in the local areas where its factories are located. For example, it has helped in the redevelopment of Moss Side in Manchester in the

UK. Kellogg's is also active in encouraging healthy eating and promoting breakfast cereal as a method of improving diet.

Legal bodies

Businesses have to work within legal frameworks. For example, they have to pay taxes. So UK organisations which collect taxes, such as HM Revenue & Customs, are stakeholders in a company like Kellogg's. Businesses can be investigated if they trade unfairly. If larger businesses are thought to be exploiting their customers because they have too much market power they may be investigated by a government body called the Competition Commission.

Kellogg's is subject to food and health and safety laws in the UK and its manufacturing plants must conform to the strict standards laid down. All these legal bodies are stakeholders in businesses like Kellogg's.

Source: adapted in part from www.kelloggs.co.uk.

Checklist ✓

1 Name SIX main groups of stakeholders in a business.
2 Why might the owners of a company be interested in its performance?
3 Explain the difference between the different types of customer who might be a stakeholder.
4 A food manufacturer is having problems buying ingredients from abroad to supply to a supermarket. Why might it be concerned about the reaction of the supermarket to this situation?
5 Explain THREE ways in which employees might be affected by a loss made by a business.
6 How might a business (a) benefit and (b) harm the local environment in which it operates?
7 Suggest ONE way in which (a) local government, (b) central government and (c) the Competition Commission might be affected by a business's activities.

key terms

Stakeholder - an individual or group which is affected by a business and so has an interest in its success or failure.

TRAIN CONDUCTORS' INDUSTRIAL ACTION

In 2007 senior conductors working for Central Trains voted to strike in a dispute over rotas. Staff who belonged to the Rail, Maritime and Transport union (RMT) were planning to stage a one day walkout on 24 February.

At the centre of the dispute was the Crew Plan. This is a computer programme designed to manage the shift patterns of workers. It had already been introduced in 9 out of 15 depots to replace the former paper rostering system. The union wanted the system scrapped. The firm, which admited to some 'teething problems', said all the information was computerised and it could not 'turn back the clock'.

Initially, the conductors voted 235 against 89 to stop issuing tickets to passengers. But the firm said it would dock workers' pay by up to 50 per cent if this action went ahead. So the union suspended the action and announced a one day strike. It claimed that 550 workers would walk out.

RMT boss Bob Crow accused the company of making the situation 'far worse' by threatening to cut pay. 'The industrial action we had planned to start on Monday would have allowed Central to continue to operate trains,' said Mr Crow. 'But once more they have shown that they are not in the least interested either in settling the dispute or in ensuring that passengers can travel.'

Central Trains said that they had put two deals to the RMT which were agreed nationally by the union, but were rejected by local negotiators. The firm's operations director, Andy Thomas, said they were committed to finding a 'sensible resolution' to the dispute. 'We have not escalated this dispute at all - we have simply responded to every new industrial action the RMT has said that they will pursue and made every effort to keep services running for our passengers.' The firm said it would wait for confirmation of details of the strike before announcing the disruption passengers will face.

Source: adapted from http://news.bbc.co.uk, 15.2.2007.

1 Identify the stakeholders of Central Trains mentioned in the article.
2 What might have been the objectives of each stakeholder in February 2007?
3 Discuss whether there is conflict between the stakeholders in the business.

THE AIMS AND OBJECTIVES OF BUSINESS

Making decisions

A business needs to decide what are its objectives. Is it just to survive? Does it want to make the largest possible profit? Perhaps it has set itself a number of targets, such as sales growth or increasing market share. To find out what are these objectives, it is important to understand who controls a business. If it is the owners, they are likely to want to see profits maximised. If it is the workers and management, they may be more interested in good pay and working conditions, and the survival of the business.

Costain is an international engineering and construction group. It operates in a number of sectors including water, rail, retail, nuclear and oil and gas. It builds everything from new railway stations to new bridges. Its vision is to be 'Number One' in all that it does. To achieve that, it has a number of different objectives.

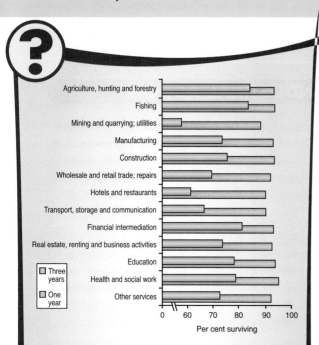

Source: adapted from DTI, Small business service.

Figure 1 *Percentage of businesses surviving one year and three years*

1 What type of business had (a) the least chance of survival and (b) the best chance of survival over (i) one year and (ii) 3 years?
2 Explain TWO factors that might influence the survival of a business in its first year.
3 Explain why businesses that are hotels or restaurants may find survival in the first year difficult.

Aims and objectives

The AIMS of a business are what it wants to achieve in the long term, its ultimate purpose. Aims are often described in general terms, such as 'To be the market leading supplier of garden products in the UK'. Costain's aim is to be 'Number One' in all its operations. The OBJECTIVES of a business are its goals - the outcomes or targets of the business. Meeting its targets will allow a business to achieve its aims. Objectives are often measurable, such as 'To increase profits by 10 per cent over the next three years'. In 2007 Costain set out seven objectives designed to achieve its aim.

Survival

One important objective of most businesses is survival. To survive, the business has at least to break even over time. This means that it makes neither a profit nor a loss. If it continually makes a loss, it will almost certainly go out of business. For example in 2006, Tower Records, went out of business having first declared itself bankrupt in 2004. Its objective over the two years is likely to have been survival.

Profit maximisation

Businesses will want to do more than just survive. They will want to make profits. PROFIT MAXIMISATION should benefit the shareholders, the owners, because they will then receive a dividend (a share of the profits) at the end of the year. In 2005, for example, Costain paid £23.6 million to holders of shares.

For a sole trader, profit is the amount earned from the business. A sole trader would obviously prefer to earn £20 000 rather than £10 000 a year for the same amount of work.

Britvic Soft Drinks is one of the two leading soft drinks businesses in Britain. Its brands include Pepsi, Robinsons, Tango and Britvic brand. Innovations such as J2O and Fruit Shoot have helped Britvic become the largest supplier of still soft drinks, the faster growing category in the soft drinks market, while remaining the number two supplier of carbonates. In 2006 Paul Moody, the chief executive, said there had been a significant fall in Britvic's sales of fizzy drinks in the first two months. Carbonated drinks make up about half of Britvic's sales. As a result, earnings would be at 'the lower end of market expectations', with analysts expecting after-tax profits of £40m-£46m for the financial year. Some argued that the decline in fizzy drinks could be offset by growth in other areas. Britvic's still range includes fruit juices such as Robinsons and Britvic, and Pennine Spring water.

Source: adapted from the *Financial Times*, 3.3. 2006.

1 What does Britvic produce?
2 What profits was Britvic expected to make in 2005/06?
3 Why might Britvic have still had a problem in 2006 even though it made profits?
4 Outline (a) two possible objectives for soft drinks and (b) two possible objectives for carbonated drinks that Britvic might have had in 2006. Explain why it might have had these objectives.

Sales and other objectives

Many businesses set a number of objectives, each of which is an indicator of how well the business is performing.

Growth in profits Businesses performing well will want to see a growth in profits. In 2007, for example, Costain stated that it wanted a double digit (i.e. 10 per cent or more) growth in profit over the year.

Growth in sales turnover Businesses that are performing well will also want to see increase in their turnover or revenue from selling products or services. In 2007, for example, Costain said that it also wanted to achieve double-digit growth in sales turnover over the year.

Increase in market share Another objective of business might be to increase its market share. For example, a consumer products business might aim to increase its market share for one of its soap powder brands from 7 per cent to 10 per cent. So if total sales of all soap powders were £1 billion, it would aim to increase sales of its brand from £70 million to £100 million.

Expansion of the product range Selling a wider variety of products into more markets could be an indicator of a successful company. In the 1990s, Richard Branson considerably expanded the Virgin brand name from its base in records and then airlines to cola drinks, train services, and bank accounts.

Selling into more areas of the country or the world In 2007 Costain stated that it 'wanted to develop even stronger positions in our key targeted markets'. For example, its objective was to expand the number of projects carried out by its property development operation in Spain.

Corporate image and public service Public or corporate image is vitally important for some large companies, like oil companies. If their corporate image is poor, they face losing sales. Pressure groups, like environmental groups, may also keep attacking the business. So having a good corporate image and being seen to be providing a public service to customers is likely to be in the best long term interests of the company.

Stakeholder objectives

In a large business, like a plc, the shareholders, directors, managers and workers are likely to be different people, with different objectives. All businesses have to balance the objectives of different groups with a stakeholding in the business. The owners of the business, consumers, workers and others have a 'stake' in the business because the business affects them. They are '**stakeholders**'.

Owners Shareholders are likely to want the greatest gain from their shares in the company. This is most likely to happen if the company maximises its profit.

Workers Employees are interested in how much they earn, their conditions of work, etc. Better pay and conditions of work mean increased costs for the company. This could lead to a lowering of profit. Costain has a 'zero tolerance for accidents'. The construction industry has a relatively high accident rate and Costain has put worker safety as a high priority. Equally, it wants to 'provide a challenging and stimulating working environment where people enjoy their jobs, can fulfill their potential and are recognised for their efforts'.

Customers Customers want better quality products at lower prices. In 2007 Costain said that it wanted to 'ensure we achieve improved customersatisfaction scores by providing excellent and innovative project and framework solutions'. That means its objective is to provide a high quality product for its customers.

Government, the environment and local communities Other stakeholders include government, environmental groups and local communities. Government, for example, might have job creation as an objective for businesses. This is because it wants to see unemployment reduced. Environmental groups might want businesses to aim to have zero impact on the environment. Local communities might not want to have large, noisy factories built in their area.

Cheese making

Michelle Kenna makes goats' cheese. Her business started off from small beginnings. She and her family had just moved to a house with a very large overgrown garden. Being the daughter of a farmer, she suggested that they buy a pair of goats to control the problem. Before long, she had a small herd and was selling goats' milk to locals.

Milk, though, was never going to make a substantial profit. She needed to add value to it and for this she turned to cheese making. She converted part of the house into a cheese making 'parlour' at a cost of £15 000 and bought £10 000 worth of equipment. One of the advantages of cheese making from home was that she was able to combine a job with bringing up her children.

Since the first cheeses were produced ten years ago, the business has grown slowly. Today, she sells £12 000 worth per month on average and employs four part-time staff. She really enjoys working with her team whom she regards more as personal friends than employees. Her range of cheeses gives her immense satisfaction. These vary from smoked cheeses, to soft goats' cheese covered in walnuts, to varying strengths of plain goats' cheese.

Despite the growth, the business barely makes any profit after she has paid herself a wage of £10 000 a year. But she doesn't complain. The most satisfying thing for her is when customers come to her dairy saying that they don't like goats' cheese or only eat French cheeses and end up walking out having bought an armful of her cheeses.

1 What is the product range of the business?
2 What do you think is the aim/s of the business? Give evidence for your answer from the article.

Wordprocessing
3 A local businessman visits the shop and is extremely enthusiastic about the cheeses. He offers to buy up the business for £30 000 if he is allowed to carry on using the premises rent free for the next thirty years. He will keep Michelle on to run the business and pay her a salary of £13 000 per year. He will also put an extra £20 000 into buying some new equipment.
   (a) Write a letter from Mr Pritchard, the American, to Michelle offering to buy the business. In the letter, explain the advantages of the purchase. Wordprocess your letter if possible.
   (b) Write a reply to Mr Pritchard from Michelle refusing the offer. Give reasons for your refusal.

All businesses want to engage in **wealth creation**. But different stakeholders will have different views about what type of wealth should be created. Should it be profits, or jobs or beautiful, environmentally friendly buildings for example? Also, different stakeholders will fight over who gets that wealth. The final outcome in a large company might be a compromise between the different stakeholders.

So it might **profit satisfice**. This means that it makes enough profit to keep shareholders happy, but doesn't aim to maximise profit.

It might then give all the directors far more expensive company cars than is necessary to keep them happy. It might also pay higher wages than is usual in the industry to keep the workers happy. Then it might spend more than legally required to cut its environmental pollution to satisfy environmental groups.

Objectives of small business

In a small business, like a sole proprietorship or a partnership, the owners, managers and workers are likely to be the same people. Many small businesses aim to maximise their profits. However, they may be happy with making some profit and then pursuing other objectives, like sales growth. Many people own businesses because of the flexibility it gives them in terms of working. They may be prepared to accept lower profits if, for instance, they can take time off when they feel like it. In practice, owners of small businesses tend to work much longer hours than if they were an employee working for someone else. However, they often have more choice about when they work.

A few businesses value their independence very highly. For instance, a worker co-operative set up to promote environmental products might not want to take an order to supply scientific instruments to the nuclear industry.

Objectives of public sector enterprises

Public sector enterprises, like the Post Office or a local council leisure centre, are unlikely to be aiming to maximise profit. Their owners, central or local government for instance, might expect them to make a certain level of profit, or at least cover their costs. However, they are likely to have other objectives as well, such as providing a high quality service.

Public sector enterprises often don't make as high a profit as a private sector business. One reason for this is because they produce a range of goods or services, some of which are sold at a loss in the public interest. For instance, Royal Mail makes a loss on letters collected from and delivered to rural areas. It wouldn't want to charge more for delivery to, say, a village in Wales than to Westminster in London because this would be seen as unfair by most people.

Source: information from Costain, *Annual Report and Accounts*, 2006, www.costain.com.

The Game Group

The Game Group Plc is Europe's leading specialist retailer of computer software and video games. It states that 'We aim to constantly review and improve the unique offerings and services that customers see as our unique selling proposition, and therefore maintain our position as the leading specialist retailer in this growing market. In the coming years this will include:

- People. We are expanding the range of training opportunities for all our staff, and developing our management teams in the UK and Europe.
- Stores. The controlled expansion of our store base in Europe, including the refurbishment of our French stores, and the store opening programme in the UK, Spain and Sweden, will ensure customers have easy access to our stores, in all territories.
- Logistics. We have built a state of the art Distribution Centre to service the UK & Eire stores. We moved in June 2004, and we believe it's given us the most effective and responsive logistics operation in the industry... .
- Communication. Installing broadband in all our stores and upgrading our IT systems in the UK & Eire will allow us to communicate more effectively, and understand even better what our customers require.'

It also states that 'Within our Distribution Centre we recycle all cardboard and plastic materials and we ensure that all our stores comply with local authority disposal and recycling recommendations'.

Source: adapted from www.gamegroup.plc.uk, 2006.

1 In your own words, explain the aim of the business.
2 (a) What stakeholders can be identified in the statement from the business? (b) What objectives might these stakeholders have?
3 Explain how meeting the objectives of stakeholders might help the business to achieve its aim.

key terms

Aims - in business, the long term purpose of the business.
Objectives - in business, the goals or targets of a business.
Profit maximisation - aiming to make the highest level of profit possible.

Checklist ✓

1 Most businesses must aim at least to break even. Why is this true?
2 Why might the aim of a business be to maximise its profits?
3 (a) What is meant by 'sales maximisation'? (b) Why might a business want to maximise its sales?
4 What conflict of objectives might there be between different groups in a large company?
5 What is the difference between profit maximisation and profit satisficing?
6 What might be the objectives of a small business?
7 How might the objectives of a plc differ from those of a public sector enterprise?

SUMMARY CASE STUDY

CLIMBING TO SUCCESS

Prakash Raj and Jenny Baker feel that they have the best of both worlds. On the one hand, for six months of the year they are out climbing in the Himalayas. On the other hand, they earned £80 000 between them for the privilege of doing so.

They climbed their way into their business ten years ago when an old university friend of Jenny's offered to pay all the expenses of a climbing trip to Nepal for the three of them. From that experience, Prakash and Jenny thought that others might offer to pay them if they could join their climbing expeditions. They advertised in a specialist climbing magazine and ten people went on their first expedition each paying £2 000.

Ten years on, sales are £1 million with 600 people booked in over the year for a variety of trips. The business now employs 18 trek leaders.

For Jenny, money is not very important even though she earns £40 000 a year, has the latest Land Rover and owns half a business which she believes could be sold for £300 000. For her, what's important is that she can carry on climbing. Prakash is more interested in the business side. 'I enjoy working with the office team in Kendal and seeing the company grow.' At the same time, like Jenny, he spends six months of the year leading expeditions. 'It might make more business sense for me to spend all my time in the office, but where would the fun be then?'

1 Prakash and Jenny's business was recently called a 'package tour company' by a friend. Do you think this is a fair description of their business?
2 Compare the business objectives of Prakash and Jenny. Give evidence from the article to support your answer.
3 One of the trek leaders employed by the company has recently inherited a large sum of money. He thinks the company has great growth potential if it were better managed. He has offered to buy one third of the shares in the company from Prakash and Jenny for £100 000. Should they accept? In your answer, put down the advantages and disadvantages for Prakash and Jenny.

Making decisions

A person wanting to set up in business has to decide what legal form the business organisation should take. This will depend on many factors.
* How many people are going to own the business?
* Can the owner take the risk of having unlimited liability?
* What will be the tax position of the business?
* Does the owner want to be in complete control of the business?
* Does the owner want all the profits from the business?
* Does the owner want complete privacy in the affairs of the business?
* What will happen to the business in case of the owner's illness or death?

Rich Perry is a national record plugger. He previously worked for music businesses BMG, RCA and Sony but eventually he decided to set up on his own. Music businesses often like to use independent promoters like Rich because they 'live and die' by their decisions. Large record companies have promotion teams which only promote their own records. But Rich chooses to promote only the music he really believes in.

Sole traders

Rich set up a SOLE PROPRIETORSHIP, a business which he alone owned. He became a SOLE TRADER or SOLE PROPRIETOR. His business is getting the music of artists he represents played on radio stations such as Radio 1 and Kiss.

To set up properly in business, sole traders need money. They may borrow from a bank or use their own savings. In Rich's case he may not have needed a lot of money to start because the service he provides requires little machinery or equipment. Instead he is using his skills and contacts in the radio and music industry to promote records and get them played. A sole trader who was a retailer may need to rent premises and buy stock. A plumber would need transport. A builder would need equipment. These would all need to be paid for.

One of the disadvantages of being a sole trader is that the owner has UNLIMITED LIABILITY. This means that the owner has to pay for any losses made by the business. If Rich makes a loss instead of a profit, he would have had to find the money from somewhere. He may be forced to sell his belongings or perhaps even his house. For a sole trader, there is no difference in law between the profits and debts of the business and the finances of the individual owning the business. Legally, they are one and the same.

Inwood

Brian Inwood is a furniture maker. He worked on his own as a sole proprietor, making high quality pieces like tables in oak. In the first few years of trading he did well. By showing at big exhibitions in the UK and the USA, he received a number of commissions. In his first year, he managed to make a £9 000 profit on sales of £30 000. His best year was his third when he sold £80 000 worth of furniture and made £35 000 in profit. However, orders began to dry up. The economy went into recession and people could no longer afford to buy expensive handcrafted furniture. Sales slumped and in his fifth year he made a loss of £15 000. He was forced to sell his stock of wood and move out of his rented premises. He was afraid that he would run up more debts and risk losing his house. So he got a job working for a furniture making company.

1 'Brian Inwood is a sole proprietor.' What does this mean?
2 What did the business sell?
3 Who received the profit from the business in its first year?
4 Explain, using the idea of 'unlimited liability', why Brian Inwood closed his business.
5 Suggest TWO ways in which Brian Inwood might have saved his business from closing.

Woollen cot mattresses

Hanna Jacobs didn't want her newly born child to sleep on a foam mattress. She was scared of the research evidence linking foam mattresses with infant cot deaths. She had a friend who ran an organic farm and who suggested that she make a wool mattress from her sheep. The mattress was made. Then a friend of Hanna's asked her if she could make a wool mattress for her. From that point, a business was born.

Hanna had a lot of problems on the way. She had to find the money to buy the looms to spin the organic wool as well as rent premises. She had to work long hours to build up the business. However, she got a great deal of satisfaction making a product with which mothers felt safe. She enjoyed working with the two part time workers she took on. The finance side of the business was always a worry. But she had always made a profit and she felt she could cut costs very quickly if new orders ever failed to come through. She was proud of the fact that she was her own boss and enjoyed dealing with the problems that any business faces in day to day trading. What's more, the business was flexible enough to give her the time to bring up her children.

DTP

1 Hanna has been interviewed by a reporter from a local newspaper. The reporter is running a feature on the advantages of being a sole trader. Write a short article based on the facts in the case study. If possible, produce the article as it might appear in a newspaper using a desktop publishing package.
2 Hanna is thinking of expanding her product range by making other wool products, like cot mattresses for ordinary sized beds.
   (a) What might be: (i) the advantages; and
   (ii) the disadvantages of this for her?
   (b) Do you think she should do this and why?

The advantages of being a sole trader

As Figure 1 shows, many businesses in the UK are sole proprietorships. There must therefore be some important advantages to setting up this type of business.

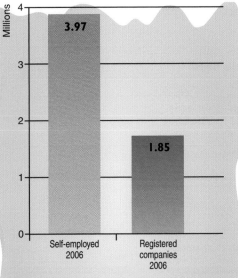

Source: adapted from ONS, *Monthly Digest of Statistics*; Small Business Service.

Figure 1 *Most self-employed people are sole traders, the rest being partners in partnerships. The number of self-employed people outweighs the number of companies in the UK.*

Easy to set up One important advantage is that it is easy to set up. A sole trader can set up in business immediately. There are few, if any, complicated forms to fill in or procedures needed to set up. Rich would have found it relatively easy to set up after leaving his job with large record companies. However, Rich would have to fill in an income tax return for HM Revenue and Customs, which collects income tax, recording the profits of the business. Businesses also have to register for Value Added Tax, a tax on the sale of products. A business that was converting a building for its use would have to get the approval of the local council.

Easy to run Any business is difficult to operate successfully, but a sole proprietorship is easier to run than other types of business. The owner is in sole charge and doesn't need to get the agreement of other owners to make changes to the business. Lawyers and accountants don't have to be employed as part of the business. Rich, for example, makes his own decisions about when he works and what records he chooses to promote.

Tax advantages A sole trader is taxed in a different way to other types of business. National Insurance contributions (NICs) are a tax on a worker's earnings. Rich would have saved money by being a sole trader instead of setting up a limited company and having to become an employee of the company.

Control The owner is in sole charge and so can make whatever changes are necessary as the business operates over time. Rich didn't have to call shareholders' meetings or get the agreement of other directors or managers to make changes.

Capital A business nearly always needs some capital to start trading. Rich might have needed only a little money to start as his business does not have large amounts of equipment and he could work from home. The amount of money needed to set up a sole proprietorship is often small and can be just a few hundred pounds.

Profits All the profits of the business are kept by the sole trader. They don't have to be split up amongst several or perhaps even millions of other owners or shareholders. This means that there is a link between effort, success and money earned. The harder a sole trader works, and the more successful the business, the more can be earned. Rich has considered taking on a partner but prefers to work alone so that the profit is not split.

Privacy Only HM Revenue and Customs need to know how well a sole trader is doing financially. The business doesn't have to publish any information which could be seen by the general public or other businesses.

Labour relations The larger a work organisation, the bigger the scope for misunderstanding and

Sole traders usually work long hours, especially when they first set up in business.

problems. Many sole traders work on their own. Rich for example, does not employ any other people to help him. Other sole traders employ one or perhaps several workers. However, because the team of workers is so small, relations between the workers and the employer are likely to be good.

Flexibility Many sole traders have some choice about when they work. Rich, for instance, could organise his work so that he could visit a friend in the day and work later in the evening.

The disadvantages of being a sole trader

Being a sole trader also has disadvantages.

Unlimited liability Being a sole trader can be risky. If things had gone badly wrong, Rich might lose any money he has put into the business, his house and any other high value items he owned.

Lack of continuity Because Rich is the business, there is no guarantee that it will survive when he no longer wants to carry on running it. He might be able to sell it to someone else. He might, for instance, pass the business on to a friend. However, a business could simply stop trading and all its assets (everything of value that could be sold) sold off.

Illness If Rich were to have an illness, his business would stop operating. There would be no-one to promote records for the business. His income and profits would then stop.

Long hours Many sole traders work very long hours to keep their business afloat. Rich works his '9 to 5 day'. But he argues that after that his work really begins. He has to see new acts and listen to music in studios. He also has to socialise with people who are playing the records to develop relationships or meet with businesses hiring him to

promote their records. He hardly ever takes holidays.

Difficulty of raising capital Some people have the money already to start up a business. They might have some redundancy money, for instance. Most small businesses, though, find it difficult to get suitable start up capital. They also find it difficult to get money to expand their business.

Limited specialisation Rich does all his own work. He is the head of human resources, accounting, IT and even head of administration and ordering stationery. A larger business, however, could afford to

buy in specialist workers. A supermarket employs shelf stackers, accountants and lawyers. So, Rich might find that some of his costs are higher than those of larger businesses because he can't gain the advantages of the division of labour. Rich does pay an accountant to do his annual accounts.

Limited economies of scale A sole trader who was a builder may hire a lorry by the day. A large construction company could own its lorries because this is cheaper if they are kept in use all the time. But the sole trader would only

Shona Mackie wants to set up in business. She has asked a friend who knows about business for advice. One of the things her friend talked about was tax and fees for setting up and running a company rather than being a sole trader. This advice is summarised in Table 1. Shona hopes to earn £300 a week from the business in the first year.

1 Look at Table 1. Would she be better off from a tax and fee viewpoint becoming a sole trader or setting up a limited company?

Table 1

	Sole trader	Limited company
Legal fee to set up in business	None	At least £50
Prepare accounts fees for audit	None	At least £500
Income tax	Payable twice yearly	Payable monthly, immediately after the money has been earned
National Insurance contributions	*Class 2 contributions* £2.20 per week **plus** *Class 4 contributions* 8% on income earned between £100 a week (£5 225 a year) and £670 a week (£34 840 a year) and 1% on any extra income.	*Class 1 contributions* Employees contributions at 11% on weekly income of between £87 and £670 and 1% on any extra income. **plus** Employers' contributions at 12.8% on weekly income above £100.

The difficulties of boatbuilding

Kim Chang trained as a boatbuilder three years ago. Before that, he had spent four years as a boat repairer in Bristol. However, his dream had always been to make traditional small wooden boats.

When he completed his training, he spent £1 000 on a single mahogany log and started his boatbuilding business. This one log built his first boat. However, despite it being much admired at boat exhibitions, he couldn't sell it at the asking price of £10 000. He built a second boat in marine ply, but this too failed to sell despite again getting a lot of positive comments in the boat press and at exhibitions. His start up capital was now almost exhausted as a result of the cost of going to exhibitions and the materials bought. But for the income that his wife was bringing in from her job, he couldn't have survived.

In the end, he was forced to take a £12 000 contract to repair a motor cruiser. This was not the work he wanted to be doing. But at least it was in the boat trade and it was earning him money. He was working long hours to complete the contract on time. He was very afraid of what would happen if he fell ill because there was a penalty clause on the contract which fined him if he didn't complete on time.

The good news came one month before the end of the repair contract deadline. He managed to sell his second marine ply boat for the asking price, £4 000.

1 What does Kim Chang's business produce?
2 Kim Chang is seriously considering giving up the business and taking a job. Suggest reasons why.
3 What advice would you give to Kim to persuade him that he should carry on with the business?
4 Why might a larger boat builder be able to make boats more cheaply than Kim?

need lorries some of the time. This is an example of economies of scale. In general, the larger the business, the more scope there is to reduce costs per unit produced. Sole proprietorships are nearly always small businesses. So they often don't have the cost advantages that large businesses enjoy because of large scale production.

Source: adapted in part from BBC Bitesize.

SMALL BUILDINGS

Chris Davenport was made redundant from his job eight years ago. He used his redundancy payment to set up in business making wooden outdoor buildings. These are more substantial than just garden sheds. They are properly insulated, permanent structures which can be used for anything from an office to a classroom. They are built to be an attractive feature in, say, a garden. Because they are well designed, using high quality materials, they are more expensive than a typical prefabricated temporary building.

Chris has built up his business over time. In the first year, he sold £53 000 worth of products. Today, sales turnover is averaging £300 000 per year. This has not been without its problems. Three years ago, with the economy in recession, orders seemed to dry up and the business made a loss for the year of £20 000. Without a sympathetic bank manager, who increased the overdraft by £15 000, the business would have been in serious trouble.

However, Chris has never thought of giving up. He enjoys running his own business and being his own boss, even if he does have to work long hours. His 6 workers are highly valued. Without them, he would not be able to deliver the quality product that he guarantees to deliver to customers.

One problem facing the business is Chris's age. As he gets older he knows that he might have a period of long illness or even die. None of his family work in the business.

1 (a) Explain FOUR advantages for Chris of being a sole trader. Use evidence from the passage to support your answer.
   (b) Explain FOUR disadvantages for Chris of being a sole trader, again supporting your answer with evidence from the passage.
2 During the recession, Chris considered cutting his prices by reducing the quality of his structures. Discuss whether this would have been a good strategy for Chris to adopt.
3 (a) Suggest how Chris can deal with the potential problem for his business of illness or even death.
   (b) Are there any potential disadvantages to your suggestions?

Making decisions

A person setting up a business has to decide whether to run it alone or with others. This to some extent will depend upon:

• how much control they want over the business;
• whether they are prepared to share the profits;
• whether they can get the necessary money to start up the business.

The person also needs to decide whether he or she is prepared to accept the risk of unlimited liability.

Gallant Richardson is partnership estate agency based in the centre of Colchester, Essex. It was set up 13 years ago by John Gallant and Mark Richardson. They had both worked in partnerships before. When they set up their own partnership together they felt that this was the type of business organisation that suited them.

Partnerships

The law says that in a GENERAL or ORDINARY PARTNERSHIP there can be between 2 and 20 partners. PARTNERS are the joint owners of a business. The business has two partners - John and Mark. The partners have unlimited liability. This means that they have to pay any debts of the business, even if they have to sell their house and other valuable personal possessions. In a partnership, all the partners are liable for the debts even if the debts have been caused by another partner. For instance, if one partner in an estate agency bought new computers, all the partners would be liable to pay off the debt even if the partner hadn't got their permission to order the stock.

Deed of partnership

When partnerships are first set up they often draw up a DEED OF PARTNERSHIP. This is a legal contract which sets out:

• who are the partners;
• how much money (or capital) each partner has put into the partnership;
• how profits should be shared out. Mark and John share profits equally 50/50;
• how many votes each partner has in any partnership meeting;
• what happens if any of the partners want to withdraw from the

James Appleton and David Harris became involved in the oyster business in the 1980s. James had inherited some land by the sea and decided to grow oysters. David provided some financial capital and ran the sales side of the business. The two partners knew that the first few years would see almost no income coming into the business as their oyster park became established. However, James began to build up a trade in shellfish, buying from local fishermen and selling on to restaurants.

In 1989, they borrowed money from the bank and bought some buildings to convert into a restaurant specialising in sea food. The move was almost disastrous for the business because the economy went into a deep recession between 1990 and 1992. Sales in the restaurant were only 50 per cent of what had been forecast. Between 1990 and 1992, the restaurant lost £50 000. Fortunately, the oyster side of the business was beginning to take off. Even so, the partners lost money from the business in those years.

Since then, though, the business had become very successful. In 1996, a second restaurant was opened, and by 2007 sales of oysters exceeded £1 million. The partners are now looking for further opportunities for expansion.

1 In 2007, what products and services did the partnership make?
2 Who owns the business?
3 (a) Explain why the business had difficulties between 1990 and 1992.
  (b) The business lost money during this period. How were the two partners affected financially by this?
4 Discuss ways in which the business could now expand profitably.

Sandwiches with a difference

Mad Max runs a sandwich bar in Birmingham but it's a sandwich bar with a difference. Where else would you find a 'Mad Max Madras Express' - a roast beef sandwich, topped with a cabbage and peppers salad, and dressed with curried mayonnaise? His sandwich bar has been a roaring success, offering a number of different types of exotic and delicious tasting sandwiches and other snacks. In two years, he has doubled sales.

Now he wants to expand by opening another sandwich bar. He hasn't got the money to buy or even rent a second bar, and so he has found another person who is willing to enter a partnership with him. Mad Max would help the new person set up the new sandwich bar and provide all the recipes.

1 What would be the advantages to Mad Max of getting a partner?

2 Mad Max has approached you as a solicitor to draw up a deed of partnership.

(a) What are the essential points which must be covered in the deed of partnership?

(b) What terms would you advise Mad Max to offer his new partner in the partnership agreement? (For instance, how should the profits be distributed? What should happen if Mad Max finds that the new partner is not offering a good service at the new sandwich bar?)

Wordprocessing

(c) Draw up a simple partnership agreement. You could use a wordprocessing package to present the agreement.

the business. The affairs of the partnership can be kept private because only the tax authorities need to be told how much the partners are earning and what is the profit of the business. Partnerships tend to be small, so that there are often good relations between partners and any workers employed. John and Mark feel that a partnership allows them to support each other and one can cover for the other if they take days off.

Partnerships can have advantages over sole proprietorships. Forming a partnership is one way for a sole proprietor to get extra capital for the business. Two people can normally raise more money to start or expand a business than one. Getting extra partners willing to invest money in the business is a way of financing expansion. A partnership is also a way of adding expertise to the business. John and Mark have over 60 years' experience between them in the local property market. John in particular enjoys the selling side of the business.

Some partnerships have sleeping

Figure 1 *An extract from the deed of partnership of Heyes.*

business or retire, or if new partners are brought in;

- what happens if one partner dies. For example, Gallant Richardson has insurance to pay the estate of a partner who dies.

If there is no deed of partnership, the law says that every partner is equal. Each partner then gets an equal share of the profit and has the same voting power as any other partner. For example, Figure 1 shows a deed of partnership for Heyes, an accountancy firm. Carlton and Amerie Heyes put up all the starting capital for the business. They have an equal say in how the business should be run. Gemma Cleaves, their daughter, has no vote in the business but is entitled to receive 20 per cent of the profits. Carlton and Amerie each receive 40 per cent of the profits. If there were no deed of partnership then Gemma would be

entitled to 33 per cent of the vote and the profits. Carlton and Amerie may think this is unfair given they have put in all the starting capital.

The advantages of a partnership

Partnerships have many of the advantages of a sole proprietorship. They are very easy to set up and run. John and Mark just put in their tax return to HM Revenue and Customs each year. They don't have to employ solicitors or accountants to help run the business. In practice, most do use these professional services because their businesses are larger and more complicated than sole proprietorships. Profits belong to the partners, who usually work in

THIS DEED OF PARTNERSHIP is made, the 1st day of January – 2007

BETWEEN
1. CARLTON HEYES of 125 Gatesmead Road, Newcastle (Mr Heyes); and
2. AMERIE HEYES of 125 Gatesmead Road, Newcastle (Mrs Heyes);and
3. GEMMA CLEAVES of 2 Wayland Drive, Bedlington (Ms Cleaves);

WHEREAS
(1) Mr Heyes, Mrs Heyes and Ms Cleaves have agreed to enter into partnership together to practise as an accountancy firm.

partners. These are partners who, whilst owning part of the business, play little or no part in its day to day working. When joining the partnership, these partners provide vitally needed money to help set up or expand the business. Some partnerships, although few in the UK, are limited liability partnerships. This is similar to an ordinary partnership except partners have unlimited liability. It is often used for financial businesses dealing with large amounts of money.

The disadvantages of a partnership

Partnerships mean that people have to work together. However, sometimes people disagree. When partners in a business disagree, it can be a problem for a business. Partners must also be able to trust each other. Fortunately in Mark and John's case they both share the same vision for the business. They want it to grow in the same way and have the same ideas about how it should be run. They also tend to agree with each other, but if they do not, then they will not take on an idea.

At Heyes, the business in Figure 1, Carlton and Amerie want to keep control of the business in case Gemma wants to organise the business in a different way. They have arranged for Gemma not to have any voting rights in the business. In the long term, though, they hope that Gemma will take charge of the day to day running of the business. They can see a time when they are retired and have become sleeping partners. The deed of partnership would then be rewritten giving Gemma full voting rights and a greater share of the business. Eventually, they hope Gemma, their daughter, will inherit the business and take on other partners or pass the business on to their grandchildren. This will solve a problem that many small businesses face: who will carry on the business when those who set it up retire?

Carlton and Amerie have sorted out some of the problems that might arise in the future through the deed of partnership. However, some partnerships don't have a deed of partnership. This can lead to great problems if they break up. Even with a deed of partnership, there can be problems if there are disagreements amongst the partners. For instance, what would happen if partners fall out over how to develop a business? What would then happen to the business?

Partnerships in business

Most partnerships are relatively small businesses. Shops, farms and catering businesses account for half of all partnerships in the UK. Many of these partnerships, particularly in farming, are family partnerships.

You need to do this exercise as a group with 2 or 3 others. You are about to set up a business in your school or college. You may be going to run a real mini-company and already have decided on a business idea. If you haven't, assume that you are going to sell stationery - pens, pencils, paper, note pads, plastic wallets, etc.

If you are running a real mini-company, you need to make the decisions below. If this is a role play, share out the roles shown with the photographs between the members of your group.

You have decided to organise your business as a partnership. Draw up a deed of partnership. As a group, you need to decide on matters such as:
- who will own the business?
- who will get profits from the business and in what proportion?
- who is going to put up the capital (the money) to buy stock for the business to sell and how much capital is needed?
- what happens if one of the group doesn't do anything in helping to run the business?

Remember, these are just some of the issues you need to take into account when drawing up your deed of partnership.

Faisal - hardworking, a natural leader, has two part time jobs, willing to put £20 into the business to start it off.

Susan - meticulous, likes everything organised properly, always on time and well prepared, doesn't like people who don't pull their weight, has £300 in the building society.

Claire - not very reliable, gets excited about work to start with, often stands up for 'her rights', never had a job, thinks her mum will put some money in.

Wayne - not very interested, only in the group because he's got to be, sometimes doesn't get on with others in the group.

In some professions, like medicine, accountancy, the law and architecture, it is standard for businesses to be partnerships. Doctors, dentists, accountants and other professionals like to keep their business affairs private. However, they need to offer the range of services their customers expect.

Source: adapted in part from BBC Bitesize.

Copas Partnership

The Copas Partnership is a family-run business, based in Cookham in the heart of the Thames Valley, where the family can be traced back to 1698. Today the business is managed by Tom Copas, and two of his daughters, Tanya and Fenella. Originally a farming enterprise, over the years the Partnership has evolved into a diverse rural business, with interests in property, turkey production, farming and the Henley Regatta. For example, over the years, the Copas Partnership has redeveloped a number of its redundant farm buildings for alternative use. It now has a portfolio of office and storage facilities for rental purposes.

Source: adapted from www.copas.co.uk.

1 What business activities is The Copas Partnership involved in?
2 Explain how the The Copas Partnership may have solved TWO problems faced by Partnerships.
3 Discuss whether The Copas Partnership should expand into new areas of business in future.

key terms

Deed of partnership - the legal contract which governs how a partnership will be owned and organised.
General or Ordinary partnership - a business organisation which has between 2 and 20 owners, all of whom have unlimited liability.
Partners - the owners of a partnership.

Checklist ✓

1 Who owns a partnership?
2 'Partners have unlimited liability.' What does this mean?
3 If there is no partnership agreement, how are profits distributed in a partnership?
4 What might be written in a deed of partnership?
5 What advantages do partnerships share with sole proprietorships?
6 Why might a partnership be a better form of organisation than a sole proprietorship?
7 What are the disadvantages of partnerships?
8 Why is disagreement between partners a problem in a partnership?

SUMMARY CASE STUDY

JUGGLING WITH FINANCE

Sophie and Bill Waites run a juggling business. For ten years, they ran juggling parties for children where they would do some funny sketches and tell some jokes with juggling as part of the act. This was done in their spare time whilst both had full time jobs in a manufacturing company.

Then they decided to put the skills they had acquired in their full time jobs to set up a business manufacturing juggling equipment. They knew that they would need help on the marketing side to sell the equipment to wholesalers who in turn would sell it to shops. A friend introduced them to Pat Irvine, a marketing consultant. Impressed with the proposal, he agreed to come in as a partner. Sophie, Bill and Pat each put up £10 000 start up capital for the partnership.

The business was a success. In its first year, it sold £80 000 worth of equipment and a £20 000 profit was made. But Sophie and Bill found Pat almost impossible to work with. Although he had been successful in gaining orders, he didn't seem to be putting very much time into the business. They felt that he was now losing interest and allowing other business opportunities to occupy his energies. They were afraid that orders would start to fall off.

Pat was very angry when they confronted him with this. He said that he was mainly responsible for the success of the business. When Sophie and Bill offered to buy him out, he said the partnership was now worth £100 000. Unfortunately, no deed of partnership had been drawn up.

1 What is a partnership?
2 What skills did each partner bring to the business?
3 Suggest why Sophie and Bill now face problems because there is no deed of partnership for the business.
4 Discuss: (a) why the partnership might have a value of £100 000; and
   (b) what problems this would give Sophie and Bill.

Making decisions

Businesses have to decide on the legal form the organisation should adopt. They could be an unlimited business (a sole proprietorship or a partnership) or they could be a joint stock company with limited liability. The choice is likely to be determined by:

- the size of the business and how easy it is to get extra money to finance growth;
- whether the owners want limited or unlimited liability;
- the extent to which the owners want privacy about the affairs of the business;
- how prepared is the business to deal with the extra work involved in running a limited liability company;
- the tax implications.

James Rix and Bianca Rix and Gemma Mash run the Fox & Hounds restaurant in Cambridgeshire. They are the directors, shareholders and owners of the business that runs the pub, called The RixyMash Pub Company Ltd. The company was set up in 2005. They had just 6 weeks from taking over the pub to have it ready to operate as it had not been open for a period of time before they took it over.

Limited liability

The RixyMash Pub Company Ltd is a **limited company**. It is owned by the three people who founded the business, James Rix and Bianca Rix and Gemma Mash. The owners of a company are called the SHAREHOLDERS. They have LIMITED LIABILITY.

Limited liability is important for James, Bianca and Gemma, the shareholders, if the company goes out of business leaving debts (i.e. the company becomes **insolvent**). They will only lose the money that they have put into the company (the value of their shares). But they won't be forced to sell off their own personal possessions, like a house, to pay off the company's debts. This is because a limited company has a separate identity in law from its shareholders. To show that it has a separate legal identity, a limited liability business is normally called a COMPANY. It is also important

Mining problems

The Strongfellow Mining Company Ltd was founded four years ago by five miners made redundant from a local coal pit. The mine they bought with their redundancy money for £100 000 was an old stone mine, producing high quality stone which sold at a premium price. The mine was in a reasonable state of repair. During the first year, they were able to run it without having to invest in any new equipment. Having paid themselves £12 000 each in wages, the mine made a small profit of £8 000 in that year.

Encouraged by this, they decided that the company could be more profitable if it could sell another stone. They found a quarry about ten miles away. The owners of the quarry didn't want to sell but were prepared to accept a mixture of rent for the site and a royalty on sales. This suited Strongfellow Mining because they then wouldn't have to find the capital to buy the site.

However, it took 18 months to get planning permission. Buying equipment cost a lot more than expected and the quarry proved more difficult to work than planned. The quarry wasn't fully operational even one year after opening. The time and effort put into the quarry meant that output of stone from the mine fell sharply. So sales revenue for the company went down just when they needed more cash to repay the rent and overdraft on their loan. Four years after they first set up, the company was forced into liquidation (i.e. it was forced out of business). It owed £150 000 to the bank and to a variety of suppliers. After sale of assets, £50 000 was still owing.

1. What does it mean to say that The Strongfellow Mining Company was a 'limited company'?
2. Why did the company get into financial difficulties?
3. (a) How much did the company owe to its bank and suppliers when it went into liquidation?
   (b) Suggest what assets of the company could be sold to pay its debts.
4. What did the five shareholders lose because the company went into liquidation?
5. Who gained and who lost out because The Strongfellow Mining Company was a limited liability rather than an unlimited liability business?

to raise finance. Banks would not loan money to James, Bianca and Gemma unless they set up a company which had limited liability.

The RixyMash Pub Company Ltd has been doing well since it first opened the Fox & Hounds. However, this doesn't take away the risk of a loss. The company could make a loss in any one year in future. Owners of a business prefer to have limited liability if it has large debts.

You have decided with a friend to set up a company. You may already have a business idea. If you don't have an idea, assume that you have decided to set up a company selling costume jewellery in your school or college.
1 Draw up a Memorandum of Association for the company as follows.

> The Companies Act 1985
>
> Company Limited by Shares
> Memorandum of Association of _____(name of your company)
> The Company's name is _____ .
> The Company's registered office is _____
> (unless you have decided otherwise, put the home address of one of the shareholders).
> The Company's objectives are _____
> (description of your trading activity).
> The liability of the Members is limited.
> The Share Capital of the Company is £ _____ (figure for your starting share capital) divided into _____ shares of £1 each.

2 Now draw up the Articles of Association. Use the following heading.

> The Companies Act 1985
>
> Company Limited by Shares
> Articles of Association of_____ (name of your company)

Write one sentence about each of the following under your heading: (a) which of the shareholders has a vote and how many votes each shareholder has; (b) what proportion of the profit will go to each shareholder; (c) the duties of the company directors (e.g. they have the right to authorise the company to borrow money); (d) who will act as chairperson for the AGM and where it will be held.

The Registrar General

The Registrar General (or Registrar of Companies) keeps records on all UK limited companies. Four documents have to be sent to the **Registrar of Companies** to set up a limited company.

• The MEMORANDUM OF ASSOCIATION gives details about the name of the company, the address of its registered office, a statement that the shareholders will have limited liability, the type and amount of share capital and a description of the business activities of the company which in the case of The RixyMash Pub Company Ltd is the running of the Fox & Hounds restaurant.

• The ARTICLES OF ASSOCIATION give details about the voting rights of the shareholders, how the profits will be distributed, what are the duties of the directors of the company and what procedures will be followed at the annual general meeting (the AGM).

• FORM 10 gives details of the first directors, secretary and the address of the registered office. Directors must give their names and addresses, date of birth, occupation and details of other directorships they have held within the last five years.

• FORM 12, a statutory declaration of compliance with all the legal requirements relating to the incorporation of a company. It must be signed by a solicitor who is forming the company, a director or the company secretary.

The Registrar of Companies has to issue a **certificate of incorporation** before a company can start trading, i.e. start up in business. Every year, a limited company has to send audited accounts and various other documents to the Registrar of Companies at Companies House. These can be seen by anyone who asks to see them. The affairs of the business, therefore, can't be kept private like a sole proprietorship or a partnership. Anybody can know what the sales of the company were and what profit was made according to the last set of accounts sent to Companies House.

Ltd and plc

There are two types of limited company - PRIVATE LIMITED COMPANIES and PUBLIC LIMITED COMPANIES. Private limited companies add Ltd after their names as in The RixyMash Pub Company Ltd. Public limited companies add plc after their name as in HBOS plc, the financial company formed after the merger of Halifax and Bank of Scotland.

Differences between private and public limited companies

There are important differences between private limited companies and public limited companies.

Sales of shares The shares of a plc must be tradable on a stock exchange. HBOS plc, for example, is **listed** on the London Stock Exchange. New smaller plcs in the UK tend to get a listing on AIM (the Alternative Investment Market). A listing means that the stock exchange is prepared to allow the shares of the company to be bought and sold through the stock exchange. There is no open market for the shares of private companies like The RixyMash Pub Company

Bharat Nalluri and Suzanne Frazer are partners in a business which designs and makes equipment for the disabled. They started the business two years ago and spent the first year researching and developing products. Sales began in the second year.

By the end of that year, the business was turning over £8 000 worth of orders per month. The partners felt that the business needed more capital to expand. They thought that £200 000 would enable them to move to larger premises, buy more machinery and extend their marketing efforts. They started looking for an individual or another business prepared to invest £200 000 in the business.

1 What is the difference between a partnership and a limited company?

2 Both partners think that they would need to become a limited company to attract the extra capital needed. (a) Why would limited liability be attractive to the individual or business putting up the £200 000? (b) Suzanne would prefer to see the £200 000 come from a relative or friend. Do you think this is likely? Explain your answer carefully.

Ltd. This might be a problem for them if they want to raise a large amount of finance.

Share capital A plc by law must have at least £50 000 in share capital to start up. A private company can start up with just one share of £0.01 in share capital. In practice, new plcs today have to have a market value of millions of pounds in order to get a listing on a stock exchange.

Size and number of shareholders The number of shareholders is likely to be far greater in a plc than in a private limited company. The RixyMash Pub Company Ltd has just three shareholders. In 2006 HBOS had 2 205 843 shareholders. Plcs tend to have more shareholders because they are bigger companies. There is no open market for shares in private limited companies. Anybody wanting to sell shares in a private limited company has to have the permission of the majority of shareholders. This can make it

difficult to sell shares to people outside the business. Anyway, the major shareholders in a private limited company are likely to work in the business and wouldn't want to sell. James, Bianca and Gemma, for instance, are unlikely to want to sell shares in The RixyMash Pub Company Ltd to outsiders.

Control In theory, shareholders control a limited company. Each year, at the annual general meeting, they elect DIRECTORS to represent the interests of shareholders. The board of directors will appoint MANAGERS to run the company. The most important manager, the managing director, is also automatically a director of the company as well. Some of the other managers will also sit on the board of directors. The shareholders, the directors and the managers in a private limited company are often the same people because the company is small. However, in a plc, the directors and the

managers are likely to own only a small fraction of the shares of the company. This means that the people who are responsible for the day to day running of the company (the managers), and the long term direction of the company (the directors), are different from the shareholders.

In theory, the directors are elected by the shareholders at the annual general meeting of the company to defend the shareholders' interests. In practice, what the shareholders want and what the directors want and what the managers decide to do might be different. This is known as the divorce of ownership and control. This might affect the goals of the company. This is not the case at The RixyMash Compnay Ltd. There are just three shareholders who are directors in The RixyMash Pub Company Ltd. James & Bianca have 50 per cent between them and Gemma has 50 per cent. They take dividends in proportion to the amount they own.

The advantages and disadvantages of becoming a limited company

The great advantage of being a limited company is that it is easier to attract extra shareholders to invest money in the business because of limited liability. This means that the business can grow and become large.
One disadvantage is that information about the company has to be given to the general public. More information has to be given if the company is a plc than if it is a private limited company. Giving information is also costly. It may cost £500 a year to prepare a report and accounts for a private limited company. The minimum cost for a plc is over £100 000. The published report and accounts of a plc alone costs tens of thousands of pounds to prepare, print and distribute.

?

Table 1 shows details of the share prices of selected retailing groups.

1 On 18 March 2007, what was the share price of (a) Next; (b) Kingfisher; (c) Tesco?

2 The market capitalisation of the company shows how much the company is worth according to its share price. What was the total value in millions of pounds on 18 March 2007 of (a) Carphone Warehouse; (b) Sainsbury; (c) Marks & Spencer?

3 The number of shares issued times the share price is equal to the market capitalisation of a company. Use a calculator or a spreadsheet to find out how many shares there were in March 2007 to the nearest thousand in (a) Debenhams; (b) DSG International; (c) Home Retail Group; (d) Next.

Table 1 *Share prices of retail companies, 18 March 2007.*

	Today's price pence	Market capitalisation £million
Carphone Warehouse	294	2 634
Debenhams	180.25	1 548
DSG International	174.5	3 215
Home Retail Group	443.75	3 893
Kingfisher	269.5	6 301
Marks & Spencer	690	11 725
Next	2 065	4 688
Sainsbury	556	9 635
Tesco	431.75	34 271

Source: adapted from the Sunday Times, 18.3.2007.

Another disadvantage of being a plc is the cost of complying with stock exchange rules. The London Stock Exchange imposes a variety of rules on companies seeking a listing. These are meant to protect future shareholders by giving them more information about the business. The advantage of getting a listing on the Alternative Investment Market (AIM) is that regulations are less strict and so it is cheaper for a company to get a listing. On the other hand, the shares are seen as higher risk and it might be more difficult to raise money through new share issues. It is also sometimes claimed that shareholders in a plc are only interested in making short term profits. They are not interested in taking the long term view. So the company is discouraged from investing money in projects which will be profitable in the long term but not in the short term.

Source: BBC Bitesize.

Checklist ✓

1 What does 'limited' mean if it refers to a company?

2 A company goes out of business leaving debts of £100 million. How much will the shareholders of the company have to pay as a result?

3 Who owns a company?

4 What documents does a company have to give to the Registrar of Companies before it can begin trading?

5 What document does the Registrar of Companies issue which allows a company to start trading?

6 How can a company check to see whether another company has made a profit or a loss recently?

7 What is the role of (i.e. what is the job of): (a) a director; (b) a manager of a company?

8 If a company has 'Ltd' after its name, what does this mean?

9 What are the differences between a private limited company and a public limited company?

10 Why is it easier to attract new shareholders to a plc than a Ltd company?

11 What is meant by the 'divorce of ownership from control'?

SUMMARY CASE STUDY

J SAINSBURY

J Sainsbury plc is made up of Sainsbury's supermarkets, convenience stores, an Internet home based delivery service and Sainsbury's bank. Look at Table 2.

Table 2 *Shareholders by size of shareholding, 25.3.2006.*

Number of shares owned	Number of shareholders	% of shareholders	Number of shares (millions)	% of shares
500 and under	91 457	64.9	11.9	0.7
501-1 000	18 742	13.3	13.7	0.8
1 001-10 000	28 748	20.4	71.9	4.2
10 001-100 000	1 409	1.0	37.7	2.2
100 000-1 000 000	423	0.3	162.6	9.5
Over 1 000 000	141	0.1	1 413.7	82.6
Total	140 920	100	1 711.5	100

Note: figures have been rounded.
Source: adapted from J Sainsbury, *Annual Report and Accounts*, 2006.

1 How many shareholders did the company have?

2 How many shareholders owned (a) less than 500 shares and (b) more than ten thousand shares?

3 How many shares in total did (a) small shareholders owning less than 500 shares hold and (b) large shareholders each owning more than one million shares hold?

4 'J Sainsbury is owned by nearly 141 thousand shareholders but in practice it owned by a fraction of that number.' Do you agree with this statement? Give evidence from the table.

5 Banks and other nominees own nearly 55% of shares. (a) How many shares does this group own? (b) How does this illustrate the possible 'divorce of ownership from control'?

Making decisions

Most businesses are set up to make a profit for the owners. However, not every business today has this as its main goal. Some businesses prefer instead to concentrate on benefiting customers, or workers, or perhaps on caring for the environment. These businesses might consider setting up as Co-operatives.

The Co-operative Group, often known as the Co-op, is one of the largest co-operatives in the world. It employs over 69 000 people and has over 3 000 outlets. Most businesses are in business to make a profit. The Co-operative Group is in business to meet the needs of its members.

The first societies

The first retail Co-operative society was formed in Rochdale, Lancashire, in 1844. A group of workers joined together to buy food and other goods collectively. These were then sold to working families. Profit from the shop, the dividend, was distributed back to the workers according to how much each had spent. By the end of the nineteenth century, there were 1 400 Co-operative societies in existence, with goods provided by the Co-operative Wholesale Society.

Co-ops compared to plcs

The Co-operative Group is in some ways similar to public limited companies like Sainsbury's or Tesco. They both have limited liability. Both are separate legal entities, which can own property and be sued.

However, there are also important differences. Public limited companies are owned by shareholders and they are run to make a profit for their shareholders. Each shareholder receives a share of the profit and

has a vote at the AGM of the company in accordance with the number of shares they own. Plcs want satisfied customers because they can create profit for the owners of the company.

Co-operatives were originally founded to serve the needs of members. Making a profit was less important than providing a high quality service. Profit was given back to customers who were members of the society as a dividend. It was paid out in proportion to how much they had spent at the society. This is also

the case today at the Co-operative Group. Each member has only one vote at the society's AGM however many shares they might own. The Co-operative Group is democratically owned. It also spends money in the community on schemes such as environmental projects and education projects.

The Co-op today

Today the Co-operative Group operates in a number of business areas. Details are shown in Figure 2. It is sometimes referred

1 What, according to the extract, were the advantages of shopping at the Rochdale Society?

2 (a) How did the dividend system work?
  (b) Why did it encourage people to join the society and shop there?

The Rochdale Equitable Pioneers Society original store, today a museum.

On the night when our store was opened, the 'doffers' came out strong in Toad Lane inspecting the scanty arrangements of butter and oatmeal.

Since that time two generations of 'doffers' have bought their butter and oatmeal at the shop, and many a wholesome meal, and many a warm jacket, have they had from that store, which articles would never have reached their stomachs or their shoulders, had it not been for the co-operative weavers.

Mr. Charles Howarth proposed the plan of dividing profits among the members in proportion to their purchases. At the end of the first quarter the Rochdale Society did pay a dividend of 3d in the pound. In 1844 the number of members was 28, amount of capital £28...In 1857 the number of members was 1,850, the amount of capital £15,142.

Note: a 'doffer' was a young boy who worked in the mills.

Source: George Holyoake, *The History of Co-operation in Rochdale*, 1878.

to as a CONSUMER or RETAIL CO-OPERATIVE.

Competition

Where they compete against similar organised businesses, businesses that are now part of the Co-perative Group have done well over the past 50 years. For instance, Co-operative Funeralcare is the UK's largest funeral director. Travelcare is the UK's largest independent travel services provider. Co-operative Pharmacy is the fourth largest UK pharmacy operator. The Co-operative Insurance Society and the Co-operative Bank are both very successful.

Figure 1

Source: adapted from www.tescocoperate, www.co-op.co.uk.

1 What are the differences shown in the diagram between Tesco plc and The Co-operative Group?

The food business, however, has faced growing competition from supermarket chains like Sainsbury's and Tesco for a number of reasons.

- The supermarket chains have grown so large that they can buy in bulk and sell at prices equal to if not cheaper than Co-operative food stores.
- Many of the Co-operative food stores are small local shops which may be expensive to run.
- As chains like Sainsbury's and Tesco opened bigger and bigger stores, the Co-operative societies were not able to compete directly. They couldn't raise large amounts of money through issuing new shares on the stock market to pay for new stores.
- They also didn't want to close their local small shops because they felt that they were providing a service to local people. The service was particularly useful to poor and old people, or people such as parents with young children who didn't want to travel to large superstores. Such people didn't own cars and so couldn't get to and from the new supermarkets easily.
- The dividend, which kept customers loyal to Co-operatives in the past, became less and less important as shoppers could see lower prices at large Tesco stores or low price stores such as Aldi or Lidl.

Today Co-operative food stores have introduced a number of policies that adopt an ethical and member-based stance. These will be attractive to customers for a variety of reasons.

- They are emphasising their community roots by operating smaller local stores which complement large superstores rather than competing directly. .
- They stress a commitment to 'responsible retailing'. This includes, for example, the labelling of products that have been genetically modified, are suitable for vegans or have animal ingredients. In 2005 the

UK CO-OPERATIVE MOVEMENT FACTS AND FIGURES

Food Stores The UK leader in community shopping.
Number of outlets: 1,713
Number of employees: 43,963

Co-operative Pharmacy The fourth largest UK pharmacy operator, providing a high standard of community healthcare services across the UK.
Number of outlets: 372
Number of employees: 2,893

Co-operative Funeralcare The UK's largest funeral director, at the forefront of moves to improve client service, reassurance and information.
Number of outlets: 609
Number of employees: 2,871

Travelcare The UK's largest independent travel services provider, with a commitment to offering open and honest advice to our customers.
Number of outlets: 358
Number of employees: 2,038

Shoefayre Footwear shops selling at competitive prices.
Number of outlets: 283
Number of employees: 2,389

Farmcare The UK's largest commercial farmer. It was formerly known as CWS (the Co-operative Wholesale society) Broadoak. The group farms over 85,000 acres - owned by both the Co-operative Group and private landowners. It supplies Co-op stores.

Property division In addition to its trading properties, the Co-operative Group's property and development business holds a substantial portfolio of investment properties currently valued at over £280m.

The Co-operative Bank Provides a variety of financial and banking services. Noted for its ethical stance.
Number of outlets: 119
Number of employees: 4,271

CIS Co-operative Insurance Services (CIS) is a life assurance and general insurance business with over five million customers.
Number of employees: 6,214

CFS Co-operative Financial Services (CFS) is an Industrial and Provident Society, which brings together the Co-operative Insurance Society (CIS) and The Co-operative Bank under common leadership.

Smile A full-service Internet bank, winner of many awards for customer service.

Figure 2 The Co-operative Group

Co-op banned a range of colours and monosodium glutamate (MSG) in its own-label food because of possible links to food intolerance.

- It sells Fairtrade products. These are products where a fair price is paid to suppliers in Third World countries. Fairtrade 'guarantees a better deal for Third World producers'.

Worker co-operatives

Worker co-operatives are different from retail co-operatives. A WORKER CO-OPERATIVE is a business which is owned by its workers, the producers in the business. Edinburgh Bicycle Cooperative is a worker co-operative. It designs its own cycles and has them manufactured. It also sells leading brands of bicycles and cycle clothing from its stores in

Edinburgh, Aberdeen, Newcastle and Leeds. It offers free delivery to addresses in the UK. It also has workshops where repairs can be carried out. In 2006 the Edinburgh Bicycle Cooperative had 46 members. Every full time Edinburgh Bicycle worker becomes a Co-op member, with an equal share in the business, after serving a 1 year 'apprenticeship'

Co-operatives UK estimates that there were less than 400 worker owned and controlled co-operatives in the UK in 2006. These tend to be relatively small businesses. Over half have an annual turnover of less than £250 000.

The workers are also the owners of the business, and so they have to make decisions about how it should be run. Normally there are more meetings in a worker co-operative than in a limited company because of this. In many worker co-operatives, each worker is entitled to one vote when it comes to making a decision, even if workers own different numbers of shares in the business. In others, like in a limited company, the number of shares owned determines how many votes a worker is entitled to use. At Edinburgh Bicycle, each worker only owns one share and so only has one vote. The workers/shareholders enjoy limited liability.

The advantages and disadvantages of worker co-operatives

Worker co-operatives have several advantages, all linked to the fact that the workers own the business.

- There is less likely to be a conflict of interest between owners and workers because the profits made by the business go to the workers or are invested back in the business to ensure its long term success.

Halliwell C. Ltd

Halliwell C. Ltd is a small worker co-operative with 12 members. The Co-operative also employs a further 4 workers who are not members. It manufactures industrial fastenings, including bolts and nuts.

Geoff is the manager. He is responsible for the day to day running of the factory. Bob is responsible for sales. This isn't a full time job, so he can also often be found on the shop floor working alongside the other members. Carol is the secretary. She is not a member of the Co-operative, but she is married to Bob who is a member.

All the members, apart from Geoff and Bob, are paid what they would earn in a normal company. The rules of the Co-operative state that no worker member should be paid more than twice the wage of the lowest paid worker member. Geoff admits that he could earn more if he got a job in a normal company. Bob too is probably underpaid compared to a full time sales executive and he has to share the only car owned by the company with other members when he is not using it for business purposes.

Each month there is a members' meeting when important policy issues are discussed. Most meetings are fairly uncontroversial. However, there is usually a fair amount of disagreement when each year the Co-operative has to decide what to do with its profits. Geoff tends to want to put all of it back into the business to finance investment. Some of the members, though, press for it to be distributed to members.

1 Explain: (a) who owns Halliwell C. Ltd; and (b) how decisions are made in the business.
2 Geoff is seen looking at adverts for managers in the local newspaper. (a) Why might he be tempted to move job? (b) Why might he want to stay with the Co-operative?
3 Bob wants Carol, his wife, to become a member of the Co-operative. Carol is currently paid less than any of the shop floor workers and her wage is only one third that of Geoff's. Under the rules of the Co-operative, she would have to pay £3 000, the amount each of the other members paid, to buy in. Any worker leaving the Co-operative would only get what they put in to become a member, i.e. £3 000. Last year, the Co-operative paid each member £1 500 as a bonus out of the profits made. The company, if sold, is currently valued at £200 000. The rules of the Co-operative state that it could be sold if three quarters of the members agree. The proceeds of the sale would be distributed equally to each member. Carol's membership is to be discussed at the next meeting. What arguments do you think might be put forward by members: (a) in support of Carol's application; and (b) against it?

- The business is likely to be conscious of its place in the community. For instance, Edinburgh Bicycles offers day classes in bicycle maintenance to its customers. Other Co-operatives may give a proportion of their profits to charity.

However, there can be problems with worker co-operatives.

- It is usually difficult to persuade other workers to establish a worker co-operative because it is much easier to set up a partnership.
- New workers usually have to become owners of the business, but they might find it difficult to raise the money to buy a share in the business. At Edinburgh Bicycle, this is not a problem because no worker is allowed to buy more than one £1 share in the business. Any worker who has worked for the Co-operative for more than a year is entitled to become a member of the Co-operative.
- Very successful worker co-operatives often end up being sold to other limited companies, with the worker-owners only too happy to pocket the money gained from selling their shares.

- If the worker co-operative needs extra money to expand the business, it can't look to new shareholders to finance that expansion. This means that worker co-operatives often find it difficult to grow. At Edinburgh Bicycles, the Co-operative has relied on overdrafts and bank loans, as well as retained profit, for finance.

- Worker co-operatives often set limits on the amount that top workers can be paid. The workers who found the Co-operative often believe that all workers should be paid roughly the same for the same amount of work.

Source: BBC Bitesize, www.co-op.co.uk, www.edinburghbicycle.com.

Key terms

Consumer (or retail) co-operative - a business organisation owned by customer shareholders and which aims to maximise benefits for its customers.
Worker co-operative - a business organisation owned by its workers who run the business and share the profits among themselves.

Checklist ✓

1 Explain why the first Co-operatives in the UK were organised.
2 What are the differences between a consumer or retail co-operative and a public limited company?
3 Why have consumer or retail co-operatives found it hard to compete against large supermarket chains like Sainsbury's?
4 What other areas are co-operatives increasingly operating in?
5 Who owns a worker co-operative?
6 How are decisions made in a worker co-operative?
7 What are the advantages of worker co-operatives?
8 What are the problems of worker co-operatives as a form of business organisation?

SUMMARY CASE STUDY

UNITED CO-OPERATIVES AND THE CO-OPERATIVE GROUP

In 2006 United Co-operatives was the largest regional co-operative society in the UK with a turnover of £2.5 billion and 16 500 staff employed across the Midlands and Northern England. Anyone can become a member for £1 providing they live within the Society's trading area, are over 16, shop with the business and agree to the co-operative values. They get an equal share in the Co-op which has a 'one member one vote' system.

As a member-owned business, it wants to share its success with the people who have helped create that success. It has an Active Members' Benefit Scheme card which earns points based on the value of purchases and the trading group in which shopping takes place. In order to qualify for a possible payout under the Scheme, people must to collect at least 500 points during the year. Table 1 shows the schemes rewards. Figure 3 shows the organisation of the business in 2006.

In February 2007 the boards of United Co-operatives and the Co-operative Group agreed to recommend to their members that they approve a merger between the two societies. It would create the world's largest consumer co-operative, with a turnover of £9 billion. It was argued that the proposed merger would be good for members, staff and customers. Peter Marks, the Chief Executive of United Co-operatives said that the two societies' activities were geographically complementary and that the merger would ensure growth and allow the business to fulfil its social goals in the communities in which it operated.

1 United Co-operatives is a member-owned business. Explain what this means.
2 What might be the (a) benefits and (b) problems of the Active Members' Benefit Scheme card for members?
3 Explain ONE similarity and ONE difference in the organisation of United Co-operatives and a plc.
4 Explain why a merger between the two businesses might 'be good for members, staff and customers'.
5 The new business would sell ethically produced products. Discuss whether customers would be attracted by this.

Table 1 *Active Members' Benefit Scheme*

Purchase made in		Number of points awarded
Food stores	£1	1 point
Pharmacy branches	£1	1 point
Travel branches (excludes Travelcare outlets)	£10	1 point
Motor dealerships	£50	1 point

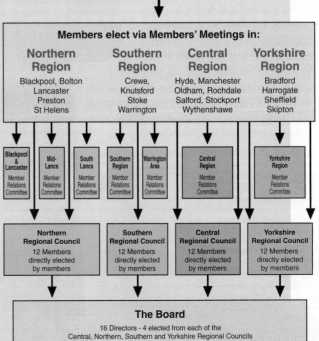

Figure 3 *United Co-operatives' structure 2006*
Source: adapted from www.united.coop, www.co-op.co.uk.

Making decisions

You want to go into business. Do you:
- want to reduce the chance of failure considerably?
- want help to set up and run your business?
- find yourself short of money to put into the business to start it up?
- want to be part of a regional or national chain of businesses?

Are you not too bothered if:
- you don't have full control of your business?
- you have to pay a fee or a share of the profits to another business?

If your answer is yes to all these questions, then you may want to consider buying into a franchise.

Toni&Guy is an international company which offers a creative hair styling service. Toni&Guy Hairdressing was founded in London over 40 years ago by Toni&Guy Mascolo. Its styles are varied to reflect customers' different face shapes and lifestyles. In 2006 there were around 250 UK salons and 400 salons and training academies across the world. The annual turnover of the business exceeds £115 million.

?

1 These businesses operate franchises. What is meant by a 'franchise'?
2 The largest number of franchises is found in food outlets, property care and home care services, walk-in retailers, motorist services and business services. Are any of the businesses shown here in these industries? If so, which?
3 You are considering becoming a franchisee. (a) Which of the franchises shown in the photographs would most appeal to you? Explain carefully why.
(b) What sort of person might you need to be to be a successful franchisee? For instance, would you need to be hard working or independent? Would you need business experience and an ability to deal with people? Think of as many characteristics as possible and explain why they are important.

Franchisors and franchisees

Toni&Guy is an example of a FRANCHISE. Toni&Guy is the FRANCHISOR. This means that it earns revenue by giving other businesses, the FRANCHISEES, the right to sell goods or services using its name. These other businesses, which sign a franchisee agreement, could be large or small. In Toni&Guy's case, these are the part owned salons which provide hair styling services. For example, Gary France worked for Toni&Guy for 15 years as art director before he and his wife took over the Toni&Guy franchise in Kensington. They own 49 per cent of the franchise.

The Toni&Guy franchise developed because, having trained its staff, it wanted to make use of their skills to expand. Rather than having them set up in competition as rivals, it allowed them to remain part of the Toni&Guy family as

Oscar Pet Foods

1 What service does this franchise offer?

2 What benefits does the franchisor give the franchisee?

3 What would be the minimum cost in the first year to the franchisee of buying and operating the franchise?

Company Name: Oscar Pet Foods

Main Category: Pet Services, including home delivery of pet food and nutritional and behavioural advice

Sub Category: Sales and Distribution

No. of Outlets: 87

Minimum Investment: £11,995 plus VAT

Royalties/Fees: £100 per month (inclusive of VAT)

Training and Support: 8 days in-house plus field training, with ongoing support

Our Franchise Opportunity

As a credible franchisor, Oscar Pet Foods will

- offer support before you decide, when you decide and as you continue,
- provide a unique brand in an exclusive territory, with the chance to expand at no extra cost,
- provide the buying power to compete with supermarkets,
- offer free consultation with technical experts in the event of any queries,
- supply a computerised customer management system, including a personal website and intranet discussion forum.

Source: adapted from www.thefranchisedirectory.net/.

---

franchises.

There are many examples of franchise operations, such as Prontaprint, McDonald's, Snappy Snaps and Dyno-Rod. The franchisor is likely to be a national or even an international company. It will have developed a product, whether a good or service. Rather than selling it directly to customers, it chooses to use other businesses to do the selling.

What the franchisor provides

There are certain benefits to a business of become a franchisee. These may include the following.

Training Toni&Guy has always stressed the importance of training. It has academies around the world where it provides basic and advanced training. It is rigorous about the professional standards of its hairdressers and colour technicians operating in its salons. Also, all franchisees have to have worked at Toni&Guy first.

Equipment Tony&Guy sells equipment to its franchisees including hair styling equipment, televisions and its 'salon genius system' computerised till.

Materials to use in the production of a good or service Franchisees can only use Toni&Guy products, not other brands.

Finding customers Tony&Guy help franchisees find customers through national advertising. It also provides publicity material to each franchisee such as posters. The brand name of 'Tony&Guy' also brings in customers.

Back up services A whole range of back up services are provided. These include advice, loans and insurance cover.

A brand name Tony&Guy is known nationally because of its size and advertising. Branding can be crucial to the success of the franchisee. Toni&Guy has regional managers that check that staff wearing uniforms, pictures are correctly used windows and that that staff are being trained, to make sure standard is same wherever in the world the service of offered.

Exclusive area Each franchisee is given a geographical area from which to operate. So you won't find two Tony&Guy salons in the same high street. This means that franchisees are not in direct

competition with each other.

Branded goods or services to sell At Tony&Guy's, this includes branded shampoos and other hair care products.

The cost to the franchisee

The franchisor doesn't provide all its services for nothing. Franchisors often charge a fixed sum at the start of the franchise agreement to cover the costs of starting up a new branch. Then they charge either a fee (a proportion of the value of everything sold) or they charge higher prices for the products they sell to the franchisee than they would if bought in an open market. For example, Gary France has a renewable 5 year contract for the Kensington branch. He pays a monthly royalty of 10 per cent of turnover for his 49 per cent share of the business.

Advantages and disadvantages for the franchisee

For the franchisee, franchising is a relatively safe way to start a business. Only 6-7 per cent of franchisees fail. In other types of business, the failure rate is about 50 per cent within the first two years. The difference in failure rate comes about because:

- the franchisor carefully selects people from those who want to buy a franchise; this tends to eliminate people who are unsuitable for the business;

- the franchisor sets out at the start how much money the franchisee needs to put into the business; many new businesses fail because the owners badly underestimate the amount of money they will need to survive in business.

- the franchise formula has already been tried out and tested and has been successful; the franchisee only has to repeat the success of other franchisees.

- the franchisor provides on-going support and can help the franchisee sort out any problems such as quality control or tax problems.

On the other hand, the franchisee doesn't have the freedom to operate that an ordinary business would have because of the franchise agreement. In particular, the franchisee can't sell the business without the franchisor's permission. In some franchises, the franchisor can end the franchise without reason and without having to give any compensation. The franchisee is also tied to making payments to the franchisor. Successful franchisees often feel that they are being overcharged by the franchisor.

Advantages for the franchisor

For the franchisor, there are two main advantages.

- The franchisee puts up money at the start and during the running of the business. This means that the franchisor doesn't have to find that money to run its business. It can therefore expand at a faster rate than it might otherwise.

Razzamataz

Razzamataz Theatre Schools is a franchise. It was set up in 2000 with just 25 students and 3 teachers. Today hundreds of students attend the schools across Cumbria and Scotland and the business is continually growing. Before starting the business Denise Hutton had been a professional dancer, choreographer and gymnast for over 10 years, performing around the world on cruise ships, in pantomimes, summer seasons, European and UK tours, the Millennium Dome and the London Palladium. At the schools, children between the ages of 5 and 18 receive top class dance, drama and singing lessons from a wide range of professional and experienced teachers – many of whom are professional performers in their own right.

Its promotion states 'If you're an energetic, motivated and fun person who enjoys working with youngsters, possibly with a background in dance, drama or stage then a Razzamataz Theatre Schools franchise could be just the opportunity you're looking for!

Source: adapted from www.thefranchisedirectory.net/.

1 What services does this franchise provide to customers?
2 What types of people might be suited to running a Razzamataz Theatre Schools franchise?
3 Why might a potential franchisee consider that this could be a successful franchise to buy into?

- The franchisee is as keen and motivated to make a success of the business as the franchisor. This might make the whole business more successful than if the franchisor simply employed staff to run branches of the business.

Does a franchise work?

Not all franchises work. The franchisor might have a poor business idea and mislead people into buying a franchise. Both the franchisor and the franchisees might then go out of business. Equally, franchisees might not provide a good product or service because they run the business badly. In a well run franchise, the franchisor monitors quality and could tell the franchisee to improve or risk losing the franchise. However, in a badly run franchise, poor quality could be a major problem, dragging down both the business of the local franchisee and the national business of the franchisor.

Source: adapted in part from BBC Bitesize, www.growthbusiness.co.uk, uk.businessesforsale.com, www.hwca.com.

Countrywide Signs

Countrywide Signs is a franchise which provides a sign service for property and estate agents. Maintenance and retrieval of boards is important, as the estate agents want their boards to retain the smart appearance that reflects their public image. Retrieval is also vital as these boards cost money to produce.

Whatever the economic climate and the position of property prices, people need to move home. Families grow, families shrink, employment moves individuals around, people need larger houses, people need smaller houses. It is estimated that the UK market for siting, erection and maintenance of signs is worth £20 million. Countrywide Signs plan to achieve at least 20% of that market within the next two years and expand its coverage to a countrywide network of franchisees.

Source: adapted from www.thefranchisedirectory.net/.

1 What type of franchise operation is being offered by Countrywide Signs?
2 Why might the business feel that it could be a successful business?
3 (a) Why might Countrywide Signs want to expand its franchise operations? (b) What might be the long term disadvantages for Countrywide Signs of expanding through the use of franchising?

Checklist ✓

1 What is the difference between a franchisor and a franchisee?
2 What may the franchisor provide for the franchisee?
3 How does the franchisor make a profit?
4 What are the advantages of a franchise for the franchisee?
5 Why might a person decide not to become a franchisee but set up his or her own business in competition with a franchise?
6 Why are businesses willing to franchise their valuable business ideas to other businesses?
7 Why might franchising be a problem for; (a) the franchisee; and (b) the franchisor?

key terms

Franchise - the right given by one business to another to sell goods or services using its name.
Franchisee - a business which agrees to manufacture, distribute or provide a branded product.
Franchisor - the business which gives franchisees the right to sell its product, in return for a fixed sum of money or a royalty payment.

SUMMARY CASE STUDY

SERVICEMASTER

Merry Maids - domestic cleaning services

Merry Maids are looking for mature couples or individuals to acquire ownership of a Merry Maids Franchise. They should have the skills to manage a fast growing business as well as managing the cleaning staff who work within it. The cleaning staff will be employees of the franchise. They are among the greatest assets of the business. Working in pairs, they will deliver an efficient and quality service to customers. The initial franchise fee charged by Merry Maids includes an exclusive and unique service worker selection program to make sure you bring the right people into your business. Also included in the initial franchise fee is the equipment, supplies and exclusive Merry Maids' cleaning products to equip four two-person cleaning teams. Each cleaning team, when properly trained and scheduled, can clean two to three homes a day.

Franchise Fee: £13,500 (Plus VAT)
Equipment Package: £5,450 (Plus VAT)
Royalty fee: 7%

TruGreen

TruGreen is a franchise opportunity that allows enterprising individuals to enter the profitable and growing lawn care market and provide specialist services. The franchise benefits from the respected professional standing of its parent company, ServiceMaster Limited. It operates with low overheads and attractive margins and is an enjoyable and potentially rewarding business. TruGreen offers a franchise that:
• You can work from home, with low overheads, plus great Monday to Friday daytime hours.
• Your franchise will be in the service sector with exceptional growth predictions.
• No cash flow problems and high profit margins.
• No selling, you just provide the quotations.
• 90% repeat customers, in your own territory.

Franchise Fee: £12,000 (Plus VAT)
Equipment Package: £9,500 (Plus VAT)
Royalty fee: 10%

Source: adapted from www.theukfranchisedirectory.net/,www.servicemaster.co.uk, www.franchise-uk.co.uk

ServiceMaster is a successful US franchise which came to Britain in 1959. Today it has over 700 franchises. It offers 6 franchisee opportunities including Merry Maids and TruGreen.

Jim and Dot Truepenny are looking to operate a franchise. Jim is 52 and has just been made redundant from his job as a maintenance supervisor, responsible amongst other things for health and safety. Dot works in a garden shop and they are both keen gardeners. Jim has was given a redundancy package which included a payment of £22 500.

1 What services are being provided by Merry Maids and TruGreen?
2 Why would be the cost to Jim and Dot of running a Merry Maids franchise?
    3 Which of the two franchise opportunities do you think would most suit Jim and Dot? Explain your reasons carefully.

Making decisions

As businesses grow in size, they might find that their national markets are too small for them. They may begin to export their products. Later they might find it to their advantage to switch some production to foreign countries. At this point they can be called multinational companies. These companies must decide how to operate successfully across several countries, faced with a variety of different local legal, tax and social situations. They must decide on the most profitable location to produce and where it is profitable to sell.

BP is one of world's largest energy companies. Based in Britain, it provides its customers with fuel for transportation, energy for heat and light, retail services and petrochemical products for everyday items. In 2005, its worldwide sales were $262 billion.

Multinational companies

BP is a MULTINATIONAL COMPANY. This means that it operates not just in the UK but in other countries around the world. It owns companies, petrol outlets, refineries and sites everywhere from China to Algeria to Kuwait and Australia. It sells its products to consumers, businesses and governments worldwide.

A UK multinational will almost certainly be a plc. All major industrialised countries have their own multinational companies, owned by shareholders in their own countries, but operating internationally. Some multinationals have major shareholders in several other countries as well.

Company structure

Multinational companies often have complicated structures. There is likely to be a PARENT COMPANY. BP plc is a parent company. This is a company with

shareholders which owns other companies. These other companies are called SUBSIDIARY COMPANIES. In 2007, BP owned

or part-owned over 1,500 other companies. In Trinidad and Tobago, for instance, BP plc wholly owned BP Trinidad (LNG) and 70%

Ford

Ford is one of the world's largest vehicle manufacturers. Based in the US, its annual sales in 2005 were $177.1 billion (equivalent roughly to £93 billion). Some of the brands owned by Ford include Mazda, Jaguar, Aston Martin, Volvo, Landrover and Mercury. In Britain there are two big Ford car factories. One is in Dagenham, Essex and another in Hailwood, Liverpool. Ford also has an interest in financial services. For example, it provides financing for car purchases in 36 different countries.

1 What makes Ford a 'multinational company'?
2 Ford, a US company, has often grown by buying foreign businesses. What evidence of this is there?
3 Setting up a car factory costs millions, perhaps even hundreds of millions of pounds. How does Ford's size help it to set up and operate dozens of car factories?

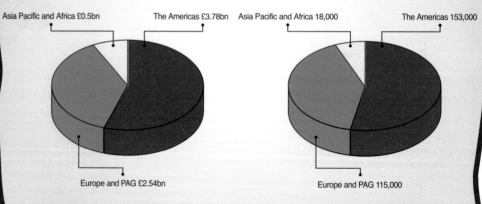

Asia Pacific and Africa £0.5bn   The Americas £3.78bn   Asia Pacific and Africa 18,000   The Americas 153,000

Europe and PAG £2.54bn   Europe and PAG 115,000

Figure 1 *Sales of trucks and cars per region (thousands)*

Figure 2 *Employees per region (excludes those in financial services)*

Source: adapted from Ford, *Annual Report and Accounts*, 2005.

of BP Trinidad and Tobago, both oil exploration companies.

One reason why a UK multinational may have subsidiaries in other countries is because tax may be lower in these countries. Also, each subsidiary company will have limited liability. It might also be argued that separate local companies can meet the needs of its customers more easily.

Benefits of larger size

Companies often become multinationals because size can help them compete against other businesses. Size can lead to lower costs of production, perhaps because of economies of scale. The company may also be able to locate production more cost effectively. Of more importance to BP is that size can lead to better products. Not many businesses have the expertise and resources to engage in oil exploration. BP is also in the forefront of technology. For example, BP is developing the world's first industrial scale project to generate electricity from hydrogen. The hydrogen is manufactured from natural gas to create 'decarbonized fuels', reducing carbon dioxide emissions by around 90%.

Problems facing multinationals

A multinational needs to develop strategies to cope with a number of different problems.

Size BP employed 97 000 people in December 2006. Only 16 900 of these worked in the UK with 20 200 employed in the rest of Europe. This is not surprising since much of BP's revenue is generated outside the UK. With some 1 500 subsidiary companies and thousands of sites worldwide, BP needs to find ways of making everyone work together to achieve the goals of the company. The sheer size of the company and its geographic spread mean that good communication is essential.

Law and politics BP owns businesses in over 100 countries and sells products in many more. This means that it needs to understand at least 100 different legal systems. It is also constantly dealing with government, both at a local level and a national level. It needs permission to operate refineries and open petrol stations. It might need government approval to employ workers. It must pay tax to the local government. Permission might also have to be obtained to import and export its products, as well as pay bills and send profits from one country to another. BP is also subject to a wide variety of environmental regulations because its exploration and refining processes affect the local environment.

Exchange rate fluctuations
Multinationals may sell products and earn profits in a large number of different currencies. However, the values of currencies are constantly changing against each other. If the value of the pound against other currencies changes, this can have an important effect on profits and the values of overseas sales of a multinational. For instance, in 2006 the US dollar was relatively weak against other currencies. This was not good for BP because oil, BP's main product, is traded in dollars.

Source: adapted in part from the BP plc, *Annual Report and Accounts*, 2006.

key terms

Multinational company - a business which operates in at least two countries, usually both selling products and producing them in these countries.
Parent company - a company which owns and controls other companies (called **subsidiary companies**).

SUMMARY CASE STUDY

ASTRAZENECA

AstraZeneca is one of the world's leading pharmaceutical companies, with a broad range of medicines designed to fight disease in important areas of healthcare. The company is active in over 100 countries with growing presence in important emerging markets. Its head office is in London and it operates major research and development (R&D) sites in Sweden, the UK and the US. In 2006, AstraZeneca's sales totalled $26.5 billion, with an operating profit of $8.2 billion. It employed 66 000 people.

AstraZeneca spends over $16 million every working day on the research and development of new medicines that meet patient needs. Total R&D spending in 2006 was $3.9 billion. The company employs around 12 000 people at 16 research and development centres in 8 countries. It has 27 manufacturing sites in 19 countries and over 66 000 employees (58% in Europe, 27 per cent in the Americas and 15 per cent in Asia, Africa and Australasia).

Source: adapted from www.astrazeneca.com.

1 Why can AstraZeneca be called a 'multinational company'?
2 Suggest why companies like AstraZeneca operate in a large number of different countries worldwide.
3 What evidence is there to suggest that AstraZeneca is in the forefront of technology?
4 Discuss TWO problems that AstraZeneca may have to deal with operating as a multinational.

Checklist ✓

1 Name FOUR multinational companies.
2 What is the difference between a parent company and a subsidiary company?
3 Why might companies become multinational companies?
4 (a) What problems do multinational companies face and (b) how can they overcome these?

Making decisions

Government must decide what is to be provided in the public sector of the economy and what is to be produced in the private sector. If it is to be produced by the public sector, should it be produced by private sector businesses or by state owned businesses? What should be privatised and what should be kept in the public sector?

The BBC is a large broadcasting organisation in the UK. In 2006 the corporation had an income of around £4 billion. Around £3.1 billion of this was raised from television licence fees. The remainder was generated from the sale of programmes, co-production deals, publishing activities and the provision of media monitoring services. The BBC employs over 25,000 people in its organization. It is a popular employer attracting around 90,000 job applications in 2006.

The public sector

The BBC is part of the PUBLIC SECTOR of the economy. The public sector is run and owned by the state. The two most important parts of the **state** are **central government** and **local government**. Central government is controlled from London. The Prime Minister is in overall charge of central government. Citizens elect MPs (Members of Parliament) to supervise central government. Local government is the government of counties, districts, parishes and boroughs throughout the UK.

Producer, provider and buyer

The public sector is a provider, producer and buyer.

Provider The public sector in the UK provides a large range of services, illustrated in Figure 1, from health and education to defence and the police. Part is provided free of charge to consumers, like secondary school education. Prices are charged for the rest. For example the BBC often sells DVDs of its programmes.

Producer The public sector produces some of the goods and services it provides, like defence, education and health care. Because the BBC is owned by the public sector, it also therefore provides radio and television programmes.

Buyer The public sector buys the rest of what it provides from private sector businesses, including tanks, new roads and places in old people's homes.

Public corporations

The BBC is a PUBLIC CORPORATION. This is a type of business organisation recognised in law, like a **public limited company** or a **co-operative**. A public corporation is owned by central government, i.e. the government is the only shareholder. Like a public limited

1 Look at Figure 1. Who provides:
(a) the army; (b) dustbin collection;
(c) unemployment benefit; (d) primary schools;
(e) NHS hospital operations; (f) social workers;
(g) higher education?

2 Williams Holdings is a private sector UK company which makes fire and safety equipment and building equipment, including Yale locks and Cuprinol wood preservative. What business opportunities are there for the company of selling to the public sector?

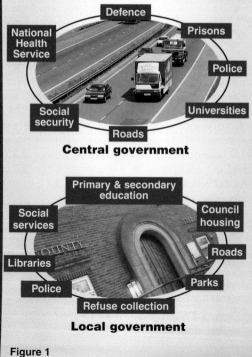

Figure 1

company, it has a **board of directors** (or the BBC Trust in the case of the BBC) which oversees the running of the corporation.

The government sets **goals** for public corporations to achieve. These are likely to be different from a private company. This is because the government itself has far more objectives than a private company which is most likely to want to maximise returns to the owners of the business. The objectives of the BBC are laid out in a Royal Charter which came into force in 2007.

Privatisation

In 1979, the list of public corporations was much longer than it is today. It included the gas industry, the electricity industry, the railways, British Telecom, British Aerospace, Rolls Royce, British Airways and British Steel.

During the 1980s, most public corporations were PRIVATISED. This means they were sold off by the government to private buyers. So they are now PRIVATE SECTOR companies owned by private shareholders. The opposite of privatisation is NATIONALISATION. This occurs when the state buys a company from its private sector shareholders. Many of the companies privatised in the 1980s and 1990s, such as British Steel and British Rail, were nationalised between 1945 and 1951.

The BBC is the only large public corporation apart from the Post Office to stay in the public sector. Should the BBC be sold off to the private sector? It is unlikely at the moment. There is a number of issues which are important in deciding this.

Costs Most private sector companies aim to make profits. More profit is better than less profit. One way they can make more profit is by keeping their costs as low as possible. Public corporations, on the other hand, have had little incentive to keep costs as low as possible because profits may not be important. In

Competition and the Post Office

For 150 years the Post Office enjoyed operating as a monopoly. No other company was allowed to deliver letters or packets for less than £1. This means that the Post Office did not face any competition in its letter service. However, in January 2006 the law was changed. Now, any licensed operator can deliver mail to business and residential customers. Royal Mail welcomed the move, claiming it is 'ready for a fair fight', while regulator Postcomm claimed it will 'improve the state of the nation's postal service' and improve reliability.

In addition to potential new operators, such as TNT Mail, the British arm of Dutch company TPG, the Post Office already faces competition. There are other forms of communication such as email, telephone and fax.

Some people think the Post Office should be privatised. At the moment the Post Office has to give some of its profits to the government, which owns it. This limits the amount the Post Office can keep for investment. It is also restricted in the prices it can charge. For example, it makes standard charges for letter delivery regardless of the costs involved.

Source: adapted from Post Office website.
1 What is meant by: (a) privatisation; (b) monopoly; and (c) competition?
2 What competition does the Post Office face?
3 Explain why privatising the Post Office might make it able to compete better against its rivals.
4 It costs far more to collect and deliver letters to rural areas than urban areas. Do you think that the Post Office should be allowed to adjust letter prices to reflect these differences in costs?
Explain your answer carefully putting down advantages and disadvantages to those involved.

practice, the companies and industries which have been privatised, like gas and electricity, have seen falls in costs. This means they are more **efficient** as producers. So, if the BBC were privatised, it could be that its costs would fall too.

Prices If costs fall after privatisation, this gives companies the opportunity also to cut their prices to customers. Some industries and companies which have been privatised have operated in competitive markets. Competition between businesses often forces businesses to set low prices. This is because, otherwise, they would lose customers and sales to other businesses. Telephone charges in the UK have fallen since privatisation, for instance, because BT has been forced to compete with other businesses like Vodafone and Orange. Where there is no

competition, as in the water industry, the government set up **regulatory bodies**. These are:
- OFWAT for the water industry;
- OFGEM for gas and electricity;
- ORR for the rail industry;
- OFCOM for the telephone and broadcasting.

These regulatory bodies lay down rules for how businesses in the industry can compete. They also tend to fix maximum prices that firms can charge so that the consumer is not charged too much.

If the BBC were privatised it would probably have to charge viewers and listeners. It may charge subscriptions in the way that Sky does for its satellite channels. It may also raise revenue from advertising like most other commercial broadcasters. Since there is competition in the market, the BBC would have to set prices to win and retain audiences.

The product Public corporations were usually monopolists. Without any competition, they didn't have a particularly strong incentive to provide goods and services that customers wanted. Privatisation can change this. If the company is still a monopolist, one way of earning more profit is to sell more. This means finding out what the customer wants to buy and providing it. Although the BBC operates in a competitive market, without the licence fee, it may be pressurised into providing a better service than it does now. Perhaps the quality of programmes might improve. On the other hand, it might try to increase its efficiency by cutting out some services. For example, it might close down loss making services ie, where audiences are relatively low such as BBC Radio 3. Programmes for minorities might be axed. Such cuts would be considered undesirable by many – even though they might not use the services. However, as already stated, at the moment, there are no plans whatsoever to privatise the BBC. The BBC is not currently a profit seeking organisation.

Other public sector enterprises

Public corporations, like the BBC, are only one of many examples of PUBLIC SECTOR ENTERPRISES, businesses which are owned by the state.

Public corporations are owned by central government. However, local authorities also own many public sector enterprises, such as local leisure centres, cemeteries, crematoria, airports and market halls.

Local authorities may run these MUNICIPAL ENTERPRISES for profit, or at least expect them to break-even financially. Some, though are run at a loss. Local authorities subsidise them to achieve a range of different objectives. For example, a

Network Rail

The rail industry has experienced a number of ownership changes during its fluctuating history. Train services were supplied by British Rail, a nationalised industry, up until 1996 when it was broken up and sold off in parts. The largest part was Railtrack, the rail infrastructure which included the railway lines, stations, bridges, signals and property. Transport services were provided by private operators such as Virgin Trains, Stagecoach and North Western.

In 2002, Railtrack was at the point of bankruptcy, and was taken back into the public sector. The government refused to grant Railtrack any more funds. It now operates as Network Rail, a not-for-profit company. During its time in the private sector Railtrack was heavily criticised for paying up to £700 million in dividends to shareholders despite continually missing operational targets, losing money and relying on subsidies. It was criticised for its lack of investment in the infrastructure and its general inefficiency. Railtrack was also very unpopular with rail passengers due to continual delays, cancellations and accidents.

1. Who owns Network Rail?
2. Why do you think Railtrack went bankrupt?
3. Network Rail is regulated by ORR (the Office of Rail Regulation). Discuss the role of ORR.
4. Discuss whether the privatisation of Railtrack was a success or not.

municipal leisure centre may offer free or subsidised entrance for senior citizens or the disabled. It may run swimming classes for children at a loss. Activities may be targeted at ethnic minority groups to try to get them to participate more in sports activities.

There is also a growing number of public sector enterprises which are not owned either by central of local government. One example is health Trusts which organise health care in a local area. Another is many Foundation Schools in England and Wales.

PUBLIC PRIVATE PARTNERSHIPS (PPPs), sometimes called PUBLIC/PRIVATE SECTOR PARTNERSHIPS, is a term used to describe the working together of the public sector and the private sector. A partnership might, for example, be set up to regenerate a run down area. Or a new hospital might be built using PRIVATE FINANCE INITIATIVE (PFI)

funding. PFI is where a private company builds and runs a building like a hospital or a school, or a road, and then rents the use of the building to central government, a local authority or a hospital trust.

Government policy today is to increase private sector involvement in providing goods and services in the public sector. This is because it is argued that the private sector is often more efficient than the public sector. Getting the private sector involved will cut costs and lead to better services being provided.

Opportunities for businesses

Privatisation Privatisation has created new businesses. At the point of privatisation, the electricity industry was split up into over ten different companies, for instance. Many privatised businesses were then **taken over** by existing private sector businesses. However, there are many other ways in which changes made by the government can affect businesses.

Deregulation Government makes a large number of rules about how businesses can operate. Laws like the **Health and Safety Acts** protect workers from unsafe working conditions. Laws like the **Trade Descriptions Act** protect consumers from poor quality goods and services. Deregulation occurs when the government removes some of these rules. In the 1980s, for instance, the government changed the rules about buses. Before, bus companies, mainly owned by local authorities, were given local monopolies. No other bus company could set up in competition. Today, any bus company can provide local or national services. This has greatly increased competition in the bus industry. It provided a business opportunity for companies like Stagecoach to set up in business and expand. It also posed a threat to existing bus companies. The bus companies owned by local authorities tended to lose customers.

Contracting out Many services are now paid for by government but provided by private sector services. For instance, local authorities in England have to put out refuse collection to **tender**. The company putting in the lowest bid - the cheapest price - to provide the service gets the contract. This gives businesses the opportunity to win new orders. Everything from places in old people's homes to catering in hospitals has been put out to tender.

key terms

Municipal enterprises - businesses which are owned by local authorities and which get at least part of their revenues by charging customers for services.
Nationalisation - the purchase by the state of a private sector business.
Private Finance Initiative - a government scheme where a private sector business pays for the construction and running of a building or other piece of infrastructure and then rents the building to the public sector.
Private sector - the rest of the economy apart from the public sector, owned and controlled by private individuals and businesses.
Privatisation - the sale of state-owned businesses to the private sector.
Public corporation - a public sector enterprise owned by central government.
Public Private Partnerships of Public/Private Sector Partnership (PPP) - activities where the public sector and private sector businesses work together to provide goods and services.
Public sector - part of the economy owned and controlled by the state or government.
Public sector enterprise - a business owned by the state which sells what it produces to the private sector.

SUMMARY CASE STUDY

CONTRACTING OUT IN THE NHS

The NHS was set up in 1948 and is now the largest organisation in Europe. It is recognised as one of the best health services in the world by the World Health Organisation. Health care is free at the point of delivery and is funded by the government, from taxation. However, there need to be improvements to cope with the demands of the 21st century. The NHS is changing the way it works to make sure patients always come first. This has brought about some big changes in the way the NHS is structured and the way in which the different organisations within the NHS relate to each other. One of these changes has been the contracting out of a number of non-clinical NHS activities such as cleaning, the provision of hospital meals and laundry. More recently it has allowed private sector hospitals to carry out clinical work. For example, to help reduce waiting lists the government agreed to contract out certain non-emergency services, such as MRI scanning or elective procedures, such as cataract surgery and knee operations, to the private sector.

Source: adapted from NHS website.

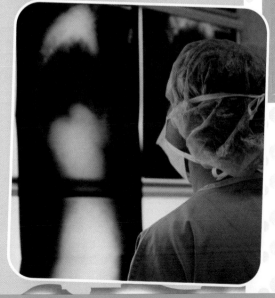

1. What is meant by contracting out?
2. In addition to contracting out, how else might private sector businesses benefit from NHS activity?
3. Why has the government chosen to contract out activities in the NHS?
4. Discuss whether you think the NHS should be privatised.

Checklist ✓

1 What is the public sector?
2 What is the difference between central and local government?
3 Give FIVE examples of goods and services produced by the public sector.
4 Give TWO examples of services bought by the public sector from the private sector.
5 (a) What public sector enterprises might a local authority run? (b) Are there any examples of these in your area?
6 What is the difference between nationalisation and privatisation?
7 What is a regulatory authority in a privatised industry?
8 What is the difference between deregulation and contracting out?

THE INTERNAL ORGANISATION OF A BUSINESS

Making decisions

Every business has to decide how to organise itself. In a large business, there might be hundreds of thousands of workers to be organised. The business must decide:
* how workers will be put into groups to work together;
* who is going to be in a position of authority, giving orders;
* how many workers will be supervising the work of others and how many will be producing the output of the business;
* how messages will be passed through the business so that employees are kept informed.

Fitzgerald Lighting manufactures fluorescent lighting for domestic, commercial and industrial use, along with emergency and amenity lighting. Started in 1972 with two employees, it has expanded to employ over 500 people in 2007. The majority are based at headquarters in Bodmin, Cornwall, where all production takes place. The business has sales and distribution depots in Upminster, Birmingham, St.Helens, Belfast, Edinburgh, Dublin and Bodmin.

Organisation

At Fitzgerald Lighting, workers specialise, each taking on a ROLE, a given job of work. Some workers are administration or sales staff, some are skilled workers, whilst others are managers. Workers need to know:
* what jobs they are supposed to do;
* who is in charge of them;
* who they are in charge of;
* how they relate to the wider ORGANISATION.

This can be shown on an ORGANISATION CHART.

 Draw an organisation chart for your school or college. You will need to find out how the school or college is organised. The organisation chart is likely to be complicated because there is a number of different functions being fulfilled by different workers in the hierarchy. You might find that the same teacher or lecturer needs to be put into two separate places on the chart - as a subject teacher and as a tutor for instance.

Organisation charts

Figure 1 shows an organisation chart for Fitzgerald Lighting. At the top of this HIERARCHY, the series

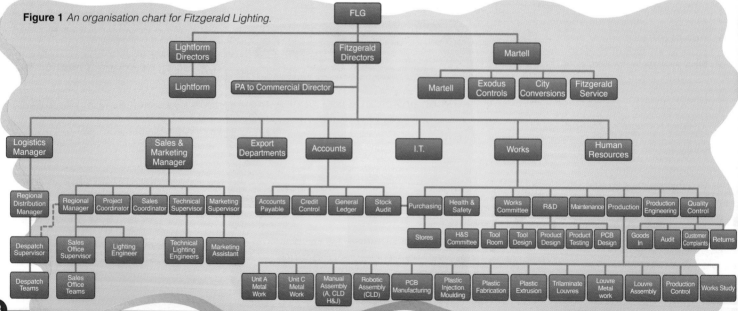

Figure 1 An organisation chart for Fitzgerald Lighting.

of layers in the organisation, are the directors. Next in the hierarchy are the managers, including for example the sales and marketing manager and the logistics manager. At the bottom of the hierarchy are the production workers, despatch team and sales office team. Workers in a hierarchy have a LINE MANAGER. This is someone immediately above the worker, to whom he or she reports.

The business is organised by FUNCTION. This means that Fitzgerald Lighting is organised according to what people do in the organisation. So, the department responsible for sales and marketing is led by the sales and marketing manager, whilst the logistics manager is responsible for distribution. An operations manager and production manager are responsible for all the different aspects of production.

Because there tend to be more people the lower down you go in the organisation, a hierarchy is often said to be a **pyramid**.

The chain of command

The person at the top of the organisational pyramid is in a position of AUTHORITY over workers lower down the pyramid. So a director has authority over the managers. He or she can give orders to workers lower down the hierarchy, his SUBORDINATES. For instance, he or she could tell the production manager to increase production. In the organisational pyramid, there is therefore a CHAIN OF COMMAND from the top to the bottom.

The length of the chain of command

The length of the chain of command at Fitzgerald Lighting is typical of manufacturing companies. For instance, Figure 2 shows the layers in the hierarchy from the managing director to the assemblers and packers. The longer the chain of command, the more difficulties a business can face.

- Messages can get lost or distorted as they go up and down the chain of command, rather as in a game of Chinese whispers.
- Managing change can be another problem. In a sole proprietorship change is simple. The sole trader decides to change and acts on that decision. In a large organisation, the chairperson might decide on change but it might be resisted further down the hierarchy. The longer the chain of command, the more groups there are to resist that change.

Delayering

Some large businesses try to resolve the problems of a long chain of command by flattening it. This is called DELAYERING. They cut out large numbers of middle managers, pushing responsibility and decision making down the line. In a factory, for instance, supervisors and quality control inspectors can be eliminated if workers are organised into groups and made responsible for their own work in terms of output and quality.

This EMPOWERMENT of workers can motivate them more. However, it usually means that workers have to be better trained to cope with the extra responsibilities. Workers might have to be paid more because they are doing a more responsible job. Delayering should lead to workers becoming more productive. Fewer workers are needed to do the same amount of work. Businesses can then DOWNSIZE, making workers redundant whilst producing as much as before.

Span of control

The Sales and Marketing Manager at Fitzgerald Lighting cannot be expected to organise or supervise every single sales worker. This job would be too large. Instead, he only controls the work of his five immediate subordinates – the regional manager, the project coordinator, the sales coordinator, the technical supervisor and the marketing supervisor. These are shown in Figure 1.

The number of people that a worker directly controls is called a

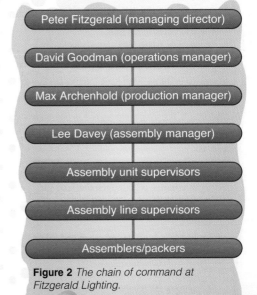

Peter Fitzgerald (managing director)

David Goodman (operations manager)

Max Archenhold (production manager)

Lee Davey (assembly manager)

Assembly unit supervisors

Assembly line supervisors

Assemblers/packers

Figure 2 *The chain of command at Fitzgerald Lighting.*

In 2007 Tesco has 2,710 supermarkets, supercentres, and convenience stores worldwide. In 2006 it had sales of £41.3 billion and profit before tax of over £2.2 billion and employed over 450 000 people. Sir Terry Leahy became its chief executive in 1997. He argues that its hierarchy is relatively flat. 'Anyone can make it here. There are only six layers between the person who works on the checkout counter and me.' Tesco's record in retaining staff has improved vastly in the past decade. Turnover was nearly 100 per cent a year when Leahy became boss. In 2006 it was 30 per cent.

Soure: adapted from *The Guardian*, 8.1.2006, www.tescocorporate.com.

1 What is meant by the Tesco hierarchy?
2 'Tesco has a relatively flat hierarchy for such a large organisation.' Explain what this means.
3 Discuss the (a) advantages and (b) disadvantages for Tesco of having a flat hierarchy.

SPAN OF CONTROL. The span of control of the Project/Sales Manager is therefore five employees, whilst for the span of control of the accounts manager is the 10 employees in the accounts team.

The span of control: how big?

The span of control varies depending upon circumstances.

- The more complex the supervision task, the smaller the span of control. The supervision task can be complex if checking work is difficult and time consuming. It can also be more complex if the workers which need supervising are not particularly good at their job.
- The span of control has to be small if communication with subordinates is time consuming. The operations manager and production managers can supervise employees in the works department more effectively because they are based in Bodmin than they could if subordinates were scattered across the world.

- The better the supervisor, the more people he or she can supervise.
- The more the supervisor DELEGATES his or her work, the greater can be the span of control. Delegation means passing down responsibility to subordinates to complete tasks. Delegation frees up a supervisor's time to supervise the work of more workers. It also empowers subordinates. Workers further down the chain of command are likely to be more motivated. This is because they are being shown trust and can use their own talents and skills more.

Formal groups

Employees of Fitzgerald Lighting are organised into departments and sections, examples of FORMAL GROUPS. These are groups set up by the organisation to carry out tasks.

There are many advantages to organising work through formal groups.

- Each group and possibly even each worker within a group can

specialise, leading to higher output and lower costs.
- The group has a clear position within the organisational structure of the business. This means that other groups know which group to turn to when they need help. For instance, finance matters can be referred to the accounts manager. Knowing who is doing what in an organisation saves time and therefore ensures lower costs.
- Communication in the organisation is helped, again because there is a clear structure.
- Workers can act as a team, receive support from others in the group and also have their work supervised.

Informal groups

An INFORMAL GROUP is a group which is not set up by the organisation but comes into existence by itself. A group of friends at Fitzgerald Lighting who play squash together would be an example.

Informal groups can be good for business. People who form a group tend to get on well together and may work better as a result.

Informal groups can sometimes lead to information getting through which otherwise would get clogged up in an inefficient chain of command.

Informal groups can also be bad for the business. Most medium to large businesses have groups of people who spend their time together moaning about other workers and bad decision making by their bosses. The group may set out to prevent needed change in the business because the members of the group don't want that change.

Whether good or bad for the business, the one thing that the business can not do is prevent informal groups being formed. The business therefore has to take these groups into account when managing change and making decisions.

Source: information from Fitzgerald Lighting.

Jeff Simmons is a call centre manager for a computer company. He has a team of 12 telephone staff who take calls regarding a variety of issues ranging from sales to payments. He also supervises the work of a team of 3 staff who answer queries regarding the technical operation of the system and 5 staff who make visits to homes or businesses to sort out maintenance or installation problems. Each day Jeff prepares a list of work that the maintenance staff have to do. If staff are called out and extra jobs have to be carried out, they need to report back to Jeff for him to approve the jobs.

Each week Jeff holds a meeting to highlight issues that have occurred over the past 7 days. He draws up an agenda and, at the end of the meeting, makes a decision on the procedures that staff will need to follow in future. Staff have recently felt that this restricts their ability to answer queries over the phone and some customers have complained about the lack of service. Last week after a dinner time discussion, the sales team agreed to approach Jeff about this problem.

1 What is a call centre manager?
2 Draw a simple organisation chart showing Jeff's chain of command and the span of control.
3 Explain how (a) a formal group and (b) an informal group operates at the call centre.
4 Discuss whether delegation might help Jeff to be more effective.

Bender Forrest

Figure 3 shows an organisation chart for Bender Forrest, a specialist manufacturer of stainless steel piping, vessels and fabrications.

1 Who is at (a) the top and (b) the bottom of the chains of command?
2 Who would the accounts supervisor issue instructions to?
3 Who would be subordinate to the quality assurance manager?
4 Explain the (a) advantages and (b) disadvantages to the business of removing the piping side and fabrication side foremen's jobs from the hierarchy.

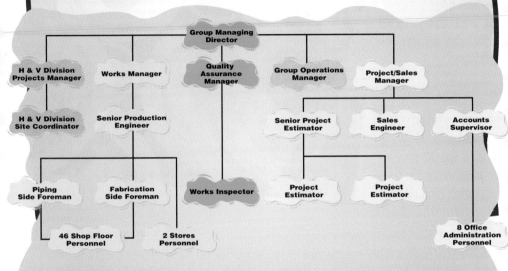

Figure 3 *An organisation chart for Bender Forrest.*

key terms

Authority - the right to decide what to do in a situation and take command of it.
Chain of command - the path (or chain) down which orders (or commands) are passed. In a company, this goes from the board of directors down to shop floor workers.
Delayering - removing layers of management and workers in a hierarchy so that there are fewer workers in the chain of command.
Delegation - passing down of authority for work to another worker further down the hierarchy of the organisation.
Downsizing - when a business employs fewer workers to produce the same amount through increases in productivity which can be achieved through delayering.
Empowerment - giving more responsibility to workers further down the chain of command in a hierarchy.
Formal group - a group created by an organisation to complete a specific task.
Function - tasks or jobs. Organisation by function means that a business is organised according to tasks that have to be completed, such as production or finance.
Hierarchy - structure of different levels of authority in a business organisation, one on top of the other.
Informal group - a group of people who join together outside the formal structure of an organisation.
Line manager - employee who is responsible for overseeing the work of others further down the hierarchy of an organisation.
Organisation - the way in which a business is structured for it to achieve its objectives.
Organisation chart - a diagram which shows the internal structure of an organisation.
Role - a job of work given to a worker which he or she is expected to complete.
Span of control - the number of people who report directly to another worker in a superior position.
Subordinate - workers in the hierarchy who work under the control of a more senior worker.

SUMMARY CASE STUDY

BA RESTRUCTURING

In 2005 the target of taking £300m out of British Airways' employee costs set in 2003 was not looking likely. Willie Walsh, the former commercial pilot who had saved Aer Lingus from financial collapse, was brought in as chief executive officer to save the project. At first sight his management cuts were sweeping. There was to be a 50% cut in senior managers from 414 to 207 and a 30% cut in middle managers from 1,301 to 911, for example. Mr Walsh said that the cuts were 'part of a restructuring designed to simplify the airline's core business, provide clear accountability and remove duplication.' They came at a time when all BA operations were under one roof at Terminal 5 instead of expensively spread over various terminals.

Analysts commented that he was trying to simplify the business and that BA was over-managed. One suggested that 'There will be a whole layer of management, that is surplus, when you are not supervising two terminals. With a simpler business overheads and supervisors can be cut back.' But some argued 'Is losing so many skilled and experienced senior and middle management the best strategy to restructure the group?'

Source: adapted from the *Financial Times*, 1.12.2005.

1 Who would have been Willie Walsh's subordinates?
2 'BA may have been able to delayer the organisation'. Explain what this means.
3 How might (a) the chain of command and (b) the span of control change if the business had delayered?
4 What do you think might have been the (a) benefits and (b) problems of the changes made at the company?

Checklist ✓

1 Draw an organisational chart for a company with 32 workers, a board of directors, a managing director, and four managers each of whom have two assistant managers. Each assistant manager controls the same number of workers.
2 Explain the term 'middle management'.
3 'The chain of command is very long.' What does this mean?
4 What are the problems of having a long chain of command?
5 In a plc, who has authority over: (a) the managing director; (b) a manager; (c) shop floor workers?
6 'The span of control of the managing director is very small.' What does this mean?
7 What factors determine the best number for a span of control of a manager?
8 What are the advantages of organising work through formal groups?
9 Why can informal groups be (a) an advantage; and (b) a disadvantage for a business?

Making decisions

Every business must decide how to organise itself. If it is a medium to large sized business, it will almost certainly organise itself into departments. It then has to decide what departments to create and what work or functions each department will have. The commonest departmental structure is to have departments which cover marketing, production, personnel and finance. But this will not be appropriate for every business. How will it organise itself best to create greatest efficiency?

Lynam Castings is a large engineering company based in Walsall in the West Midlands. With a turnover of £40 million a year and a workforce of 750, it has survived global competitive pressures by specialising in low volume, difficult-to-make precision parts. It is organised on a traditional departmental basis.

Departments

In a very small business, individual workers are likely to perform several tasks. A sole trader, for example, might be a painter and decorator, but also be responsible for marketing and sales and accounting. In larger businesses, workers begin to specialise. In medium to large sized businesses, specialised workers are likely to be grouped together by function in

DEPARTMENTS. The traditional way of organising a business is to have four departments: production, marketing, personnel and finance. These are the four departments which are found at Lynam Castings.

The production department

The PRODUCTION DEPARTMENT at Lynam Castings is responsible for research and development of

products, and organising production. Service businesses are unlikely to have a research and development section. But for a manufacturing business like Lynam Castings, research and development is an essential part of the creation of products. Customers ask for parts to be designed for their specific needs. The research and development section at Lynam Castings then produces initial designs and, if necessary, will make prototypes and test these.

Once a design has been finalised, production can take place. There are many ways of organising production. For example, if the volumes of production are high enough, it might be possible to make a product on a production line. At Lynam Castings, volumes are small and each order requires a slightly different product to be made. So the parts are made in batches.

The workers in the production department at Lynam Castings are organised hierarchically. At the top there is the Production Manager

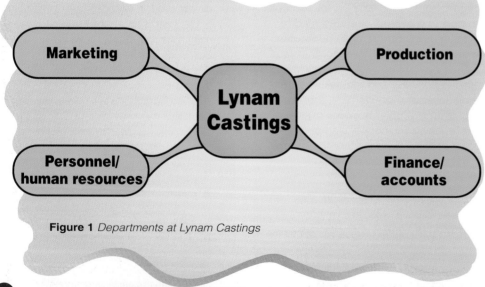

Figure 1 *Departments at Lynam Castings*

The production department is responsible for R&D and manufacturing.

where the customer may want to buy is also essential for products such as soft drinks. For some products, advertising in the media such as television may be vital.

The personnel or human resource department

The PERSONNEL or HUMAN RESOURCES DEPARTMENT is responsible for recruitment, training, terms and conditions of service, contracts, disciplinary and grievance procedures, resignations, industrial relations negotiations and dismissal. It deals with all issues to do with the workforce.

Lynam Castings, like many engineering companies, has difficulties recruiting sufficiently skilled production workers. Much of

whilst at the bottom there are workers such as machine operatives.

The marketing department

The MARKETING DEPARTMENT at Lynam Castings is the department responsible for selling the product. A marketing department might have to make decisions on market research, product planning, packaging, pricing, sales promotion, advertising and the distribution of the product.

Lynam Castings is constantly looking for new customers. It has a team of sales representatives who are responsible for finding new clients. They have an in-depth knowledge of companies in the UK which could provide new work and contact them regularly. Overseas, they attend trade fairs and seek to expand their network of customers. The marketing department is responsible for pricing products, although it works closely with both the finance department and production department on this.

Businesses which make consumer products, like cars, soap powders or soft drinks, may have extensive market research departments which attempt to find out the needs of customers and

then develop product ideas to satisfy those needs. Issues such as packaging may also be important. Getting the product to a place

Tariq Engineering

Tariq Engineering is a medium-sized engineering company in Leicester. It makes metal components for a range of customers but 67 per cent of the products are parts for aircraft seats. Ernie Tomlinson is the production manager and is responsible for the following functions.

Production and planning - involves setting standards and targets for each section of the production process. The quantity and quality of products coming off a production line will also be closely monitored.

Purchasing – involves making sure that the materials, components and equipment required to keep the production process running smoothly are provided.

Stores – involves stocking all the necessary tools, spares, raw materials and equipment required to service the manufacturing process.

Design and technical support – involves researching new products or modifications to existing ones, estimating costs for producing in different quantities and by using different methods. It will also be responsible for the design and testing of new product processes and product types, together with the development of prototypes through to the final product. The technical support department may also be responsible for work study and suggestions as to how working practices can be improved.

Works - involves the manufacture of products. This will include the maintenance of the production line and other necessary repairs. The works department may also have responsibility for quality control and inspection.

Source: adapted from www.thetimes100.

1 What is a production department?
2 Which of the above functions involves: (a) buying a spare part for a machine; (b) deciding on daily production targets for each section in the factory; (c) testing a new product to see if it stands up to sub-zero temperatures.
3 Ernie is thinking of merging the stores and purchasing function. Discuss the possible advantages and disadvantages of this proposal.

Café Queen

Café Queen is a chain of coffee shops. Most of the shops are located in the North and the Midlands. However, a few have been opened in the Southeast recently. The layout and atmosphere in the shops are specifically designed to be cosy and intimate, while at the same time providing people with their own personal space to use as they wish. Many people use Café Queen for business meetings. However, in recent years the chain has seen earnings fall.

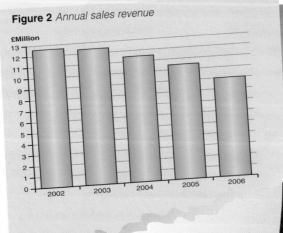

Figure 2 *Annual sales revenue*

1 Describe how sales have changed between 2002 and 2006.
2 The marketing department has been told to find out why sales have fallen. How might they do this?
3 Outline briefly TWO possible reasons for the fall in sales revenue.
4 (a) Explain TWO ways in which the marketing department could halt the fall in sales.
   (b) How might the finance department be affected by these two measures?

its existing production workforce is aged 45 plus. Recruitment is therefore a major challenge for the company. It does offer some training internally to unskilled workers who have the potential to develop engineering skills. But much of the training budget goes on workers in the marketing, personal and finance departments.

The company is considered to be a good employer locally and turnover of staff is relatively low. There is a steady trickle of workers who retire from the company each year reflecting the age structure of the workforce.

Around 60 per cent of the workers are represented by trade unions. Trade union membership is strongest in the production department where almost all workers are trade union members. The personnel department has good relations with trade union representatives who, for example, would advise members if the company were to issue a formal warning against an employee.

The finance department

The FINANCE or ACCOUNTS DEPARTMENT is responsible for paying wages and salaries, invoicing customers and paying suppliers, keeping accounts, preparing cash flow statements, as well as financial forecasting.

A business like Lynam Castings has a legal obligation to pay its bills. It is contractually obliged to pay its

workers at the times specified in the contracts of employment signed when workers start their jobs. Failure to pay suppliers could see the company taken to court.

The finance department must also issue bills, or invoices, to its customers. When customers don't pay on time, it must chase up these late payers. If the business is a retailer, the finance department would be responsible for the cash collected each day from customers and process cheques, debit card and credit card payments.

By law, businesses have to keep accounts, for example for tax purposes. The finance department at Lynam Castings keeps a variety of accounts recording the flow of money into and out of the business on a day to day basis. From these, annual accounts showing sales, costs and profits are produced. The finance department also produces a balance sheet which shows what the company owned and what it owed at the end of its financial year. The finance department will be asked on a regular basis to draw up financial forecasts. These are predictions about what will happen to the finances of the company in the future. It is important for the directors and the senior managers of the company to anticipate any future financial problems and deal with them now before they get out of hand.

Brecon Insurance

Jackie Peak works for a large insurance company based in South Wales. She is employed in the human resources department and is involved in recruitment. However, she has had a change of heart regarding her future career recently and thinks that her skills would be better suited to working in the finance department. She has asked her line manager about a possible transfer.

1 What might be the role of the human resources department in a company like Brecon Insurance?
2 What skills might Jackie need if she is to work in the finance department?

Relationships between departments

All the four departments at Lynam Castings are interdependent. They must all work together if the company is to be successful. For example, over the past twelve months the marketing department has secured £5 million worth of orders from new customers. As a result, the production department needed some new equipment and two extra workers to cope with the orders. The personnel department was responsible for recruiting the new members of staff and for drawing up contracts of employment. The orders had financial implications. Cash would be needed up-front to pay for the new equipment, raw materials and the wages of the two workers. On the other hand, the new orders brought in extra revenues. The customers were invoiced. One customer paid late after having to be chased up by the finance department. All the transactions were recorded in the accounts of the company.

Another recent example concerned cost cutting. The marketing department reported that it could lose some contracts in future because the company's prices were not the lowest in the market. The board of directors took the decision to cut costs and prices by seeking efficiency gains across all departments. The main outcome was that 50 workers, mainly in personnel, finance and marketing, lost their jobs. The personnel department was responsible for organising the redundancies. Fortunately it was able in many cases to lose staff through early retirement or not replacing staff who left for other reasons. The finance department had fewer workers to pay. Workers in the production department noticed that it took longer for queries to be dealt with by both the personnel department and the finance department.

Checklist ✓

1 What is a department in a business?
2 Describe THREE tasks carried out by the production department.
3 Who is likely to be (a) at the top and (b) at the bottom of the hierarchy in a production department?
4 Briefly explain the role of the marketing department in (a) market research and (b) promotion.
5 List SIX functions of a human resources department.
6 How might the work of the human resources department help the business to reduce staff turnover?
7 Explain the difference between (a) paying bills and (b) issuing bills which are functions of the accounts department.
8 How might a decision to cut back on television advertising affect: (a) the advertising department (b) the production department (c) the human resources department and (d) the accounts department?

SUMMARY CASE STUDY

CARDEAL PLC

CarDeal plc is a 'car supermarket'. It sells 250 cars a week through its telesales and Internet business, and a further 450 from its Birmingham, Oxford, Glasgow and Cardiff sites. With sales of accessories and brokered car-finance packages, CarDeal achieved sales of £198.7 million in 2005.

The marketing and sales department is responsible for setting targets for sales staff in telesales and on the sites. Bonuses are paid to staff for meeting and exceeding these targets. The marketing department works closely with the finance department to come up with an incentive scheme which will both motivate sales staff, and at the same time retain good profit margins for the company. It is quite complicated because it includes sales of cars, accessories and car-finance packages. However, the final scheme seems to work well. Sales staff are happy and the company is making record profits.

Due to the success of the company CarDeal has had to recruit 56 new staff this year. About a third of these were to be employed in the finance department to deal with the growing number of transactions.

1 Explain what is meant by 'interdependence' between departments at CarDeal.
2 State THREE possible functions of the finance department at CarDeal.
3 Explain TWO reasons why CarDeal produces accounts.
4 Discuss whether it would have been better for CarDeal to put all the 56 new staff into the marketing and sales department.

Making decisions

Businesses need to recruit the best possible workers. To achieve this, they have to decide what procedures to adopt for recruitment and selection. For instance, how will they attract workers to apply for the job? How will they choose which applicants to appoint? Will they use interviews? Will they use other methods of selection? What use will they make of references?

Office Angels is a specialist supplier of secretarial and office support staff. It provides recruitment services for many businesses, from small, medium and large businesses to household names such as Marks & Spencer, Capital One and the BBC. It has branches throughout the UK and an online database of part time, full time, temporary and permanent office jobs, such as secretaries, managers and public sector finance jobs. Its consultants find out the needs of businesses and try to match them with suitable candidates.

Why recruit and select?

Businesses need workers. How many workers they employ depends upon what tasks need to be done, the cost of the workers and how much they can afford to pay. A business might carry out **human resource planning** to find out how many workers and what type of workers are needed. Recruiting workers with the right skills and at a wage or salary the business can afford is very important.

Recruitment

Businesses wanting to recruit workers have a variety of ways in which they can seek applicants. INTERNAL RECRUITMENT occurs when a business appoints someone to a post who is already working for the organisation. EXTERNAL RECRUITMENT is when a person who is not already working for the business is appointed.

Jobcentres One way of doing this is to notify a local Jobcentre of the vacancy. Jobcentres are paid by the government. They are responsible for helping workers,

including the unemployed, to find jobs or get training. They also provide a service for businesses which want to recruit workers. The services they provide are mostly free.

Employment agencies Office Angels is an employment agency. It advertises jobs on behalf of businesses. Many employment agencies specialise. For instance, there are agencies that deal mainly with permanent or temporary work, nursing jobs or executive posts. This helps businesses looking for these types of workers to find them more easily. Unlike Jobcentres, agencies charge clients for their services.

Office Angels is a supplier of secretarial and office support staff. Businesses ring to register vacancies. Office Angels consultants then visit the business and take details about the position, including job role, salary and benefits, and the level of skills and experience required.

Consultants can advise on a suitable salary and give advice on market trends. Office Angels holds details of large numbers of people looking for work. It may be able to recommend suitable candidates for the job. Each week it registers around 2 000 new job seekers. Office Angels consultants also phone companies 'speculatively' offering candidates registered that week.

Note: OTE = ordinary time earnings
Figure 1 *Job advertisement at Office Angels*

In 2006 research by Totaljobs.com showed that the number of jobseekers using the Internet rose from 8.7m to 14m over the period 2000-06. 70% of the UK working population was looking for jobs online. The reason for the growth was the ability to search many jobs at the click of a button. It was suggested that drivers, secretaries and part-time workers are just as likely to look online as retail and project managers.

In 2004 a survey by reed.co.uk, a private recruitment agency, found that 72% of businesses felt the Internet was effective in recruitment, compared to 42% per cent in 2000. In large businesses more than 1 in 3 felt it was more effective than any other method. The reason given was its low cost. Half of organisations with over 5,000 staff said they were spending over a third of their recruitment budgets on the Internet. This survey suggested that 'professionals' were most effectively recruited over the Internet. Nearly half of all those surveyed found the Internet useful for this type of employee. In 2000 businesses only tended to use the Internet to recruit graduates or IT staff.

Source: adapted from www.onrec.com, https://recruiter.totaljobs.com.

1 Reed is an example of a private recruitment agency. How might a business like Woolworth's or Ford use a private recruitment agency?
2 Explain the advantages of using the Internet rather than a newspaper for (a) jobseekers and (b) businesses.
3 A car manufacturer is recruiting a marketing manager. A small independent dress making shop wants to recruit a part time assistant. Do you think that they should use Internet recruitment, national newspaper advertising and local newspaper advertising? Explain your answers carefully.

You know what you want. We know how to get it.

Not one to dither, you've already sussed out what kind of job it is you're after. You know the area, the hours you'd like, the working culture that suits you best and the kind of benefits that really float your boat. Now all you need to do is track down the job. Why not talk to us. We deal with any industry you care to name, so we can advise you on new openings, shifts in the market and ways to go about bagging your dream job. What's more we believe in being upfront. We'll tell you if your dreams are achievable, or at least could be achieved with a bit of a skills tweak and some choice training courses. In fact we'll discuss everything with you first...and we certainly wouldn't send out your CV without your say-so. That's just the way we are. And it seems to work as 75% of our candidates come to us through recommendation.

- **Secretaries/PAs** • **Customer Services Administrators**
- **Receptionists** • **Financial Assistants** • **Office Juniors**
- **Much more!**

So come see us today or call 01293 539000 or email: **crawley@office-angels.com**
Office Angels Ltd, 2-4 Queensway, Crawley, West Sussex RH10 1EJ. (Employment Agency)

officeangels
RECRUITMENT CONSULTANTS

www.office-angels.com

CELEBRATING 20 YEARS OF OFFICE ANGELS

Figure 2 *Office Angels advertisement*

Advertising Businesses can advertise to fill vacancies. There are many places that a business might advertise. Office Angels, for example, advertises vacancies for its business clients in branch windows and inside its 97 UK branches. Figure 1 shows an advert for positions with businesses in Reading. Office Angels has interbranch advertising, which means that a vacancy in one branch may be filled by a candidate from another.

Businesses can advertise on their own websites or a specialist website. Office Angels uses Total jobs as well as other sites. Its branches also advertise in local newspapers to attract people from an area. Businesses that want to recruit from all over the UK might advertise in a national newspaper or magazine. Websites and newspapers can reach a large number of people. Different newspapers and magazines can also reach different readers. There is a charge for placing an advert in newspapers or on websites. Office Angels advertises the service it offers using flyers and magazine adverts. Figure 2 shows an example of an advertisement.

Office Angels also makes use of technology. For example, it advertises its services using email and the small messaging service (SMS) which sends text messages to mobile phones.

Word of mouth

The most important way in which people find out about jobs is through word of mouth. Somebody may know that a job is vacant and tell the person who actually applies for the job. If a vacancy can be filled by word of mouth, it can save on advertising costs. Businesses will find it easiest to fill vacancies by word of mouth when there are plenty of suitable workers looking for a job. This could be, for instance, at a time of high unemployment. Word of mouth is important for Office Angels. People who visit its branches may tell others about vacancies or the services offered by the organisation. Office Angels' research indicates that over 75 per cent of candidates choose Office Angels as a result of personal recommendation.

Cut out TEN different job advertisements from one or more newspapers or magazines. They should be for a wide variety of jobs. Some should be large display advertisements, others should be small adverts.
1 Compare the advertisements. Do they all give salary levels? Do they all give an address and a telephone number? How much detail about jobs do they give? Do they state what experience and qualifications are needed?
2 Which advertisements do you think are going to get the most enquiries? Explain your reasons carefully.

Application

Some jobs may only attract a few applicants but other jobs attract lots of people. In urgent cases a business may interview and make a decision quickly. If the job is unskilled, the business may interview immediately anybody who rings up or calls in.

For most jobs, though, there will be a formal procedure. Applicants write in, email, visit or ring up to get **particulars** of a job. These are likely to be a general description of the business, together with details of the job. These details may include a JOB DESCRIPTION. This sets out what the person appointed to the job will have to do.

To write a job description a business may carry out JOB ANALYSIS. This is a study to find out what the job entails. The skills and knowledge shown in a job description are often reworded into a PERSON SPECIFICATION. This is a profile of the person most suited to the job. An example of a job description and person specification for a corporate receptionist is shown in Figure 3.

The particulars will explain how the applicants would apply. For some jobs applicants are asked for a CURRICULUM VITAE (CV) and a letter of application. A CV is simply a document, often one or two sides of A4 paper, which gives the main details about the applicant, such as name, address, age, qualifications and employment history. The letter of application is a letter in which the applicant explains why he or she wants the job and is particularly suited to that job.

Alternatively, the applicant will be asked to fill out an APPLICATION FORM. This asks for information which would typically be contained in a CV. It can also include space for a letter of application. Office Angels asks all job seekers wishing to register with the business to fill out an application form. It then holds applicants' details in case suitable jobs become available.

Selection

Having received letters of application and CVs businesses are in a position to start the process of **selection**. A business

may have many applications for a job. It will **shortlist** a small number of people for the job based on the person's specification and then invite them for an **interview**. The interview is very important because it allows the employer and the applicant to meet. The employer is trying to find out whether the person would make a suitable employee. The employee is trying to find out whether the business is right for him or her.

The registration process for job seekers at Office Angels lasts around one hour. It includes an in-depth interview. In the interview an Office Angels' consultant will discuss the job history and expectations of the applicant. The consultant will try to find out not only the skills of the job seeker but also about their personality. Finding out as much as

Figure 3 *Job description and person specification*

Job Title: Corporate receptionist
Reporting to: Administration officer
Job Outline: Dealing with orders and enquiries received by phone/fax and processing same through computer based systems.

Responsibilities:
Answering all calls through a switchboard
- Taking messages
- Meeting and greeting customers
- Dealing with incoming and outgoing posts and ensuring post gets to the relevant person
- Ensuring the stationery order is done on time and all sections have placed their orders
- Ordering couriers and taxis and ensuring that they are here on time
- Keeping the reception area tidy
- Responsible for ensuring all telephone extensions and switchboard faults are dealt with promptly and efficiently
- Meeting room arrangements including co-ordination of catering arrangements, equipment and other requirements
- General administration duties.

Person specification
The ideal candidate will have
- Previous corporate reception/switchboard experience
- Impeccable smart appearance
- Strong computer skills, including typing speed of 45 words per minute
- Excellent communication skills
- Experience of working in a fast paced environment.

Telephone interviews

Kevin Peters was looking for a management job. He had climbed as far as he was going to go in his current organisation and had been combing the ads for months. Just before Christmas, he spotted a very promising job. He sent in his CV and a covering letter.

A few days later, his mobile phone went in the middle of a day's shopping. It was the company to which he had sent his application. At first he thought they were just ringing to make an appointment but then they started asking questions about his current job and experience. After a few minutes, he realised he was in the middle of a preliminary interview.

He didn't get on the short list to be invited to a face to face interview. This didn't surprise him. He had felt distracted on the phone and didn't sell himself very well at all. If he had had a face to face interview, he would have been prepared and psychologically ready for the questions he would have been asked. As it was, he didn't feel that he had been fairly treated.

1 Explain the importance of the following in getting a job:
   (a) 'combing the ads'; (b) sending in your CV and letter of application; (c) getting onto a shortlist; (d) being interviewed.
2 Why did Kevin Peters fail to perform well in his telephone interview do you think?
3 How well do you think you would perform in a telephone interview? Give reasons for your answer.

possible about the applicant will help Office Angels to match suitable applicants to jobs which become available at businesses.

When a suitable applicant has been selected they will be offered the job subject to **references**. These are reports on the employee from his or her current or last employer or from someone who knows them and can say something about them.

School leavers, for instance, might ask someone from their school to be a referee. The reference is the final check that the information given by the applicant at the interview and on the application is correct. Office Angels helps the recruitment process for businesses by checking the references of applicants.

Source; information from Office Angels.

Thinking of becoming a hairdresser?
Grants of Newcastle

is now interviewing school leavers for its two year hairdressing and beauty training programme, leading to vocational qualifications.

Apply by letter, including a CV to Janet Williams, Grants, Heaton Road, Newcastle.

We are an equal opportunities company.

Sharon White has sent a letter and her CV in response to the advertisement.
Grants has received Sharon White's letter.
Do you think it should invite her for interview? In your answer, consider: (a) who else might be applying; (b) the sort of post being offered, and (c) the training involved.

---

71 Addycombe Terrace
Heaton
Newcastle Upon Tyne
6 June 2007

Dear Mrs Williams

Ive seen the advert you put in the newspaper and I want to apply for the job, I am very interested in haredressing and beauty. I can come to an interview this week but next week Im going on holliday.

Yours sincerely

Sharon White

Sharon White

CV

Name	Sharon White
Address	71 Addycombe Terrace, Heaton, Newcastle Upon Tyne
Date of birth	1 April 1992
Age	16
Qualifications:	exams taken this summer GCSE English, Maths, Science; History, Child Care, Business Studies

---

Checklist ✓

1 Why do businesses need to recruit workers?
2 Distinguish between internal and external recruitment.
3 Describe THREE different ways in which a business could recruit externally.
4 An applicant for a transport lorry driver's job is sent a job description. What is a job description?
5 What is the difference between a job description and a person specification?
6 How might a business ask applicants to send in details about themselves and why they want to apply for a job?
7 Why do businesses often ask for references for an applicant?

SUMMARY CASE STUDY

GALLIFORDTRY

1 Describe the job that is being advertised.
2 To apply, you are asked to forward a CV. (a) What is a CV? (b) Describe THREE characteristics that the business might be looking for in a suitable applicant which might be found on a CV and on a person specification. (c) Having received CVs, how is the business likely to select a candidate?
3 The job was advertised in Personnel Management, a magazine aimed at people with an interest in human resources. What are the advantages and disadvantages of advertising in this way rather than (a) a job centre, (b) a local newspaper (c) using a website or a recruitment agency?
4 Draw up a list of FOUR questions that might be asked of each candidate. For each, explain why you think it is an important question.

Human Resources Manager

Excellent Salary + Car/Allowance + Benefits

Galliford Try is one of the UK's leading construction and house building companies and as such we are involved in some of the country's most exciting major construction projects. We have an immediate vacancy for an HR Manager within our Infrastructure businesses, based at our offices in Wolvey, who will be responsible for:

- The provision of an HR service to line managers covering such issues as recruitment, reward, learning and development and employee relations.
- Engaging with the Board on people related issues that will add value to the business.

Supported by an HR Advisor and HR Assistant, this is an excellent opportunity to join an organisation committed to people oriented solutions and will appeal to the most business focused HR professional.

Applicants must be CIPD qualified or equivalent, with proven experience in the aspects of this role outlined above, preferably gained within a 'multi-site operation'. Excellent communication and organisation skills are prerequisites.

In return we can offer real career development opportunities within an expanding organisation, along with an excellent salary and benefits package that will include bonus, car or car allowance, pension and private medical insurance.

Interested candidates should forward their CV including salary details to
Howard Walker, Group Human Resources Director,
Galliford Try Services, Wolvey, Hinckley, Leicestershire
LE10 3JH or E-mail howard.walker@gallifordtry.co.uk
Closing date for applications Tuesday, 21 November 2006
Galliford Try is an equal opportunities employer

Making decisions

Businesses want their workers to work hard and produce goods and services of a high standard. Workers are more likely to do this if they are well motivated. How can businesses motivate their employees? Should they try to motivate workers simply through pay? Or are they going to appeal to the needs of workers other than pay, such as being given responsibility or achieving their own goals? How can businesses create an environment where their workers are putting all their efforts into making a success of the business?

Ugo Foods Group produces fresh pasta and noodles. It supplies Waitrose and its products are also served in first class and club class sections of airlines, and in leading restaurants such as Wagamama and Strada. Ugo employs 81 staff and has been trading since 1929. The family business is based in Borehamwood and its turnover is £5.4 million. In 2006 Ugo Foods came 5th in a *Sunday Times* survey of the 'Best Small Companies to Work For'.

The importance of motivation

A company like Ugo Foods Group needs to MOTIVATE its workers. A well motivated workforce is more likely to work hard. This will help a business improve the quality of its product, keep its costs down, make a profit and remain competitive. There is a number of different ideas about what motivates workers.

Basic needs

One idea, first put forward by Frederick Taylor in *The Principles of Scientific Management*, published in 1911, is that workers are motivated mainly by pay. **The scientific management school** argues that pay should therefore be linked to performance, for instance through the use of **bonuses** linked to sales or **piece rates**.

This view says that workers, like the staff at Ugo, go to work mainly to earn money to survive. Without money, staff at Ugo wouldn't be able to buy food, clothes, shelter and heating essential to satisfy their basic human needs.

Higher needs

People, however, have other needs. An American researcher called A H Maslow put these in order of importance (a HIERARCHY OF NEEDS) as can be seen in Figure 1.

Physiological needs Staff at Ugo Foods Group want to satisfy their basic human needs (called physiological needs by Maslow). Ugo achieves this through paying its workers a wage.

Safety needs Workers want to know that they won't be made

P3

P3 is a charity which operates services and creates opportunities for vulnerable and disadvantaged people. P3 provide services such as supported housing, accommodation for homeless people, outreach teams, link worker schemes and community support projects for people recovering from mental illness. They also provide a wide range of youth services and support hundreds of people every day, to take control of their own lives and move from social exclusion to inclusion. They employ 160 staff and have a turnover of £4.2 million.

In 2006, the organisation came first in a *Sunday Times* survey of the 'Best Small Companies to Work For'. Staff feel looked after by managers, they can grow with the company and are compassionate about their work. They feel fairly paid and are happy with their benefits. There is also a very strong team spirit at P3. 'If there is a job to be done, people just pull together. We just do it', said Martin Kinsella, chief executive. 91 per cent of the staff at P3 said they love working for the charity.

Source: adapted from www.timesonline.co.uk/best100

1 Worker motivation is very high at P3. Why do you think this helps make the organisation successful?
2 P3 is a charity. How might this improve worker motivation?
3 Discuss other reasons why workers are extremely well motivated at P3.

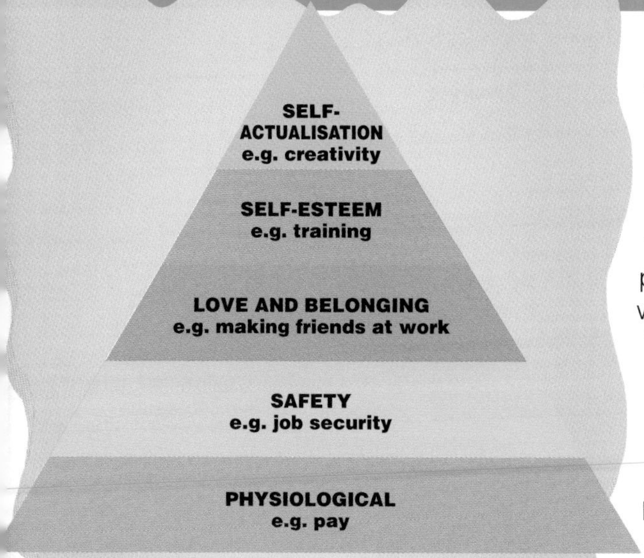

Figure 1 *Maslow's hierarchy of needs.*

redundant and that their working environment is safe. As a slowly expanding business, staff at Ugo Foods Group know that they are unlikely to be made redundant. Safety of workers and customers is also a key priority of the business.

Love and belonging This is a higher order need. People want to feel accepted as part of a group, like a family at home or a team in a workplace. They want to be trusted and be able to support others. Ugo

Foods Group has a supportive culture. Managing Director Paul Ugo, whose Italian immigrant grandfather started the business said that being good with people got him through when he first started. 'There's a belief out there that you can't have a business with a heart, but that's rubbish – and we're proof'. A trained psychologist and hypnotherapist, he sees personal development as the key to a happy workforce. The effect of this is shown by the very low staff turnover – just 11 per cent, considerably less than the national average. Staff at Ugo also say that management take a genuine interest in employees as individuals.

Self-esteem needs People want to feel that others respect them for what they can do. They want to respect themselves too, feeling that they have achieved something and are good at a task. For instance, at Ugo Foods personal achievements are celebrated – certificates line

the walls, from Basic Food Hygiene Awards to internal long service prizes.

Self-actualisation This is the highest order need, according to Maslow. It is the ability to realise your full potential. At Ugo Foods, if the firm feels someone has potential, they will be hired even if they don't have all the skills, and will be supported while learning. Employees at Ugo feel that they can make a difference to the company. Ideas are always listened to and taken seriously.

Fulfilling needs

When businesses try to motivate their workers, they need to be aware of three things.
- If a worker is well paid, pay is no longer a motivator. A worker is motivated by achieving the next level within the hierarchy of needs. Only the highest level, self-actualisation, can in itself carry on motivating workers who have achieved this.
- If a need is not satisfied, then it can lead to demotivation. For instance, workers threatened with redundancy or who are worried that their boss thinks their work is poor are not going to be well motivated.
- If a lower order need is not met, then meeting higher order needs becomes irrelevant. If staff felt they were poorly paid, this would demotivate them however much their other higher order needs were being met.

Human relations

Frederick Taylor believed that pay was the main reason why people worked. They needed to be closely supervised and told what to do. This was because workers would tend to do as little as possible and would not necessarily work in the most efficient way. They also didn't want to accept responsibility, such as organising their own work.

These views were called Theory X by another American researcher,

---

Red Gate Software

Cambridge-based Red Gate Software has the feeling of a family company. Employing just 58 workers it provides software tools for database professionals. Keeping staff happy is important to the company. It has a special fund for its engineers that subsidises everything from Japanese lessons to yoga classes. Half of the workforce cycle to work and the offices are equipped with a television and table football. Staff feel that the firm really tries to help its employees. They feel supported by their managers and think that their workload is fair. Staff turnover at the company is an incredibly low 2 per cent.

With a non-contributory pension scheme, people feel they are fairly paid. More than 38 per cent of employees earn £35 000 per year or more. This is above the national average. There is also a free gym and free health care scheme. Also, after a period of probation all staff are entitled to company share options. A social committee runs a 'feelgood fund' that subsidises fun, including punting on the river Cam, wine-tasting and bowling nights, as well as away days to London, Paris and Amsterdam.

Source: adapted from www.timesonline.co.uk/best100.

1 List Maslow's five needs in his hierarchy of needs.
2 How does Red Gate Software meet its staff's (a) physiological needs; (b) love and belonging needs?
3 What evidence is there that staff are happy at Red Gate Software.

Douglas McGregor. However, he argued that a company like Ugo Foods Group would fail to motivate workers if they adopted Theory X views. This is because workers want their higher needs fulfilling when they go to work. He called this view Theory Y. This says that workers, like those at Ugo Foods Group, will be motivated to work if they are given responsibility and allowed to make decisions. This **Human Relations School** of thought says that workers work best in conditions where they are trusted, and where they are given an opportunity to fulfil themselves. These views are shown in Table 1.

Job satisfaction

Another American researcher, Frederick Herzberg, came to similar conclusions. He suggested that some factors about a job, shown in Table 2, would motivate workers and give them JOB SATISFACTION. This is the amount of enjoyment, satisfaction or pleasure that a worker gets out of doing a particular job. Ugo Foods Group wants its staff to enjoy their work. For instance, at Ugo a survey showed that 83 per cent of staff are naturally happy with their work/life balance. 'If you walk around, I can guarantee that most people will be smiling', says Paul Ugo. Employees are also encouraged to attend meditation classes to help them take a step back from daily pressures.

Frederick Herzberg also found what he called hygiene factors could demotivate workers if they were not met. Workers at Ugo Foods Group would be demotivated if they didn't receive a reasonable wage. On the other hand, once a Ugo's employee was reasonably paid, offering them higher pay would not motivate them. According to Herzberg, hygiene factors can demotivate but not motivate.

Job enlargement and job enrichment

The work of people such as Maslow and Herzberg has led to ideas that workers' jobs could be made more satisfying through:

- job enlargement - instead of a worker doing one small task every day, they would be able to do a variety of tasks. This would make the work less monotonous and boring;
- job enrichment - where workers are given some opportunities to choose how to complete a particular job of work, usually working in a team.

Source: adapted from www.timesonline.co.uk/best100.

Table 1 McGregor's Theory X and Theory Y.

Theory X	Theory Y
Workers are motivated by money	Workers are motivated by many needs
Workers are lazy and dislike work	Workers can enjoy work
Workers are selfish, ignore the needs of organisations, avoid responsibility and lack ambition	Workers can organise themselves and take responsibility
Workers need to be controlled and directed by management	It is up to management to allow workers to be creative and apply their job knowledge

Table 2 Factors which motivate and demotivate workers.

Motivating factors	Demotivating or 'hygiene'
Sense of achievement	Pay
Chance of promotion	Working conditions
Responsibility	Company rules and policy
Nature of the job itself	Fear of redundancy
Recognition by management	Treatment at work
Personal development	Feelings of inadequacy

'Before I started this job, I used to work on an assembly line. It was like school. We sat in rows and if we wanted to go to the toilet we had to put up our hands and ask.'

'All I was doing was putting extra bits on to a product and passing it on every 7 minutes. It was too boring and we were making a lot of mistakes.'

'Every 15 minutes, I mount a magnetic head on a tape-drive, and then test it, glue it and clamp wires round it. This is better than my previous job where I sat by a conveyor-belt and put screws into machines 158 times a day.'

'We experimented with workers changing jobs every hour. It was more interesting, but the number of products we produced per hour went down and there were more mistakes. We had to abandon the system.'

1 What is assembly line work?
2 What problems about assembly line work are talked about in the quotes above?
3 Discuss how the higher needs of assembly line workers' might be met.

Power Technology Solutions

Power Technology Solutions (PTS), provides services to blue chip companies in the high-voltage electrical power systems industries, including leading utilities and distribution network companies. It has annual sales of £4.6 million and employs 65 staff.

The company is run by Duncan Mansfield and Daniel Ferguson. Staff are inspired by their leadership and feel they truly live the values of the company. Employees enjoy the teamworking approach taken by the company and feel that their managers care about them as individuals. They are proud to work for the company.

Staff get 20 days training in their first three years with the company. This contributes to their personal development and helps them to feel valued by their employer. 80% of staff are happy with their pay and benefits and they believe their workload is fair and rarely boring. Perks include performance-related pay, bonuses, health care, sabbaticals and a pension scheme. Laptops and a broadband connection are provided for those who choose to work from home or do flexible hours. Staff are said to be happy with the work/life balance.

Source: adapted from www.timesonline.co.uk/best100

1 Do you think workers are motivated by money at PTS?
2 How does PTS meet the self-esteem needs of its employees?
3 How does PTS provide job enrichment for its workforce?
4 According to Herzberg, to what extent will the perks provided by PTS help to motivate staff?

key terms

Hierarchy of needs - placing needs in order of importance, starting with basic human needs.
Job satisfaction - the amount of enjoyment, satisfaction or pleasure that a worker gets out of doing a particular job.
Motivation - in work, the desire to complete a task.

Checklist ✓

1 Why is a motivated workforce important for a business?
2 What, according to Frederick Taylor, motivates workers to work?
3 What is the role of management in motivating workers according to the scientific management school?
4 Explain FOUR higher order needs according to Maslow.
5 Explain what needs you think would be met if you took on a paper round.
6 What is the difference between Theory X and Theory Y?
7 (a) What are 'hygiene factors'? (b) What, according to Herzberg, motivates workers?
8 How could an employer increase the amount of job satisfaction gained by its workers?

SUMMARY CASE STUDY

WOODS

Woods is a national chain of shoe shops. It is looking for a full time shop assistant for one of its stores. It has interviewed the five candidates below. Some of the comments made at the interviews are shown next to each candidate.

Rachael Boswell - You are offering good pay and I need the money. I'm very keen on doing overtime. I'm sure the job will be OK. I've done a number of different jobs before. Some of them have been much worse than this. I've had some terrible managers in my time. I hope the one you put me with will be better.

Sean McDermott - I know my qualifications aren't very good. I messed around at school a lot. Then I had some awful work placements. But the last one in a shop was great. It really opened my eyes. I want to get on. I want to go right to the top. I want to be in charge and make big decisions. I know this sounds stupid because this is just a job at the bottom of the ladder. But you've got to start somewhere, haven't you?

Belinda Tombs - It looks as though my branch is going to go. They call it 'rationalisation'. I've been looking around because I could see this coming. There's nothing worse than turning up every day thinking that this is the day when you'll get your redundancy notice. My boss says she'll give me a good reference. I pride myself on being a good worker. I like everything to be perfect. My boss says I'm too much of a perfectionist. I don't really need the money.

Efia Charles - Being at home all day can be very depressing. I used to work in a shop before I had the children. I'm really looking forward to getting out of the house and back to work again. I really enjoyed the friendships with the rest of the staff. You always had a few awkward customers and a lot of the work was rather boring, but some customers were really nice. What are the opportunities for promotion?

Josh Nichols - I've just got married. My wife says I've got to settle down and get a decent job. She works in a shop too and says its OK. It will bring in the money and that is what's most important isn't it? What are your overtime rates? I expect I'll get used to dealing with the public. Do you give free uniforms or anything like that?

1 What do you think will motivate each candidate to do the job?
2 On the evidence of the interview comments, which candidate would you choose for the job? Explain your reasons carefully.

Making decisions

Leadership is important for a business. A business rarely does well unless it has an effective leader. There are many different styles of leadership, each of which has its own strengths and weaknesses. A larger business has to decide what sort of person it wants to lead it. In a small business, the leader may have to change his or her style to make the business run effectively.

Mike Manners has always been a keen skier. For many years he took his holidays in resorts in France, Italy and Austria. He even lived in France for a number of years and competed in race meetings. In 1985 he returned to live in the UK and realised that more people were taking skiing holidays rather than beach holidays. He realised there was a gap in the market. He started to import skiing products from abroad and set up a wholesale business to sell these to the growing number of ski and outdoor shops that were setting up. He employed ten workers in his warehouse. In 2001 Mike handed over the business to his daughter, Gina.

Leadership

Mike was a LEADER of his business. Leadership is difficult to define precisely, but usually involves:

- setting targets or goals for a business. A captain may set goals or point targets for a team, for example. Mike set monthly targets for sales to retailers for his sales team in the warehouse;
- organising work and appointing key personnel in the management hierarchy. For example, leaders in large businesses often appoint key managers with the vision to run their organisations. Mike appointed Carl to run the office sales team and ensure that targets were being met;
- monitoring work to see whether goals were being achieved and, where necessary, motivating workers to achieve these goals. Mike had regular meeting with staff to tell them what he wanted and rewarded them with a bonus each year depending on the performance of the business.

Types of leader

There are different types of leadership style that might be used in a business.

- Autocratic leadership.
- Paternalistic leadership.
- Persuasive and democratic leadership.
- Consultative and democratic leadership.

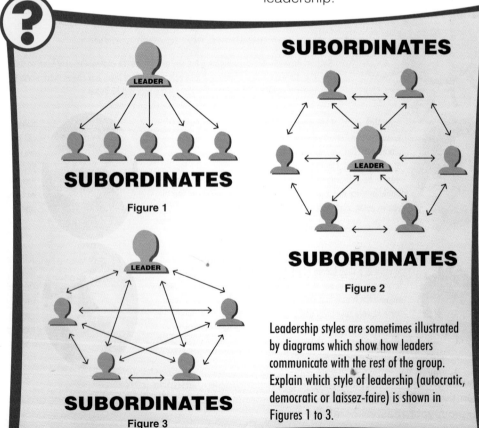

Figure 1

Figure 2

Figure 3

Leadership styles are sometimes illustrated by diagrams which show how leaders communicate with the rest of the group. Explain which style of leadership (autocratic, democratic or laissez-faire) is shown in Figures 1 to 3.

- Laissez-faire leadership. Each style will have certain advantages and disadvantages.

Autocratic leadership

An AUTOCRATIC LEADER is one who makes all the key decisions in the business. The leader than tells the group working under him or her what to do. The role of workers lower in the hierarchy is to carry out the orders of the leader.

Communication tends to flow from the leader to subordinates and back again. There is little need for subordinates to communicate with one another because they receive orders from above. If the leader is making the right decisions there can be very effective leadership because the leader is having a powerful influence on the organisation under him or her. However, it can mean that subordinates feel frustrated and become demotivated because they can't fulfil their **higher order needs** indicated in Maslow's hierarchy of needs.

Mike used an autocratic leadership style. He thought that his experience of working in France and his knowledge of what skiers wanted meant that he was the only person to make important decisions. He also wanted to keep control on the business. Many of the sales team were young and he felt that they would need guidance. Mike found that the business expanded rapidly in the 1990s as more people took skiing holidays. But each year one member of the sales team and a warehouse worker would leave. He would then have to train new workers.

Paternalistic leadership

A PATERNALISTIC LEADER is similar to an autocratic leader. He or she will make all the important decisions in a business. They tell employees what they want and expect this to be carried out. This means that they retain control of the business.

Employees can be **demotivated** under an autocratic style of leadership. However, paternalistic leaders usually have the welfare of the workforce in mind when making decisions. They are concerned about how their employees feel at work. They may decide, for example, to make less profit one year by spending on improved facilities for staff. Staff tend to remain loyal and can be motivated as a result.

Persuasive and democratic leadership

A DEMOCRATIC LEADER is one who shares some of the decision making with subordinates. Persuasive leaders, like autocratic leaders, make decisions alone. But then they 'persuade' workers under them to accept their decisions through discussions and reasoning.

Workers are more likely to be motivated under this type of leadership because they feel more involved in decision making. However, decision making can take longer because the leader has to spend time persuading others.

In 2001 Mike decided that he wanted to retire. He passed the business to his daughter Gina, who had been working alongside him for a number of years. Gina had a different style of leadership. She was far more willing to listen to the views of the people she had worked with for a number of years. She made all the key decisions and could be seen as this type of leader. However, it is more likely that she is a consultative and democratic leader.

Consultative and democratic leadership

This type of leader is a different type of democratic leader. Consultative leaders 'consult' or ask for other people's opinions before coming to a decision. The final decision that they make will take into account what subordinates have said. More time probably will be taken when making a decision than with a persuasive leader, but equally

Robert Maxwell

Robert Maxwell did things very much his own way. During the 1970s and 1980s he built up a multi-billion pound business empire. Some have commented that it was like a medieval court, with Maxwell as the leader. People who opposed his rules were banished, while those who flattered him stayed.

He was notorious for attempting to bully people into doing what he wanted. Few people would stand up to him, including the board of directors of the companies which he part owned and ran.

In 1992, he was found drowned. Within weeks, his empire crumbled as it emerged that it owed billions of pounds. Even worse, it was discovered that he had been illegally transferring money from one company to another company in his empire, attempting to keep them afloat. Over a billion pounds of that money belonged to the pension funds of Maxwell-owned companies. The people who were paid to protect ordinary shareholders and pensioners, the directors of these companies, and all the other financial specialists involved, had failed to spot the massive fraud taking place.

Source: adapted from the *Financial Times*, various.

1 What type of leader (autocratic, democratic or laissez-faire) was Robert Maxwell? Explain your answer.
2 Why do you think that a democratic leader would have been more likely to have been found out if they had been attempting to steal billions of pounds from the companies they ran?

workers feel even more motivated with an effective consultative leader.

Gina had worked in the business with the sales and warehouse team for a number of years. She recognised that they had experience and skills that she could draw upon. So she held monthly meetings. At these meeting every employee was allowed to raise issues and put forward suggestions for improvements. In 2002 the business increased its turnover by 25 per cent. Some of the ideas that employees had suggested were used by Gina and she felt that this had improved the service offered to customers. In the next 3 years no staff left the business.

Laissez-faire leadership

The term Laissez-faire means 'leave it be' and is used to describe a leader who leaves his or her colleagues to get on with their work. A LAISSEZ-FAIRE LEADER is one who makes very few decisions. These leaders allow workers under them to make their own decisions. Although this allows subordinates (workers under them) to be highly creative, laissez-faire leadership can also lead to a feeling by subordinates that noone knows or cares about what is going on. Another unofficial or informal leader often appears in the organisation who gives the organisation a sense of direction.

In 2006 Gina decided that she wanted to move away from the area where the business was situated. She could have moved the whole business to another area. But this would have meant changing the address and she may have lost clients. So she moved, but left the business at the same location. She only visited twice a year just to check things were going well. Tim, the sales manager, started to make daily decisions in her absence. As long

Interview 10 people.
- Ask them to identify a situation where they had to make a decision that affected other people.
- Find out whether they made the decision themselves, using guidance from others or left the decision to others.
- Categorise the decision making style.
- Find out whether the decision was successful or not. Identify the factors that influenced the success or otherwise of the decision.
- Evaluate whether the leadership style chosen was suitable or whether another style may have been more effective.

as the business made a satisfactory profit, Gina did not feel the need to interfere too much. Gina's style had perhaps changed to a laissez-faire leadership style.

The business did well in 2006, although it did have to sack one worker. He was found to be stealing and selling products himself.

Democratic leadership

Up to the 1990s, the commonest form of leadership in business was autocratic. Then a revolution began which set about the process of modernising and democratising businesses. Empowerment was the buzzword as people were encouraged to take responsibility and become accountable. However, many individuals were simply not ready for empowerment. They hadn't been trained, their own leadership style hadn't developed and, let's face it, some people actually prefer to be told what to do.

Source: adapted from www.coaching-life.co.uk.

1 What is meant by 'democratising' a business?
2 Suggest TWO reasons why a democratic leadership style may not be successful.
3 A business that sells office equipment to businesses has recently experienced problems in the sales team. Customers have complained about the time taken for decisions to be made. A new sales manager has been appointed who feels that a more democratic leadership style is needed. Explain how this might affect the operation of the sales team.

Checklist ✓

1 What qualities might a leader have?
2 Explain why the head chef in a large restaurant could be described as a 'leader'.
3 What are the differences between an autocratic leader and a laissez-faire leader?
4 Compare TWO types of democratic leadership.
5 Explain what type of leadership you think might be most effective in: (a) a rock band; (b) the army; (c) a school; (d) a car manufacturer; (e) a hairdressing salon.

key terms

Autocratic leader - a leader who tells others what to do without consulting them.
Democratic leader - a leader who seeks the views of other workers before making a decision.
Laissez-faire leader - a leader who tends to allow others to make their own decisions and only occasionally makes decisions for others.
Leader - someone who organises others and makes decisions.
Paternalistic leader — like an autocratic leader makes all the decisions but takes into account the welfare of workers in making decisions.

SUMMARY CASE STUDY

JENKINSONS

Jenkinsons is an advertising agency. It employs 30 workers. They work in two teams - the design team and the team of consultants and advisors to clients. They often have to meet important deadlines. Clients have to launch advertising campaigns at the right time so that they maximise the impact on the market. Clients often change their minds and want detailed amendments to the campaigns. The business is owned by four freinds. They all started as designers and appreciate the needs of an ever changing business.

1 What is meant by leadership style?
2 Explain THREE factors that could affect the leadership style at Jenkinsons.
3 Advise the business on a leadership style that might be suitable for the business.

There is no one 'right' way to lead or manage that suits all situations. To choose the most effective approach you must consider:
- The skill levels and experience of your team
- The work involved (routine or new and creative)
- The organisational environment (stable or radically changing, conservative or adventurous)

You own preferred or natural style.

Source: adapted from /www.mindtools.com.

Making decisions

Businesses employ people. These employees need to be paid, so a business must decide what payment system to use. The decision is likely to be based on:
- what payment system is most suitable in the circumstances;
- which system will be most cost effective;
- what will best motivate workers to work hard and achieve a high standard of work.

Tesco is the largest supermarket chain in the UK. In 2006 it had over 30% of the total market. It is reckoned that £1 in every £8 spent in UK retail sales is spent in Tesco. The chain enjoyed sales of £38.259 billion in 2006 and made a profit before tax of £2.21 billion.

Reasons for working

Why do people work? Why might they choose to work at Tesco?
- At its most basic, people work in order to provide themselves with the basic necessities to survive, like food and shelter. In a modern economy, people work because they are paid. They can use the money to buy these necessities.
- People also work to be able to afford the luxuries of life, like a larger house, or foreign holidays or a night out.
- Other researchers, like Maslow, Herzberg and McGregor, say that people also work to fulfill a variety of other needs. For example, they are motivated to work because they enjoy their job. Or they enjoy working with other people. Or they like being in a position of responsibility. Or they like achieving goals.

Why people work affects how employers like Tesco reward their workers.

Payment systems

Tesco employs around 270,000 workers in total. Most of these are employed in the company's supermarkets but others work from their head office in Cheshunt,

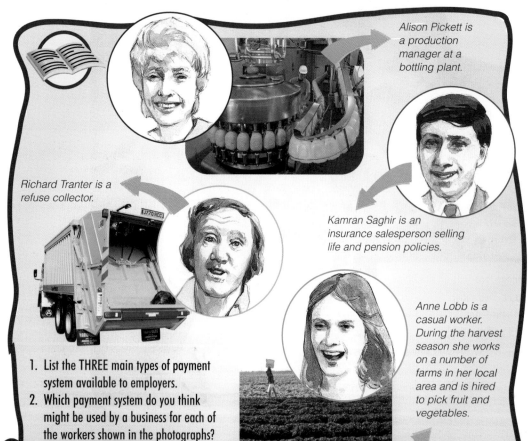

Alison Pickett is a production manager at a bottling plant.

Kamran Saghir is an insurance salesperson selling life and pension policies.

Richard Tranter is a refuse collector.

Anne Lobb is a casual worker. During the harvest season she works on a number of farms in her local area and is hired to pick fruit and vegetables.

1. List the THREE main types of payment system available to employers.
2. Which payment system do you think might be used by a business for each of the workers shown in the photographs? Give reasons for your choice.

Benefits at Firefly Communications

Firefly Communications is a public relations (PR) company. It has annual sales of £4.2 million and employs 53 staff. Most staff earn between £15,000 and £35,000 pa and feel fairly paid relative to others in the same industry. Most employees are accounts executives. This means they look after the PR needs of a particular client or clients.

The London-based company offers its employees a number of perks. For example, it invests £300 per employee a year in a well-being programme, including stress-relieving massages and cash for treatments such as acupuncture and homeopathy. New fathers have two fully-paid weeks of paternity leave and emergency leave is available for problems to do with children. There are crèche facilities for employees' children, there is a gym and after five years service people become eligible for a five-week fully paid sabbatical. Staff are also allowed to finish early on Fridays and bank holidays. On the social side, company founder Claire Walker and her husband, host an annual summer barbecue, cooking and laying on drinks and games.

Source: adapted from www.timesonline.co.uk/best100.

1 What of payment system is probably being used at Firefly Communications?
2 Using examples from the case, explain what is meant by a fringe benefit.
3 (a) Explain the advantages of such benefits to Firefly Communications and its employees. (b) Are there any disadvantages to the benefits provided?
4 Discuss the extent to which fringe benefits can motivate workers.

Hertfordshire. Tesco uses a number of different PAYMENT SYSTEMS. These are different ways of paying workers.

Time-based systems MANUAL WORKERS or BLUE COLLAR WORKERS are workers who tend to do manual work like stacking shelves, operating tills, serving customers and cleaning in Tesco's stores. They have tended to be paid WAGES on a time based system. They are paid 'so much' per hour worked. If they work longer than the agreed basic working week, such as 38 hours, they usually get OVERTIME. This is often paid at a higher hourly rate, such as time-and-a-quarter or double time. This means that they are paid 1.25 or 2 times the BASIC PAY per hour for every hour of overtime worked. For instance, at Tesco the basic working week is 36.5 hours. The basic hourly rate for established staff is £6.01 for grade c staff (general/customer assistants), £6.15 for grade d staff (fishmongers/delivery service assistants), and £6.52 for grade e staff (skilled bakers). This means that a grade c worker would get £219.37 (36.5 x £6.01). Last week

he worked 2 hours overtime at time-and-a-half. Therefore, the GROSS EARNINGS or GROSS PAY of a grade c worker would be £219.37. Tesco also pays premiums to night workers. These are £1.22 for hours worked between 10pm and 12pm, and £1.81 for hours worked between 12pm and 8am.

Salaries NON-MANUAL or WHITE COLLAR WORKERS tend to be paid SALARIES. A non-manual worker is one who does non-physical work, like an accountant or purchaser at Tesco or a teacher. Salaries tend to be paid monthly rather than weekly as with wages. Salaried workers are paid for doing a particular job. No overtime is usually paid because salaried workers are expected to work for as long as it takes to do their job. Salaried managers at Tesco are likely to work for more than the 36.5 hour basic week.

Results-based systems Some workers are paid according to how much they produce. Workers on PIECE RATES are paid for every item they produce. If they produce nothing during the day, they get paid nothing. Sales staff may be

paid on COMMISSION. For every sale they achieve, they get paid a certain amount. Some sales staff are paid totally on commission, and so if they sell nothing, they get paid nothing. Others are paid commission as a BONUS. Bonuses are given as a reward for doing well. Non-sales staff may be given bonuses if, for instance, their department achieves a particular target for work. This is called a group bonus.

Other forms of payment

Workers can be paid in other ways than money. In the coal industry, for instance, it was traditional to give coal miners an amount of coal in addition to their wages. This is an example of FRINGE BENEFITS. Tesco offers its workers a variety of fringe benefits. The more senior the position you hold in a company, the more fringe benefits you are likely to receive. One of the most important fringe benefits for some

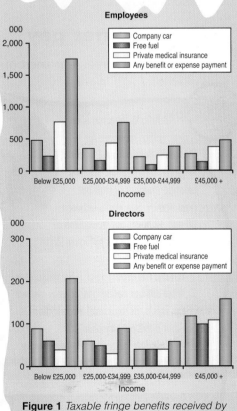

Figure 1 Taxable fringe benefits received by employees and company directors, number of recipients
Source: adapted from www.statistics.gov.uk.

workers is the subsidised company pension scheme. The company may provide a proportion of payments into the scheme so that workers can get an occupational pension when they retire. Other examples of fringe benefits are company cars, subsidised canteen meals or free housing. Fringe benefits are often given for tax reasons. The business pays less tax and other contributions in providing £1 000 worth of fringe benefits than it would if it paid an extra £1 000 in wages to a worker. Similarly, a worker may find there is a tax gain in receiving a fringe benefit rather than cash.

Fringe benefits are also used to motivate workers. The company car, for instance, is very important to many workers. Giving a car with a larger engine seems to motivate some people. At Tesco fringe benefits include a Privilege Card which entitles staff to a 10 per cent discount on purchases above £3 in the store, free Tesco shares, a save-as-you-earn scheme, an attractive pension scheme and free life assurance.

Gross and net pay

The gross pay or gross earnings of workers are likely to be different from their NET PAY or NET EARNINGS. Gross earnings are earnings before any tax and other deductions have been taken away. Net earnings are earnings after deductions. This is often called take-home pay because it is what the worker is left with to spend. The three most common deductions are as follows.

- **Income tax** - an employer like Tesco is responsible for keeping back some of its employees' pay and sending it to HM Revenue and Customs, the government department responsible for collecting income tax. This system is known as the PAYE system (pay-as-you-earn).
- **National Insurance contributions** - these are another type of tax on earnings paid to the government which entitles the worker to receive state benefits, such as Jobseekers' Allowance and state retirement pension.
- **Payments to a pension scheme**, such as a private scheme, the pension scheme of the company for which the employee works, or the additional state pension scheme (called SERPS - the State Earnings Related Pension Scheme).

Other deductions which a worker at Tesco might have are trade union membership payments or payments to a charity.

Details of these are found on a pay slip which by law must be given to every employee.

Which payment system?

Tesco has to make decisions about which payment systems to use for different groups of workers. Which payment system is used depends partly on what is possible. Tesco might find it very difficult to use piece rates for a store manager, for instance, because it is so difficult to measure output. Equally, Tesco paying its cleaners on a commission basis wouldn't be possible either because they don't sell anything. Even sales staff might not be paid commission if sales are a team effort rather than the result of the work of one individual.

Some payment systems are used because they reduce the tax bill of employers and employees. Fringe benefits are an example of this.

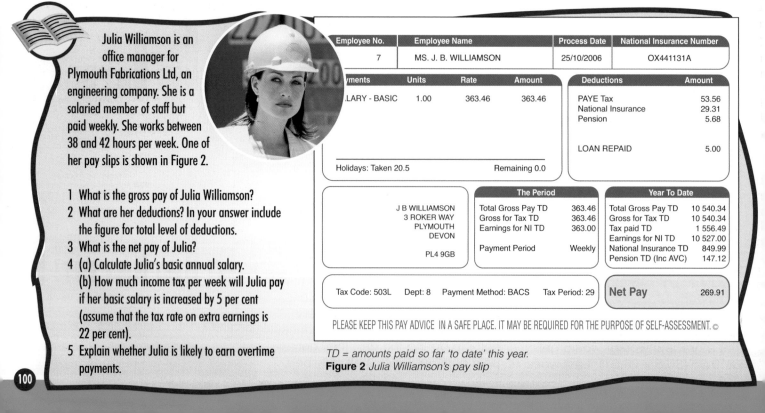

Julia Williamson is an office manager for Plymouth Fabrications Ltd, an engineering company. She is a salaried member of staff but paid weekly. She works between 38 and 42 hours per week. One of her pay slips is shown in Figure 2.

1 What is the gross pay of Julia Williamson?
2 What are her deductions? In your answer include the figure for total level of deductions.
3 What is the net pay of Julia?
4 (a) Calculate Julia's basic annual salary.
  (b) How much income tax per week will Julia pay if her basic salary is increased by 5 per cent (assume that the tax rate on extra earnings is 22 per cent).
5 Explain whether Julia is likely to earn overtime payments.

Employee No.	Employee Name	Process Date	National Insurance Number
7	MS. J. B. WILLIAMSON	25/10/2006	OX441131A

Payments	Units	Rate	Amount		Deductions	Amount
SALARY - BASIC	1.00	363.46	363.46		PAYE Tax	53.56
					National Insurance	29.31
					Pension	5.68
					LOAN REPAID	5.00
Holidays: Taken 20.5			Remaining 0.0			

	The Period		Year To Date	
J B WILLIAMSON	Total Gross Pay TD	363.46	Total Gross Pay TD	10 540.34
3 ROKER WAY	Gross for Tax TD	363.46	Gross for Tax TD	10 540.34
PLYMOUTH	Earnings for NI TD	363.00	Tax paid TD	1 556.49
DEVON			Earnings for NI TD	10 527.00
	Payment Period	Weekly	National Insurance TD	849.99
PL4 9GB			Pension TD (Inc AVC)	147.12

Tax Code: 503L   Dept: 8   Payment Method: BACS   Tax Period: 29   **Net Pay** 269.91

PLEASE KEEP THIS PAY ADVICE IN A SAFE PLACE. IT MAY BE REQUIRED FOR THE PURPOSE OF SELF-ASSESSMENT. ©

TD = amounts paid so far 'to date' this year.
Figure 2 Julia Williamson's pay slip

More importantly, payment systems reflect different views about what motivates workers. One view (the scientific management school, or McGregor's Theory X) says that pay has an effect on workers' motivation. Linking pay directly with work done should ensure that workers work as hard as possible.

The opposite view (the human relations school, or McGregor's Theory Y) says that pay is only one factor affecting workers' motivation. Tesco, like many companies today, stresses how important it is for workers to feel part of the company. Even paying wages, where workers work a fixed number of hours, can lead to 'clock watching'. Workers can feel that being at work is more important than what they do in the time they are at work. Effort and the quality of what is produced can be poor. An increasing number of workers are now paid a salary. This partly reflects changing views about motivation. It also reflects the increasing number of white collar and service jobs in the economy.

Source: adapted from Tesco website and www.ciao.co.uk/Tesco. Tesco wage rates as at 2.7.2006.

BERWICK LIFE ASSURANCE

In 2005, sales staff at Berwick Life Assurance were paid £21 000 pa plus an annual bonus based on the profits made by the company. The bonus payment for 2005 was £1 250 per employee, £2 500 lower than the year before and £5 600 lower than in 2003. During this period staff turnover amongst the sales team had risen from 15% to a massive 62%. This was beginning to trouble the company, causing recruitment costs to rise significantly.

It was clear that staff were leaving because pay was poor relative to other firms in the industry. The problem was obviously the bonus payments. Profits had fallen at Berwick because of errors made by the senior management. For example, they had to pull out of a misguided overseas expansion project which cost the firm dearly. Senior managers had also wasted money moving to plush new premises.

In 2006, a new system of pay was introduced. This involved a basic salary of £15 000 and £200 commission for every assurance policy sold by a salesperson. The management also said that sales staff could work any hours they choose and not have to report into the office each morning. In 2005, Jenna Pearson was one of the staff who had joined an employee committee to raise the issue of pay with the senior management. In 2006, she sold 76 life assurance policies.

1 Calculate Jenna's gross pay in 2006.
2 Explain what deductions are likely to be made out of Jenna's gross pay.
3 What might be the impact of the new payment system on staff turnover?
4 How might the new pay deal motivate workers? Use theories of motivation in your answer.

Checklist ✓

1 What is the difference between a time-based payment system and a salary payment system?
2 How does a results-based system work?
3 What is the difference between piece rates and a bonus?
4 List FIVE common fringe benefits given by companies.
5 Why do businesses give fringe benefits to their employees?
6 What is the difference between gross and net pay?
7 What are the most common forms of deductions from workers' pay?
8 What factors affect which type of payment system is used by a business?

Making decisions

In a modern economy, a business needs well trained workers if it is to remain competitive. Businesses therefore have to identify their training needs. They have to decide how much they can afford to invest in their workers. They also need to decide who should receive training and what sort of training is needed.

Vodafone Group Plc is the world's leading mobile telecommunications company. It was set up in September 1991. The business provides a wide range of services, including voice and data communications. In September 2006 it had an annual turnover of £15.6 billion and in December 2006 it had 198.6 million mobile phone customers. Its vision is to be 'the world's mobile communications leader'. Training of employees is vital if Vodafone wishes to meet its objectives.

The objectives of training

Training is a cost for a business. So it is important that businesses get 'value for money' from training programmes. There is a number of objectives of training for a business like Vodafone.

Induction INDUCTION training is usually given to new workers. New workers at Vodafone are given 4 weeks' induction training. Managers help staff to become familiar with their department, team and role, and give them an overview of Vodafone UK. They are given an Induction Checklist to help them manage their activities in the first few weeks. They can also work through an online learning module at their own pace.

Upgrading skills With technology and markets changing all the time, workers need to be adding to their existing skills. At Vodafone, a worker may need to be trained to use a new stock control system. Or the worker may need to learn new skills to get promotion.

Retraining Over time, jobs disappear or change. Workers with skills to do these jobs need retraining to do different jobs.

Creating flexibility Like other businesses, Vodafone wants its workers to be increasingly flexible in what they can do. Employees are more likely to be flexible if they have a number of skills. This **multi-skilling** can be achieved through training. For workers, training should result in greater job satisfaction because they are now able to do their job more effectively. Training also opens the door to promotion and better pay.

Methods of training

There are two main methods of training. ON-THE-JOB training occurs when workers pick up skills by working alongside other workers. At Vodafone, a new worker at a store may learn about the job by working alongside existing employees. On-the-job training is cheap and often effective. However, it is unlikely to provide in-depth training. It is also unable to help whole groups of

Preece plc

Preece is a manufacturer of transport equipment, including parking meters and emissions testing equipment.

John has just joined the company and will be working on the factory floor making parking meters.

Laura has been with the company for five years as a personal assistant to one of the managers. In a company reorganisation, this manager is changing jobs. Laura has been given a new job description which not only includes being her personal assistant but also being responsible for other office workers reporting to the manager.

Pete has been a skilled machinist. However, the introduction of new technology means that his skills are no longer needed. He has been offered a new job in logistics, getting the product to the company's customers.

Swati is an ambitious junior manager in the accounts department. She wants to gain promotion within the company.

1 Explain why each of the four workers has training needs.
2 The company has a limited budget for training. It can only afford to spend money on formal training for two of these workers. Which two do you think it should be? Explain your answer carefully.

In 2006 government plans were announced to make vocational training free up to the age of 25. They were designed to bridge England's skills shortage. The Education Secretary said that boosting skills was one of the biggest challenges facing the country. She highlighted the UK's poor international record on getting young people to stay in education and training beyond the school leaving age. At the same time a review of skills needs up to 2020 by Lord Leitch suggested that the UK was behind competitors and ranked 24th out of 29 developed nations. Other countries like India and China were rapidly improving their skills.

Source: adapted from http://news.bbc.co.uk, 26.3.2006.

1 What plans did the government have in 2006 to improve training in the UK?
2 Suggest TWO reasons why the government might have planned to improve training in 2006.
3 Rickmans is a business that makes components for the communications industry. It often takes on younger staff as they are quick to learn in a fast changing industry. Explain how the government plans might affect the business.

workers to change their skills.

To do this, OFF-THE-JOB training is needed. Workers are taken away from their jobs to be trained. This may be done within the company. A business, for example, may run an in-service course for its employees. Either experts within the company lead the course or an outside trainer is brought in. Alternatively, employees may be sent on training courses provided by outside agencies. These include management colleges, further and higher education colleges and training consultancies.

Vodafone holds workshops to explain its Code of Ethical Purchasing (CEP). It brings together supply chain representatives from most of the local operating companies to share their experiences. In 2005/06, 84 per cent of purchasing managers and employees were given in-house training using an interactive learning tool on its intranet. The training explained the CEP, the risks and challenges to its supply chain and the role of employees in implementing the CEP. Vodafone's Learning & Capability Development teams run courses that allow staff to study in a wide range of areas - computers, telecommunications, shorthand or

even for an MBA. They get free access to a Learning Resources Centre, that has books, videos, CD-ROMs and online learning modules.

Off-the-job training can be more expensive than on-the-job training. Outside trainers may have to be paid and workers can't produce anything on the days they are being trained. On the other hand, a wider range of skills can be obtained and it can provide workers with qualifications needed in their job.

Types of training

Businesses use a variety of types of training.

Induction training This has already been described above.

Modern apprenticeships Young people have specific training needs after they leave school and college. They need short term induction training. They are also likely to need longer training to bring their skills up to the level required for a particular job. Some businesses offer modern apprenticeships. These give young people:

- training for 1 or 2 years whilst at work and earning a wage;
- practical experience, skills and

knowledge;
- key skills in areas such as problem solving and new technology;
- a variety of qualifications, including a National Vocational Qualification (NVQ) level 2 (Foundation Modern Apprenticeship) and NVQ level 3 (Advanced Modern Apprenticeship).

In 2007 there were over 200 different types of modern apprenticeship in 80 different sectors, such as business administration, media studies, engineering, event management, hospitality and manufacturing. There were over 259 000 apprentices in England, working in over 130 000 businesses.

Graduate training Young people coming from university also need training. Many companies offer graduate training schemes to cater for their needs. Vodafone has a graduate training scheme. It also has a Finance Graduate Rotational Programme which gives a broad overview of the business, experience towards a CIMA qualification and three, one year placements around the business.

Staff training Groups of workers may need to be trained together. Perhaps they need to learn the skills associated with new technology (skill training). They might need to learn about new health and safety procedures. They might learn about new products available from suppliers. All retail staff at Vodafone complete a thorough training programme. This gives them the skills they need to deliver the best advice and service to customers. Vodafone says that staff work in an environment of change and empowerment, and their contribution and innovation are constantly encouraged.

Staff development Individual workers have training needs too. Vodafone runs a career advancement programme for staff at all its retail stores. This could be a route for staff to develop into managers if they have the right abilities. Vodafone holds individual performance management discussions (Performance Dialogues) each year, interim discussions twice a year and monthly one-to-one meetings. The discussions help staff to understand their strengths and areas that need developing, to create a Personal Development Plan and to help them with any problems they have.

Government and training

Vodafone has a good training record. However, many middle sized and small businesses spend little or nothing on training. They rely on schools, colleges and other businesses to do the training. They then recruit (some businesses would say 'poach' or 'headhunt') workers with the right skills and qualifications. Businesses therefore do not spend enough on training when left to themselves. So the government has to intervene, either to provide money directly for industry training or to encourage businesses to take training seriously.

The **Department for Education and Skills** (DfES) is the government department directly responsible for training. It provides funds for all government-funded training schemes. The **Learning and Skills Council** (LSC) is a public body which operates nationally and locally. Its aim is to improve the skills of young people and adults to world class standards. The LSC plans and funds education and training, including distributing government funds for training in areas such as apprenticeships.

The **New Deal** is a government initiative to provide support to unemployed people, to help them get back to work. After assessment, unemployed people are given help and advice to find a job, whilst still claiming benefits such as Jobseeker's Allowance. Employers may be given financial support for taking on unemployed people. The scheme is aimed at different categories, including 18-24 years olds, people over 25 or over 50, lone parents, musicians or disabled people.

The government plans to set up 12 **National Skills Academies** by 2008, aimed at 16-19 year olds. They are employer-led and are designed to provide world class centres training in skills required by each major sector of the economy.

The government sets **Public Service Agreement** (PSA) targets for education and training. For example, by 2008 it wanted 73.4 per cent of people aged 19 to be qualified to NVQ level 2 or equivalent (5 GCSEs). It also set a target to improve the skills of 2.25 million adults by 2010.

Investors in People is a national standard which sets out a level of good practice for the training and development of people in business. It is a key part of the government's aim to improve skills. Businesses can apply to gain the standard. Their training of staff is assessed and if they meet the standard they can display it at the business.

Government has a key role to play in training. Some argue that it needs to put more money into government funded training schemes. Others argue that businesses will always train workers if there is a need for training whether or not they get help from government. Even if this is true, government can help provide the training framework which the economy needs if it is to be successful.

Source: adapted from www.vodafone.com, www.apprenticeships.org.uk, www.dfes-uk.co.uk, www.lsc.gov.uk, www.jobcentreplus.gov.uk, www.investorsinpeople.co.uk.

UK restaurant trade

Jennie Foulkes is responsible for recruiting chefs for a chain of pub-restaurants. With the restaurant trade booming, she is finding it very difficult, so difficult that she regularly recruits from as far away as Australia. However, foreign nationals rarely stay. They want to come to England for a year, practise their language skills, see the country and then go home. She would far prefer to recruit British chefs who on average will stay four years in a post.

The problem is that there is an acute shortage of British chefs. Plenty of young people complete full time catering courses at college or go to a culinary school but only a fraction of these go on to take up a career in the catering industry. They are put off by the unsocial hours and the relatively low pay.

Jennie is considering whether a solution might be to offer an apprenticeship scheme within the company. Apprentices could be trained to NVQ level 2 or 3 and the company would get government funding for the scheme. The company might use local colleges for part of the training. Otherwise, selected chefs in some of the pub-restaurants would give on-the-job training.

1 Explain what is meant by: (a) an apprenticeship; and (b) on-the-job training.
2 Why might a 19 year old be attracted to an apprenticeship offered by Jennie's company?
3 What training needs might existing chefs have who become responsible for apprentices?
4 Do you think that such a training scheme would reduce problems of recruitment for the company? Explain your answer carefully.

Checklist ✓

1 What are the objectives of training for a business?
2 What might a worker gain from being trained?
3 What is the difference between on-the-job training and off-the-job training?
4 Where might a worker be trained off-the-job?
5 What is a modern apprenticeship?
6 What is the role of the Learning and Skills Council?
7 How might the Investors in People standard help encourage training?

key terms

Induction - period of training for workers new to a business when they find out about the business and the job they have to do.
Off-the-job training - training undertaken away from the job, either at the business or outside the business, for instance, at a college of further education.
On-the-job training - training in the workplace undertaken whilst doing a job.

SUMMARY CASE STUDY

SUPERMARKET SWOOP

In 2004 Asda announced that its staff were to start taking national vocational qualifications again. It had stopped before, claiming they were inflexible for big organisations. Other retailers were set to follow. 1 000 employees in 8 Asda outlets in north London would start work towards a new version of its in-house training qualification, which has been accredited by City & Guilds as an NVQ. Staff aged 16-24 who take part will gain a level 2 qualification as part of a foundation modern apprenticeship. Trainees will be expected to finish within 1 year. The LSC's own guidance is that foundation modern apprenticeships usually take 18 months on average. Employees aged 25 and over will work towards the NVQ level 2 on its own.

The Learning and Skills Council is contributing £500 000 to cover the cost of this pilot, which will be rolled out nationwide if it goes well. Asda suggested that the LSC changed its mind about training. It appreciated that large retailing companies were not using NVQs and modern apprenticeships because they were inflexible. The courses were changed so that students took a core plus options programme.

It was argued that the move would boost the government's chances of hitting its target for recruiting modern apprentices. This was to increase the proportion of young people under 22 starting modern apprenticeships to 28%, or about 175,000. 'We could help that. We've got 110,000 employees' said an Asda spokeswoman.

Asda staff used to take NVQs. But 10 years ago it quit. Asda decided it couldn't afford to have staff leaving the shop floor to be assessed by external examiners. So Asda set up its own training organisation, which it called the Academy. 'We didn't have a skills gap for general shop floor staff like shelf-stackers, but there was a skills shortage in the craft areas such as bakers, butchers and fishmongers.'

Source: adapted from *The Guardian*, 17.2.2004.

1 What off-the-job training has been used as a means of training Asda staff?
2 Suggest TWO reasons why Asda may have trained its staff using NVQs.
3 Why might Asda's decision have helped the government to achieve its training targets?
4 To what extent did the Learning and Skills Council play a part in influencing Asda's decision to offer NVQs to staff?
5 Discuss whether all large supermarkets should encourage staff to take NVQs.

Making decisions

Communication is vital to a business. How best can employees in a business communicate with each other and with outsiders? What makes communication effective? What are the best channels of communication?

Lloyds TSB is currently the fifth largest banking organisation in the UK. It employs around 66 000 staff and enjoyed sales of £10.5 billion in 2005. Its subsidiaries include the mortgage bank Cheltenham & Gloucester, life assurance company Scottish Widows and finance house Blackhorse. Effective communication is vital for the success of such a large company.

Senders and receivers

There are always two parties to any COMMUNICATION.
- The **sender**. An example would be Lloyds TSB sending out bank statements to its customers. It might be an employee giving financial advice to a small business. It might be the head of the personnel department giving instructions to other heads of department about how to deal with a staff problem.
- The **receiver**. This may be a shareholder getting a copy of Lloyds' Annual Report through the post. It may be a customer receiving confirmation of a loan. It may be heads of department receiving instructions from the head of personnel.
   The receiver may give FEEDBACK. The shareholder getting a copy of the Annual Report may, for instance, write a letter to the company commenting on its performance. Figure 1 shows feedback that may take place in a banking business.

Internal and external communication

Some communications are INTERNAL to the business. Examples of internal communication would be:
- one bank teller talking to another bank teller;
- the branch manager sending a memo to branch staff;
- a company director requesting her personal assistant to arrange some appointments;
- a copy of a customer mortgage application being faxed from a Bristol branch to a Cornwall branch;
- a bank teller receiving training from the branch manager.
   Other communications are EXTERNAL, where Lloyds communicates with people or organisations outside the business. Examples would be:

This letter of complaint has been sent to a rail company.
1. Who is the sender of the communication?
2. What is the sender trying to communicate in the letter?
3. Do you think that the company should reply to the letter? Put arguments for and against.

Wordprocessing
4. Assume it decides to reply. (a) Write the letter of reply using a wordprocessing package if possible. (b) Do you think that Mr Nichols will respond? Explain why or why not.

> 6 Greenacres Road
> Milton Keynes
> 15.5.2007
>
> I want to complain about your ticket collector. I was on the train back from London last Friday after a nice day's shopping when he asked to see my rail ticket. He said it wasn't valid because it was five o'clock and it was a cheap day ticket and demanded that I pay more money. I bought a return ticket. He really showed me up in front of the passengers. You would have thought I was a thief the way he was talking.
>
> Yours disgustedly
> P Nichols (Mr)

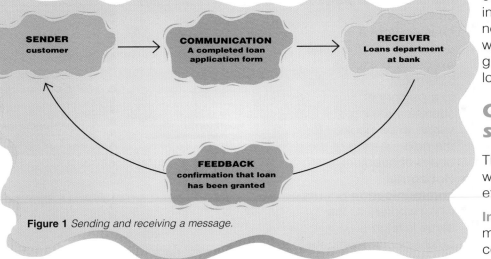

Figure 1 *Sending and receiving a message.*

- a receptionist talking to a customer;
- the chairman discussing company progress with a major shareholder;
- a building company faxing Lloyds TSB to confirm a specification to repairs on a building.

The importance of good communication

Good communication is essential to any business. For instance, at Lloyds TSB:

- accurate advertising brochures avoid disappointed customers;
- a clear instruction by a manager makes sure that a task gets done;
- an accurate memo from the personnel department might help clear up a misunderstanding.

Poor external communication can lead to dissatisfied customers, a poor business image and problems with suppliers. Poor internal communications can lead to workers not understanding what they have to do, poor motivation of the workforce and duplication of effort. Overall, poor communication can lead to a loss of sales as

customers are not satisfied. It also increases costs because work is not completed in the most efficient way. Mistakes are made and things get overlooked. All this may lead to lower profits.

Communication skills

There is a number of key factors which make a communication effective.

Information What is communicated must be accurate. It must be complete, giving all the information necessary. It must also be simple and clear, so that the receiver can understand the information as quickly and easily as possible.

Sender and receiver The message must be sent from the right people to the right people. A memo sent to all employees dealing with details about a new product which is received only by those working in the London branches may be an example of poor communication.

Time and place Communication must take place at the right time and right place. A 2006 Lloyds TSB advertising leaflet might be useless if it is sent out in 2007 because the interest rate is likely to have changed, for example. A notice about fire safety which nobody can read because it is pinned too high up is in the wrong place. An urgent memo from head office mustn't arrive at branches three weeks later.

Method The method of communication, must be right. Methods include face to face communication, memos, telephone calls and the use of information technology.

Barriers to communication

Not all communication is effective. There is a number of reasons why communication breaks down. The person sending the communication

Lindsey Myers, Accountants

Lindsey Myers is an accounting business which employs assistant accountants who work together in offices in Nottingham. The business provides accounting services for other small businesses. Its keeps the books of local shopkeepers, garages, doctors and electricians, for instance. These businesses are more likely to use Lindsey Myers than larger accountancy firms because its services are more suitable for their needs.

1 What service does Lindsey Myers offer its customers?
2 Give FIVE examples each of: (a) external communications; and (b) internal communications which Lindsey Myers might have.
3 Make a list of points which Lindsey Myers might use when trying to win new custom for the business. In your list, include some ideas about why communication might be better in a small business than in a larger accountancy practice.

might not explain themselves very well. The receivers might not be capable of understanding the message because they lack understanding of technical jargon. The receiver might not hear the message because he or she is not paying attention or chooses to focus in on part of the message, but not all of it. Messages can get distorted if they go through too many people like in a game of Chinese whispers. Equipment might break down or not be working very well. A fax machine may have a fault or a telephone line might be very noisy.

Channels of communication

Information passes along CHANNELS of communication. These are channels which are recognised and approved by the business and by employee representatives such as trade unions. There are two main types of **formal communication**.

- **Vertical communication** is communication up and down the hierarchy of the business. For instance, a worker at a Lloyds TSB call centre might seek

authorisation to waive a customer's bank charges from a supervisor. Or the chief executive of Lloyds TSB might send a note to a personnel secretary asking a venue to be booked for the next meeting of the board of directors.

- **Horizontal communication** occurs when workers at the same level in a business communicate formally with each other. One branch manager might consult with another branch manager about a report they have both been sent, for example. Often, communication doesn't get passed along official channels in the organisation. INFORMAL COMMUNICATION is called communication through the GRAPEVINE. For instance, a manager in the foreign currency department may have a friend who works in mortgages. When they chat and exchange gossip about what is going on in the company, they are passing on

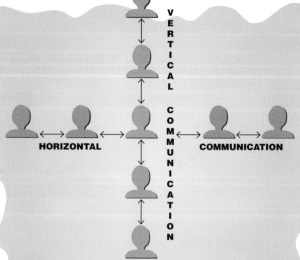

Figure 2 *Horizontal and vertical communication.*

information through the grapevine. Channels of communication should be clearly laid down by a business. If they are not, then vital information can get sent to the wrong people, or get lost. Communication through the grapevine can sometimes be a problem because messages may get distorted the more people they go through. On the other hand, the grapevine can be very useful. A manager may know that to do his job properly, he needs as much information as possible. This might mean getting more information than he 'officially' receives.

In general, the fewer the number of stages through which a communication passes (i.e the shorter the chain of communication), the less likely it is that a message will be misinterpreted. One of the possible advantages of a small company compared to Lloyds TSB is that, with very few people employed, it may be easier to communicate effectively. This is why Lloyds TSB has to work hard to maintain the effectiveness of its communication systems.

Source: adapted from Lloyds TSB, *Annual Report and Accounts*, 2005.

1 What makes the front cover of a travel brochure an effective piece of communication?

2 Write a short report suggesting how and where brochures might be distributed. For instance, should a travel business post a copy to every house in the country? Should it be distributed to all travel agents in Europe? When writing your answer, bear in mind that distribution costs should be kept as low as possible and that the brochures should reach those people most likely to use the service.

Your school or college is likely to be a business organisation. It has formal channels of communication. Find out the formal channel(s) of communication for the following situations.

1 A pupil or student is persistently late for business studies lessons.
2 A pupil or student needs a bus pass.
3 A teacher or lecturer wants to order some business studies textbooks.
4 A teacher or lecturer wants a white board installed in the teaching room.
5 A pupil or student needs afternoon release to be able to appear in a show running for two weeks at the local theatre.

SUMMARY CASE STUDY

BT

Public limited companies have to send their shareholders a copy of their Annual Report and Accounts every year by law. The statement below is an extract taken from BT's *Annual Report and Accounts*, 2005.

1 Who is the receiver of the communication?
2 Is this an example of internal or external communication? Explain your answer.
3 Describe the purpose of the communication.
4 Discuss the extent to which this communication is effective. In your answer, write about what makes a communication effective and what might be the barriers to communication.

Chairman's message (an extract)

Our results for the 2005 financial year were strong. New wave revenues grew by 32% to £4.5 billion, and now represent nearly a quarter of our business. Earnings per share have more than doubled over the past three years and net debt is more than £20 billion lower than in 2001. Earnings per share in the 2005 financial year, before goodwill amortisation and exceptional items, grew by 7% to 18.1 pence. While continuing to invest for the future, we generated free cash flow of £2.3 billion, up 10%.

The news on dividends is positive. We are recommending a full-year dividend of 10.4 pence per share, a pay out ratio of 57% of earnings before goodwill amortisation and exceptional items, compared to 50% last year. We continue with our progressive dividend policy. The dividend for the 2006 financial year will be at least 60% of underlying earnings: subject to the group's overall financial position, we expect our pay out ratio to rise to around two-thirds of underlying earnings by the 2008 financial year.

Source: adapted from BT, *Annual Report and Accounts*, 2005.

key terms

Channel of communication - the path taken by a message, such as horizontal communication, vertical communication or grapevine communication.
Communication - messages passed between a sender and a receiver, through a medium such as a letter or a fax.
External communication - communication between the business and an outside individual or organisation like a customer, a supplier or a tax inspector.
Feedback - response to a message by its receiver to the sender.
Formal channels of communication - channels which are recognised and approved by the business and by employee representatives such as trade unions.
Informal communication or communication through the grapevine - communication through channels which are not formally recognised by the business.
Internal communication - communication within the business organisation.

Checklist ✓

1 In communication, what is the difference between a sender and a receiver?
2 A company sends out a brochure to a customer. What feedback might it expect to receive?
3 What is the difference between internal and external communication?
4 List FOUR external communications which a local newsagent might send or receive.
5 Why is good communication important for a business?
6 What makes communication effective?
7 What is the difference between vertical and horizontal communication?
8 Why is communication through a grapevine both useful and a possible problem for a business organisation?

Making decisions

Every business needs to communicate. People within the business need to communicate between themselves. The business needs to communicate with outsiders such as customers, suppliers and government. So businesses have to decide what is the most effective means of communication. Is it a letter, a fax, a set of minutes or a telephone call, for instance?

Office Angels is a specialist supplier of secretarial and office support staff. It provides recruitment services for many businesses, from small, medium and large businesses to household names such as Marks & Spencer, Capital One and the BBC. It has branches throughout the UK and an online database of part time, full time, temporary and permanent office jobs, such as secretaries, managers and public sector finance jobs. Its consultants find out the needs of businesses and try to match them with suitable candidates.

Body language

When two or more people meet, many messages are passed by the way they act and react physically. For instance, an Office Angels consultant may smile and nod when interviewing a candidate. This could be interpreted in different ways. It might relax the interviewee. Equally, a passive expression may be seen as a lack of interest. The way we laugh, frown, walk and dress are all examples of **non-verbal** communication.

Verbal communication

Verbal or **oral** communication is when two or more people talk together. They may meet together informally. For instance, two staff may discuss a problem over timing of interviews, an example of **face-to-face** communication. A person who gets a job through Office Angels may recommend this to another person, an example of **word of mouth** communication. An employee might ring up head office to ask when new desks or equipment might be delivered. Ringing up would be an example of **telephone** communication.

Examples of more formal types of verbal communication at Office Angels might include:

- a consultant **meeting** with a business to discuss the employees it needs;
- a consultant **interviewing** applicants for a job;
- employees attending a **training course** where new software is explained ;
- a manager attending a **conference** to find out about developments in future employment trends;
- a group of managers **teleconferencing**, where more than two people can join in and listen to a conversation over the telephone;

Look at the photographs.
1 What does each of the photographs show, do you think, about how each worker is feeling?
2 A manager is to deliver a verbal warning to a worker. The worker has been persistently late to work for no good reason. The verbal warning will be given in the presence of the worker's union representative. (a) What information might be given to the worker in the verbal warning? (b) What non-verbal messages might the manager give to the worker during the interview? You might carry this out as a role play exercise.

- directors **videoconferencing**, where they can see and hear each other through video cameras, telephone lines and monitors.

Verbal communication can be effective. A consultant at Office Angels who makes a telephone call can contact someone immediately. They can return the call if they are not there. The conversation can be confidential. The two parties can exchange views quickly and easily. The receiver of the message can also question anything not understood or give instant feedback. This is important when discussing complicated issues.

The larger the number of people involved, the less likely it is that there will be feedback. For example, in a meeting with all staff at an Office Angels branch, some will not give any feedback at all.

Visual communication

Office Angels makes use of visual communication. Visual communication can take place within and outside the organisation A manager, for example, might be sent a **bar chart** by head office showing sales figures by different branches. The manager might read a **newspaper article** which shows employment trends of Office Angels on a **line graph**. The manager might convert spreadsheet data about costs or budgets into **pie charts**.

A manager might also view visual information about the business on television or via the Internet. This might be a **video** or **film** about the success of Office Angels on a business programme.

Office Angels uses **posters** and **window displays** in its branches to advertise to people looking for jobs. It has a business **logo** and company image **design** which is instantly recognisable. This involves the use of the colours pink and blue in its promotions. It places **advertisements** in newspapers and magazines to attract business clients. It also sends out **flyers** advertising its services.

Visual images and colourful designs can improve communication. They may affect people's perceptions or feelings about something in a way that written information might not. For example, showing a training video to an Office Angels consultant may give a clearer picture of a skill. A film showing happy employees getting a job via Office Angels and colourful visual window displays can be effective in attracting people to use its services.

Written communication

Written words are a useful means of communication. Because they can be stored on paper or on a computer, they can give a permanent record of the communication. In contrast, there is unlikely to be a permanent record if an Office Angels consultant has an informal talk with a colleague about the employees a business wants to hire. Written communication can also reach large numbers of people. A company newsletter, for instance, can be sent to all employees.

Written communication can be very detailed. This is important for Office Angels. Consultants need to record many details when they meet businesses to discuss the types of employees they are looking for. These include the types of skills, the personality and other features that the business feels are important. Written communication is also vital when advertising jobs. It will show what the job involves, conditions of work and pay, and the skills and experience that people looking for jobs will need.

There are many types of written communication.

What methods of communication are being used by Office Angels in the photographs?

Letters A letter is versatile and can convey plans, instructions, comments and analysis, for instance. A **personal letter** is one which is sent with the understanding that it will only be read by the named receiver. An **open letter** is one where the sender wants anyone who is interested to read the letter. The letter might be faxed to the receiver via a fax machine, to be printed out by a fax machine at the receiver's end. Most businesses today are likely to e-mail a letter, as explained later.

Memorandum A memorandum or memo is a short letter, usually giving instructions such as a request for information. Memos are sometimes written on standard forms.

Circular or newsletter A circular is a communication which is sent to a number of people. For example, the head office at Office Angels might send a circular to branches with information about changes in recruitment practices. Some companies send regular newsletters to all branches or employees giving the latest information about the business.

Forms Forms are designed to make sure that all the information required is included in a communication. For instance, Office Angels has standard application forms that have to be filled in by all people wishing to be placed on its register of people looking for jobs. These include details about the applicant such as personal details, experience and qualifications.

Minutes These are a written record of a meeting. Someone at the meeting makes a note of what is discussed and then writes it up. Minutes are important because they might be consulted. If there is any dispute about what was said at the meeting, the minutes might clarify what really happened and act as a permanent record. Because they are referred to, it is usual for people at a meeting to confirm the minutes. This means that they agree that the written minutes accurately reflect what was said at the meeting.

Reports A report is an extended piece of writing on a particular topic. Limited companies like Office Angels must submit their accounts to the Registrar of Companies each year to show how the business has performed over the last 12 months. Public limited companies often include these in an Annual Report and Accounts to show stakeholders how the business is operating. There are other types of report. A branch manager might submit a report to head office about the performance of his or her branch. Reports may contain, graphs, charts and photographs as well as words.

Kept in the picture

Telephone and video conferencing are not for amateurs. When IBM, one of the world's largest computer companies, wants to hold a conference, it uses an outside company to organise it. That company is Geoconference, which employs just 40 people.

George Mackintosh, the managing director of Geoconference, explains that it is not difficult for three or four people to make a conference call by telephone. But staging a conference for more than that 'requires something more than your telephone normally gives you. It requires an operator and a whizzy box'.

The operator connects all the people participating in the conference, keeps them on hold and puts them through to the chair of the conference at the scheduled time. The operator then monitors the conference to make sure that the participants remain connected. He then ends the connections when the session is over. For video conferencing, Geoconference uses its own equipment including a computer to set up the links.

Naturally, telecom companies like BT provide teleconference and videoconference management facilities. But Geoconference believes that it can supply both a better service and a keener price than the major telecom companies.

Source: adapted from the *Financial Times*.

Bill Kale is a director of a medium sized household and personal products company. It manufactures a range of goods including shampoo, soap, deodorant and perfume as well as household cleaning products and washing powders. The company has six factories, four scattered round the UK, one in Ireland and one in Hungary, as well as a head office in London. At the moment, management from the factories and at head office only talk on a one to one basis over the telephone. Twice a year, the senior managers from each factory hold a one day conference in London to discuss issues. On top of that, managers from each factory spend on average ten days scattered through the year at head office on company matters.

1 Write a short report for Bill Kale, outlining the benefits of teleconferencing and videoconferencing compared to what happens now. Explain how you would decide whether it was financially worthwhile to change to more tele- and videoconferencing.

INTERNAL MEMO

From	Bill Kale	Date 4/5/2007
To	Stephen Deane	Ref
Subject	FT article on conferencing	

What do you think? Following our recent discussion, do you think we ought to get in touch with Geoconference to talk about a contract?

Use of ICT

Information and communications technology (ICT) today is a vital part of communication in most businesses. It comes in different forms.

E-mail Most businesses today make use of e-mail. It is a quick and easy way to send written communications such as letters, memos, minutes, circulars, figures and photos produced in **word processing**, **spreadsheet** or other computer software. It can be sent to one person or many people, who can respond immediately. A business may email people inside the organisation or those outside.

Databases These are computer records that contain detailed information. Office Angels keeps a comprehensive database of all applicants that register with the business. This can be searched when clients are looking for people with particular skills. It also has a comprehensive database of jobs that are available and clients looking for candidates.

Websites Many businesses today have websites on the **Internet**. A website can be used to give information about the business and its products. It can also be used by customers to contact the business. The Office Angels website at www.office-angels.com gives information to employers and job seekers on how to register with the business. Some businesses have **intranets**. These only allow employees within a business to pass information to each other electronically, or give limited access to people with security passwords.

Small messaging service The small messaging service (SMS) is where messages are sent to mobile phones or other mobile devices such as pocket PCs. Businesses make use of this in promotion. Office Angels uses SMS to provide jobseekers with details of vacancies, called job alerts.

EPOS Electronic point of sale (EPOS) systems allow businesses to record and store information about sales as customers pay at the till and bar codes are scanned on products. Businesses, like retailers, can use the system to give them information about stock levels, sales and new orders.

Information and communication technology is often quicker and easier to use than paper communication. It is also more powerful, enabling far more information to be handled than would be possible using pen and ink.

Source: information from Office Angels.

Checklist ✓

1 Why might a manager use verbal communication to pass a message to another manager rather than write them a memo?
2 What are the disadvantages of verbal communication?
3 List and then describe in words THREE pieces of visual communication you can find in this book.
4 Why might a manager present sales figures over the past five years in the form of a graph rather than in words?
5 What is the difference between a letter and a memo?
6 When might a business use a circular?
7 Explain TWO reasons why an employee might send an email asking if another employee can attend an urgent meeting taking place tomorrow.
8 List THREE types of information that a business might communicate on its website.
9 What makes an instruction manual effective?

ANN RAWLINGS

Ann Rawlings is head of marketing in a medium sized limited company manufacturing ceramics, based in Stoke-on-Trent. Below is an entry in her diary for Tuesday 5 June.

1 For each entry in her diary, describe the types of communication she is likely to have used.
2 A potential new customer has approached the company. Ann has to decide whether to:

- go and meet the customer in London;
- ask the customer to come and meet her in Stoke-on-Trent;
- set up a teleconferencing or videoconferencing discussion (where people can talk to each other or see each other on screen if they have the correct equipment);
- e-mail details and image attachments
- send promotional material about her company and its products through the post.

Which of these ways of communicating with the potential customer do you think she should choose? Give reasons for your answer, thinking about cost, time spent and effectiveness of the communication.

5 June

Tuesday

8.30 Briefing meeting with Claire about the day
8.45 Respond to incoming mail and e-mail
9.15 Contact John Tyler in London
9.30 New product committee meeting
12.00 Lunch meeting with representatives from Sealware plc
14.00 Interviews for deputy assistant marketing
15.30 Update client list
16.00 Preparation for board meeting in 7 days time
18.00 Home

Making decisions

Management and workers need to decide how they should relate to each other. They both have common interests, such as ensuring the survival of the business. However, they also have conflicting objectives, such as the size of pay increases or the quality of working conditions. Workers need to decide whether to join a trade union to protect their interests. Management needs to decide whether it will work with trade unions and how to communicate with workers. Both management and trade unions are responsible for relations between workers and managers in business.

Levens Construction is a construction and engineering business. It specialises in the building of commercial property such as shops. This is a smaller market than the house building market, but the business has been successful as a result of its innovative designs. Started in 1976, today it employs 173 people.

Unions at Levens

The employees at Levens are represented by two trade unions. The majority of workers are represented by Amicus. This is the largest manufacturing, technical and skilled workers union in the UK. It has over 1 million members. A small number of senior workers belong to UCATT, the Union of Construction, Allied Trades and Technicians. This is the only specialist construction workers union in the UK and has 125 000 members.

Communication

The management at Levens communicates with its workforce over a whole range of issues, such as pay, holidays, working conditions and contracts of employment, redundancies and staffing levels. INDUSTRIAL RELATIONS is the term used to describe the relationship between the two groups.

All the workers at Levens are members of a TRADE UNION. Trade unions exist to protect the interests of their members. At Levens, trade union representatives negotiate on behalf of members with the management. This negotiation is called COLLECTIVE BARGAINING. It is 'collective'

because many shareholders are represented by just a few managers.

Equally, many workers are represented by just a few trade union representatives. Collective bargaining provides a **channel of communication** between workers and management.

Members' services

The T&G is Britain's biggest general union and can offer its members the very best services. These range from support and advice to financial assistance, both at work and at home, all for a minimal monthly subscription. In addition, the T&G boasts a range of top-class facilities for work functions and leisure use.

T&G Care

T&G members get unrivalled assistance from their union. T&G Care is a comprehensive package of benefits and services available, with support at work as well as special deals to let members make the most of their income.

Support at work

The T&G represents workers in every type of workplace throughout the UK and Ireland. Members benefit from legal representation and advice, research, journals and information, education services, and a dedicated health and safety team. The union also offers a unique support service to professional drivers: DriverCare. Find out more about how the T&G supports its members at work.

Legal and financial support

When accidents or illness happens, the T&G supports its members through its T&G Care Assistance scheme. It also offers a range of money-saving deals to meet insurance and financial needs through T&G FamilyCare. There are extra legal services available to members too, such as its legal helpline CareXpress. More details about legal and financial support.

Facilities

The T&G has superb facilities in London and on Britain's sunny south coast, in Eastbourne, suitable for conferences, seminars and holidays. Members convalescing after illness can also enjoy the recuperative amenities at its Eastbourne Centre.

STOP THE UNDERCUTTING **STOP** THE ABUSE

Equal rights for agency workers
Support the temporary and agency workers bill. British labour law fails to protect agency workers. Paul Farrelly MP's Temporary and Agency Workers (Prevention of Less Favourable Treatment) bill would outlaw discrimination against agency workers. Get involved in the campaign and get your MP to back the bill on March 2nd.

New on our site

Gate Gourmet and beyond
End discrimination against the missing million
T&G on National Skills Academy for Manufacturing

Figure 1 *Benefits of T&G*
Source: www.tgwu.org.uk.

1 Tariq Mohammed in a member of the T&G. He has recently been ill and missed work for a time. He has been threatened by his employer that he could be sacked unless he improves his attendance. How might being a member of the T&G help Tariq:
   (a) while he is off work ill;
   (b) when he returns to work;
   (c) if he is sacked by the business?

Trade unions

Workers at Levens belong to trade unions because they provide a range of services.

- They negotiate with employers and employers' associations over conditions of work, including pay, hours of work, holidays and safety.
- They give legal protection to workers, offering advice about issues such as unfair dismissal. If matters are serious enough, they will employ legal experts to defend members in court.
- They provide monetary benefits. These vary from union to union. They can include strike pay, accident and death insurance, mortgages and loans.
- They act as pressure groups. They try to pressure employers, their associations and government to bring in further benefits for workers. They also resist changes which are likely to harm workers' interests.

At Levens, like other businesses, union members elect SHOP STEWARDS to represent their interests. A shop steward is an unpaid volunteer. He or she deals with problems of members either directly or by passing the problem on to someone who is better able to sort it out. Shop stewards act as a channel of communication between workers and management.

John Riley is the Amicus shop steward at Levens. He passes on information from the union to members at the business, for example through the union bulletin board. He advises members on areas of concern and deals with grievances on issues such as:

- pay – including pay rises, overtime pay and bonuses;
- conditions of work – such as hours, holidays and shift working;
- health and safety at work;
- redundancies;
- equal opportunities.

Alongside the voluntary workers of the unions are full time officials.

These are paid by the union to give advice to members, shop stewards and branches.

Each year a union holds an **annual conference**. This is the annual general meeting (AGM) of the union. Representatives are elected by members to go to the conference. The **motions** passed at the conference become union policy. The full time officials of the union then have to follow that policy.

Many unions belong to the **Trades Union Congress (TUC)** or in Ireland the Irish Congress of Trade Unions (ICTU). This body acts as a pressure group, representing union interests in discussions with government and other organisations.

Employers' associations

Levens belongs to an EMPLOYERS' or TRADE ASSOCIATION. Employers' associations represent the interests of business. Levens is a member of the Federation of Master Builders which represents over 13 000 building companies in the UK.

Like trade unions, employers' associations act as pressure groups, representing their members' interests to government and other organisations. They give advice to member businesses. They can also be involved in research and development for the benefit of members. Some employers' associations negotiate industry-wide pay agreements with trade unions. Here minimum pay levels are set by yearly negotiations. Businesses are free to pay more than the minimum if they want. This may be the case if there are **skills shortages**. In the past, in the construction industry, there has been a lack of construction workers with skills. High wages have had to be paid to recruit workers with the right skills.

At national level many trade associations and large businesses belong to the **Confederation of British Industry (CBI)**. Like employers' associations, it is a pressure group representing the interests of British businesses to the government and the European Union.

Membership gender gap closes

A March 2005 report *A woman's place is in her union* revealed that the 'gender gap' in union membership between women and men fell over the period 1997-2003. The report said that 29.3% of working women and 29.4% of working men were union members in 2003. The figures represent a growth in female union membership of 312,000 to 3,475,000 over the six-year period. Male membership fell by 193,000 to 3,592,000. Much of the growth in female membership may be accounted for by increases in public sector employment and a greater desire by young women to become union members.

The TUC report also highlighted benefits for women working in unionised workplaces over non-unionized workplaces. These include higher rates of pay for women, equal opportunities policies with monitoring of promotions and reviews of selection procedures to identify indirect discrimination, and better access to parental leave and financial help with childcare. The TUC general secretary said it was an impressive achievement that unions have closed the gender gap amongst their members ... not least since many women work part time - 'a group that unions have always found hard to recruit'.

Source: adapted from www.eiro.eurofound.eu.int.

1 What is a meant by 'a gender gap ' in union membership?
2 (a) What happened to the proportion of (i) female workers who were union members over the period 1997 - 2003, (ii) male workers who were union members over the period 1997-2003 (iii) the gender gap?
  (b) Suggest TWO reasons for this change.
3 Why might unions have found it difficult to recruit part time female workers?
4 A union is seeking to attract part time workers. What benefits might it use to attract such workers to become union members?

Industrial action

Nearly all worker-management problems are sorted out peacefully. However, occasionally an issue arises which sets workers against management without any agreement. Various forms of INDUSTRIAL ACTION can then be taken to try to force the other side to back down. Workers, for instance, can:

- go on strike – perhaps a one day strike, a strike where key workers do not come in to work, or more seriously, an all out strike by all workers;
- ban overtime work;
- boycott work, such as refusing to work with new machinery;
- work slowly (a go slow) or work to rule (only do work on a job description) which reduces productivity.

Management too can take action against workers. In particular it can lock out workers, either sacking them and employing new workers, or stating that only workers who are prepared to accept management terms will be allowed to resume work.

If management and workers are in dispute they can bring in the Advisory, Conciliation and Arbitration Service (ACAS) or in Northern Ireland the Labour Relations Agency (LRA) to help resolve the disagreement. These are independent bodies, financed by government, which are responsible for giving advice to both businesses and employees about industrial relations matters. They also provide CONCILIATION services. This means that they are prepared to help management and workers come to an agreement when they are in dispute. Finally, they provide an ARBITRATION service. This is where management and workers agree to allow an outside person, the arbitrator, to make a decision about something in dispute.

Industrial relations

Industrial relations at Levens in the 1970s were not always good. There were **unofficial** strikes – strikes not backed by a trade union. There was also a small number of **wildcat** strikes – very short strikes that flared up over issues and then were quickly resolved.

In the 1980s and 1990s the climate of industrial relations changed for a number of reasons.

- The government introduced laws that made it more difficult to take industrial action. For example, unions had to call a secret ballot and win at least 50 per cent of the vote in favour before they could call a strike. Secondary picketing was banned. This was where workers from other factories or offices would stand outside a business trying to persuade workers not to cross the picket line.
- Between 1979 and 2006 there was a 3.8 million fall in the number of jobs in manufacturing, the sector of the economy where trade unions were strongest. This partly explains the 6.0 million fall in trade union membership over the same period. Fewer members weakened the power of unions.
- With so much unemployment in the economy, workers were afraid to take industrial action in case they lost their jobs.
- Employers became tougher. In a number of key strikes employers won the dispute. This discouraged trade unions from taking action.
- Some employers **de-recognised** unions. Workers could still join a union but management would not allow the union to represent workers in negotiations (i.e. it no longer recognised the union for bargaining purposes). This put businesses in a stronger position when bargaining with individual employees.
- Some businesses negotiated **single union agreements**. They would agree to recognise one union. This would simplify negotiations and mean the company wouldn't be drawn into disputes which were between unions rather than between unions and management. They would often be introduced alongside no-strike deals, where workers agree never to strike in return for compulsory arbitration when management and workers can't agree.

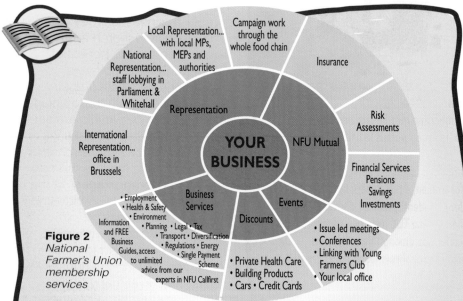

Figure 2
National Farmer's Union membership services

Local Representation... with local MPs, MEPs and authorities

National Representation... staff lobbying in Parliament & Whitehall

Campaign work through the whole food chain

International Representation... office in Brussels

Representation

Insurance

YOUR BUSINESS

NFU Mutual

Risk Assessments

Financial Services
Pensions
Savings
Investments

Business Services

Events

Discounts

• Employment
• Health & Safety
• Environment
• Planning • Legal • Tax
• Transport • Diversification
• Regulations • Energy
• Single Payment Scheme

Information and FREE Business Guides, access to unlimited advice from our experts in NFU Callfirst

• Private Health Care
• Building Products
• Cars • Credit Cards

• Issue led meetings
• Conferences
• Linking with Young Farmers Club
• Your local office

The NFU offers a range of membership categories for those individuals and businesses that are connected to the farming and growing industries or who are interested in the countryside.

Source: www.nfuonline.com.

Helen Mills runs a farm in Northumberland. She is considering expanding production in future. Explain FOUR ways in which her membership of the farmers' union NFU might benefit the business.

Bus workers strike

In December 2005, Amicus members at First Bus in Cheshire voted to suspend strike action planned for three separate days in a bid to solve a pay dispute. This followed meetings between Amicus, the employers and ACAS. Amicus members had earlier taken action in November in Chester and the Wirral. Amicus warned that if the offer was not accepted by members further strikes would take place. An overtime ban would remain in place.

Source: adapted from www.amicustheunion.org.

1 Explain the difference between strike action and an overtime ban.
2 Suggest TWO reasons why the two sides may have involved ACAS in the dispute.
3 Explain how the law might affect further strike action by members of Amicus.
4 Discuss whether employees should disrupt such an important service as bus travel which could potentially leave people stranded.

Changing industrial relations

After the year 2000 industrial relations at Levens changed in two main ways.

The Employment Relations Act 1999 forced businesses with over 21 employees to automatically recognise unions if the majority of workers were members of the union. Levens therefore had to recognise Amicus in negotiations. However, it also chose to recognise UCATT as some of its key workers were members. It felt this would improve industrial relations at the business. It might also prevent lots of individual negotiations, which could be costly and time consuming

The Employment Act 2002 allowed workers to request flexible working practices. Levens introduced a system where workers could start and then finish work early to pick up children from school. Workers felt more motivated as a result and the business was able to work in shifts so that more work was carried out.

Levens also noticed that a large multinational construction business in the UK had set up a EUROPEAN WORKS COUNCIL. This is a body made up of employee representatives and management which discusses issues such as conditions at work, redundancies, investment and training. Levens is considering buying a construction company in Holland and is thinking of setting up such a council for all workers.

key terms

Arbitration - a method of settling a dispute which involves both parties agreeing to put their case to an independent outside arbitrator and accept his or her judgement as to how the dispute should be settled.
Collective bargaining - when the representatives of workers, such as a trade unions, and the representatives of the business negotiate on issues such as pay and working conditions.
Conciliation - process of helping two parties to a dispute to discuss and settle their dispute.
Employers' or trade association - an organisation which represents the interests of the businesses which are its members.
European Works Council - a body designed to inform and consult employees in companies which operate at European Union level.
Industrial action - direct action, such as strikes or lockouts, taken by employees or employers in the course of an industrial dispute to put pressure on the other side to agree to their demands.
Industrial relations - the relationship between businesses and their workers.
Shop stewards - trade union members elected by workers in a place of work to represent their interests to management.
Trade union - an organisation which represents the interests of the workers who are its members.

NO VOICE AT WORK

Three years after the majority of UK workers won the right to be represented by a union, 6m employees in small firms are still being denied a voice at work. A TUC report says that nowhere else in Europe is there a similar bar to unions wanting to represent people in businesses with 21 or less employees.

The TUC report says there are 5.4 million employees working for businesses with less than 19 staff. Over a fifth (21.8 per cent) of the UK workforce is employed by small firms. Female workers are more likely than men to be denied a voice by the small firms' exemption, as almost a third of UK women employees, compared to 26 per cent of men, work here.

Although unions have no legal right to recognition in small companies, it is often such workers who need protection most. Small businesses usually have lower rates of pay, bigger gender pay gaps, and poorer health and safety records than larger companies which recognise unions. Despite evidence suggesting that small employers can gain a great deal from working with unions, there are no proposals for change yet. The TUC general secretary said 'The Government has paid too much attention to the irrational fears of the small business lobby. In practice, many small employers have good union relationships, and as a result have better personnel procedures and trained workforces, safer workplaces and are less likely to face employment tribunals.'

Source: adapted from www.tuc.org.uk.

1 What is meant by 'union recognition'?
2 Suggest THREE reasons why small businesses might need union recognition.
3 (a) What group is most likely to be denied union recognition?
   (b) Suggest TWO reasons why this group might not be recognised by unions.
4 What might be the 'irrational fears of small employers' in recognising unions?
5 Jack Banners runs a small bakery employing 10 staff who are all members of the same union. He has no union recognition and so workers have asked if he will negotiate with their union. Do you think he should agree to recognising a union?

Checklist ✓

1 'Collective bargaining provides a channel of communication.' What does this mean?
2 What is the purpose of a trade union?
3 State THREE areas in which a union may negotiate with employers on behalf of its members.
4 Explain the difference between a trade union member, a shop steward and a full time union official.
5 Describe THREE types of industrial action that a trade union might take.
6 What is the difference between conciliation and arbitration?
7 Why might a business want to recognise a trade union?
8 What are the advantages to a business of working with trade unions?
9 What are the advantages to a business of agreeing to flexible working practices?

Making decisions

There is a number of laws which relate to employing workers. Some affect how a business recruits workers. Others protect workers when they are employed. Businesses must have policies and procedures to make sure they stay within the law.

Zoe Calame, Colin Reeves, Ethan North and Li Weifeng work for Advantage North West, a business that designs and makes promotional materials such as lighting, props and stands in Manchester. They are all designers at the business. Their job involves thinking of ideas for promotional campaigns and advertisements, and producing the initial designs for clients.

The law

Businesses have to obey the law. If they fail to obey, they risk two things:

- they can be prosecuted by a number of government departments and agencies, such as the Health and Safety Executive, and possibly fined;
- they can be sued by people or other businesses which have lost out as a result of their actions. Damages might then have to be paid.

Getting a job

When Zoe, Colin, Ethan and Li applied for their jobs they had certain rights in law. These rights try to give all applicants EQUAL OPPORTUNITIES when seeking work. In particular employers are not allowed to DISCRIMINATE because of sex, racial origin, age or disability. Advantage North West, for instance, could not have advertised for a 'male designer, because this would have been against the Sex Discrimination Act 1975.

It could not have advertised for a designer of European origin as this would have been against the Race Relations Act 1976. It could not have advertised for a designer aged 20 as this would have been against the Age Discrimination Act 2006.

The Disability Discrimination Act 1995, amended in 2005, says that employers are not allowed to discriminate against disabled people when recruiting or promoting. Disabled applicants must be given a job when they are clearly the best applicant. The only exception to this is if there are 'substantial reasons' for not doing so. These reasons might include, for example, having to make hugely costly adjustments to a building so that one disabled person can do the job there.

The Disability Discrimination Act says that small and medium sized businesses have to make 'reasonable adjustments' so they do not discriminate against disabled employees. For instance, Ethan suffers from arthritis which prevents him from driving. However, he is an excellent designer and his job does not require him to drive. Asking for a driving licence when the job requires no driving would be discrimination. His arthritis also means that he can have gripping problems. The company agreed to alter certain equipment to help him use the computer keyboard. This might be a reasonable adjustment.

Figure 1 shows how laws have helped to promote greater equal opportunities between men and women, although it could be argued that discrimination does still exist to some extent.

Playing unfair

After a new coach was appointed by a professional rugby club, the coach told a player that he would not be selected for the team however well he played. The coach gave the player no idea that his performance was not up to scratch. No other player was treated like this. The player felt that his treatment must have been as a result of his Caribbean background. So he took his complaint to an employment tribunal.

The tribunal decided that it had not been given any explanation as to why the player was not given a chance to compete on the team. At a later meeting the player was awarded a five figure sum in damages for loss of earnings and injury to feelings. The club was ordered to reinstate him on the same terms as his last contract. The MD and coach were ordered to give written apologies and issue a press release as a public apology.

Source: adapted from www.cre.gov.uk.

1 'The rugby club failed to give all players equal opportunities'. What does this mean?
2 (a) How did the club suffer initially as a result of the decision? (b) Suggest how else the business might suffer in future.

Then	Now
Only one in four of both boys and girls in England & Wales passed five O levels by the time they left school.	49% of boys and 59% of girls in the UK gain five high grade GCSEs or equivalent by age 16.
Nine out of ten men and six out of ten women of working age were in employment.	Employment rates are 79% for men and 70% for women of working age.
Around one in ten professionals were women.	Women hold two-fiths of professional jobs.
The gap between women's and men's full-time hourly pay was 29%.	Women earn on average 17% per hour less than men for full-time work.
Two-thirds of workers in public administration were men and 55% of workers in the distribution sector were women.	The workforce in wholesale & retail is almost equally split between women & men, as is that in public administration & defence.
Half of mothers with dependent children worked, including over a quarter of mothers of under fives.	Two-thirds of women with dependent children work and 55% of those with children under five.

Figure 1 *Work changes, 1970 to 2006*
Source: adapted from *Facts About Men & Women*, Equal Opportunities Commission, 2006.

Starting work

Zoe, Colin, Ethan and Li signed a CONTRACT OF EMPLOYMENT with Advantage North West before they started work. This is an agreement between the employer and the employee.

It includes conditions such as rates of pay, hours of work, holidays, pension contributions, and the amount of notice that must be given if the worker wants to leave or if the employer wants to make the worker redundant. Under the Employment Rights Act 1996, employees must be given a written statement of the conditions within two months of starting work.

Under the Equal Pay Act 1970 female employees must be paid the same rate of pay as male employees if they are doing the same job, a similar job or a job with equal demands. So Advantage North West could be acting illegally if it paid Ethan or Colin more than Zoe because they were male employees, when all their jobs were equally demanding in terms of skills, effort, tasks and responsibility. The Minimum Wage Act 1998 also sets out minimum wages that must be paid to employees. A new employee aged 19 was taken on in the workshop on Jan 1 2007. He was paid £4.45 per hour, the rate for 18-21 year olds at the time.

Protection at work

Figure 2 shows that work can be a dangerous place to be. Advantage North West, like any business, needs to conform to the Health and Safety at Work Act 1974. This lays down standards of **health** and **safety** that must be met. The workshop is visited by inspectors from the Health and Safety Executive, the body responsible for checking that the 1974 Act is being followed. For example, the business must ensure that dangerous materials used in the making of props are safely stored. The business also has a health and safety policy which it must display, and must ensure that employees comply with the policy.

Another aspect of safety is the **length of time** employees work. The Working Time Regulations 1998 say that employees can not be made to work longer than 48 hours on average a week, although there are exceptions. There is other

Jo Keely has just been appointed at Nelson-James Ltd, a haulage company. She has been sent a written statement showing conditions of her contract of employment to sign.

1 Give THREE conditions of employment mentioned in the contract.
2 What would happen if Jo Keely wanted to leave the company, according to the contract?
3 After six months at work, Jo Keely was reprimanded by her line manager on safety grounds for carrying out a minor repair. Jo disagreed. Where might Jo have found out whether she was allowed to carry out the repair?

Statement of main terms and conditions of employment

Nelson-James
Unit 57
Calleva Park
Industrial Estate
Reading

Ms J Keely
3 Fairfield Drive
Aldermaston
Reading

Dear Ms Keely

I have pleasure in confirming your appointment as a haulage operator with effect from 1 June 2007.

Pay and hours of work Your wages will be at the rate of £10.20 per hour. Your basic pay per week will be £337.40. Overtime will be paid at time and quarter up to six o'clock in the evening Monday to Friday and time and a half at other times. Your hours of work will be 37 hours. The company reserves the right to choose when you work those hours between 8 a.m. and 6 p.m. Monday to Friday.

Annual Leave Your annual leave entitlement is 20 working days plus statutory bank holidays.

Notice Your appointment is terminable by 4 weeks notice on either side.

Continuous employment For the purpose of the Employment Protection (Consolidation) Act, the start of your period of continuous service is 1 June 2007.

Disciplinary As an employee of Nelson-James, you are protected by its Disciplinary Policy, a copy of which may be obtained from the Personnel Department.

Health and Safety at Work Your attention is drawn to the Company's 'Statement of General Policy', a copy of which may be obtained from the Personnel Department.

Yours sincerely

Mr M Murphy
Human Resources Manager

Form of Acceptance

I hereby accept the appointment mentioned in the foregoing Contract on the terms and conditions referred to in it and return one copy signed.

Date .... Signature ....

119

protection. By law employees must also be given paid annual leave. Advantage North West gives five weeks leave, although the minimum by law is 4 weeks. Regulations also say that employees must be given a 20 minute break every 6 hours worked.

Li's wife has just had a baby and he is taking two weeks' **leave**. The Employment Act 2002 says that parents are entitled to maternity and paternity leave with pay. It also says that workers may work flexible hours. Zoe and Ethan have asked if they could start earlier and finish in time to pick up their children from school. If the business can not find a valid reason why not, it must agree to this.

Advantage North West must also be aware of **equal opportunities**. If an employee applied for a senior post in the business he or she must have the same chance as any other employee. It would be illegal to discriminate against Zoe because she was a woman and employ Ethan, discriminate against Ethan because he was older and employ Li, or discriminate against Li because he was from an ethic minority and employ Colin.

Advantage North West employs 50 workers. Workers have the right

to belong to **trade unions**. The Employment Relations Act 1999 says that any business employing over 21 workers must **recognise** trade unions if the majority of workers want this. All four employees belong to the T&G union. This represents workers' interests in pay bargaining. It would also support them if they took **industrial action**, such as a strike.

Leaving work

The law also affect workers when they leave their job.

Finding a new job Workers who have found new jobs have to resign from their posts. They will then have to 'work out their notice'. Their contracts of employment state how much notice workers need to give employers when leaving. Contracts

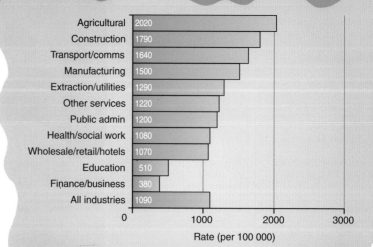

at Advantage North West say that a month's notice must be given.

Retirement Most workers pay into a pension scheme so that they can receive a pension when they retire. The law doesn't force a business to have a pension scheme but Advantage North West has one. Zoe, Colin, Ethan and Li make monthly payments into a scheme with Norwich Union. The business also makes payments into their schemes. They will also receive a state pension when they retire. They make employees' National Insurance contributions into the state scheme each month. The business makes employers' National Insurance contributions.

Redundancy A business may make workers redundant if it faces difficult trading conditions. Three years ago the business faced falling orders and made 5 workers redundant. Under the Employment Rights Act 1996 a business can only make workers redundant if their job 'no longer exists'. Nearly all workers made redundant are entitled to redundancy payment. A period of notice must be given before redundancy takes place.

Dismissal In law, workers can be dismissed (i.e. sacked) if they are unable to do the job or there is misconduct. Last year a worker was found to be taking regular lunch

	Rate (per 100 000)
Agricultural	2020
Construction	1790
Transport/comms	1640
Manufacturing	1500
Extraction/utilities	1290
Other services	1220
Public admin	1200
Health/social work	1080
Wholesale/retail/hotels	1070
Education	510
Finance/business	380
All industries	1090

Figure 2 *Estimated rates of reportable non-fatal injuries to workers, average 2003/04 - 2005/06*
Source: adapted from Health and Safety Executive.

Flexible Foods

Northern Foods is a member of the Employers' Alliance for Work-Life Balance. It has introduced a range of flexible working policies, including paternity leave, flexible shift-working, compassionate leave, and, at one or two sites, after school clubs. Fox's Biscuits, for example, offers 80 different shifts, allowing parents to combine work and childcare responsibilities. The 9 am to 4 pm shift is popular with parents who need to get children to school in the morning. Other employees, such as students or those with out of work commitments such as voluntary work, also benefit. The company has introduced a new maternity policy for management and supervisors. Asked why Northern Foods has taken these initiatives, Phil Ward, Corporate Affairs Executive, feels instinctively that it is a good thing to do. 'One of the biggest issues facing the growth of the business is recruitment. So we have broadened our thinking about how we can get more people to apply and stay in the business. Flexibility is the key to our approach. Instead of saying these are the hours, we ask people what hours they are prepared to work, and do what we can to make it possible'.

Source: adapted from www.eoc.org.uk.

1 Using an example from the case, explain how legislation might have affected Northern Foods.
2 Explain TWO benefits to the business of its approach.
3 A food manufacturer which does not have shift work is hoping to recruit 30 new staff. Should the business allow them all to work flexible hours?

Unfair dismissal?

Mike King was a sheet metal worker at Leefields Ltd. He was dismissed last year after the company told him that he took too long with his work. Mike took his case to an employment tribunal and won an unfair dismissal case.

The tribunal heard that the first time the employee felt his job was in jeopardy was on the actual date he was dismissed. Although the tribunal felt that verbal warning could be as effective as written ones, it argued that what a business feels is serious warning could be interpreted by the employee as a passing comment. Mike was awarded damages and reinstated.

Source: adapted in part from www.industrialrelations.nsw.gov.au.

1 What is meant by 'unfair dismissal'?
2 Explain why the employment tribunal decided that Mike's case was a case of unfair dismissal.
3 Suggest how the business could prevent a similar situation happening in future.

breaks in excess of what he was entitled to. Before dismissal warnings must be issued. The business first issues a formal verbal warning to the worker. But he carried on exceeding his lunch break time and so Advantage North West issued a written warning. With no improvement in the situation the business finally sacked him.

In more serious cases, a worker can be sacked immediately, for example in cases of gross misconduct such as failure to observe safety regulations, theft or fighting. A designer was sacked at Advantage North West when he was found to be drunk at work and attacked a fellow worker.

If Advantage North West had not gone through the correct procedures of verbal and written

warnings, the worker taking too long over lunch breaks could have taken his case to an EMPLOYMENT TRIBUNAL on grounds of unfair dismissal. An employment tribunal hears claims about matters to do with employment and deals with issues such as **unfair dismissal**, discrimination at work and sexual harassment. It is like a court but unlike most courts lawyers do not have to be used. People can argue their own case in front of the tribunal. The tribunal is informal, with members listening to presentations and asking questions to find out about what happened. The idea is that the law is accessible to every worker. The tribunal has the power to order a business to pay damages or compensation to workers if it is breaking the law or reinstate workers in cases of unfair dismissal.

SUMMARY CASE STUDY

CARPETCLEAN

Richard Astles runs a 'green' carpet business. He specialises in recycling old carpets for new uses although he also sells new carpets. He has been particularly successful in buying large areas of carpet from businesses with office premises which have gone bankrupt and cutting them down into smaller sizes. Often parts of the carpet will be as good as new. At other times he uses cleaning materials to ensure the carpets are in first class condition.

Richard employs 10 people in his business. Two people work in administration, two in sales, and the others work in cleaning, cutting and delivering carpets. Richard is now looking to expand. He wants to hire another sales person, hoping to find new markets of which he is currently not taking advantage. Richard is aware that he must be careful to pay the new person the same rate as his current sales people as they will be doing the same job. Richard has produced an advertisement to go into both local papers and also into magazines with a 'green theme'. He will also advertise in trade journals.

Richard is also looking for ways to motivate his workforce and increase productivity. He has recently reviewed both his health and safety policy and his work arrangements. He has decided to allow workers to vary their hours. He has also extended the lunch break by ten minutes and now carries out regular checks that all materials are being used and stored correctly.

Source: adapted from www.cre.gov.uk, www.eoc.org.uk, www.hse.gov.uk.

1 Explain why Richard must be careful to 'pay the new person the same rate as his current sales people'.
2 Explain THREE ways in which equal opportunities legislation might affect how Richard advertises for the new salesperson.
3 (a) Explain the benefits and problems for the business in changing its operations.
(b) Do you think that Richard has made the right decision to change operations?

key terms

Contract of employment - an agreement between the employer and employee about the conditions under which the employee will work, including rates of pay and holiday entitlements.
Discrimination - favouring one person rather than another. In the UK, it is illegal to discriminate in most jobs on grounds of gender or race.
Employment tribunal - court which deals with the law relating to employment.
Equal opportunities - where everyone has the same chance.

Checklist ✓

1 'Businesses are not allowed to discriminate on grounds of gender or race.' Explain what this means.
2 What help does the law give to disabled people wanting to work?
3 What information does a contract of employment contain?
4 A man and a woman are paid different rates of pay for doing exactly the same job in a company. Is this legal? Explain your answer.
5 What help does the law give to workers on health and safety issues?
6 What does the law say about (a) trade unions and (b) working time in a workplace?
7 On what grounds can a business dismiss a worker?
8 Describe the work of an employment tribunal.

Making decisions

The costs and revenue of a business will determine the profit it makes. If the business wants to maximise profits, it needs to earn the highest possible revenue and to reduce cost to a minimum. To do this, it must know where its revenues are coming from and what are its costs.

Tettenhall Glazing is a small business owned by Shana Barghouti. She employs her brother, Amun, and another worker, Josh, to make windows. Most of her work comes from individual households which ask her business to replace individual windows in their properties. But she also gets some work from local building companies which subcontract window work to the business.

Profit

Shana Barghouti is a sole trader. She wants her business to grow and make profits. Her PROFIT is the difference between the value of what she sells (her SALES REVENUE or TURNOVER) and her costs of production. This is calculated over a period of time, like six months or a year.

Profit = Sales revenue - costs

In practice, there are many ways of expressing **profit**, such as gross profit, net profit, profit before tax and profit after tax, each of which has a very precise definition. All of them, however, are a measure of some type of revenue minus some type of cost.

Sales revenue or sales turnover

Shana Barghouti is very interested in the **sales revenue** or **sales turnover** of her business. This is the value of the sales of the business. When she first started the business, sales had been poor and she had failed to make a profit. However, over time, sales revenue had grown and the business began to make a profit. This was a sign that the business was doing better.

Shana Barghouti charges an average £800 for making and installing a window. If she sells 10 windows in a week, her weekly sales turnover would be 10 times £800, which is equal to £8 000. If she sells 500 windows a year, her yearly sales turnover would be 500 times £800 which is £400 000.

Windows come in all shapes and sizes. A small window might sell for just £400. A large window might be £2 000. This shows that there are at least two ways of calculating sales turnover.

?

Kingfisher plc in 2006 was the world's third largest home improvement retailer. In the UK, it owned B&Q. DSG International plc in 2006 was Europe's largest specialist electrical retailing group. In the UK, it owned Currys, PC World and Pixmania.

1 Calculate the profit for Kingfisher plc for each year between 2002 and 2006.
2 Calculate the costs for DSG International plc for each year between 2002 and 2006.
3 Which company do you think performed best over the period 2002 to 2006 and why?

Table 1 *Kingfisher plc, turnover and costs for each year to 28 January*

£ million

	2002	2003	2004	2005	2006
Sales turnover	5 119	6 136	7 044	7 656	8 010
Costs	5 091	5 535	6 473	7 008	7 778

Table 2 *DSG International plc, turnover and profit for each year to 29 April*

£ million

	2002	2003	2004	2005	2006
Sales turnover	4 502	5 368	6 051	6 554	7 072
Profit[1]	257	276	366	337	303

1 Profit on ordinary activities before taxation.

Source: adapted from Kingfisher plc and DSG International plc, *Annual Report and Accounts*.

Haycraft Dry Cleaning Services

Rosemary Haycraft runs a dry cleaning business. But it is not just any ordinary dry cleaner. Its premises are on an industrial estate and it relies for most of its custom from internet and telephone orders. Customers either email or telephone and the clothes are collected from the customer's home or business address. They are then returned to that address. It takes the hassle for customers out of having to visit a dry cleaning shop twice to drop off and collect their clothes. In 2006, the business had sales worth £300 000 and dry cleaned 10 000 garments.

1 (a) What was the sales revenue for Rosemary Haycraft in 2006?
  (b) How many garments did her business clean?
  (c) Calculate the average price of each garment cleaned.
2 If this average price stayed the same, how many garments would she have had to dry clean in order to achieve sales revenues of (a) £450 000; (b) £600 000; (d) £750 000?
3 Explain why sales revenue is important to Rosemary Haycraft.

- Sales turnover is equal to the **average price** of the products **times** the number (or **volume**) sold. At an average price of £800, selling 100 windows, turnover would be £80 000.
- Sales turnover is equal to the sum of the sales turnover of each different window sold. For example, if Shana Barghouti sold 10 windows at £800 each and 5 windows at £400 each, her total turnover would be £8 000 (10 x £800) plus £2 000 (5 x £400) making a combined total of £10 000 .

Fixed and variable costs

Shana Barghouti has to pay a number of different costs. She has to pay for the wood and glass to make windows. She pays herself a wage and also has to pay wages to her two other workers. There is the rent to pay on the small industrial unit where she makes windows, as well as costs like the telephone and electricity. She runs a van to transport materials and windows. The business also sometimes has a small overdraft at the bank on which she has to pay interest.

Some of the costs stay the same however much is produced. For instance, it costs the same in rent whether 10 windows are made in a week or none. Costs which don't vary with output are called FIXED COSTS.

One very important fact to realise about fixed costs is that they have to be paid even if nothing is produced. If the business closed down for six weeks over the Christmas period due to lack of orders, it would still have to pay all its fixed costs during this period. A fixed cost line is shown in Figure 1. It shows that the business has to pay out £100 000 each year however much is produced.

Some costs vary directly with the amount produced. For instance, the total cost of wood used goes up if more windows are made. Costs which vary with output are called VARIABLE COSTS. A variable cost curve is shown in Figure 2. This shows that the average variable cost per window made was £500.

TOTAL COSTS are the sum of these different types of cost. It is usual to assume that all costs are fixed or variable. So total costs equal fixed costs plus variable costs. A total cost line is shown in Figure 3. It is drawn by adding together the fixed and variable cost lines.

Direct and indirect costs

Some fixed costs are called **overhead costs** or **indirect costs**. Variable costs are then called **direct costs**. For a small business, fixed and overhead costs are likely to be the same. However, strictly speaking, in a large business like a

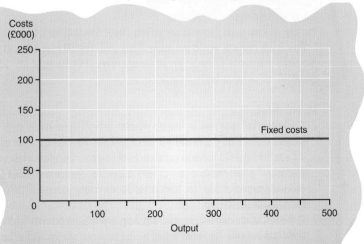

Figure 1 *Tettenhall Glazing's fixed costs. Whatever the level of output, fixed costs stay the same. This is why the fixed cost line is horizontal on the diagram.*

public company or a multinational, fixed costs and overhead costs have different meanings. Direct costs are the costs of production like wood in windows. Indirect costs are all other costs like office costs or advertising.

Shana keeps a constant watch on costs. If costs rise when sales revenue stays the same, her profits will be squeezed. Reducing costs, on the other hand, with revenues constant will lead to a rise in profits.

Shana uses costs when pricing products. She knows that in the long run the business needs to set prices which will covers its total costs. However, sometimes when business is slack, she is prepared to sell windows at a price which at least covers the variable cost, but doesn't include all of the fixed costs of production. This is because any order which helps pay off at least some of the fixed cost is worth taking if the alternative is that the business would be idle for some of the time. This is known as **contribution cost pricing**.

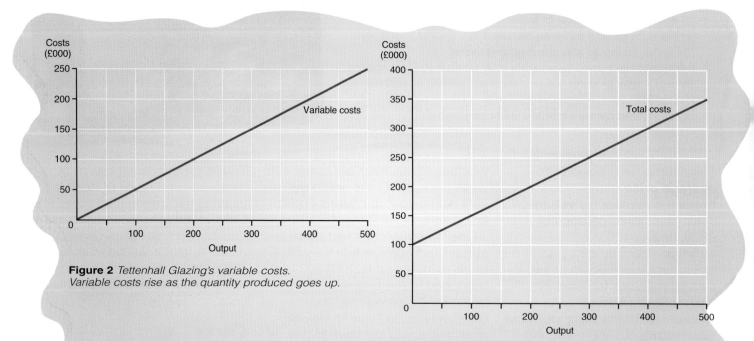

Figure 2 *Tettenhall Glazing's variable costs. Variable costs rise as the quantity produced goes up.*

Figure 3 *Tettenhall Glazing's total costs.*

The CakeMake Company

You are finance director of the CakeMake Company. Your mini-company idea has been to make cakes and sell them to adults at various school functions, such as school concerts, jumble sales and open evenings.

You are making some financial projections about revenues for a future school fete.

1 How much revenue would you make if you sold: (a) 60 fairy cakes at 5p each? (b) 20 large chocolate gateaux at £2 each? (c) 30 sponge cakes at £1.00 each? (d) 50 chocolate brownies at 20p each? (e) all of (a) to (d)?

Spreadsheet

2 You know that your task as finance director, projecting revenues, costs and profits, would be simpler if you used a spreadsheet package. Enter the data for price and sales of each type of cake on a spreadsheet in order to calculate total revenue. Calculate what would happen to total revenues if prices changed to: (a) fairy cakes 10p, chocolate gateaux £3, sponge cakes £1.50 and chocolate brownies 30p; (b) fairy cakes 3p, chocolate gateaux £1.50, sponge cakes 75p and chocolate brownies 15p.

3 If the cost of making a fairy cake was 2.5p, a chocolate gateaux £1.25, a sponge cake 60p and a chocolate brownie 12p, what would be the total cost of making the batch of cakes for the fete?

4 What would be the profit at each of the three levels of prices?

5 Assuming that you could sell all the cakes, which level of prices would you choose to charge and why?

key terms

Fixed costs - costs which remain the same whatever the level of output of the business.

Profit - the difference between sales revenue and costs.

Sales revenue or turnover - the money value of the sale of products by a business.

Total costs - all the costs incurred by a business over a period of time. It is equal to fixed cost plus variable cost.

Variable costs - costs which vary directly with the output of the business.

Many businesses offer leisure facilities to customers. Sometimes cinemas, theatres and concert halls are only open for part of the day. Look at the photographs.

1 Explain what you think the fixed costs of these businesses might be.
2 Explain what might be their variable costs.
3 How do these businesses earn revenue?
4 (a) Suggest TWO ways in which the businesses could increase their revenue.
  (b) What are the likely effects of these suggestions on: (i) fixed costs; and (ii) variable costs?

Checklist ✓

1 How is profit calculated?
2 A business increases its profit but costs too have increased. What must have happened?
3 A business sells dresses at an average price of £10. What is the sales turnover of the business if its weekly sales are: (a) 10 dresses; (b) 100 dresses; (c) 898 dresses?
4 The monthly turnover of a company is £2 million. The turnover of its tractor division was £0.5 million. What was the monthly turnover of the rest of the company?
5 What is the difference between a fixed cost and a variable cost?
6 List: (a) two fixed costs; and (b) two variable costs which a music shop is likely to face.
  Which of the following are likely to be (i) fixed costs and (ii) variable costs for a garden centre:
  (a) fertilizer; (b) a new car park; (c) ice creams; (d) plant pots; (e) the manager's salary; (f) a new potting shed; (g) new tables and chairs for the restaurant?

SUMMARY CASE STUDY

PETS HAVENS

Pets Havens is a business which is now two years old. Set up by Kevin and Emma, it provides a mobile pet-grooming service. They decided there was a gap in the market in their local area of Bournemouth and hope to expand the business to cover other services such as providing kennels for overnight accommodation for pets.

To start the business, they took out a loan for £20 000 repayable over five years. Most of this was used to pay for two vans. A small van transports equipment to allow grooming in the client's home. A large van acts as mobile premises and 'doggie makeovers' are given in the van itself. Around £5 000 was used to buy equipment for the business and set up a website. Kevin and Emma are paying back the loan at a rate of £400 per month.

They have a variety of other costs which stay the same however much work they complete. For example, they pay an accountant to sort out their finances. They have to pay insurance on their vans and for their business. They also advertise in Yellow Pages. These costs add up to £5 200 a year.

Each visit they make to a client costs money too. There are petrol costs as well as the cost of shampoos and other grooming materials. These costs work out at £5 per session.

The average price they charge clients is £20 per session. Kevin and Emma complete around ten sessions a day, which, by the time you take holidays into account, is 2 000 sessions a year.

1 Make a list of Kevin and Emma's (a) fixed costs and (b) variable costs in running their business which are mentioned in the article.
2 (a) How many pet grooming sessions do they sell each year? (b) What is the average price paid by customers for each pet grooming session? (c) What is Kevin and Emma's total sales revenue for the year?
3 Kevin and Emma have worked out that their total fixed costs are £10 000 per year. Explain how they have calculated this.
4 (a) What is their variable cost per pet grooming session? (b) What is their total variable costs per year?
5 Calculate the value of their total costs - their total variable costs plus their total fixed costs.
6 How much profit do they make over a year by giving 2000 pet grooming sessions?
7 Would they have made a profit if they had only completed 400 sessions in a year? Explain your answer.
8 What might be the advantages and disadvantages for them of expanding their business to offer kennels for overnight accommodation of pets?

Making decisions

Businesses have to decide how much to produce. Nearly all businesses need at least to break even in order to survive. One way in which businesses can plan is to draw up budgets. Once a draft budget is drawn up, the business must decide whether or not it is going to change its plans because of what the budget shows. Another way is for businesses to calculate the break-even point of production. Will sales levels be high enough for the business to cover its costs and make a profit?

Olivia Rollay is planning her spending over the next four weeks. Her dad, Wayne, is planning his spending for the next 12 months. He runs a business, Rollay Boxes, which manufactures stackable plastic storage boxes used in schools, offices and homes. They are doing this on Budget day, the day when the Chancellor of the Exchequer, the person responsible for the government's finances, is announcing the government's tax and spending plans for the year. They are all calculating a budget.

Budgets

A BUDGET is a **forecast** of what might happen. Table 1 shows Olivia Rollay's budget. She gets £80 a month from her parents and earns £40 a month from a part time job. Her monthly income is therefore £120. She plans to spend it on clothes, food and going out. She hopes to have £10 left over to save.

The budget shown in Table 2 for Rollay Boxes is more complex. Wayne Rollay has been manufacturing plastic stacker boxes for five years and sales have been steadily increasing. He forecasts that he will be able to sell 100 000 boxes next year. At £2 each, this will give his business total sales turnover of £200 000.

Out of that, he has various costs to pay. His raw material costs, such as plastic, come to 50 pence per box. Making 100 000 boxes will therefore cost him £50 000 in raw materials. His wage bill for himself and three employees comes to £60 000. Then he has rent to pay for his industrial unit which comes to £25 000 per year. Administration costs, such as paying for an accountant to do his books, come to £15 000 a year. Finally, other costs, including a company car for himself, come to £20 000.

The budget shows that the estimated profit for the year is £30 000.

Uncertainty

A budget is only a forecast. Many things can happen which could make the actual outturn different from what was budgeted. For instance, Wayne may find that he doesn't sell 100 000 boxes next year. Or the cost of his raw materials may go up in price. The Chancellor of the Exchequer may put up the rate of employers' National Contributions that he has to pay for for each of his employees. The Bank of England may put up interest rates, increasing the interest payments on his overdraft. Or Wayne may decide half way through the year to lease a less expensive company car.

Budgets are vital for a business because they help it to plan its finances. If Wayne Rollay had produced a budget which showed that he would make a £20 000 loss instead of £30 000 profit, he would have had to consider what to do.

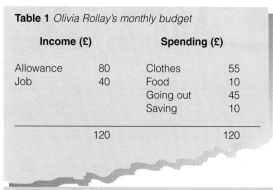

Table 1 *Olivia Rollay's monthly budget*

Income (£)		Spending (£)	
Allowance	80	Clothes	55
Job	40	Food	10
		Going out	45
		Saving	10
	120		120

Table 2 *12 month budget for Rollay Boxes*

Revenue (£)		Costs (£)	
Sales	200 000	Raw materials	50 000
		Wages	60 000
		Rent	25 000
		Administration costs	15 000
		Other costs	20 000
			170 000
		Profit	30 000
	200 000		200 000

Wayne Rollay has not had a good year. Instead of making a £30 000 profit as he budgeted in Table 2, he in fact made a £10 000 loss. He sold the 100 000 boxes he predicted but both his sale prices and costs proved disappointing

1 Table 3 shows what actually happened to Rollay Boxes in its next year of operations. Compare it with the projected budget in Table 2. What is the difference between what Wayne Rollay budgeted for and what actually happened? Suggest why the outturn was different from the forecast.

2 Is Rollay Boxes now in difficulty?

3 Wayne Rollay has drawn up a budget for the next 12 months. Write down this budget assuming that:
(a) he sells 120 000 boxes at £1.50 each;
(b) his raw material costs are 50p per box ;
(c) he makes one worker redundant and saves £15 000 on his wage bill;
(d) all other costs remain the same as in the outturn for the last year shown in Table 3.

4 (a) According to this new budget, will Rollay Boxes be in financial difficulty? Explain your answer. (b) Suggest TWO ways in which Wayne Rollay could improve his financial position.

Spreadsheet

5 Use a spreadsheet package to draw up a range of budget forecasts for next year based upon the year's outturn in Table 3.
(a) Get a printout showing the budget for sales of 80 000, 90 000, 100 000, 110 000 and 120 000 boxes assuming prices to his customers of £1.80, £1.90, and £2.00. Assume the price of the cost of raw materials are 60p per box and the other costs remain the same.
(b) Now, assuming a sales price to his customers of £1.80, draw up a spreadsheet showing a range of budget forecasts if raw material costs per box are is £0.50, £0.60, and £0.70 with all other costs the same.

Table 3 *12 month outturn for Rollay Boxes*

Revenue (£)		Costs (£)	
Sales	180 000	Raw materials	60 000
		Wages	65 000
		Rent	25 000
		Administration costs	15 000
		Other costs	25 000
			190 000
		Loss	(10 000)
	180 000		180 000

Would the loss simply be temporary? Should he try to increase sales or reduce costs to get him back to profitability? Would he be better off in the long term finding a different product to manufacture?

Break-even

Wayne Rollay had forecast a profit of £30 000 for next year. However, the actual profit may be less than this if he sells fewer boxes or his costs are higher. He wants to know at what point he would just BREAK EVEN. The break-even point is the one where he would neither make a profit nor a loss. He is going to use the figures in his draft budget in Table 2 as a basis for his projections.

The simplest break-even calculation involves total revenue, total fixed costs and total variable costs.

Total revenue Total revenue can be calculated by multiplying average revenue and the quantity sold. The average revenue in this case is the price of each box

which is £2. Table 4 shows how total revenue rises as the number of boxes sold rises. At 20 000 sales, it is £40 000. At 60 000 sales, it is £120 000. At 100 000 sales, it is £200 000.

Total variable cost The only variable cost for the business is the cost of raw materials such as plastics. This is £0.50 per box. So if Wayne sells 20 000 boxes, the total variable cost would be

Budgeting at High Valley School

The economics and business studies department at High Valley School has been given £4 000 to spend on books and other resources by the headteacher. The department would like to buy the following textbooks: 100 copies of *GCSE Business Studies* by Alain Anderton at £17 each; 50 copies of *Economics for GCSE* by Alain Anderton at £20 each; 10 copies of *A Level Business Studies for AQA* by Alain Anderton at £22 each; 20 copies of *Economics* by Alain Anderton at £25 each. These prices include any discount given. The department needs to spend £500 on paper and exercise books. It would like to buy £300 worth of computer accessories including disks. It needs to set aside £500 for photocopying over the year. It would also like to have £300 for buying single books and resource packs. The head of department is grateful that her £4 000 budget doesn't have to cover her new applied GCSE courses for which there is a separate budget.

1 Draw up a draft budget for the department. Set it out as in Tables 1 and 2.
2 The department can't overspend its £4 000 allowance given by the headteacher. Explain whether the budget shows there is a problem for the department.
3 How could the head of department resolve any problem?

20 000 x £0.50 or £10 000. Selling 100 000 boxes would give a variable cost of 100 000 x £0.50 or £50 000.

Total fixed cost All the other costs are fixed costs. They do not vary whether he sells 20 000 or 100 000 boxes. So Wayne's total fixed costs are £120 000.

Table 4 shows that the break-even point, where total costs equal total revenue, is at 80 000 boxes per year. If sales are more than this, the business will make a profit. If they are below this level, the business will make a loss.

Break-even charts

The information in Table 4 can be shown on a graph, called a BREAK-EVEN CHART. In Figure 1, the total revenue line starts at 0 because with no sales, there is no revenue. It rises as every extra sale brings in an extra £2 of revenue.

The total cost line does not start at 0. This is because, whatever the number of sales, there will always be fixed costs of £120 000. The total fixed cost line is therefore a straight horizontal line across the chart. However, total variable cost

does increase as sales increase. It is equal to the distance between the total cost line and the total fixed cost line. In this case, it is equal to total cost minus £120 000. The total cost line (equal to the sum of total fixed cost and total variable cost) starts therefore at £120 000 and then rises.

The BREAK-EVEN POINT is where the total cost and total revenue lines cross. This is at a sales level of 80 000 and at a total cost and revenue level of £160 000. To the right of the point, Rollay Boxes will make a profit whilst to the left it will make a loss.

The number of sales above the break-even point is known as the MARGIN OF SAFETY. It is the range of output over which a profit can be made.

Table 4 Break-even analysis for Rollay Boxes

£ per year

Sales	Total revenue (average price, £2, x quantity sold)	Total fixed cost	Total variable cost (£0.50 x quantity sold)	Total cost (fixed cost plus variable cost)	Profit/loss (total revenue minus total cost)[1]
20 000	40 000	120 000	10 000	130 000	(90 000)
40 000	80 000	120 000	20 000	140 000	(60 000)
60 000	120 000	120 000	30 000	150 000	(30 000)
80 000	160 000	120 000	40 000	160 000	0
100 000	200 000	120 000	50 000	170 000	30 000

1 Losses are shown by putting bracket around the number.

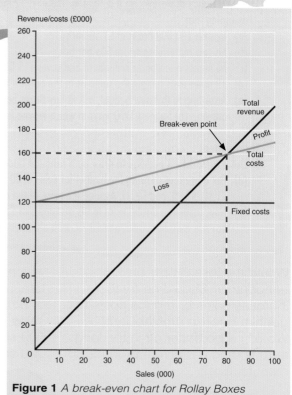

Figure 1 A break-even chart for Rollay Boxes

The Boutique Hotel

Elliot John runs the Boutique Hotel. They have 15 rooms and can accommodate up to 25 visitors. The average guest pays £50 per night for bed and breakfast. In addition, they spend £10 on an evening meal. Most costs are the same whether the hotel is full or half empty; these are the wages of staff, business rates, repairs, etc., which come to £750 per day. Some bills, however, vary according to the number of rooms occupied, such as heating and lighting and laundry bills. These variable costs on average come to £6 per guest. The food cost for the hotel of an evening meal comes to £4 per meal.

Table 5

£ per night

Number of guests	Total revenue	Total fixed cost	Total variable cost	Total cost
5				
10				
15				
20				
25				

1 Complete Table 5, showing revenues and costs changing as the number of guests per night change.
2 Draw a break-even chart from your calculations in Table 5. Remember to put quantity (i.e. the number of guests per night) along the horizontal axis and costs and revenues on the vertical axis.
   You must have a total revenue line, a total fixed cost line and a total cost line on the graph.
3 Mark the break-even point on the chart.
4 It is June. The average number of guests staying per night so far this year has been 10.
   (a) Explain whether or not you think Elliot has a problem.
   (b) How could Elliot reduce the break-even point do you think?

Using break-even charts

Break-even charts can be constructed to show the break-even point on past production. This gives a guide to what the current break-even point might be. However, Wayne Rollay was using break-even analysis to forecast profit. Any forecast is more than

likely to be wrong because the figures on which the forecast is based will change in reality.

For Wayne Rollay, the forecast was very important. It allowed him to see what risks he was taking over the next 12 months. As the first year went by, he had a good understanding of how he was doing and whether or not he was heading for a profit or a loss. The

bank manager who originally gave him an overdraft facility also wanted to see Wayne's **business plan**. This included the break-even forecast. The bank manager used it to discuss whether he would be likely to meet the sales targets needed to break even and be able to afford the overdraft.

SUMMARY CASE STUDY

STAYFRESH BAKERIES

Stayfresh Bakeries bakes bread and sells it to wholesalers. On average, each loaf is sold for 50p. Figure 2 shows production in millions of loaves of bread.
1 What is the break-even point of sales?
2 What is the current margin of safety (in quantity of loaves) if production is 1.2 million loaves?
3 How much profit is the business currently making?

Draw the axes for a break-even chart running from 0 to 1.5 million loaves on the horizontal axis and 0 to £750 000 on the vertical axis. (You will find this easier if you use graph paper.)
4 Stayfresh Bakeries gives staff a pay rise and buys new machinery. This increases fixed costs by £50 000 a year. Plot the new fixed cost line on your diagram.
5 The cost of flour goes up. This increases the variable cost of a loaf of bread by 8 per cent, from 25p per loaf to 27p. Plot the new total cost line on your diagram.
6 Stayfresh Bakeries increases its prices by 4 per cent, from 50p per loaf to 52p per loaf to cover these increases in costs. Plot the new revenue line on your diagram.
7 What has happened: (a) to the break-even point; and (b) to profit on sales of 1.2 million loaves?
8 The aim of the company is to make £50 000 profit per year. Suggest how the business could do this.

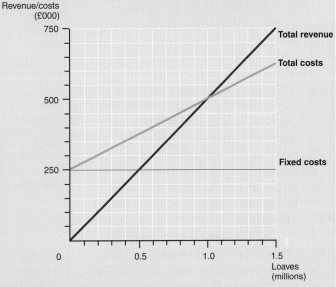

Figure 2 *A break-even chart for Stayfresh Bakeries*

Checklist ✓

1 'A budget is a forecast.' What does this mean?
2 Each March, the Chancellor of the Exchequer announces The Budget. What is in The Budget?
3 A business draws up a budget which shows that its costs over the next month will be £1 000 whilst its revenues will be £900. It wants to make a profit during the month. How can this information help in its planning?
4 Why might an actual business' finances be different from what it planned in its budget for the period?
5 Three lines are normally drawn on a break-even chart. What are they?
6 Why is the fixed cost line on a break-even chart horizontal?
7 How much profit does a business make at its break-even point?
8 A business is currently producing 1 000 units per week and it is making a profit. Its break-even point is 600 units per week. (a) What is its margin of safety? (b) How would its margin of safety change if the break-even point: (i) rose to 800 units; (ii) dropped to 300 units?
9 Why do businesses calculate their break-even points?

Making decisions

How does a business and its competitors assess whether it is trading successfully? How does an individual or a pension fund manager know which companies to invest in on the Stock Exchange? How do the tax authorities know how much tax to charge a company on its profits? One way is for them to look at the profit and loss account of a business. The business itself can also use its profit and loss account to help it make decisions now and to plan for the future.

Smallbone plc manufactures and sells kitchens, bathrooms, bedrooms and flooring in both the UK and the USA. Through its three subsidiary companies, Smallbone of Devizes, Paris Ceramics and Mark Wilkinson Furniture, it offers products at the luxury end of each of its markets. Each year, by company law, it has to produce a set of accounts. One account is the profit and loss account.

Use of profit and loss accounts

The PROFIT AND LOSS ACCOUNT is a record of revenues and costs of the business over a period like a year. It shows how much profit the business has made over the past year and what has happened to the profit.

The profit and loss account is a record of **past** costs and revenues. However, it can still help people in the business to make decisions about the future because the account says something about where the business has been in the recent past. On the whole though, other financial data, such as cash flow forecasts, are far more useful than the profit and loss account in helping businesses make these decisions.

More importantly, the profit and loss account is a summary of recent business events for the owners of the business and anyone who might want to invest in the business. Shareholders in limited companies, for instance, are particularly interested in trends in profits because this determines, in part, how valuable is their share of the business. Profit and loss accounts are also used by the tax authorities to assess a company's tax. Other businesses may also look at a company's profit and loss account for the previous year to judge whether it is safe to give it credit.

The profit and loss account of Smallbone plc is shown in Table 1.

The profit and loss account can be split into **three** parts:

Table 1 *Profit and loss account for Smallbone plc 2005*[1]

	£ million
Sales turnover	35.7
Cost of sales	(20.5)
Gross profit	15.2
Operating costs	(15.1)
Other	(0.2)
Net profit[2]	(0.1)
Taxation	0.4
Dividends	0.0
Retained profit	0.3

1 Brackets around a number mean that it is a minus value.
2 Profit on ordinary activities before taxation.

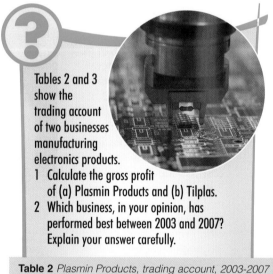

Tables 2 and 3 show the trading account of two businesses manufacturing electronics products.
1 Calculate the gross profit of (a) Plasmin Products and (b) Tilplas.
2 Which business, in your opinion, has performed best between 2003 and 2007? Explain your answer carefully.

Table 2 *Plasmin Products, trading account, 2003-2007*

					£ million
	2003	2004	2005	2006	2007
Turnover	6	9	16	18	18
Cost of sales	4	6	12	16	17

Table 3 *Tilplas, trading account, 2003-2007*

					£ million
	2003	2004	2005	2006	2007
Turnover	10	11	12	14	15
Cost of sales	5	5	6	7	8

- the trading account;
- the profit and loss account;
- the appropriation account.

Gross profit

The **first** part of the profit and loss account is the TRADING ACCOUNT shown in Table 5. The trading account is a record of sales turnover and the cost of sales.

- **Sales turnover** is the value of the sales of the business. In 2005, Smallbone plc sold £35.7 million worth of products.
- COST OF SALES was £20.5 million for Smallbone plc in 2005. This is the cost of production. For Smallbone plc, this included buying in raw materials as well as employing workers to manufacture products such as fitted kitchens or flooring. The trading account shows the GROSS PROFIT of the business. This is the profit made before the overheads of the business are taken into account. Gross profit is defined as sales turnover (one measure of revenue) minus cost of sales (one measure of costs):

Gross profit
= Sales turnover - cost of sales

In 2005, Smallbone plc had a gross profit of £15.2 million.

Table 5 *Trading account for Smallbone plc 2005.[1]*

	£million
Sales turnover	35.7
Cost of sales	(20.5)
Gross profit	15.2

Note: brackets around a number mean that it is a minus number.

Table 6 *Calculating net profit for Smallbone plc 2005.[1]*

	£million
Gross profit	15.2
Distribution expenses	(9.6)
Administrative expenses	(5.5)
Interest and other income received	0.1
Interest paid	(0.3)
Net profit/(loss)[2]	(0.1)

1 Brackets around a number mean that it is a minus value.
2 Profit on ordinary activities before taxation.

Table 4 *Trading and profit and loss account, Hurford Bakeries Ltd for year ending 28 February*

	2005	2006	2007
	£000	£000	£000
Sales turnover	4 698	4 956	5 378
less cost of sales	3 507	3 750	?
Gross profit	?	?	1 424
less Operating expenses			
Wages	583	?	630
Van depreciation	?	24	22
Other	508	482	461
Net profit	75	79	?

Hurford Bakeries

1 Copy out the profit and loss accounts for 2005-2007 and fill in the missing figures.
2 What has happened to: (a) sales turnover; (b) cost of sales; (c) gross profit; (d) net profit over the three years?
3 Do you think the company is doing well or badly? Give reasons for your answer.

Net profit

The **second** part is the actual profit and loss account. This involves calculating net profit. This is shown in Table 6. NET PROFIT is the profit made by a business after all its costs have been taken into account. So it is revenue minus both the cost of sales and all the other costs of the business, the overheads.

Not all the revenue of a business is sales revenue. Table 6 shows that Smallbone plc, for instance, received interest on money which it had deposited in the bank and elsewhere. These non-sales revenues need to be added to sales revenue in order to be able to calculate net profit.

Equally, not all costs are costs of sales. **Operating expenses** or **overheads** are the costs which are not directly related to production. Table 6 shows two different operating costs for Smallbone plc.

Distribution costs These include the costs of **marketing** and selling

products. For instance, Smallbone plc advertises its products in magazines. It also runs a number of showrooms in the UK and the USA where customers can see the products offered by the company.

Administration expenses These include the costs of employees not directly employed in production. For instance, the salaries of the directors of the company would be an administration expense. It also includes all the other costs of administering the company such as the cost of running the offices of the company in Devizes in Wiltshire.

Net profit can be calculated either as:

*gross profit + non-sales revenue
- operating cost*

or, using the definition for gross profit:

*sales revenue + non-sales revenue
- cost of sales - operating cost*

If profit is negative, and costs are greater than revenues, then the business makes a loss. In 2005, Smallbone plc made a small net loss before taxation of £0.1 million.

The appropriation account

If the business is a company, then the profit and loss account will end with figures which show where the net profit has gone. This is the **third** part of the profit and loss account, called the APPROPRIATION ACCOUNT.

Net profit can be distributed in three ways. First, part of it has to be paid to the government in taxes, mainly corporation tax, a tax on company profits. Second, the company may distribute part of the profits to its shareholders in dividends. Third, the company can retain (keep back) some of the profit to pay for new investment in the company. This **retained profit** is the main way in which businesses tend to pay for new investment in the UK.

Table 7 shows the appropriation account for Smallbone plc for 2005. Because it made a loss, it was owed £0.4 million in taxes by the government. It decided not to pay any dividends to its shareholders in 2005. This left it with £0.3 million as retained profit for the year.

Depreciation

Smallbone plc owns buildings, machines, cars and office equipment. These wear out over time and, as a result, fall in value. This wearing out is called DEPRECIATION. It is counted as a cost because the fall in value is what it is costing the business to own and operate these assets. Some businesses include depreciation in costs of sales in the trading account. Sometimes it is included as an overhead cost.

Source: information from Smallbone plc.

Table 7 *Appropriation account for Smallbone plc 2005.*[1]

	£million
Net profit/(loss)[2]	(0.1)
Taxation	0.4
Dividends	0.0
Retained profit	0.3

1 Brackets around a number mean that it is a minus value.
2 Profit on ordinary activities before taxation.

1 Explain why the value of the items shown in the photographs might fall over time.
2 Why is this depreciation a cost for the business?

Treatt plc is a chemical company which specialises in developing and manufacturing oils used by the flavour and fragrance industries. Treatt ingredients are used in products ranging from air fresheners, cosmetics, shampoos and soaps to soft drinks, confectionery and basic pharmaceutical products. In 2006, it saw its sales grow by 9 per cent to £35.4 million, although net profit before tax fell slightly.

1 A company distributes its net profit in three ways. What are they?
2 Calculate the retained profit for Treatt plc for 2005 and 2006.
3 Suggest why over the period 2005-2006: (a) taxes on profit fell; (b) the company retained part of the profit instead of distributing to shareholders.

Table 8 *Appropriation account for Treatt plc.[1]*

	£ millions	
	2006	2005
Net profit (profit on ordinary activities before taxation)	3 288	3 406
Taxation on profit	(956)	(1 070)
Dividends	(949)	(881)

1 Accounts for the year ended 30 September
2 Brackets around a number mean that it is a minus value.

Source: adapted from Treatt plc.

MANCHESTER ELECTRICAL AND WIRING COMPANY

Manchester Electrical and Wiring Company (MEWC) is a small company specialising in electrical work for households and small businesses. The work comes in on a regular basis. In 2005, however, the boss of the company fell off a ladder and had to take 8 weeks off work. This had an impact on the amount of work done by the company.

1 Copy out the profit and loss account for the company and fill in the missing figures.
2 What has happened to the company's (a) sales (b) costs (c) net profit between 2004 and 2007?
3 How has the company distributed its net profit?
4 How well did the company perform between 2004 and 2007?

Table 9 *Profit and loss account, Manchester Electrical and Wiring Company for year ending 30 September*

	2003 £000	2004 £000	2005 £000	2006 £000	2007 £000
Sales turnover	350	354	325	360	388
less Cost of sales	179	184	170	184	?
Gross profit	?	170	155	176	198
less Operating expenses					
Directors' wages	30	31	33	?	37
Equipment and vehicle hire	30	31	33	34	35
Motor Expenses	14	15	16	17	18
Other	70	68	75	64	66
Net profit	27	?	(2)	26	42
Taxes	3	3	4	0	?
Dividends	10	10	0	5	10
Retained profit	14	22	?	21	28

Brackets around a number mean that it is a minus value.

---

key terms

Appropriation account - the part of the profit and loss account which shows what has happened to net profit.
Cost of sales - costs of production such as raw materials costs, direct wage costs and changes in stock.
Depreciation - the fall in value of fixed equipment and buildings over time as they wear out.
Gross profit - sales turnover minus cost of sales.
Net profit - the profit made after all costs and revenues have been taken into account. It is gross profit plus non-sales revenue minus operating costs.
Profit and loss account - a record of the revenues and costs of a business over a period such as six months or a year.
Trading account - part of the profit and loss account which shows sales turnover, costs of sales and changes in stocks.

Checklist ✓

1 Who might look at a profit and loss account of a company and why?
2 What is included in the trading account?
3 What costs are taken into account when calculating net profit?
4 Describe THREE types of operating cost.
5 Why would an increase in non-sales revenue increase net profit but not gross profit, assuming all other costs and revenues stayed the same?
6 Explain how a company uses its net profit.
7 A company buys a delivery van for £20 000. After one year, it values the van at £15 000. Explain this depreciation in value.

Making decisions

A limited company must, by law, produce a balance sheet showing the assets and liabilities of the company on the last day of its accounting year. The balance sheet is often said to reflect the value of a business. It can be used by other businesses and individuals to judge, for instance, whether a business is safe enough to lend money to, to invest in or to buy out. A business itself can also use it to decide whether it can meet its current debts and to make decisions about the future.

JEANINGS.plc

Jeanings plc specialises in providing temporary accommodation, containers and storage facilities. For example, it provides trailers for film crews, cabins for work sites and containers for shipyards. It has a head office in Hull, but also has a number of depots around the country. Each year, it has to draw up a balance sheet which shows the value of what it owns and what it owes on 31 April.

The balance sheet

To operate as a business, Jeanings has to have ASSETS. These are what the business **owns**, such as buildings, offices, machinery, stocks and cash. Without assets, a business could not produce anything. To buy these assets, a business will need to raise funds from different **sources**. For example, Jeanings might have borrowed money, or it might owe money to other businesses for materials that it has received but not yet paid for. Money owed to others is called the LIABILITIES of a business.

The BALANCE SHEET is a record of the assets and liabilities of a business at a particular point in time. The balance sheet must balance. The assets of the business, what the business owns, must equal its liabilities, what it owes. Included in what it owes are the monies owed to the owners of the business, such as profit.

By law a limited company has to produce a balance sheet for its shareholders. This shows its assets and liabilities on the last day of its accounting year. For Jeanings, this is 31 April each year. Companies can, though, choose any date on which to end their financial year. A

Table 1 *Jeanings plc balance sheet at 31 April 2006*

	£000
Fixed assets	
Tangible assets	63 868
Intangible assets	8 935
Investments	2
	72 805
Current assets	
Stock	552
Debtors	8 334
Cash at bank and in hand	66
	8 952
Current liabilities	
Creditors: amounts falling due within one year	(29 674)
Net current assets/(liabilities)	(20 722)
Total assets less current liabilities	52 083
Long term liabilities	
Creditors: amounts falling due after one year	(23 667)
Provision for liabilities	(2 000)
Net assets	26 416
Capital and reserves	
Called up share capital	15 334
Retained profit and reserves	11 082
	26 416

Clarke's Deli was always busy. However, Mr Clarke wanted to retire and so he put the shop up for sale for £50 000. Fixed assets were valued at £15 000 and the value of stock was £20 000. The goodwill, equal to $1\frac{1}{2}$ times net profit, was £15 000.

1 Make a list of the fixed assets that such a shop might have.

2 The new owner paid £15 000 for the goodwill of the business. Do you think you would have paid the same if you had bought the business? To answer this, make a list of the costs of attracting customers if you had to set up a new business in the area. Estimate or try to find out figures for those costs.

company could, for instance, choose a financial year which runs from 1 February to 31 January.

Fixed assets

The balance sheet starts with a record of the FIXED ASSETS of the business. These assets include land, as well as buildings such as factories, offices and fixed plant. Fixed assets also include the machinery and equipment owned by a business and vehicles that it owns. Most of the value of fixed assets at Jeanings is the hire fleet of portable accommodation that Jeanings owns. Table 1 shows that the value of Jeanings's TANGIBLE ASSETS was nearly £64 million at 31 April 2006.

Not all assets are tangible, i.e. assets that you could physically touch. Some businesses have INTANGIBLE ASSETS. The most common is GOODWILL. This is usually the value of the customer contacts of the business. For instance, if the business had to be set up from scratch, it might have to spend money on advertising to build up its customer base. So one way of measuring goodwill is to estimate how much it would cost to set up the business with its customers. The value of Jeanings's intangible assets at 31 April 2006

was nearly £9 million.

Another fixed asset is investments (normally shareholdings) in other companies. They could also be loans to the government (called bonds) which earn interest for the company. Or they could be other types of long term financial investment by the company. Table 1 shows that Jeanings had investments of just £2 000 at 31 April 2006.

Current assets

CURRENT ASSETS are the assets of the business which can easily be turned into cash or are cash, i.e. they are the LIQUID ASSETS of the business. Table 1 shows that there are three main types of current asset.

Stock Stock is the raw materials and goods waiting to be processed or finished goods awaiting sale. Jeanings has fairly low stocks as it does not manufacture goods. However, it might hold some stocks of stationery or items for trailers, such as cleaning materials. Stock at Jeanings at 31 April 2006 was valued at £552 000.

Debtors DEBTORS are the people and businesses who owe the company money. In business, it is

usual to deliver goods to other businesses and then give them a minimum of 30 days to pay. For most businesses nearly all debtors are other businesses. Jeanings was owed just over £8.3 million by its debtors on 31 April 2006.

Cash The most liquid asset is cash itself. Jeanings had just £66 000 in cash held in bank accounts or in hand at 31 April 2006.

Jeanings had current assets of nearly £9 million at 31 April 2006.

Current liabilities

CURRENT LIABILITIES are what the business owes and will have to pay within the next 12 months. For most businesses, the most important current liability is the money it owes to its CREDITORS.

Just as a business has to give credit to other businesses, so it can get credit from other businesses. When Jeanings buys products from suppliers, for instance, it may not have to pay for them until at least 30 days after they are delivered. These are the **trade creditors** of the business. Jeanings also has a number of **leases** and **hire purchase** contracts used to buy its products. These are other forms of borrowing.

Businesses also borrow money from the bank via **loans** and **overdrafts**. In theory, the bank can demand that the money be repaid immediately. So short term loans and overdrafts are current liabilities.

Another important current liability is the social security payments and tax owed to the **government**. The company may have earned profit in the past on which it will have to pay corporation tax and advanced corporation tax in the future for example.

In total, Jeanings owed nearly £30 million to creditors which was repayable within one year at 31 April 2006.

Net current assets or working capital

Current assets minus current liabilities is called NET CURRENT ASSETS. Another name for this is **working capital**. Jeanings had net current assets of minus £20.7 million at 31 April 2006. The minus sign shows that its current liabilities were greater than its current assets.

After net current assets, the balance sheet shows the value of **total assets (fixed + current) less current liabilities**. This value for Jeanings at 31 April 2006 was just over £52 million. Although its net current assets were negative, these were more than offset by the large value of its fixed assets.

Long term liabilities

The LONG TERM LIABILITIES are what the business owes and which has to be paid back in more than 12 months' time. This includes long term **loans** which, for instance, might be repaid over 5 years. It could include **mortgages**. These are loans taken out where land or buildings are given as SECURITY. This means that if the firm goes out of business, the lender (usually a bank) can sell the security, in this case the land or building, and hopefully get its money back. For some companies, like Jeanings, there might be **long term hire purchase agreements or leases**. Other liabilities might be taxation owed (or deferred) from previous years, shown as a provision. Jeanings had total long term liabilities of around £25 million at 31 April 2006.

The value of **net assets** is calculated on the balance sheet as total assets less current liabilities – long term liabilities. The value of net assets at Jeanings at 31 April 2006 was just over £26.4 million.

Capital and reserves

The final type of liability of a business is the money owed to its owners. Jeanings is a plc, and so its owners are its shareholders. The shareholders put money into the business when the shares were first sold. Hence, the business owes this money to its shareholders. At 31 April 2006, the value of Jeanings's share capital was just over £15 million.

Note that this value has nothing to do with the current value of the shares on a stock market. The value of the share capital in a company reflects their value when they were first issued. The current value of the shares reflects what the business is currently worth.

Most businesses are also likely to have kept back some of their profits from previous years. This is money which is owed to the owners of the business. It is therefore a liability for the business. Instead of distributing (giving) it to the owners, the business has decided to set it aside to finance future investment, or to cover possible problems. Jeanings had retained profit and money in other reserves totalling around £11 million at 31 April 2006.

The value of capital and reserves is equal to the value of net assets on the balance sheet. So Jeanings's capital and reserves at 31 April 2006 was just over £26.4 million.

The balance sheet of a sole proprietorship or partnership is different from that of a limited company. The main difference is that there would be no share capital because there are no shareholders. So the value of the money put into the business by the sole trader or the partners would be shown where the shareholders' capital is shown in Table 1.

Blacks Leisure Group

Blacks Leisure Group is made up of two operations. The Outdoor Group comprises Millets and Blacks, the largest outdoor retailers in the UK, and Freespirit and Mambo, the leading retail chains in the newly emerging UK boardwear market. The Boardwear Division comprises the wholesale and retail arms of the O'Neill brand, one of the world's leading names in boardwear. In the year to 28 February 2006 it had sales of £297 million.

1 Copy out and complete the table filling in the missing number shown by '?'.
2 Who might be the trade creditors of the company?
3 (a) What is meant by (i) current tax liabilities and (ii) obligations under finance leases?
 (b) Why might these be liabilities for the business?
4 Write a short statement about the position of the business. In it, mention how current assets and liabilities have changed and whether the business is in a better position in 2006 than 2005.

Table 3 *Blacks Leisure Group , current assets and current liabilities, 28 February 2006 and 2005*

	2006 £000	2005 £000
Current assets	85 868	73 706
Trade and other payables	39 346	39 102
Current tax liabilities	?	3 442
Bank overdrafts	3 025	846
Obligations under finance leases	674	23
Short term provisions	581	407
Current liabilities	46 944	?
Net current assets	?	?

Source: adapted from Blacks Leisure Group, *Annual Report and Accounts*, 2006.

Renishaw plc

Renishaw plc manufactures industrial metrology (measurement) and spectroscopy (light and matter) equipment.

1 For each year since 2000 calculate the total capital and reserves of the business.
2 In 2004 the business made profit after tax of £16 million. In 2005 it made profit after tax of £25 million. How might this be reflected in the capital and reserves?
3 Explain (a) how the issue of new shares might affect this part of the balance sheet and (b) how the purchase of another company might affect (i) the retained profit of the business and (ii) the future profit of the business.

Table 4 *Renishaw plc, capital and reserves.*

£million

	2006	2005	2004	2003	2002	2001	2000
Share capital and premium	14.6	14.6	14.6	14.6	14.6	14.6	14.6
Reserves	128.1	110.9	93.1	90.6	93.1	94.7	82.5

Source: adapted from Renishaw plc, *Annual Report and Accounts*, 2006.

key terms

Assets - what is owned, for instance, by a business.
Balance sheet - the part of a business' accounts where the assets and liabilities of the business are recorded.
Creditors - the individuals, other businesses and governments to which the business owes money.
Current assets - liquid assets of the business.
Current liabilities - what the business owes and will have to pay within the next 12 months.
Debtors - people, other businesses or governments which owe a business money.
Fixed assets - what is owned by a business which it uses over a long period of time, such as buildings or machinery. Fixed assets include tangible and intangible assets.
Goodwill - the value of the customer contacts of a business.
Liabilities - for a business, the monetary value of what it owes, for instance, to other businesses or to the government.
Liquid assets - assets of the business which can easily be turned into cash or which are cash.
Long term liabilities - what the business owes and will have to pay in more than 12 months' time.
Net current assets or working capital - current assets minus current liabilities.
Security - an asset, like property, which can be sold if a borrower fails to repay a loan and the money used to pay off the rest of the loan.
Tangible assets - assets which exist in a physical sense, such as buildings or machinery, as opposed to intangible assets, such as goodwill which don't exist in a physical sense.

Checklist ✓

1 What is the difference between the assets and the liabilities of a business?
2 List FIVE fixed assets of a garage business.
3 What is the difference between the fixed assets of a business and its current assets?
4 Who might be the debtors of a business making jeans?
5 Who might be owed the money which appears as a current liability on a business' balance sheet?
6 Why is a mortgage a long term liability for a business?
7 Why is share capital a liability for a business?
8 For what might a business use its retained profit?

SUMMARY CASE STUDY

JUSTYOU LTD

JustYou is a fashionable nightclub in a smart area of Manchester. The company was founded by 4 people, each of whom put up £50 000 to finance the 200 000 shares in the company priced at £1. They bought a smart nightclub and today, together with fixtures, fittings and equipment, the premises are valued at £320 000. They had to take out a mortgage to finance buying the club and there is still £110 000 to pay on it. They also have a long term £20 000 bank loan which they used to buy some of the fixtures and fittings.

The nightclub is very successful. This year, the owners were able to retain £70 000 profit for investment in the business. The company also has £55 000 in the bank. Drink is always popular amongst the customers and most of the company's £90 000 stock is made up of drink. Some customers run credit accounts and the club is owed £20 000 by them. Current liabilities are £85 000.

1 Draw up a balance sheet for JustYou.
2 A year ago, the mortgage was £120 000, the premises, fixtures and fittings and equipment were valued at £300 000, the club had £100 000 worth of stocks of drink and was owed £30 000 by its creditor customers. Explain which of these figures you think show that the company is doing (a) better; and (b) worse today than a year ago.

Making decisions

How well is a business doing? There is a large number of ways of answering this question. Looking at profit and loss figures or studying the balance sheet are possible ways. Another is to use financial ratios. Having looked at the figures, the business needs to decide whether it is going to change its strategy. Could it perform better?

Morrisons, the supermarket chain, was founded in 1899 by William Morrison. The company has grown from a single egg and butter stall in a Bradford market, to become Britain's fourth largest chain. The company employs around 130,000 staff in its stores, factories, distribution centres and offices and has about 9 million customer visits each week. In 2005, Morrisons took over Safeway, another large supermarket. This accounts for the huge jump in sales turnover in 2005.

Gross profit

Table 1 shows that between 2001 and 2005, Morrisons increased its sales turnover from £3 511.1 million to £12 133.7 million. So, looking just at **sales turnover**, Morrisons has performed extremely well over the period. The very large increase in sales in 2005 is a result of the takeover of Safeway. However, the **cost of sales** has also risen from £2 651.5 million to £9 179.7 million. Does Morrisons need to worry about this increase in the cost of sales?

- No. Sales turnover nearly trebled during the five year period. So an increase in the cost of sales was almost certain.
- Yes. The figures might show that the cost of sales has been increasing at a faster rate than the sales turnover. Then the rise in sales will not be matched by a similar rise in **gross profit**.

One way to find out what happened to turnover in relation to cost of sales is to calculate the RATIO OF GROSS PROFIT TO SALES TURNOVER (often called the GROSS PROFIT MARGIN) where:

Ratio of gross profit to sales or gross profit margin (as a %)

$$= \frac{Gross\ profit}{Sales\ turnover} \times 100\%$$

Remember, gross profit is sales turnover minus cost of sales. So if the gross profit margin is increasing, sales costs must be falling in relation to the value of sales. This is usually a good indicator for the company. If the

Table 1 *Morrisons plc: trading account*

				£million	
	2001	**2002**	**2003**	**2004**	**2005**
Sales turnover	3 511.4	3 915.7	4 302.7	4 958.8	12 133.7
Cost of sales	2 651.5	2 944.0	3 196.3	3 695.6	9 179.7
Gross profit	859.9	971.7	1 106.4	1 263.2	2 954.0
Ratio of gross profit to sales	24.50%	24.80%	25.70%	25.50%	24.30%

Krishen Appaswamy runs a food wholesale business in Derby. He supplies restaurants, shops, hotels and pubs in the Derby area.

1 Look at Table 2. What do the sales revenue figures indicate about the performance of the business? Explain your answer.
2 (a) Calculate for each year: (i) the gross profit; (ii) the gross profit margin.
   (b) Do you think the business has being doing well? Explain your answer.

Table 2 *Sales revenue and cost of sales for Krishen Appaswamy*

					£000
	2002	**2003**	**2004**	**2005**	**2006**
Sales revenue	178	199	218	233	265
Cost of sales	99	107	114	134	162

Deenpac plc

Deenpac plc makes paper and cardboard packaging for the food industry. In 2004 the senior management team made the decision to begin exporting its products. The medium-sized company, based in Sidcup, Kent, employs 87 workers in its highly automated factory.

1 Just looking at the sales figures, do you think Deenpac plc performed well between 2002 and 2006?
2 (a) Describe how: (i) gross profit; and (ii) net profit has changed over the period.
  (b) What impact has the decision to export had on the business?
3 (a) Calculate for each year: (i) gross profit margin; and (ii) net profit margin.
  (b) Discuss possible reasons for the changes in (a) over the time period.

Table 3 *Deenpac plc: profit and loss account*

					£ million
	2002	2003	2004	2005	2006
Sales turnover	12.4	13.8	14.9	19.8	24.1
Gross profit	4.9	5.6	6.1	9.8	12.3
Overheads	3.9	4.4	4.8	7.7	9.7
Net profit	1	1.2	1.3	2.1	2.6

higher the ratio, the more profitable a business is likely to be. On the other hand, a lower ratio is often a sign that the business is not doing well.

The net profit ratio at Morrisons rose between 2001 and 2004 slightly and then fell again in 2005. The decrease in 2005 is significant. It is almost certainly due to the huge costs associated with the takeover of Safeway during the year. Hopefully the net profit margin will recover in the near future when the costs of absorbing Safeway have been exhausted. Net profit margins will fall if a business cannot control its overheads.

ratio is falling, sales costs are rising in relation to the value of sales and this could be a worrying trend for a business.

Table 1 shows that, at Morrisons, the ratio of gross profit to sales was fairly constant between 2001 and 2005. The very slight fall between 2003 and 2005 could have been due to a number of factors.

- Costs may have risen more than prices. For instance, the cost to Morrisons of buying in goods for sale may have risen slightly faster than the price at which they sold them.
- Revenue may have fallen. Increased competition may have forced Morrisons to reduce its prices by more than it would have liked. Or the company may have wanted to increase its share of the market, doing this by offering lower prices than those of its competitors. However, this is not the case because sales revenue rose.

- If sales of low profit margin products in its stores increased, but sales of high profit margin products fell, the average profit would fall.

If a company sees gross profit margins increase, this is likely to be a good sign. It could indicate better control of costs. It could be that it was able to increase its prices. Or it could be that it sold a larger proportion of higher profit margin products in its stores.

Net profit

Gross profit is important, but it doesn't include overhead costs. For the owners of a business, the final net profit figure is more important. Table 4 shows that net profit at Morrisons rose between 2001 and 2004 and then fell in 2005. The success of the company is backed up by another indicator, the RATIO OF NET PROFIT TO SALES TURNOVER or NET PROFIT MARGIN.

Ratio of net profit to sales or net profit margin (as a %)

$$= \frac{\text{Net profit}}{\text{Sales turnover}} \times 100\%$$

It shows how much net profit a business is making per £ of product sold. The higher the profit per £ and therefore the

Return on capital employed

A third ratio which is useful when looking at how well a business has performed is the RATE OF RETURN ON CAPITAL EMPLOYED (ROCE). Say you received £10 interest on money you had put into a bank account a year ago. You can't say whether you have invested your money well until you know how much you had in the account (your **capital**). If you had £20 in the account, you would have made 50 per cent on your money - a very good rate of return. If you had £1 million in the account, then you would have done badly.

Similarly, a business can't say how well it has done until it compares its profit with the amount of capital in the business. This is what ROCE shows.

$$\text{ROCE (\%)} = \frac{\text{Net profit}}{\text{Capital employed}} \times 100$$

The **capital employed** is defined as the **fixed assets** and the **net current assets**, minus any **amounts that must be repaid (including borrowing) in over a year's time** (shown on the **balance sheet**).

Table 5 shows that the return on capital employed for Morrisons

Table 4 *Morrisons' profit and loss account*

					£ million
	2001	2002	2003	2004	2005
Sales turnover	3 511.4	3 915.7	4 302.7	4 958.8	12 133.7
Gross profit	859.9	971.7	1 106.4	1 263.2	2 954
Overheads [1]	640.8	728.7	823.9	943.3	2 656.9
Net profit	219.1	243	282.5	319.9	297.1
Ratio of net profit to sales [2]	6.2%	6.2%	6.6%	6.5%	2.5%

Staff costs, depreciation, exceptional charges, interest and other operating costs.
Profit on ordinary activities before taxation.

Table 5 *Morrisons: rate of return on capital employed*

					£ million
	2001	2002	2003	2004	2005
Net profit	219.1	243.0	282.5	319.9	297.1
Capital employed	993.1	1 113.7	1 232.9	1 317.4	4 017.5
Rate of return on capital employed	22.10%	21.80%	22.90%	24.30%	7.40%

Table 6 *Accounts for Morrisons, Tesco and Sainsbury 2005*

			£ million
	Morrisons	Tesco	Sainsbury
Sales turnover	12 134	33 866	15 409
Cost of sales	9 180	31 231	14 726
Gross profit	2 954	2 635	683
Operating costs	2 657	741	668
Net profit	297	1 894	15
Capital employed	4 018	8 654	4 112
Ratio of gross profit to sales	24.3%	12.9%	4.4%
Ratio of net profit to sales	2.5%	5.6%	0.1%
Return on capital employed	7.4%	21.9%	-0.4%

increased a little between 2001 and 2004. These are good returns on capital when you consider that you would only get about 5% if you put the money in the bank.

However, you have to take into account that investing money in a business can be very risky. In 2005, the return on capital fell quite sharply. This is because of the extra costs incurred by Morrisons when it took over Safeway.

Making comparisons

So far in this unit, we have compared one year's figures of Morrisons with another year's figures. Making comparisons over time is very helpful to a business and its management accountant. However, a business can also compare itself with another similar business to see whether or not it is doing well or badly.

Look at Table 6. It shows the accounts for Morrisons and another two supermarket chains, Tesco and Sainsbury. How do these companies compare?

Starting from the top of the set of accounts, you can see that Tesco has a higher turnover than both

Morrisons and Sainsbury. In fact, sales revenue at Tesco is more than double its rivals. However, cost of sales is also much higher at Tesco. Despite its huge level of sales, Tesco does not make the most gross profit. Neither does it have the highest gross profit margin. It is Morrisons that has the highest of the three. Sainsbury easily has the lowest gross profit margin.

Looking at the net profit figures, Sainsbury is performing the worst. Tesco has the highest net profit and net profit margin. This suggests that it is the most efficient supermarket chain in 2005. Sainsbury's net profit margin is particularly low. This is explained by the upheaval experienced by the business during 2005. The company went through a period of expensive review and reorganisation.

Tesco comes out best on return on capital employed, making 21.9 per cent compared to Morrisons with 7.4 per cent and Sainsbury with -0.4 per cent. These statistics would suggest that Tesco is the best performing company overall. However, it needs to be remembered that during 2005 Morrisons acquired Safeway and Sainsbury was reorganising. These are very costly activities and will have had an impact on financial performance.

Because these three companies are plcs, stock market investors can look at these statistics when deciding whether to buy or sell shares. Sainsbury and Morrisons shares in 2005 were likely to be relatively low because of the poor profitability of these companies.

Source: adapted from Morrisons, *Annual Report and Accounts*, 2005; Tesco plc, *Annual Report and Accounts*, 2005; Sainsbury, *Annual Report and Accounts*, 2005.

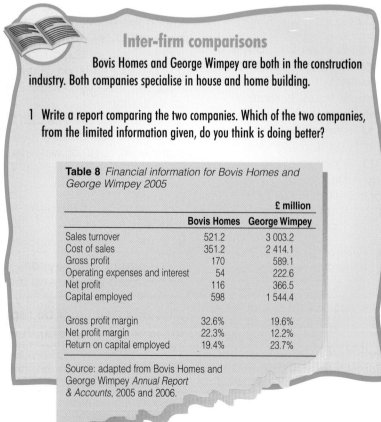

Inter-firm comparisons

Bovis Homes and George Wimpey are both in the construction industry. Both companies specialise in house and home building.

1 Write a report comparing the two companies. Which of the two companies, from the limited information given, do you think is doing better?

Table 8 *Financial information for Bovis Homes and George Wimpey 2005*

		£ million
	Bovis Homes	George Wimpey
Sales turnover	521.2	3 003.2
Cost of sales	351.2	2 414.1
Gross profit	170	589.1
Operating expenses and interest	54	222.6
Net profit	116	366.5
Capital employed	598	1 544.4
Gross profit margin	32.6%	19.6%
Net profit margin	22.3%	12.2%
Return on capital employed	19.4%	23.7%

Source: adapted from Bovis Homes and George Wimpey *Annual Report & Accounts*, 2005 and 2006.

Checklist ✓

1 The sales turnover of a private limited company importing cycle parts went up from £2m to £5m whilst cost of sales increased from £1m to £2m. What has happened to: (a) gross profit; (b) the gross profit margin?

2 Explain whether an increase in the gross profit margin is likely to be a good indicator of the performance of a business or a bad one.

3 What is the difference between gross and net profit?

4 The net profit of a plc went up from £2m to £5m whilst sales turnover increased from £20m to £100m. (a) What has happened to the net profit margin? (b) Explain whether this is a good indicator for the business.

5 Explain, using examples, what the rate of return on capital shows about the performance of a business.

6 Andrew's Ltd has a higher rate of return on capital than Maine's Ltd. Who might be interested to know this information?

key terms

Gross profit margin or ratio of gross profit to sales - gross profit divided by the sales turnover of a business expressed as a percentage.

Net profit margin or ratio of net profit to sales - net profit divided by the sales turnover of a business expressed as a percentage.

Rate of return on capital employed - net profits divided by capital employed in the business.

SUMMARY CASE STUDY

ELEGANCE

Elegance is a high quality ladies clothes chain. It operates mainly in the south east but does have stores in all other UK regions. In recent years it has been exposed to an increasing amount of competition on the high street.

1 (a) What has happened to sales turnover between 2003 and 2007?
  (b) Are these figures likely to be a sign that the company is doing well or doing badly and why?

2 (a) Describe and (b) comment on what has happened to gross profit and net profit over the period.

3 (a) Calculate the ratio of net profit to sales for each year.
  (b) What do these figures suggest about the performance of the company?

4 Calculate the rate of return on capital employed for each year and comment on its significance.

5 The *Annual Report and Accounts* for 2006-07 stated that that 'trade during the year was unsatisfactory'. Rumours were circulating that other companies might offer to buy Elegance. Discuss TWO ways in which a company taking over Elegance might improve its performance.

Table 9 *Elegance plc: profit and loss account.*

£ million

	2003	2004	2005	2006	2007
Sales turnover	112	108	106	100	91
Gross profit	10	9	8	3	1
Net profit	8	7	5	0	-4
Capital employed	9	15	25	29	15

Making decisions

Businesses need to make profit to survive in the long term. In the short term, they also need to be able to manage their day to day flows of cash. They have to decide how they can manage receipts and payments so that there is always enough cash to pay the bills of the business. Looking at how cash has flowed through the business in the past and predicting how it will in the future are both important aids to effective decision making.

Ivan Koloff spent seven years as a taxi driver saving up so that he could start his own taxi business. He wants to provide an airport service, AirportOK, from his home town of Guildford. Such services already exist but Ivan thinks they are unreliable. He was once kept waiting at Gatwick Airport more than two hours for a pre-booked taxi back home. He also plans to target business customers and hopes to build up a regular customer base of frequent-fliers.

Disc-Pro

Disc-Pro is a manufacturer of hard discs. Next year, it predicts that:
- its wage bill will be £1 million;
- sales of products will be £7 million;
- the cost of parts and raw materials will be £3 million;
- advertising and other marketing costs will be £1 million;
- all other costs will be £1 million;
- interest received on investments will be £0.2 million.

1 (a) Which of these are receipts for the business? (b) What is the total value of receipts forecast?
2 (a) Which of these are payments or outgoings for the business? (b) What is the total value of payments forecast?
3 What is the forecast net cash flow of Disc-Pro?
4 If Disc-Pro had cash of £1 million at the start of the year, how much would it have at the end of the year?

Surviving the first month

Ivan managed to save £19 000 during his seven years as an employee. However, he will also need a bank loan of £6 000 to meet the set-up costs and to see him through the first few 'difficult' months of trading. The loan and his savings are RECEIPTS for the business in the first month. Receipts are the cash flowing into a business. In later months, his receipts will be the money he gets from taxi fares.

His OUTGOINGS or PAYMENTS are the monies which he has to pay out. In his first month, he plans to buy a Mercedes to give the service the image it needs to attract business customers. He will also need to build a web site to promote his business and take online bookings. Ivan also plans to do some heavy advertising early on to raise awareness of his airport service.

So in his first month, July, he forecast his outgoings would be £20 300, made up of:
- £15 500 for a Mercedes;
- £600 for website design and construction;
- £900 for advertising in local newspapers and mailshots to local businesses;
- £2 300 for other set-up costs such as insurance and business cards.

Table 1 shows the cash flow forecast for the first month, July. His receipts are put first. Then comes his payments. Net cash flow, £5 700, is the difference between receipts of £25 000 and payments of £19 300. A positive net cash flow shows that more money will come into the business in his first month than goes out.

His opening balance would be £0. This is the amount of money in the business at the start of the month. During the month his net cash flow is £5 700. So by the end

Table 1 Cash flow forecast for AirportOK

	July (£)
Receipts	
Bank loan	6 000
Savings	19 000
Total	25 000
Payments	
Mercedes car	15 500
Website design	600
Advertising	900
Other set-up costs	2 300
Total	19 300
Net cash flow	5 700
Opening bank balance	0
Closing bank balance	5 700

The Bristol Better Crust

The Bristol Better Crust is a bakery run by two partners. They specialise in baking high quality breads for sale to hotels, restaurants and delicatessens. Table 2 shows their cash flow for February.

1 (a) Copy out Table 2 and fill in and calculate the cash flow figures for March assuming that: wages are £21 000; van expenses are £2 000; sales of bread are £110 000; drawings of the partners (the amount they pay themselves from the business) are £5 000; flour and other materials are £55 000; rent and rates are £5 000; and other costs are £18 000.

2 Fill in the table for April assuming that: wages are £22 000; van expenses are £1 500; sales of bread are £105 000; rent and rates are £5 000; drawings of the partners (the amount they pay themselves from the business) are £5 000; flour and other materials are £52 000; and other costs are £26 000.

Table 2 *Cash flow forecast for The Bristol Better Crust (£).*

	February	March	April
Receipts			
Sales of bread	100 000		
Total	100 000		
Payments			
Flour and other materials	50 000		
Wages	20 000		
Rent and rates	5 000		
Van expenses	1 000		
Other costs	15 000		
Drawings of the partners	5 000		
Total	96 000		
Net cash flow	4 000		
Opening balance	22 000		
Closing balance	26 000		

of the month he will have £5 700 (the opening balance, £0, plus the net cash flow, £5 700) left in the business. This is his closing balance.

His second month

In the second month, he plans to start trading. This means there will be extra costs. He will have to begin the loan repayments, and buy fuel, and meet other running costs for his Mercedes. Table 3 shows his cash flow forecast for the second month.

Because the business is new, sales are expected to be low. It takes time to get a business established and build up a customer base. However, Ivan is encouraged by the interest shown in AirportOK. There was even a small article in the local newspaper commenting on the new service due to begin. He

Table 3 *Cash flow forecast for AirportOK, August (£)*

	August
Receipts	
Sales	1 000
Total	1 000
Payments	
Drawings	1 000
Loan repayment	200
Fuel and other running costs	300
Advertising	900
Other costs	200
Total	2 600
Net cash flow	-1 600
Opening balance	5 700
Closing balance	4 100

cautiously predicted that sales would be £1 000 in the first month. Ivan will also have to start taking money out to live on. This is called DRAWINGS.

His payments total £2 600. So his net cash flow, the difference between receipts and payments, is - £1 600. Money is therefore going to flow out of the business. His opening balance for the month is £5 700 (equal to last month's closing balance). His closing balance is £4 100 (£5 700 - £1 600).

September to December

Over the next four months Ivan hopes that the business will become more established. He plans to increase drawings a little as trade picks up. He also plans to continue heavy advertising. He believes that continual adverts will help to establish the name and nature of the business – AirportOK. In December Ivan thinks he might be quite busy. Even though business trade might dwindle, he thinks that people going abroad during the Christmas period might use the service. He also

plans to start advertising in nearby Woking.

Table 4 shows his cash flow forecast for the whole period from July to December. Under receipts, cash from taxi fares are shown in August through to December. They are forecast to rise as the business becomes more established. Under payments, he has to continue paying for advertising, fuel and other costs. There is also loan repayments and drawings to be added. One of the largest costs at the moment is advertising. Ivan thinks it is important to keep reminding the public about the service. Fuel and other running costs will obviously go up as Ivan gets busier.

The net cash flow is negative between August and October. This means that money will be flowing out of the business in these months. However, according to the forecast, the cash position of AirportOK is predicted to be sound for the period shown. By December, Ivan expects to have £5 100 in the bank. Ivan thinks that this is because he put plenty of money in the business at the beginning. One of the problems

Table 4 *Cash flow forecast for AirportOK for July to December*

	July	Aug	Sep	Oct	Nov	Dec
Receipts						
Bank loan	6 000	0	0	0	0	0
Savings	19 000	0	0	0	0	0
Sales		1 000	2 000	3 000	4 000	6 000
	25 000	1 000	2 000	3 000	4 000	6 000
Payments						
Mercedes car	15 500	0	0	0	0	0
Website design	600	0	0	0	0	0
Other set-up costs	2 300	0	0	0	0	0
Advertising	900	900	900	900	900	1 000
Drawings	0	1 000	1 200	1 200	1 200	1 500
Loan repayment	0	200	200	200	200	200
Fuel and other running costs	0	300	500	700	900	1 400
Other costs	0	200	200	200	200	300
Total	19 300	2 600	3 000	3 200	3 400	4 400
Net cash flow	5 700	-1 600	-1 000	-200	600	1 600
Opening bank balance	0	5 700	4 100	3 100	2 900	3 500
Closing bank balance	5 700	4 100	3 100	2 900	3 500	5 100

when setting up a small business is that owners often fail to put sufficient capital in at the start.

The next year

By 31 December, Ivan had put £19 000 of his own money into the business. He had also taken out a £6 000 loan which has only partly been repaid. He only has £5 100 of that money left in cash. He has also kept drawings quite low during the start-up period. However, Ivan knows that it can be difficult when starting a new business. The following year, he is confident that the position will improve.

He knows that if he provides a good service to business customers they are likely to book again. Existing customers will tell their friends and other business colleagues - this will generate further bookings. He also plans to attract more customers from Woking and employ another driver to keep the car on the road 24 hours a day, 7 days a week. So, in a full year, he hopes to generate £100 000 sales revenue.

Advertising costs are likely to fall once people in the area know about the service. However, Ivan will have to pay wages to another driver and of course, fuel and other running costs will rise. He also plans to take out £2 000 drawings each month. So his total payments are forecast to rise too from the first year. His net cash flow over the year is forecast to be positive (£20 000). Overall, he predicts that he will end the year with £25 100 in cash. This is shown in Table 6.

The use of a cash flow forecast

Ivan needed to make a cash flow forecast for a number of reasons.
- He needed it for his own planning. From his forecast, he knows that sales revenue will be week at the start. He will also have spent £19 000 of his own money on the business, taken out a £6 000 loan and yet only has

Sam Walker was unemployed. He decided to set up in business as a market trader dealing in antiques. Table 5 shows how well he did over the first seven months of running the business. He received a grant of £1 000 to set up the business. He also arranged an overdraft facility, which allowed him to borrow up to £300 from his bank account. Each month, his drawings from the business, the amount he paid himself in wages, were £200. Look at the figures carefully.

1 (a) What happened to: (i) sales; and (ii) costs over the seven months? (b) Explain whether these figures showed that the business was doing well or badly.
2 (a) What happened to cash flow during this time? (b) Do these figures indicate the business was doing well?
3 When did Sam Walker have to use his overdraft facility?
4 Explain whether the business: (a) has made a profit over its first seven months; and (b) is likely to make a profit in the future.

Table 5 *Cash flow forecast for Sam Walker (£).*

	June	July	Aug	Sept	Oct	Nov	Dec
Receipts							
Grant	1 000	0	0	0		0	0
Sales	500	600	700	800	900	1 000	1 000
Total	1 500	600	700	800	900	1 000	1 000
Payments							
Setting up	300	0	0	0		0	0
Rent	120	120	120	120	120	120	120
Stock	500	350	400	450	500	550	500
Drawings	200	200	200	200	200	200	200
Other exps.	100	110	120	130	140	150	150
Total	1 220	780	840	900	960	1 020	970
Net cash flow	280	-180	-140	-100	-60	-20	30
Opening bank balance	0	280	100	- 40	- 140	- 200	- 220
Closing bank balance	280	100	- 40	- 140	- 200	- 220	- 190

£5 100 in cash left after 6 months. However, he will have seen growing sales. If his predictions are right for the second year, his drawings can increase and the cash balance at the end will be £25 100.
- He needed it for the bank. Before he started setting up the business, he needed to borrow some money. It was important for the bank to see how cash would be managed in the business to see whether the business had a chance of survival. Without a cash flow forecast, he would not have got a loan from the bank.
- He would also have needed it had he applied for a grant to set up the business from government, perhaps with help from his local Business Link.

Cash flow statements

Ivan made his cash flow forecast before he set up in business. Once

he started operating, he kept monthly CASH FLOW STATEMENTS. These showed how much money was actually flowing into and out of the business each month. He kept these for a number of reasons.
- It was one way of monitoring the performance of the business. If sales were down, for instance, this could show up as a worsening of the cash flow.
- It helped him identify crisis points.

Table 6 *Cash flow forecast for AirportOK for January to December of the second year of operation*

Receipts	
Sales	100 000
Total	100 000
Payments	
Wages	20 000
Advertising	2 000
Drawings	24 000
Loan repayment	2 400
Fuel and other running costs	30 000
Other costs	1 600
Total	80 000
Net cash flow	20 000
Opening bank balance	5 100
Closing bank balance	25 100

If the cash in the business were falling much more rapidly than his cash flow forecast predicted, he knew he would have to do something immediately to stop the fall.

- He used it to compare performance from month to month and year to year. For instance, he could see that his cash flow position was better in December than in November. In December there was an extra £1 600 in the bank. In his second year of trading, sales increased and he was able to see improvements month by month compared to the previous twelve months.

Cash flow and profit

Profit and cash flow are different.

The amount of cash a business has at the end of the year is not profit. For example, at the end of the second year Ivan had £25 100 in the bank. However, this was not the amount of profit made. One reason is because there was £5 100 already in the bank at the beginning of the year. Another reason is that Ivan took £24 000 out of the business for himself in drawings. This would have to be added to profit. Profit is the difference between sales turnover and costs. It has to be calculated separately. Profit is not normally shown on a cash flow forecast.

Sometimes it is possible for a profitable business to collapse because it runs out of cash. For example, what if Ivan's Mercedes was written off in a crash in October? He could not have bought a new Mercedes with the £2 900 cash left. He may eventually receive a payout from an insurance claim, but this often takes a while and in the meantime he may have lost his customers. His business may have collapsed – not because it was unprofitable, but because he did not have enough cash to resolve a crisis.

This shows that businesses can potentially be profitable but collapse because they have cash flow problems. Equally, a business can have a stable cash flow position from month to month. However, unless receipts are greater than payments, the business will not make a profit.

PARINDER KAUR

Parinder Kaur wants to set up in business making soft furnishings for customers on an individualised basis. In her business plan, she predicts that to start with nearly all her orders will be for curtains and pelmets. Later on, she hopes to branch out into more complicated work.

She is going to work from home, so her fixed costs will be low - just £200 per month. One main fixed cost will be adverts in the local newspaper. The main variable cost will be the cost of material for the curtains. On average, she expects her variable cost to be half the amount she charges her customers for a particular job. For instance, on a job where she charges £200, she expects £100 of that to be the variable cost of materials.

Every order is individual and so she keeps no stocks. When she buys material, it is immediately made up into the order. She also expects her clients to pay immediately the order is fulfilled.

Spreadsheet

(The cash flow forecast which you are asked to prepare in questions 1-5 could be more easily done using a spreadsheet package.)

1. She is prepared to put £200 into the business in the first month to start it up. She predicts sales in the first month, March, will be £200 whilst material costs will be £100. Fill in her cash flow forecast for March in Table 7.
2. In April, she expects to pick up more orders. She thinks sales will be £300 whilst material costs will be £150. Complete her cash flow forecast for April.
3. In May, June and July, she expects to have sales of £400 per month with material costs of half that amount. Complete her cash flow forecast for these months.
4. In August, with so many people on holiday, she expects to get only £200 worth of orders with £100 material costs. (a) Complete her cash flow forecast for the month. (b) She faces an important problem in this month. What is it?
5. In the remaining four months of the year, she forecasts £600 worth of sales and £300 worth of material costs per month. Complete Table 7 for these months.
6. Is the problem in August important given what she predicts will happen in the last four months of the year?
7. Parinder expects to work 20 hours a week on her business between September and December. The only money she receives is the profit made by her business. (a) Do you think that her business is successful? (b) Suggest TWO ways in which Parinder might increase her profits.

Table 7 Cash flow forecast for Parinder's soft furnishing business (£).

	Mar	Apr	May	Jun	Jul	Aug	Sept	Oct	Nov	Dec
Receipts										
Cash inflow	200									
Sales										
Total										
Payments										
Fixed costs										
Material costs										
Total										
Opening balance										
Closing balance										

---

key terms

Cash flow forecast - a prediction of how cash will flow through a business over a period of time in the future.
Cash flow statement - a statement showing how cash has flowed through a business over a period of time. It includes a summary of receipts and payments during each period of time.
Receipts - the monies flowing into a business.
Payments - the monies flowing out of a business.

Checklist ✓

1. (a) A newsagent receives cash from its customers. List FIVE different items which bring in cash to the business.
   (b) A newsagent pays out money. List FIVE different people or organisations which it might pay.
2. A business starts out the month with £200 cash. It ends the month with £300 cash. How much cash is carried forward to the next month?
3. What is the difference between a cash flow statement and a cash flow forecast?
4. A business has a negative cash flow at the end of a month. (a) What does this mean? (b) Why might this be a problem for the business?
5. Why can a business be fundamentally profitable but go out of business because of a cash flow problem?

Making decisions

Businesses need assets to produce goods and services. They need fixed assets like offices, factories and vehicles. They also need circulating assets (or working capital) such as cash, stock or payments due shortly. A business doesn't want too much tied up in working capital. Money invested in stocks could be earning interest in a long term investment, for instance, or it could be used to buy a new machine. On the other hand, too little working capital could lead to it going out of business. A shop with no stock to sell isn't going to earn any profit. So the business has to decide how much working capital it needs to be successful.

Northern Foods is one of the UK's leading food producers. It has a proven reputation for quality and innovation. Some of its well known brands include Pork Farm pies, Fox's biscuits and Goodfella's pizzas. It operates three divisions - Chilled, Bakery and Frozen. In 2005-6 the company had sales of £1 438.2 million.

Working capital

Northern Foods needs **fixed assets** to manufacture its food products. These are the machines, factories, offices, etc. which the company owns. But it also needs WORKING CAPITAL to pay for day to day expenses, such as bills. Working capital is what the business owns, which is either cash or could easily be turned into cash minus what it owes, which needs paying shortly. For Northern Foods, working capital is:

- the value of the cash in the business as well as cash held in the bank;
- the stocks of the company, such as raw food products waiting to be turned into pies, pizzas, sandwiches, puddings and biscuits and the finished products waiting to be sent to customers;
  - the debtors of the company, the businesses which have received goods from Northern Foods but have yet to pay for them;

minus

- money owed to the bank which might be repaid within the next 12 months;
- what it owes to other businesses for goods and services that it has received but not yet paid for (its creditors);
- other monies owed which are payable within a year, such as to the government in tax or to its shareholders in dividends.

There is a formula to calculate working capital. It is defined as the difference between **current assets** and **current liabilities** (terms which are found on the balance sheet of the business). So working capital is:

current assets - current liabilities

or:

(cash + debtors + stock) - (bank overdraft + creditors + other monies owed)

Working capital is the value of **net current assets**. This is the current assets of the business left over after the current liabilities have been taken away.

The working capital cycle

Every business has a working capital cycle. Look at Figure 1. Northern Foods manufactures food products using raw materials. Some are bought with cash. Some are delivered now by **creditors** and paid for 30 days later. It also hires workers and equipment. The products are sold to customers who usually get 30 days to pay for them. So customers become debtors for Northern Foods. The

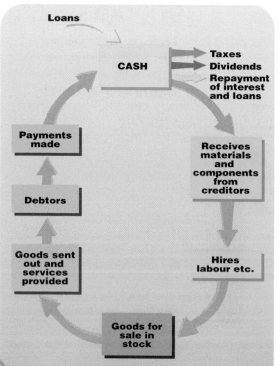

Figure 1 *The working capital cycle.*

Bisco

EITHER chart the flow of working capital round your business and estimate or record the level of working capital in the business at a point of time in its operation, OR complete the following case study.

Bisco is your mini-company. You plan to make and sell biscuits within your school. For your first day, you plan to make 90 Shrewsbury biscuits. The four members of the business have each put £0.50p into the mini-company as start-up capital, but you know this won't cover the cost of the ingredients to make the first batch of biscuits. So you have persuaded your parents to lend you all the money to buy the ingredients and you have promised to pay back the money once you have sold the biscuits. To make the 90 biscuits, you need 350 gm of margarine, 350 gm of castor sugar, 3 small eggs, 700 gm of plain flour, and 2gm of ground cinnamon. Unfortunately, when you come to buy the ingredients, you find you can't buy 350 gm of margarine, 350 gm of castor sugar etc. - you to have buy bigger packs. The size of packs and their prices are shown in Figure 2.

You sell each biscuit for 5p. On your first day, you sell 80 out of the 90 biscuits. Two people buy a biscuit and promise to pay you the next day.

1 Calculate your current assets at the end of the first day. Record your answers by copying out Table 1.
2 Calculate your current liabilities at the end of the first day.
3 At the end of the first day, what is the value of: (a) your working capital; (b) the total amount of cash that you have?
4 Why does your business need working capital to carry on trading?

Table 1 *Current assets for Bisco*

	(£)
Cash	
Start up capital	?
First day's takings	?
Total cash	?
Debtors	?
Stock	
Unsold biscuits	?
Ingredients	?
Total stock	?
Total current assets	?

Figure 2

amount of working capital if its stock levels are very high and it owes little to the bank. But if it doesn't have enough cash to pay its day to day bills, then it faces a cash flow problem.

On the other hand, a business might have £100 million in the bank in cash today. It is cash rich today and it has no cash flow problem. But if it has to pay a bill for £200 million in a week's time and its other current assets, like stocks, are worth only £50 million, then it has a working capital problem today. It doesn't have enough current assets to cover its current liabilities. As a result, it is likely to get into financial difficulties in the future.

Current ratio

Another way in which Northern Foods can find out whether it has enough working capital is for it to work out its CURRENT RATIO. This is the ratio of current assets to current liabilities:

$$Current\ ratio = \frac{Current\ assets}{Current\ liabilities}$$

The higher the ratio of current assets to current liabilities, the higher the amount of working capital in the business. The higher

customers will then pay Northern Foods. The cash coming into the company has to pay for the raw materials that it originally bought. It also has to pay for the wages of its workers, its overheads, taxes, repayments on loans and dividends to shareholders. So current assets and liabilities, like cash, stocks, debts, credits and bank loan repayments, are constantly going round the financial system of the business.

The need for working capital

To survive, businesses need working capital. They need enough current assets left over, after allowing for current liabilities, to pay for the day to day bills of the business.

It is considered good practice in the average business for current

assets to be between 1.5 and 2 times the value of current liabilities. This allows a business to cope with a sudden crisis. For instance, Northern Foods might suddenly get an unexpected tax bill from the Inland Revenue. Or a major customer might go out of business leaving unpaid bills with Northern Foods. If it has enough current assets compared to current liabilities, it will be able to carry on paying its day to day bills, even though working capital is reduced.

Working capital and cash flow problems

Problems with shortages of working capital can be different from cash flow problems. A business, for instance, might have a large

Table 2 *Working capital, Northern Foods, 1 April 2006*

	£ million	£ million
Stock	69.7	
Investments[1]	9.6	
Debtors	175.3	
Cash	40.7	
Current assets		**295.3**
Trade creditors	231.0	
Taxation	25.0	
Bank loans and overdrafts	1.4	
Current liabilities		**257.4**
Working capital		**37.9**

1 Investments such as shares in other companies which could be sold for cash.

Andy Clarke doesn't always get things right. His small engineering business is not doing as well as he had hoped. He wanted it to make enough money for him to buy a Mercedes. Instead, he has to drive around in the ten year old van belonging to the business. He has written you a letter saying that he has found the solution to his problems -increase the working capital of the business. To achieve this, he intends to get more cash in the business by:

(i)   increasing his overdraft with the bank;

(ii) reducing his stocks by 50 per cent;

(iii) delaying paying his bills (his creditors) by a month.

Wordprocessing

Write a letter back to him, explaining:

(a) the difference between cash and working capital;

(b) why none of these three measures will increase his working capital;

(c) the possible effects of the measures on (i) the costs and (ii) the revenues of the business and therefore on (iii) the profit of the business.

the ratio, therefore, the safer is the business.

The part of the balance sheet which shows the working capital for Northern Foods is shown in Table 2. At 1 April 2006, the current ratio for the company was £295.3 million ÷ £257.4 million,

which is equal to 1.15 to 1. As already mentioned, accountants usually advise that a typical business should have a current ratio of 1.5 to 1 to 2:1. If it is less than this, the business runs the risk of not being able to pay its bills and going out of business. The

ratio for Northern Foods is lower than the 'safe' range often given in textbooks. However, the company does have £40.7 million in cash. So this might compensate for a low ratio. It is also true that businesses don't want too high a current ratio because current assets earn little or no interest and money might be better used elsewhere.

The acid test ratio

Stock is part of the working capital of the business. However, it might be difficult to sell off stock quickly if the business faced a cash crisis. For instance, Northern Foods might find it difficult to sell quickly half its stock valued at £69.7 million. If it needed cash it might have to sell its stock at low prices and only get a fraction of the book value of £69.7 million. So a better measure of whether a business has enough working capital might be the ACID TEST RATIO. This excludes stock from current assets in calculating the ratio of current assets to current liabilities:

Acid test ratio =

$$\frac{Current\ assets - stock}{Current\ liabilities}$$

Like the current ratio, the higher the acid test ratio, the safer is the business and the less likely it is to become insolvent. On 1 April 2006 Northern Foods' current assets minus stock were £295.3 million - £69.7 million = £225.6 million. The acid test ratio was £225.6 million ÷ £257.4 million, which is equal to 0.88:1. This is slightly different from its 1.15:1 current ratio. A typical business should have an acid test ratio of between 0.5:1 and 1:1. So, Northern Foods looks a safe business with its acid test ratio within the recommended range.

Source: adapted in part from Northern Foods, *Annual Report and Accounts*, 2005/6.

Enodis

Enodis manufactures food making and kitchen equipment in a number of factories in the UK, US, Continental Europe and Asia. It sells exclusively to the corporate sector and its brands include Cleveland (steamer cookers), Frymaster (fryers, filtration systems, holding cabinets), Icematic (refrigeration) and Ice-O-Matic (ice makers).

1 What is the difference between: (a) a debtor and a creditor; (b) 'cash at bank and in hand' and an overdraft?

2 Calculate for 2005 and 2006: (a) the current assets; (b) the current liabilities; (c) the working capital of the company.

3 Discuss what has happened to the company's working capital between 2005 and 2006?

Table 3 *Enodis working capital at 19 August 2006*

	£ million	£ million
	2005	2006
Stocks	85.3	84.8
Debtors	107.4	119.3
Investments	1.3	22.7
Cash	49.1	50.5
Trade creditors	146.4	155.2
Taxation	10.8	12.1
Other creditors	20.6	44.3

Source: adapted from Enodis, *Annual Report and Accounts*, 2006.

Inter-firm comparison

Balfour Beatty is a world-class engineering, construction and services group. One of its high profile customers is National Grid. Balfour is responsible for upgrading and enhancing both its electricity and gas infrastructure. Alfred McAlpine is also in the construction industry. It finances, designs, builds, manages and maintains buildings and infrastructure. One of its main customers is the Highways Agency. McAlpine builds and maintains many of Britain's roads and motorways.

Table 4 *Working capital of two construction companies (2005)*

		£million
	Balfour	**McAlpine**
Current assets		
Stocks	61.0	39.6
Debtors	836.0	312.6
Cash	345.0	41.0
Current liabilities	1 376.0	305.9

1 For both companies, calculate (a) the total working capital; (b) the current ratio; (c) the acid test ratio.
2 (a) Which company has the more favourable working capital position? Explain your answer.
(b) Which of the two companies might cope better with a downturn in the economy?

Checklist ✓

1 What is the difference between the current assets of a business and its current liabilities?
2 Explain what will happen to a business' working capital if: (a) its cash increases; (b) its stocks rise; (c) its creditors rise; (d) its debtors fall; (e) it increases its bank overdraft by £1 000 and uses the money to buy extra stock; (f) it sells £1 000 of stock for cash; (g) it reduces its bank overdraft because it has increased the prices of its products for sale.
3 What is the difference between cash and working capital?
4 What is the difference between the current ratio and the acid test ratio?
5 A manufacturing business finds that its current ratio falls from 2.5:1 to 1:1. (a) Why does this suggest that the business is in trouble? (b) What might have caused this fall?
6 A manufacturing business has a current ratio of 3:1 but an acid test ratio of only 0.5:1. (a) What must be its most important type of current asset? (b) Why might the business face problems in the future?

key terms

Acid test ratio - the ratio of current assets minus stock to current liabilities.
Current ratio - the ratio of current assets to current liabilities.
Working capital - current assets minus current liabilities.

SUMMARY CASE STUDY

DOMINO'S PIZZAS

Domino's Pizza Group Ltd is a wholly owned subsidiary of Domino's Pizza UK & IRL plc. It holds the master franchise licence to own, operate and franchise Domino's Pizza stores in England, Scotland, Wales and Ireland. Domino's Pizza Inc, founded in the US in 1960, is recognised as a world leader in the delivery of freshly-made, home-delivered high quality pizza. The first UK store opened in 1985.

Source: adapted from Domino's Pizzas UK & IRL *Annual Report & Accounts*, 2006.

1 (a) What is a current asset?
(b) Give three examples of stocks which Domino's is likely to hold.
(c) From Table 5, calculate current assets for 2005 and 2006.
2 (a) What is a current liability?
(b) Give three examples of current liabilities that Domino's is likely to hold.
(c) If the company had a loan which had to be repaid in 6 months' time and one which must be repaid in 5 years' time, which of these is a current liability?
3 Calculate for 2005 and 2006: (a) the working capital; (b) the current ratio; (c) the acid test ratio.
4 On the basis of your answers in 3, explain whether or not you think the company is financially sound.
5 Domino's Pizzas is continually opening new stores. Explain what impact this will have on future working capital needs.

Table 5 *Domino's Pizza UK & IRL plc, current assets and current liabilities*

		£000
	2005	**2006**
Current assets		
Stocks	2 700	2 186
Debtors	13 456	12 921
Cash	4 824	5 885
Current liabilities	13 590	13 742

Source: adapted from Domino's Pizzas UK & IRL, *Annual Report & Accounts*, 2006.

unit 38 FINANCING THE BUSINESS THROUGH CAPITAL

Making decisions

Businesses need money to start up and run their operations. One way of getting this money is for the business to attract capital - where another business or individual puts money into the business in return for a share of the ownership. If the business is already in existence, it can put back any profits made to pay for investment. The business needs to decide which is the best way of obtaining money. For instance, should a sole proprietor put in savings? If a partner or new shareholder is brought in, what will be his or her share of the profit and how much control will be left in the hands of the original partners or shareholders?

Thousands of chefs dream about owning their own restaurant. But for Natasha Williams it wasn't a dream it was an ambition. She trained as a chef in Cardiff and worked in some of the top hotels in London and Paris. She also worked in two famous restaurants - one in Oxford and one in London. Over a fifteen year period she acquired a wide range of cooking skills and developed a sound understanding of the restaurant industry. She had also managed to save up £20,000. Now, at the age of 32 she was ready to realise her ambition.

Getting started

Natasha drew up a business plan. She calculated that she would need £150 000 in total. Kitchen equipment would cost £40 000. Redecorating and refitting the rented premises would cost £60 000. She would then need £50 000 in working capital to cover day to day expenses like wages for the staff, utility bills and the rent.

Natasha had savings of £20 000 and she hoped to borrow £30 000 from a bank. The other £100 000 she hoped would come from raising capital for the business. Raising capital (sometimes called EQUITY or EQUITY CAPITAL) means:
* Natasha putting her own money into the business;
* finding people who are prepared to become joint owners of the business. These could be either partners (in a partnership) or shareholders (in a limited company). She planned to set up a partnership.

Raising capital for a small business

It is sometimes very difficult for small and medium sized businesses (like partnerships or

The Richmond Osteopath Clinic

Ben Phillips is a qualified osteopath and works for the Willowdale Osteopath Clinic in North Yorkshire. He has been working for Sam Hardwick, the owner, for 7 years. Ben felt quite strongly that he could do everything his boss was doing. Why spend the rest of his life making money for someone else? The trouble is, Ben had not saved much during his years working for Sam, preferring instead to travel. He could not afford to buy premises and the equipment needed was also expensive. However, he could rent a place and buy second hand equipment. He reckoned that £10 000 would be needed to get started. Ben had only got £3 000 and the bank would only provide a further £3 000. He was £4 000 short.

Sam got to hear about Ben's plans and to Ben's surprise suggested they might go halves on the new practice. Sam also said he would give advice on setting up and help him find suitable premises in nearby Richmond. Sam also said he would be prepared to lend the new practice more money until it got established.

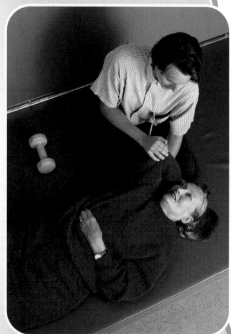

1 (a) What skills did Ben have which would help in his new business?
  (b) What skills would he have to learn if he opened a new practice?
2 What financial problem did Ben face trying to start up on his own?
3 Why do you think Sam was interested in helping Ben set up a new practice?
4 What advantages and disadvantages were there for Ben in having Sam as a partner?
5 Should Ben accept Sam's offer? Explain your answer.

Second hand shares are traded on the stock market.

private limited companies) to find someone prepared to become joint owners. When found, they are often:

- members of the family, like a parent or an uncle;
- friends who can see a good business opportunity;
- people known through work;
- people who want to set up in business and also need to find someone prepared to invest in the business.

Natasha's father was a retired head teacher who had invested a lump sum in the stock market in 2002. This sum had risen handsomely and he was prepared to put up £75 000. Natasha had a friend who was a restaurant manager. He was prepared to put in £25 000 on the understanding that he might work in the restaurant and be involved in its development. Natasha had her £20 000 of savings plus the personal loan she was taking out from the bank for £30 000. This made a total of £50 000.

Natasha would then have owned one third of the partnership (£50 000 ÷ £150 000), her father one half (£75 000 ÷ £150 000) and her friend one sixth (£25 000 ÷ £150 000). If control of the partnership were allocated according to the amount of capital put into the business, Natasha would only have one third of the votes. So she would not have full control of the partnership. She was worried that her father might not always agree with her decisions. But she had little choice because she really wanted to start the business now.

All three partners had to accept the risk of unlimited liability. However, it can sometimes be easier to find new capital for a small business if it is a private limited company, where shareholders have limited liability.

Share capital for larger businesses

Natasha Williams's problems were typical of those faced by small businesses starting up or wanting to grow. One of the reasons why larger businesses become public limited companies is because they find it easier to sell (or float) new shares in the business. A business, for instance, can raise new money through going public (i.e. becoming a public limited company). Later on, it can make a share issue (i.e. sell extra shares in the company) to raise more finance.

A new share issue by a public limited company is likely to be organised by a bank or a merchant bank. It might offer the shares for sale to the general public, or it could sell the shares to existing shareholders. It might also place the shares (i.e. sell them) with other financial organisations like assurance companies, unit trusts or pension funds which invest in shares on behalf of their savers.

One reason why investors are far more prepared to buy shares in a public limited company than in, say, a private limited company is

Sports Direct

Entrepreneur Mike Ashley netted £929 million from the flotation of Sports Direct, the group he built from a single shop to become Britain's biggest sports retailer. Sports Direct, which runs the Sports World and Lillywhites chains, said it had placed 309.6 million of Mike Ashley's shares with investors at 300 pence apiece. Mike Ashley has an option to sell up to a further 46 million shares, in which case his proceeds would rise to about £1.07 billion. But even if this option is exercised, Mike will retain a majority stake and has committed, subject to certain exceptions, not to sell any further shares for two years.

Mike Ashley is executive deputy chairman of Sports Direct, which runs 465 shops and owns brands such as Dunlop, Lonsdale and Slazenger. In the year to April 2006, the group made earnings of £145.1 million on revenue of £1.189 billion. Mike Ashley has said he wanted to float the business to help drive its expansion, particularly internationally, but has been characteristically quiet about what he plans to do with the proceeds of the share sale.

Source: adapted from http://uk.biz.yahoo.com/.

1 What is meant by a flotation?

2 Shares in Sports Direct were 'placed' on the stock market. What does this mean?

3 What are the proceeds of the flotation likely to be used for?

4 Why are investors happy to buy shares in public limited companies?

because there is an organised market for the buying and selling of second hand shares. This market is the stock market.

Types of share

Most shares issued by private and public limited companies are ORDINARY SHARES. The owners of the shares, the shareholders of the company, are entitled to receive a share of the profits. This share of the profits is called a DIVIDEND. The dividend can go up and down from year to year depending upon how much profit the company has made and how much it decides to give to its shareholders.

Limited companies can also issue PREFERENCE SHARES. These carry a fixed rate of dividend and so shareholders don't benefit from any increases in profits made by the company. However, they also don't suffer as much if the company has a bad year. Ordinary shareholders may receive no dividend that year, but

preference shareholders may be paid because they are entitled to get the first share of any profits made by the company.

Venture capital

Natasha Williams's business would have been too small to be of interest to a VENTURE CAPITALIST. Venture capital companies specialise in buying a share of small but growing businesses, most of which are private limited companies. The venture capitalist hopes that in about 5 years the business will have grown and its stake in the business can then be sold at a profit.

Retained profit

In any year, only a few per cent of all the money to finance investment in the UK comes from raising new capital. The most important source of finance is RETAINED or UNDISTRIBUTED PROFIT. This is profit which has been made by the business and is not distributed to

the owners of the business. Instead, it is kept back, or retained.

Natasha Williams, for instance, hopes to be able to expand her business once it becomes profitable by opening up other restaurants. She will therefore need more sites, more equipment, more funds for refurbishment and more working capital. A large public limited company is no different. It ploughs back profits to finance growth of its business.

Retained profit is an INTERNAL SOURCE OF FINANCE because the money has come from within the business. New capital, in contrast, is an EXTERNAL SOURCE OF FINANCE because the money comes from outside the business.

The great advantage to Natasha of retained profit as a way of financing investment is that she doesn't have to pay interest or dividends on the money. It also means that she doesn't have to find banks, new partners or shareholders, or anyone else who would be prepared to lend money or invest in the business.

Other internal sources of finance

Another way for a business to raise money internally is to sell assets. For instance, in ten years' time, Natasha might have bought her own premises. She may decide to move to bigger premises. She could then sell her existing premises to raise money to pay for the new building.

Larger businesses might be able to negotiate a sale and lease-back scheme. Here, the business sells some or all of its property to another company, like a property company. At the same time, it signs an agreement to lease (i.e. rent) back the property for a fixed annual rent. The business receives a lump sum of money which can be used to pay for expansion. The drawback is that the business now has to pay rent on the property.

Raising finance - The Print Company

The Print Company is a mini-company which plans to sell photographs of its school. It has a print of an aerial shot of the buildings and one of the directors of the company, who is a keen photographer, plans to take a number of other shots of the school. Six photographs will be mounted into a frame made by two other directors of the company with the help of their technology teacher. They are going to charge £5.99 for a set of photographs plus the frame. For £7.99, they will include a picture of any pupil or group of pupils, the photograph being taken by the photographer in the company.

In its business plan, the board of directors states that most of the frames produced will be produced to order. People will pay their money and the frames will be delivered later. However, they need to produce at least one frame for display purposes. They also want to produce another 10 for immediate sale at the next parents' evening. They calculate they need £40 for this and to cover advertising costs. They decide to make a share issue of forty £1 shares.

Read through the case study. EITHER use it to think about how you would raise capital for your mini-enterprise OR answer the following questions.

1 Who could the company get to buy the shares?
2 Why might people want to buy the shares?
3 The company successfully sells a number of photographs and makes £50 profit. Another parents' evening is coming up and the company decides that it would like to make another 10 frames for immediate sale.
(a) Where could it get the money from to finance this? (b) Discuss which would be the best way of financing the deal.

Axon

Axon is a Business Transformation consultancy that designs, implements and supports solutions to complex business issues faced by large organisations. Axon helps senior executives to develop strategies to deal with problems and make improvements. Axon helps customers to develop systems and new working practices to improve efficiency.

A shareholder has written to Axon asking why such a large proportion of the profit has been retained by the business and so little paid in dividends. Write a letter to the shareholder explaining why Axon needs to retain profits and why this might benefit shareholders in the long term. Structure your letter as follows:

1 Thank the shareholder for the letter.
2 Explain that she is correct to say that retained profits were larger than dividends in 2005. Construct EITHER a pie chart OR a bar graph to illustrate this point.
3 Explain what retained profit is used for.
4 Point out that investment in the company will now enable the company to grow and pay bigger dividends in the future.
5 End the letter by thanking the shareholder for her interest and saying that you hope this letter answers all her concerns.

Table 1 *Axon plc – where its profit went 2005*

	£000
Profit before tax distributed as:	8 128
Tax on ordinary activities	1 874
Dividends for the year	1 807
Retained profit	4 447

Source: adapted from Axon, *Annual Report & Accounts*, 2005.

MELROSE RESOURCES

Melrose Resources is an Aberdeen-based oil company. The company's interests range from high-impact offshore exploration in new hydrocarbon frontiers in Bulgaria and France, through multi-prospect exploration and development in Egypt to enhanced recovery projects in the USA.

In March 2007 it placed seven million new shares in the company to fund oil drilling projects in Egypt, Texas and Bulgaria. The shares were priced at 385p each. Melrose chairman Robert Adair and Caledonia Investments participated in the placing, subscribing to 3.6 million and 621,000 shares respectively, giving Adair a 51.8% share of the group, and Caledonia Investments 8.9%. Adair said: 'We are pleased that our major institutional shareholders have supported this fundraising, which will provide us with additional flexibility in our financing arrangements during this exciting time in the company's development.'

Source: adapted from *The Herald* 6.3.2007.

1 How many new shares did Melrose Resources sell?
2 Calculate how much money they were raising as new equity.
3 What did Melrose Resources plan to do with the money raised?
4 Why might investors have wanted to buy shares in the company?
5 (a) Give two other ways the company could have raised the money.
(b) Write a short report suggesting why issuing new shares might have been better for the company than the other two sources of finance that you have suggested.

Checklist ✓

1 Why might capital be needed to start up and run a business?
2 Who might be willing to put capital into a small business?
3 A friend of the family mentions that he is looking for someone to take a 48 per cent stake in a limited company he is setting up. You have the £10 000 he is looking for saved in a building society account. What might be: (a) the advantages; and (b) the disadvantages for you of investing money in the new company?
4 Explain the meaning of: (a) share issue; (b) going public; (c) placing shares.
5 Why are investors much more willing to invest in shares of a public limited company than in a private limited company?
6 What is a stock market?
7 What is the difference between an ordinary share and a preference share?
8 How might a venture capitalist be of help to a growing company?
9 (a) What is undistributed profit? (b) What are the advantages to a business of using retained profit to finance investment?

FINANCING THE BUSINESS THROUGH BORROWING

Making decisions

Businesses need money to start up and run their operations. They can choose to get the money by borrowing it. The business needs to decide which is the most appropriate way to borrow money. In particular, it needs to consider the rate of interest, when the money needs to be repaid, whether or not it is possible to arrange the finance and what are the implications if the business gets into difficulty repaying the loan.

Rowington Ltd is an independent gate manufacturing business. It is a small family business which makes iron gates and then fits them to driveways, gardens and business premises. It is profitable and is developing a reputation in the local area. Rowington Ltd needs money to pay for the day to day running of the business, like paying the bills and wages. It also needs money for long term finance. It is a growing company and needs money for new equipment.

External and internal sources of finance

In the previous unit, two ways of raising finance for a business were explained. These were finding **equity capital** (an external source of finance) and using **retained profit** (an internal source of finance). In this unit, other external sources of finance will be covered.

Bank overdrafts

Rowington Ltd, like nearly all businesses, has a current account at a bank. It uses the cash in the account to pay its day to day bills using **cheques**. A bank might also give the business an OVERDRAFT. This means that the bank will allow it to draw out more money than it has in its account. The maximum amount it can be overdrawn (i.e. borrow) is called its **overdraft limit**. For instance, Rowington Ltd has an overdraft limit with its bank of £100,000. It uses this to pay for the day to day running of the business, including paying for materials. Sales are higher in the summer months than in the winter months, partly because people are in their gardens more. Rowington's current account tends to be far more **in the red** (i.e. overdrawn) in the summer months than in winter months.

The great advantage of an overdraft is that money is only borrowed when it is needed. This cuts down on the interest bill. Rowington borrows far more in the summer months than in the winter months. It doesn't want to be borrowing money in the winter

Wagner's

Tom and Jill Wagner ran a successful business making cider from their own farm. They decided to expand the business by opening a bar and restaurant. They built the premises on their own land from an old barn which had been dismantled on a neighbouring farm. The cost was financed by a loan of £150 000.

They opened in September, employing a chef and an assistant chef. There was a lot of interest to start with but business dropped dramatically in November and December. This was just the time when the restaurant should have been full with Christmas parties. The bar and restaurant part of the business began to lose on average £3 000 a month. Within six months, they had run up an overdraft of £18 000.

With an overdraft limit of just £20 000, the Wagners had to act. The two chefs left and were replaced by one chef. He altered the menu considerably, making it much more linked to the Wagner's organic farming and cider activities. The number of customers doubled very quickly and the restaurant became profitable.

1 What is an overdraft?
2 On what do you think the Wagners were spending the money they were borrowing through their overdraft?
3 Explain why the Wagners 'had to act' when their overdraft was £18 000 and still rising.
4 Do you think the Wagners acted quickly enough to solve their problems? Explain your arguments carefully.

months which it doesn't need and paying interest on that loan.

Overdrafts, though, can be more expensive than they seem, particularly for small businesses. Banks often charge an arrangement fee to give the overdraft and then make a charge per quarter (three months) to maintain the overdraft limit. Banks may make higher charges for cheques issued when the account is overdrawn.

Another disadvantage is that an overdraft is also repayable on demand. The bank can **call in** an overdraft (i.e. insist that the money borrowed is repaid immediately). This means that there is a risk involved in this type of borrowing.

Trade credit

Rowington Ltd gets **trade credit** from the businesses from which it buys its supplies. It doesn't have to pay for goods until at least one month after they have been delivered. The advantage is that other businesses lend money to Rowington Ltd for at least one month 'free' of charge. The more gates that Rowington makes, the more trade credit it is likely to get as its need for supplies rises.

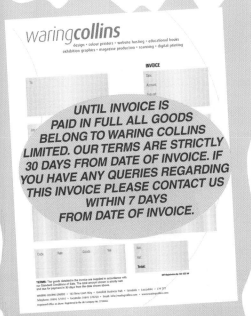

An invoice showing trade credit. Trade credit allows a business to pay for goods or services at a later date.

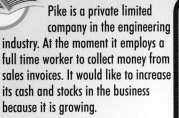

Pike is a private limited company in the engineering industry. At the moment it employs a full time worker to collect money from sales invoices. It would like to increase its cash and stocks in the business because it is growing.

1 How could Ashley Commercial Finance help Pike?

2 What disadvantages would there be for Pike if it used Ashley Commercial Finance's services?

3 An alternative way of increasing the amount of cash in the business would be for Pike to increase its overdraft with its bank. Do you think this would be better for the company rather using Ashley Commercial Finance's services? Explain your reasons carefully.

ASHLEY COMMERCIAL FINANCE

Ashley is a specialist provider of factoring or invoice finance to small businesses. We have an informal, un-bureaucratic approach to doing business. We really are the 'friend of the smaller business'. We are truly flexible and can offer a range of options to suit your needs. If you give credit to your customers and want paying more quickly we can help. Start ups, sole traders and established businesses currently use our facilities. There are many benefits to Invoice Financing with Ashley, the main ones being:

- Your business will benefit from the immediate release of cash against invoices.
- Invoice Financing will eliminate the need for you to employ a credit controller. We do all the work!
- On day one, Invoice Financing will release the agreed percentage of your existing debtor book e.g. debtors of £10 000 would release up to £8 000 on day one.
- Unlike a bank overdraft, your facility with Ashley will automatically grow with your business.

Source: adapted from Ashley Commercial Finance website.

Hence, trade credit is a way of increasing the cash in the business.

However, trade credit is not always free. Some businesses give discounts if their customers pay bills immediately. Another disadvantage of trade credit is that suppliers may stop selling goods to a business if it owes too much money through trade credit. The supplier will be afraid that the business owes too much money and may be in danger of going bankrupt or into liquidation, leaving its debt unpaid.

Factoring

Rowington Ltd uses a FACTOR to reduce the amount of money it has to borrow on overdraft. A factor is a specialist finance company. It collects the money which is owed to Rowington by other businesses and charges a fee. Remember, although Rowington gets trade credit from its suppliers, it in turn may be forced to give trade credit to the customers it supplies.

The factor will pay Rowington even if an **invoice** (a bill) hasn't been paid by a customer. Rowington is therefore guaranteed regular payment of its invoices. It also doesn't have to employ staff to

chase and collect those bills. However, a factor will only give the business a percentage of the bill, usually 80 per cent. The other 20 per cent is paid to Rowington when its customers pay the factor. The great advantage of using a factor is that it speeds up the flow of cash through a business.

Bank loans

Overdrafts, trade credit and factoring are different ways in which a business like Rowington can increase the cash and working capital flowing round the business. However, they are not suitable ways of raising money to finance the replacement of, say, £50 000 of outdated brewing equipment. This needs some form of longer term finance like a bank LOAN.

With a bank loan, the business usually borrows a fixed amount of money and then pays it back in regular fixed instalments. These repayments include the interest on the outstanding money owed. The bank may demand security on the loan. This means that the business has to pledge assets to the bank which the bank can sell if the business fails to repay the loan. For instance, Rowington Ltd could offer its premises as **security** or **collateral**.

A MORTGAGE is a type of long term loan. The money borrowed is usually used to pay for the purchase of property, such as new buildings or land. The property is then used as security for the loan.

Leasing and hire purchase

Rowington Ltd has a number of computers in its offices. It could have bought them outright, but it would have to borrow the money to do that. Instead, it has LEASED (i.e. rented) the computers from a leasing firm. Many leasing contracts also include maintenance contracts where the leasing company maintains and repairs the computers as part of the price of the rental. Leasing equipment is usually more expensive over the lifetime of the computer than buying it outright. On the other hand, it could work out cheaper if the leasing firm can buy computers in bulk and pass on the discount to its customers. There can

also be important tax advantages to renting equipment rather than buying outright.

Maintenance contracts included in a leasing deal, whilst often expensive, reduce the risk of sudden large unexpected bills if the computer breaks down.

HIRE PURCHASE (HP) is an alternative way of borrowing money. Rowington has bought two company cars on HP. It pays a fixed monthly instalment for them. Legally, each instalment is a rental payment and the finance house, a type of bank which specialises in hire purchase deals, will own the cars until the last instalment is paid.

Debentures

Large public limited companies can borrow money through the City of London by issuing DEBENTURES (also called **stocks** or **bonds**). These are usually long term loans, normally for between 5 and 25 years. Interest has to be paid on the loan.

Grants

Grants to businesses are given by a wide number of bodies including the UK government and the EU. Monies are usually distributed by local governments on a selective basis. It is usually small businesses that benefit from business grants. If the person prepares a business plan which shows that the business is likely to succeed, a 'grant' may be given for a period of time. The main advantage of a grant is that quite often the money given does not have to be repaid. It is a free source of finance. However, usually, there are qualification restrictions. For example, many grants are given on the understanding that a business sets up in a certain location or creates jobs. Also, there is often a lot of administration to do when applying for a grant. There can be a lengthy process of form-filling and waiting. It can get overwhelming and frustrating for the applicant.

Swaffham Contractors Ltd

Swaffham Contractors Ltd is owned by Linda Bennett and Ralph Carter. The company owns a tractor and carries out contract work such as ground work for arable farmers in the area. The company was set up 18 months ago using the capital shown in the pie chart. As the chart shows, Ralph's father provided some capital, however, he takes no active part in running the business. Most of the capital was used to buy a second hand Massey Ferguson tractor for £26 500 which is often worked over 80 hours a week.

The company also leases agricultural implements when carrying out contract work. Leasing has been a popular source of funding for the business. Once the tractor was purchased there was very little money left to buy important implements such as ploughs, harrows, hedge-cutters, balers and cultivators. Fuel for the tractor is purchased using trade credit. The company is sent a bill every month and then gets a further 30 days to pay.

Bank loan £5 000

Linda Bennett Share capital £10 000

Alan Carter (Ralph's brother) £5 000 share capital

Ralph Carter £10 000 Share capital

Total capital £30 000

Figure 1 *Start-up capital for Swaffham Contractors Ltd*

1 What was the start-up capital mainly used for?
2 (a) What proportion of the business does Alan Carter own?
  (b) Describe the role played by Alan in the business.
3 Using this case as an example, explain what is meant by trade credit.
4 Discuss the advantages and disadvantages to Swaffham Contractors Ltd of leasing as a source of finance.

Lesley Robinson

Lesley Robinson has just finished a course at a local college in Rochdale in the North West of England. She is young, ambitious and wants to set up a business in interior design. However, she needs money to do some market research and meet the set-up costs. She only has £1,000 of her own money. She has drawn up a business plan and thinks she needs a total of £5,000 to get started. She thinks a bank will be reluctant to lend her very much but reckons she might qualify for a business grant. She did some research on the Internet and identified the schemes below.

1 What is meant by a business grant?
2 Suggest two schemes which Lesley might be interested in. Explain your answers.
3 Discuss the advantages and disadvantages to Lesley of using grant funding.

New Entrepreneur Scholarships (NES) - England
Provides support, mentoring and finance to potential entrepreneurs

The Prince's Trust Test Marketing Grants
Provides pre-start grants to young people for market research

The Prince's Trust Grants
Provides grants for young people starting up in business

Social Risk Capital Fund - Greater Merseyside
Provides financial assistance for the formation of new social enterprises

Crisis Changing Lives Programme
Provides grants for solitary people who have been homeless to help them move towards a work based, vocational goal

Heritage Tourism Improvement Scheme - North West England
Provides grants for owners of historic houses, gardens and buildings to develop new business opportunities

North West Business Investment Scheme (NWBIS)
Provides funding for small and medium-sized enterprises (SMEs) in the North West

---

key terms

Debenture - a long term loan to a business.
Factor - a business which collects the debts of other businesses, for which it charges a fee.
Hire purchase - legally, renting equipment prior to buying it. In effect, it is a type of loan.
Leasing - renting equipment or premises.
Loan - borrowing a sum of money which then has to be repaid with interest over a period of time like 1-5 years, typically in fixed monthly instalments.
Mortgage - a loan where property is used as security.
Overdraft - borrowing money from a bank by drawing more money than is actually in a current account. Interest is charged on the amount overdrawn.

Checklist ✓

1 What does it mean if a business with a bank account has: (a) a £5 000 overdraft limit; (b) its overdraft called in?
2 Explain how a business can borrow money free of interest from other businesses.
3 How can a factor help a business increase the amount of cash it holds?
4 (a) Outline the differences between a bank loan, a mortgage and an overdraft.
   (b) A business wishes: (i) to expand turnover by buying in more stock for sale; (ii) buy a new machine; and (iii) purchase a new office building. Explain which of the three methods of financing in (a) might be most appropriate for each of these projects.
5 (a) What are the differences between leasing and hire purchase? (b) Explain which of the following a business might consider financing through a leasing agreement:
   (i) a photocopier; (ii) a company car;
   (iii) an increase in stocks; (iv) a computer system; (v) an increase in creditors.
6 Who might give a grant to a business?

SUMMARY CASE STUDY

THE FINANCE SOUTH EAST ACCELERATOR FUND

The Finance South East Accelerator Fund is a £10 million loan fund providing a source of finance for growing companies in the South East region. It can lend companies an initial £100 000 at any stage as long as they can demonstrate the potential for significant growth. A second loan of up to £100 000 can be made after 9 months.

The Accelerator Fund fills a gap between traditional borrowing and equity funding. It can be used on its own but is best used as funding alongside other sources of finance. In 80 per cent of the deals that have been agreed with companies, the Accelerator loans have formed part of a larger finance package.

The Accelerator Fund has supported companies from many different business sectors, including satellite communications, a café chain, healthcare and sports companies, a software business and a community cinema. Some of its clients are starting new businesses and others are more established - for example it has helped a company employing 50 staff with a turnover of £8 million.

Source: adapted from www.financesoutheast.com/ourfunds

1 Explain whether a loan from the Finance South East Accelerator Fund is an internal or external source of finance for a business.
2 What types of business might borrow from the Finance South East Accelerator Fund?
3 The Finance South East Accelerator Fund provide loans for businesses. What is the difference between a loan and a mortgage?
4 Discuss the advantages and disadvantages to a business borrowing money from the Finance South East Accelerator Fund.

Making decisions

Businesses need to find the right type of financing for their situation. Which type of financing would be cheapest? Which would be the most suitable? Would it put the business at any risk? What sources of finance are available?

BANK

Share Certificate

GOVERNMENT GRANTS

PARTNERS

What is the money needed for?

Natasha Williams, the chef described two units earlier would not take out a 5 year loan to pay for an increase in the electricity bill. Equally, Rowington Ltd, the brewery described in the previous unit, would not finance the building of an extension using trade credit. In general, short term financing is used to pay for an increase in **cash** and **working capital**. For instance, when Rowington Ltd gets an increase in orders for beer in the summer, it is likely to increase its overdraft and trade credit to pay for this.

The purchase of equipment or buildings (**fixed capital** for the business) is generally financed using longer term methods. Taking out a loan may be suitable for buying a company car or new kitchen equipment. Issuing new shares could be suitable for a large expansion project by Rowington Ltd.

Cost

Different types of financing have different costs. Borrowing money means that interest has to be paid. Leasing a company car costs the hire of the lease. Issuing new shares means that extra dividends will have to be paid. For Natasha Williams and Rowington Ltd, cost would be an important element in deciding which type of finance to choose.

Risk

Rowington, a limited company, can issue new shares and retain profit to increase its capital. Unlike a loan, where interest has to be paid, dividends to shareholders don't have to be given if profits fall or the company makes a loss. So borrowing is perhaps riskier than increasing the capital of the business. One way of measuring this risk is to calculate the GEARING RATIO, the ratio of loans to share capital. The formula below can be used.

$$\text{Gearing ratio} = \frac{\text{Loan capital}}{\text{Share capital}} \times 100$$

A company with more loans than share capital (i.e. a gearing ratio of over 100 per cent) would be risky. Rowington, with loans equal to 25 per cent of share capital, (a gearing ratio of 25 per cent) is relatively safe.

Henderson Group

Henderson Group, a private limited company and majority-owned by Geoffrey and Martin Agnew, is a food wholesaler. It is one of Northern Ireland's biggest employers and supplies more than 400 Spar, Eurospar, Vivo and Vivoxtra stores, some of which it also owns. Its wholesale arm supplies fresh and frozen food from a 230 000 sq ft warehouse outside Belfast. Other units include the Henderson Retail corner shop chain, and shop developer Henderson Group Property. Sales in 2005 reached £358.9 million, when the group opened 27 new stores. A further 28 are planned for this year. The company employs 1 847 staff and made a profit of £9.5 million in 2005.

Source: adapted from The Sunday Times, Top Track 250.

1 State whether the following expenditure by Henderson would require long term or short term funding: (a) buying land for new stores; (b) paying wages; (c) buying food from farmers and other suppliers; (d) buying new lorries for distribution.
2 Explain why at the moment Henderson could not sell shares on the stock market to raise finance.
3 Henderson made a profit of £9.5 million in 2005. What are the advantages of using retained profit as a source of finance?
4 What sources of finance might be suitable to fund the building of a £4 million warehouse for Henderson?

Availability of finance

Some types of finance are available to most businesses.

- Businesses, except those starting up, can use retained profit.
- Bank loans and overdrafts are frequently used. Small businesses, such as sole proprietorships, often complain though that they are charged much higher rates of interest on loans and overdrafts than larger businesses. Banks justify this by arguing that small businesses are more likely to go bankrupt or into liquidation than large businesses. Hence, lending to small businesses is more risky and they have to charge higher rates of interest to make the same rate of profit overall compared to lending to larger businesses.
- Trade credit, hire purchase, leasing and factoring are also possibilities.
- Smaller businesses, like sole proprietors or partnerships, have difficulty finding people or other businesses who might inject money as equity capital into their business. So they tend to rely on borrowing money rather than raising equity.
- Private limited companies can issue equity capital in the form of shares, but they tend to be sold to a small number of people, often family or friends. Plcs can issue shares on a stock exchange, which puts large numbers of potential investors into contact with businesses.

key terms

Gearing ratio - the ratio of long term borrowings of a company to its share capital.

Checklist ✓

1 A business has the following finance needs. Explain what type of finance would be most suitable for: (a) a new factory; (b) a company car; (c) an increase in purchases of components; (d) the take over of another company; (e) an increase in the number of workers employed; (f) the setting up of a new subsidiary company.

2 Explain why the following might be considered poor business practice. (a) A small business buys a £50 000 new machine and finances it by increasing its overdraft. (b) A hotel business takes out a loan for £30 000 repayable over five years to pay for increased staff costs during very busy holiday months in July and August. (c) A business takes out a mortgage on its factory repayable over fifteen years to pay for a £30 000 company car for the chairperson. (d) A business which has made losses for the past three years and is close to going into liquidation takes out a five year loan to pay off some of its other debts.

3 Why wouldn't the following happen? (a) A sole proprietor issues shares in her company to finance an increase in working capital. (b) A partnership issues debentures on the Stock Exchange. (c) A public limited company negotiates a £400 loan from its bankers.

4 Explain why large businesses are likely to have a greater choice of finance than small businesses.

SUMMARY CASE STUDY

PERTH HOLDINGS LTD

Perth Holdings Ltd is a Scottish-based company that makes drilling and other engineering equipment for the oil industry. It was set up in 1999 with £160 000 of share capital, owned equally between Ella McDonald and Shane MacTaggart, a £40 000 bank loan and a £10 000 local authority grant. Ella, who studied Business at Glasgow University, was adamant that the business should be properly funded at the beginning. She knew that small businesses that lacked funding in the initial stages would struggle. The company rents a factory unit on an industrial estate and leases about 80 per cent of its plant, machinery and equipment.

The company has done well since starting up. The rising oil price has resulted in a boom in oil exploration and Perth Holdings have benefited. Most of the company's recent growth has been funded through retained profit. Ella and Shane have been happy to retain around 90 per cent of the profit for investment purposes. This has avoided the need to increase borrowings significantly.

In 2006 the price of oil reached a record high and the factory was running at full capacity. Ella and Shane decided it was time to move to larger premises and cash in on the continuing boom. They drew up a business plan for expansion. They calculated that they would need to raise £200 000 to move to larger premises and update their technology. A bank agreed to loan them all the money. This is what happened and the expansion went ahead.

1 Draw a pie chart to show the start-up capital of the business.
2 What is the main advantage of using a grant as a source of finance?
3 Many new businesses struggle because they are undercapitalised (this means that there is insufficient capital at the start). How did Perth Holdings avoid being undercapitalised?
4 (a) What happened to gearing as a result of the expansion in 2006?
  (b) Would it have been better if Ella and Shane had funded all the £200 000 from retained profit rather than borrowing the money?

Making decisions

Businesses have to sell what they produce. So they have to make marketing decisions. These include:
- what product will be sold;
- what price it will be sold at;
- how the customer will get to know about the product;
- where the best place to sell the product to the customer will be.

Diageo is the one of the world's largest alcoholic drinks businesses. In 2006, it had worldwide sales of £7 260 million excluding taxes on alcohol. Its brands include Smirnoff Vodka, Johnnie Walker whisky, Guinness beer, and Baileys liqueur. It sells into 180 countries and employs over 22 000 people. It has manufacturing facilities in countries such as the UK, Ireland, the United States, Spain, Australia and India.

Marketing

MARKETING can be defined as the management process which is responsible for identifying potentially profitable products and then selling them to consumers. What does this mean for a company like Diageo?

Market research First, a business needs to understand the market into which it is selling. For Diageo, this means working with existing customers and identifying their needs. But it also means identifying new product areas. Through researching the market, Diageo can identify the products which it can sell at a profit.

The product Businesses need to have the right product for the customer that satisfies the customers needs. For Diageo, this means having a range of high quality premium drinks. They must be packaged and presented attractively, whether being bought in a supermarket or an airport or in a bar or pub. There must be a range of drinks which will appeal to every different customer group. Some drinks like Smirnoff Vodka might appeal to younger customers, whilst other drinks, like malt whisky brands, might appeal to older customers.

Price The price of a product must reflect the value that customers place on the product. Having the cheapest product on the market is not necessarily the best strategy if the product is low quality. Equally, having high prices can lose a business sales to cheaper priced competitors. The price of a product in the long term must also allow the business to make a profit by selling it. Diageo's strategy is to sell drinks for which customers will pay a premium price. To get this price, Diageo has to sell brands which are seen as being high quality and high value.

Promotion Customers need to know that a product exists to buy. Promotion is about giving them knowledge about the product. It is also about persuading them that

1 Why do you think these products need to be marketed?
2 (a) What is meant by 'the marketing mix'?
    (b) How do you think these products could be marketed? To answer this question, you need to comment on each of 'the 4 Ps'.

they want to buy the product. Diageo uses promotion to communicate with its customers and potential customers. It tells them about the range of products available. Diageo invests in promotion in order to reinforce the premium brand image of its products

Place Any successful business has to have its products available both where and when a customer wants to buy. The product must be in the right place at the right time for the customer to buy. For Diageo, this means making sure that its products are available both in retail outlets like supermarkets and off-licences, but also in bars and pubs round the world. It is constantly looking for new ways to get its products to the consumer. At the moment, for example, it is investing in distribution systems in Brazil, Russia, India and China to increase sales in those countries.

Sometimes, product, price, promotion and place are known as the MARKETING MIX or the '4Ps'. They are the fundamentals of all effective marketing.

The need for marketing

Businesses like Diageo need to market their products because there is so much choice in the market. There are so many different products on the market for customers to buy. A business would like to be in a **sellers' market** where customers have little choice but to buy from them. In a **buyers' market**, though, businesses have to compete against other businesses for sales. The greater the competition, the more businesses have to be **market orientated** and the greater is the need for effective marketing.

Diageo operates in CONSUMER MARKETS, selling **consumer goods** to other consumers. Its suppliers, like bottle manufacturing companies, operate in PRODUCER MARKETS, selling producer goods to businesses. Marketing strategies differ from market to market. For example, Diageo might use television advertising to promote its products. In contrast, a bottle manufacturing company might rely far more on its sales force to generate sales.

SUMMARY CASE STUDY

JEANS

Levi's, Wrangler and Lee, the world's most famous denim brands, are battling to maintain sales. Levi Strauss & Co, which is 156 years old, suffered eight years of falling sales until 2005. 'Classic' jeans and other denim clothes made by these companies have been squeezed. Some consumers are going down-market to buy low price jeans sold by supermarkets, like Tesco, and discount shops like Primark and New Look. Other consumers are moving up-market to buy high-fashion designer brands like Diesel, often priced at over £200 per piece.

Levi Strauss and VH Corporation, the US company that owns Wrangler and Lee, have been fighting back. They have decided to go up-market to compete with the designer labels produced by other companies. In Europe, for example, Lee has introduced its Gold Label range which retails for about £100. Levi has introduced new Blue and Red Wire brands at premium prices.

The other part of the strategy to raise sales has been to increase the number of shops operated by the denim companies. Traditionally, sales have taken place through department stores or clothes shops and brands have been sold alongside competing brands. Levi, Wrangler and Lee have had little control over how their garments are displayed and what is stocked. By selling through their own shops, Levi and VH have much greater control over what and how their products are sold. VH, for example, plans to double its number of stores worldwide by 2009 to around 1 000.

Source: adapted from *The Times*, 23.10.2006.

1 Why do Levi Strauss and VH Corporation need to market their products?
2 Using the 4Ps, explain how Levi Strauss and VH Corporation are changing their marketing to increase sales.
3 Discuss whether a better strategy for these companies would be to sell jeans as cheaply as possible.

key terms

Consumer market - a market where a business sells to consumers.
Marketing - the management process which is responsible for identifying potentially profitable products and then selling them to customers.
Producer market - a market where one business sells to other businesses.
The marketing mix - the combination of factors which help the business sell a product - usually summarised as the 4 Ps, which are price, product, promotion and place.

Checklist ✓

1 List FOUR different aspects of marketing a product.
2 What are the 4 Ps?
3 Why do businesses have to market their products?
4 What is the difference between a buyers' market and a sellers' market?

Making decisions

Businesses have to decide what to make and sell. This involves finding out who are the likely customers of the business. For instance, are they old or young, rich or poor, or Northerners or Southerners? Businesses with this sort of information are far more likely to be successful than ones who have little knowledge of their market.

PC Media is the UK's leading consumer magazine publisher, with a portfolio of brands, selling over 350 million copies each year. Its magazines reach over 70 per cent of UK women and 50 per cent of UK men, over 28 million UK adults. With more than 150 years of publishing heritage, IPC's diverse portfolio offers something for everyone - *What's on TV, Now, Marie Claire, In Style, Woman & Home, Ideal Home, Loaded, Nuts, NME, Country Life, The Field, Rugby World, Practical Boat Owner, Pick Me Up* and *TV easy* are some examples of their products.

Market segments

IPC Media knows that different readers want to read different magazines. Young males aged 18-25 might want to read *Loaded* or *Nuts*. Teenagers might want to read the music magazine *NME*. Females aged over 40 might want to read *Woman's Own* or *Woman's Weekly*. IPC Media therefore tries to cater for different MARKET SEGMENTS. A market segment is a part of a market which contains a group of buyers with similar characteristics. For example, *Yachting Monthly* is bought mainly by people who actively sail their boats.

Some businesses make products which they hope will appeal to the whole market. Birds Eye Wall's, for instance, hopes that everyone, whether young or old, male or female, rich or poor, will want to buy a Cornetto ice cream. Many products, though, are aimed at a segment of a market, like IPC's *Golf Monthly* is aimed at golfers.

Knowing who are its possible customers helps IPC Media to target different market segments. For instance, *Loaded* may be advertised on the television during a football match. A children's magazine is likely to be advertised on television between 4.00pm and 5.00pm.

Age, gender, income, area, ethnic group and occupation

Markets can be segmented according to the characteristics of buyers.

Age IPC Media offers magazines which will appeal to people of certain ages. For example, the women's magazine *Chat* is irreverent, gritty and funny and aimed at younger women while women's magazines such as *Woman* and *Woman's Weekly* are more conservative and aimed at older women.

Gender Quite a proportion of IPC's magazines are aimed at males or females specifically. For example, the readership of *Rugby World* is mainly male while *Marie Claire*, the fashion magazine, is aimed at women. That is not to say that some women do not read *Rugby World* and some men do not read *Marie Claire*.

Income This is particularly important when IPC sells advertising space to companies. High income readers will be particularly attractive to companies that want to advertise in magazines. Magazines like *Horse & Hounds*, aimed at affluent equestrians, and the *Shooting Times*, aimed at wealthy rural residents, will be popular with companies that sell expensive holidays, for example.

1 (a) Make a list of as many magazines and comics as you can think of which are bought by or for children and teenagers.
(b) By the side of each magazine or comic, write down the market segment which it targets.
2 A publishing company wants to launch a profitable new children's or teenage magazine. Which segment of the market would you suggest and why?

Table 1 *Socio-economic groups.*

Social grade	Social status	Head of household's occupation	% of total UK population (approx.)
A	Upper middle class	Higher managerial, administrative or professional such as doctors, lawyers and company directors	3.5%
B	Middle	Intermediate managerial, administrative or professional such as teachers, nurses and managers	12-13%
C_1	Lower middle class	Supervisory or clerical and junior managerial, administrative or professional such as shop assistants, clerks and police constables	22%
C_2	Skilled working class	Skilled manual workers such as carpenters, cooks and train drivers	32-33%
D	Working class	Semi-skilled and unskilled manual workers such as fitters and store keepers	19-20%
E	The poorest in society	State pensioners or widows, casual or lower grade workers, or long term unemployed	10%

The higher the income of the readers, the more companies are usually prepared to pay for advertising space.

Area Shoppers in the North East of England might have different tastes from those in the London area. People in Yorkshire and Humberside eat more fish than those in any other region in the country, for example. Businesses need to be aware of these differences when deciding what to sell and how to sell. For instance, IPC will aim *Country Life*, which contains material on architecture, the arts, gardens and gardening, the countryside, field-sports and wildlife, at rural customers and not those living in cities and conurbations.

Ethnic, cultural and religious groups In 2007 IPC did not publish any magazines aimed specifically at ethnic or religious groups. However, many of its magazines are aimed at groups of people who share specific interests or hobbies. For example, *Amateur Photographer* appeals to those interested in buying photographic equipment or wanting advice about improving their picture taking. The *Railway Magazine*, a clear and trusted voice for the railway community, covering all aspects of the scene from steam through to modern rail developments, is likely to be purchased by train-spotters.

There are radio and television programmes aimed at religious groups, such as the Sunday Programme on Radio 4. Asian Gold, a radio station based in Southall, West London, has programmes that include news bulletins (English and Asian), music, sports, poetry, comedy, and various types of traditional and modern music (ghazals, qawalis and hip-hop).

Different groups can give opportunities for businesses to sell products and services. Equally, businesses need to be careful when selling products. For example, an orthodox Jew would not buy pork and Hindus would not buy beef.

Socio-economic groupings One of the most important ways of dividing up the market is to split consumers into SOCIO-ECONOMIC GROUPS. This divides people up according to their occupations (i.e. jobs) or the occupation of the head of the household (such as the mother or father in a family).

Table 1 shows that households are split into five categories from A to E. The C category is divided into C1, lower middle class, and C2, skilled manual workers. So, for instance, Sky knows from its subscription information that 47 per cent of those in socio-economic groups A, B and C1 subscribe to Sky Sports 1.

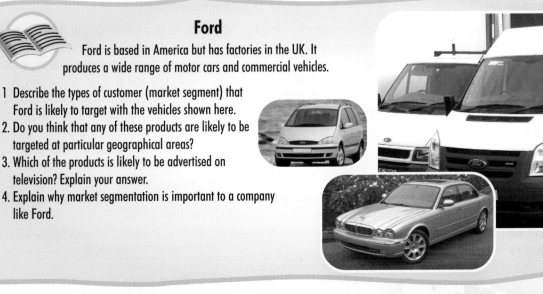

Ford

Ford is based in America but has factories in the UK. It produces a wide range of motor cars and commercial vehicles.

1. Describe the types of customer (market segment) that Ford is likely to target with the vehicles shown here.
2. Do you think that any of these products are likely to be targeted at particular geographical areas?
3. Which of the products is likely to be advertised on television? Explain your answer.
4. Explain why market segmentation is important to a company like Ford.

The market for holidays

Everyone takes a holiday from time to time. The market for holidays contains many different segments. The companies described below all sell holidays.

Pontins
Pontins offers low cost holidays in a number of resorts around the UK such as Blackpool, Southport, Prestatyn Sands and Wall Park. It provides self-catering and chalet accommodation and caters particularly for families.

Saga
SAGAtravelshop provides a wide range of holidays for the over 50s. These include touring, ocean cruising, resorts and river cruising.

Kuoni Travel Ltd
Kuoni Travel are Britain's best known long-haul luxury holiday tour operator offering a wide range of tailor-made holiday types in over 65 countries.

DR Yachting
DR Yachting provides sailing holidays in the Greek Islands for disabled people in their own-skippered yacht. The company has consulted with experts in special needs matters, in order to outfit the boats for handicapped people. For example, accessing the yacht is easy. For boarding, a 90cm wide gangway is provided in order to facilitate the access.

Source: adapted from Saga, Pontins, Kuoni Travel and DR Yachting websites.

Economic trends
Incomes are rising at between 2 and 3 per cent per year and much of the extra earning power of workers is going on services like holidays and meals out. The number of people over 50 is also rising because of the large increase in the birth rate between the mid-1940s and the mid-1960s. Pensioners have never been as well off as they are today, although there will continue to be a large minority of pensioners who will have incomes substantially below the national average. Rising incomes and rising taxes have allowed services for the most vulnerable in society, such as the disabled, to expand. Like pensioners, the disabled today have access to services which would have been unimaginable even just twenty years ago.

1 Why are there so many different segments in the market for holidays?
2 Describe the market segments that each of the above companies is targeting.
3 Discuss whether all the market segments served by these companies are likely to grow at the same rate in future.

Further down the socio-economic scale, this falls to 23 per cent of C2s, but rises to 30 per cent of groups D and E (BARB/RSMB estimates).

Other ways of segmenting the market

Businesses can analyse their markets in a large number of different ways other than just by type of consumer. One way is to assess whether customers are repeat customers or one-time customers. Repeat customers are those who keep on buying the product. They have brand loyalty. A one-time customer is a customer who buys the product once but is unlikely to do so again. For instance, for IPC, a repeat customer might be somebody who has bought the *TV Times* every week for the last 6 years. A one-time customer might be somebody who bought *Nuts* once to read on a train journey.

Another way of analysing the market is to find out whether customers bought the product on impulse or whether the purchase was planned. For instance, a shopper in a supermarket might be attracted by the cover of *Homes & Gardens* and make an on-the-spot decision to buy it. Another customer might pay by subscription for a copy of the *Angler's Mail*, to be delivered every week.

Source: adapted from the IPC Media website, www.ipcmedia.com.

EITHER answer questions 1 and 2 for your mini-company OR answer all the questions based on the Dry Flower Company.

The Dry Flower Company

Your business idea has been to make dried flower arrangements. One member of the company has a parent who is a well known local expert on dried flower arrangements. She has shown you how to make them and has promised help if you run into any problems. She has also talked to you about where to get all the dried flowers from and the baskets needed to make the arrangements.

It is the Autumn term. You have decided to sell your product, priced at £4.99, in two ways. Firstly, you have run off leaflets advertising the dried flower arrangements. You have asked your teachers/lecturers to give one leaflet to each student in their tutor group to take home to their parents. Secondly, there is an important Christmas Bazaar in November, which is very popular with parents. You have been allowed to have a stall at the bazaar.

1 What is the product that you are selling?
2 Who are your customers likely to be? For instance, are they likely to be men or women, older people or younger people, people with a high income or people with a low income?
3 Which method do you think is most likely to result in sales from your targeted customers - the leaflet or the Christmas Bazaar? Explain your answer.
4 You have decided that you want a second product to sell alongside your existing product.
(a) How could you adapt your existing product to make it appeal to a different segment of the market?
(b) Explain why it might appeal to a different market segment.

Checklist ✓

1 Why is it important for a business to know at which segment of the market to aim its products?
2 Explain what type of person by (i) age, (ii) gender and (iii) income you think is likely to buy: (a) clothes from Topshop; (b) a pair of ladies' shoes from Marks & Spencer; (c) a pint of beer in a pub; (d) a copy of the Financial Times; (e) a spaceman Lego set; (f) a Porsche car; (g) a month's holiday in Spain in February.
3 What is the difference between an A and a C1 in terms of socio-economic grouping?
4 Socio-economic group E is not usually a sales target for businesses. Why not?
5 A person in socio-economic group B might go touring in France in the summer. A person in socio-economic group C or D might go to Benidorm on a package tour. Why do you think there is a difference in the holiday destinations of the two groups?
6 What is the difference between a repeat customer and a one-time customer?
7 What is an impulse purchase?

SUMMARY CASE STUDY

SPORTS EQUIPMENT

A manufacturer of sports equipment is studying its market.
1 What is meant by 'socio-economic groupings'?
2 It wants to target advertising for its range of: (i) darts equipment; (ii) soccer equipment; and (iii) golf equipment. How might the information about socio-economic groupings in Table 2 help?
3 The manufacturer is launching two new ranges: a swimwear range and a keep fit/yoga range. (a) Who are likely to be its customers? (b) How would it market the range of products to target these customers? Base your answer around the '4 Ps' of marketing.

Table 2 *Participation in sports and games.*

Percentage in each group participating in each activity in the 4 weeks before interview

	Professional	Employers and managers	Intermediate & junior non-manual	Skilled manual & own account non-professional	Semi-skilled manual and personal service	Unskilled manual
Snooker, pool & billiards	11	12	8	17	10	9
Darts	6	5	4	8	6	6
Swimming	27	19	18	10	11	8
Keep fit, yoga	13	12	18	6	9	8
Soccer	6	3	3	6	3	3
Golf	9	10	5	6	2	2

Source: adapted from ONS, *Social Trends*.

Making decisions

Businesses need information if they are to make good decisions. One way of gaining that information is by carrying out market research. There are various types of market research. Businesses need to decide what market research methods are most likely to give them the information they need.

Nestlé is the world's leading food company. In recent years it has focused on becoming a nutrition, health and wellness company. This is the idea of supporting people to lead healthier lives. Nestlé is home to a wide range of brands including Shredded Wheat, Winalot, Nescafe and KitKat. Its Maggi brand is aimed at the 'food service sector' - chefs and the catering trade.

Product and market orientation

Many businesses are PRODUCT ORIENTATED. This means that they design and make a product, and then try to convince consumers to buy it. An example might be a drug company, like Glaxo, developing a product to help consumers with an illness and then advertising it.

Businesses can also be MARKET ORIENTATED. This is where they try to find out what consumers want before making the final product. In 2004, Nestlé noticed that sales of Maggi 'A Natural Choice', a range of culinary (cooking) products that is primarily targeted at chefs, were falling. This was because the product had come to be seen as uninteresting and old fashioned due to its dehydrated format and flavour. The product failed to meet the needs of users. Nestlé decided to carry out an investigation to get a deeper insight into chef and consumer views. Finding out about what consumers want and need, and what makes them buy, is called MARKET RESEARCH.

Why research the market?

Businesses which are mainly product orientated risk spending a large amount of resources launching a product which proves to be a failure. Researching the market helps reduce this risk. It should focus research and design effort onto products which have a chance of success in the market place. When the product is launched, a carefully researched product stands less change of failing.

Stages of market research

Market research attempts to find the answers to questions a

EASYJET founder Stelios Haji-Ioannou has reportedly pulled the plug on plans to revolutionise the movie business with a chain of bright orange no-frills cinemas.

The entrepreneur has closed his sole EasyCinema venue, in Milton Keynes, after three years of operation. Mr Haji-Ioannou blamed the failure of the cinema on high rents. The site's landowner, UCI, was recently bought over by Terra Firma, which also owns Odeon cinemas. He reportedly said: 'Now that Odeon, who have become both our landlords as well as our competitors, are demanding a totally unrealistic rent we have decided to let them operate the cinema.' The entrepreneur had hoped to create a national cinema chain with tickets selling for as little as 20p during quiet periods.

Source: adapted from www.mkweb.co.uk

1 How might the information in Figure 1 have influenced Stelios Haji-Ioannou in his decision to open a cinema in 2003?
2 Using this case as an example, explain what is meant by:
   (a) desk research; and (b) secondary data.
3 After reading 65 scripts a film producer has drawn up a short list of two. One is a children's film about a school teacher who persuades his pupils to compete in a round-the-world cycle race. The other is a film about two people who went to the same school and meet again after many years, which is likely to appeal to the over 40s. If you were the film producer wanting to maximise the potential audience, which one would you choose to make? Explain your answer.

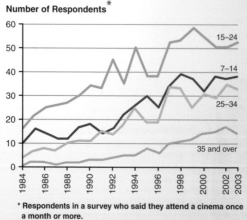

Number of Respondents*

15–24
7–14
25–34
35 and over

* Respondents in a survey who said they attend a cinema once a month or more.

Figure 1 *Cinema attendance by age*
Source: adapted from *Social Trends*, 2005, Office for National Statistics.

business might have about its market. For example, Nestlé carried out some research to find out why sales of Maggi, were falling.

The market researcher must then decide what information might help answer this question. Nestlé wanted information about the views of chefs and other consumers who bought Maggi. They wanted to know what people thought of the product. The market researcher then decides how best to collect this information. In this case Nestlé researchers spoke face-to-face with chefs and held open discussions.

The information is then collected and analysed. Finally, the business has to make a decision about what to do in the light of the information gained.

Desk research

DESK RESEARCH involves the use of SECONDARY DATA. This is information which is already available, both within and outside the business.

Information within the business
Businesses collect information routinely. Invoices, for instance, will tell them how much they sell and who they are selling to. Nestle will have records of sales of all their products. It was these records which showed that sales of Maggi were falling.

Information from outside the business
Businesses can also collect information which is available from sources outside the business. Figure 2 shows some of these sources. Nestlé may use market research reports which discuss trends in the various markets they operate in. They might be able to calculate their share in each market if they can obtain figures for sales of products from rival companies.

Field research

FIELD RESEARCH involves the collection of PRIMARY DATA - information which no one has yet collected. It is collected specially for the particular piece of research. Primary data is collected through direct investigation, usually through observation, survey or experiment. Nestlé used field research when talking to chefs and consumers about Maggi.

Observation

Looking at and recording what people do and how they behave can be important. For instance, a supermarket may find that sales in one aisle in the store are very poor. By observing people, it would be possible to see whether the problem was that shoppers were avoiding the aisle. However, observation can't tell the supermarket anything about why shoppers are behaving in this way.

Surveys

A SURVEY usually involves asking questions of RESPONDENTS - people or organisations who reply to the questions asked. Nestle, for instance, used a survey to find out what chefs and consumers thought about Maggi. The survey showed that the market was split into a number of segments. The chefs interviewed fitted into four main segments. These are shown in Figure 3.

There are different ways of conducting surveys. A postal survey, where QUESTIONNAIRES

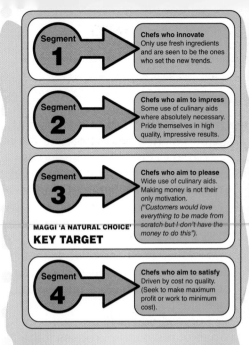

Figure 3 *The market segments identified in the survey carried out by Nestlé*

are sent through the post, or newspaper surveys, where readers are invited to fill in and return a questionnaire in a newspaper, are cheap. Telephone surveys, personal interviews, and consumers' panels are more expensive because an interviewer has to be employed to interview customers. However, only a fraction of customers sent a postal survey will respond. A much larger proportion of those approached will take part in telephone and personal interviews. The interviewer can also help the respondents understand what questions mean and how they should be answered.

If the interview is in a person's home, products, packaging, etc. can also be shown so that reactions can be recorded. A consumer panel, where a group of people meet together, allows researchers to see how people react in a group situation to a product or idea. In the case of Maggi, the chefs and consumers were involved in open discussions about the product. Four different market segments were identified as a result of the discussions and it

> ○ **Internal sources** - such as sales invoices, reports, accounts.
>
> ○ **Government** - published statistics, such as consumer spending figures; reports such as Monopolies and Mergers Commission Reports
>
> ○ **The media** - reports in newspapers, magazines, on radio and on television.
>
> ○ **Trade associations** - statistics or reports published by national organisations such as the TUC, the CBI or chambers of commerce, or industry associations such as the Engineering Employers Federation or the National Farmers Union.
>
> ○ **Research organisations** - reports prepared by specialist market research organisations such as Mintel or Mori; articles published in academic journals such as university journals.

Figure 2 *Sources of secondary data.*

was clear that segment 3 provided the best opportunity for the Maggi product. The research helped Nestlé with ideas for developing the brand. It was proposed to create a product with more natural qualities for 'chefs who aim to please' who want their cooking to be as fresh tasting as possible. The research also helped Nestle to identify a target market. Maggi 'A Natural Choice' target was to be 'chefs who aim to please'. Their prime aim is to provide delicious, wholesome foods that customers enjoy. These chefs enjoy their work and have a pride in the satisfaction they give customers.

Surveys can only be useful for market research purposes if the questions asked are appropriate. For instance, sometimes it is important to ask closed questions. These are questions which have a definite answer. An example would be: 'How many cartons of Maggi did you buy last week?' Other times, the market researcher might want to find out about opinions and allow the respondent to develop an answer. It is best then to ask open questions, which have many possible answers. For instance, 'Why do you like the packaging of Maggi?' is an open question.

Sampling

A survey cannot ask every customer for their opinion. Only a fraction or SAMPLE of customers can be surveyed. To be useful, the sample chosen must be representative of all consumers (the population).

In a random sample, every potential respondent has an equal chance of being chosen. Random numbers can be used to do this or it can be done by 'picking people out of a hat'. It is often quite difficult to construct a truly random sample. So a cheaper and quicker method is to use a systematic sample. This is where, say, every 100th or 1 000th person on a list like a telephone directory or the electoral register is chosen. A systematic sample is not truly random though

---

Malvern Safari Park

Malvern Safari Park carried out some research to find out why visitor numbers were falling. Visitors to the park had fallen from 56 400 in 2001 to 49 400 in 2006. A survey was carried out using telephone interviews. 1 000 telephone numbers were chosen at random from the local telephone directory. Table 1 shows answers to five key questions from the survey and Table 2 shows a selection of comments made by the people interviewed.

1. What is the aim of the research carried out by Malvern Safari Park?
2. Explain whether the research carried out by Malvern Safari Park is primary or secondary.
3. Using examples from the case, explain the difference between open questions and closed questions in a survey.
4. Analyse the data for Malvern Safari Park and suggest reasons why the number of visitors have fallen in recent years.

Table 1 *Answers to five questions from the survey*

1. Have you ever been to Malvern Safari Park?
   YES 18%   NO 82%
2. Have you ever been to any other safari park?
   YES 21%   NO 79%
3. Would you visit Malvern Safari Park if it was cheaper?
   YES 44%   NO 56%
4. Have you heard the radio advert for the park?
   YES 7%   NO 93%
5. Have you seen the newspaper advert for the park?
   YES 29%   NO 71%

Table 2 *Comments made by some of the people surveyed*

'There's no public transport to the park since the bus service was withdrawn'.

'It's too expensive – it would cost me and my family over £80 to go for the day'.

'There aren't any tigers in the park'.

'I didn't even know there was a safari park at Malvern'.

---

and therefore the results may be less reliable.

In a quota sample, the sample is broken down (or stratified). For example, Nestlé might want to launch a new chocolate bar. Previous research has shown that 1 out of 10 people who buy similar chocolate bars are aged 5-15, 3 out of 10 are aged 16-24 years, 4 out of 10 people are aged 25-34 and 1 out of ten people are aged 35 and over. It intends to interview one thousand people in a survey about the new chocolate bar. If it used quota sample techniques, 100 people would be aged 5-15, 300 would aged 16-24 and so on.

One problem with a quota sample is that any people who fit the description can be asked to complete the survey. So Nestlé wanting to find 300 people aged 16-34 to complete a survey, could ask the first 300 16-34 year olds who came out of a McDonald's in London. This may not be very representative of all 16-34 year olds nationally.

A stratified random sample may get round this problem. It is a quota sample where all the respondents, the people being interviewed, must

be chosen at random. For the sample to be random, Nestlé would have to find some way of selecting 300 people aged 16-34 through pure chance.

Experiments

Market researchers can use experimental techniques. To launch a new product is often very costly. It is important for a company like Nestlé to make sure the new Maggi product is exactly to the taste of its customers. One approach that manufacturers like Nestlé use is to test products as they are being developed to check that they are likely to succeed. For example, during the research it was discovered that chefs wanted products with less salt - but how much less? Nestlé would have to carry out tests to ensure that the salt content of Maggi was exactly what chefs wanted. Chefs would have to be invited to attend tasting sessions to ensure that salt levels were perfect. Such tests reduce the risk of failure when launching new products.

Some companies use test marketing. This is where a product

Database and wordprocessing

Conduct a survey about crisps.

1 Before you start asking questions, you need to do two things. (a) Draw up your questionnaire. This should cover: (i) how many packets people eat; (ii) what are their favourite flavours and brands; (iii) where they buy crisps from; (iv) what influences them to buy a particular flavour and brand; (v) whether they think crisps are a healthy part of their diet. You could write your questionnaire using a word processing package. (b) Decide what type of sample you will use. You are likely to want to get responses from people of different ages and of different genders.

2 Conduct your survey.

3 You now need to analyse your findings. You could enter your results on a computer database and the program would then do much of the work for you.

4 Write a short report. You could use a wordprocessing package for this. (a) The report should outline briefly the questionnaire and the sample you chose to use. Were there any problems you found with the survey? (b) Briefly present the main findings of the survey. (c) A small but growing chain of supermarkets is thinking of launching own brand crisps. What does your survey suggest is important if sales are to be high?

is sold in a region before being launched nationally. If the product proves to be a success in the test market, a national launch is likely to follow. Nestlé produced one tonne of the new Maggi product for trials before going into full production.

Decisions

The purpose of market research is to help a business come to a decision. Nestlé knew that sales of Maggi were falling. They wanted to know why and what could be done about it. It found that customers thought the product was now uninteresting and old fashioned due to its dehydrated format and flavour. Nestlé also found that the market was divided into four segments and that a 'new improved' Maggi product could be targeted at one of these. Nestle launched the Maggi 'A Natural Choice' range in 2005. It is now lower in salt and made using sunflower oil. In addition, where possible the range benefits from having no added MSG, is gluten free and contains no artificial colours or flavours. Market research helped Maggi to reverse a worrying sales trend.

Source: adapted from www.thetimes100.co.uk.

key terms

Desk research - finding out information from secondary data.
Field research - the process of collecting primary data.
Market orientated business - a business which develops products which have been researched and designed to meet the needs of consumers.
Market research - the process of gaining information about customers, competitors and market trends through collecting primary and secondary data.
Primary data - information which has been gathered for a specific purpose through direct investigation such as observation, surveys and through experiment.
Product orientated business - a business which develops products with little or no market research and which it hopes will prove successful in the market.
Questionnaire - a list of questions to be answered by respondents, designed to give information about consumers' tastes.
Respondent - person or organisation answering questions in a survey.
Sample - small group out of a total population which is selected to take part in a survey.
Secondary data - information which already exists, such as accounts and sales records, government statistics, newspaper articles or reports from advertising agencies.
Survey - research involving asking questions of people or organisations.

SUMMARY CASE STUDY

INTERNET SURVEYS

An increasing number of businesses are using Internet surveys to gather data. This involves providing a link to a questionnaire on a company website and inviting customers or other users to complete it. The main benefit of Internet surveys is time. A much faster survey process can be expected as an Internet survey can be completed quickly - the respondent keys in the data which is then fed straight back for immediate analysis. Survey costs are lower, thanks to the absence of printing and postage, and the keying in. Internet surveys are often fun to complete because they may be interactive. They can also be accessed 24/7 and be completed at the convenience of the respondent. Internet surveys also make it easy to give feedback. Results can be e-mailed to respondents, as their e-mail addresses have already been noted, or they can be published on a website as a news item, to attract visitors.

However, there are problems with Internet surveys. The sample used may not be reflective of the total population because surveys are only presented to Internet users. The views of others will be neglected even though they may be potential customers.

Source: adapted from www.snapsurveys.com

1 What is an Internet survey?
2 Explain why an Internet survey is an example of field research.
3 Explain whether an Internet survey would benefit a company selling to: (a) customers in isolated areas; (b) undeveloped countries such as Bangladesh, Sudan and Vanuatu.
4 Discuss the advantages and disadvantages of Internet surveys.

Checklist ✓

1 Explain the difference between a market orientated and product orientated business.
2 What is the purpose of market research?
3 List the stages of market research.
4 What sources of information are available to someone undertaking desk research?
5 Distinguish between field research and desk research.
6 A shopping centre wants to find out how many shoppers visit the centre. How could it gather this information?
7 What differences are there between a postal survey and personal interviews in surveys?
8 A business wants to take a random sample of people in the London area. How could it do this?
9 A chocolate manufacturer wants to find out if a new bar of chocolate is going to sell well in the UK. How could it find this out without having to go to the expense of launching the product nationally?

Making decisions

Businesses have to decide what product or range of products they are going to sell. They also have to decide what quality of product they wish to make and sell, what name to give to the product and how it is to be packaged. A further decision is whether to attempt to brand the product.

JVC is a global design, development and manufacturing company. In 1976 it invented the VHS video system and produced the first VHS home recorder. Today it manufactures a range of consumer electronic goods including LCD and projection televisions, video cameras and audio systems.

The product range

JVC sells a RANGE of products. In 1976 it invented the VHS video system and produced the first home recorder. This is still part of the company's total PRODUCT MIX. Today it manufactures a wide range of electronic products. For example, it produces DVD players and recorders, televisions and audio products used in the home and in vehicles. These are shown in Figure 1.

JVC produces a range of televisions, for example, because different consumers want different products. JVC can then sell more and make more profit by satisfying different consumers' wants.

Product differentiation

Producing a range of televisions, for example, allows JVC to DIFFERENTIATE its products. Each television will be different. For instance, JVC manufactures a 178cm high definition professional quality television. This might be bought by a bar or club showing sport. It also manufactures a 102cm, high definition LCD, widescreen television with exclusive sound features. This might be bought for the home by a film or music enthusiast. Its 51cm, widescreen television might be bought by a family that wants a flat screen television in the kitchen or bathroom, or a student living in a flat. Consumers in Europe often buy televisions with only basic features.

Ways of differentiating the product

There is a number of important ways in which businesses make their products different from each other.

Design, formulation and function

The different products manufactured by JVC have different characteristics. Televisions are made with different sized screens. Some are 20 inch, some are 26 inch and some are 40 inch. Headphones have different designs. Some cover the ears and others are in-ear designs. Amplifiers manufactured for vehicle sound systems have different outputs. Some are 580 watt and some are 900 watt. CD changers have different functions. Some allow MP3 players to be connected. Each year JVC introduces new designs with

1 How are these four products differentiated from each other?

2 What consumer needs and wants does each product satisfy?

3 There has been a suggestion that burger chains, like McDonald's or Burger King, should sell ethnic food, such as Chinese spring rolls or Indian curries. Explain whether you think these would be as popular and as profitable as the food in their current product mix.

Vegiburger £0.85

Cheeseburger £0.79

Big Mac £1.99

Burger £0.69

Product range

DVD/Home cinema
Home cinema system
DVD recorder
DVD player
Receiver

Television
HD-ILA Hybrid TV
Widescreen TV
Plasma TV
LCD TV
Digital set top box

Audio
Portable audio
Hi-fi component
Micro system
Mini system

Mobile entertainment
Head units
CD changers
Amplifiers
Speakers
Monitors
Accessories

Accessories
Computing (ie card readers, adaptors, cables, software)
Speakers
Headphones
Camcorder (ie DVD
burners, cables, memory cards, lenses
Home cinema (ie cables)
D-ILA
Audio

Recording decks
VCR combinations
S-VHS
VHS

Camcorder
Everio
Mini/DV digital
Compact analogue

Figure 1
JVC product mix
Source: adapted from
www.jvc.co.uk.

improved visual and audio functions, cosmetic features and improved functionality.

Similarly, car manufacturers produce a range of cars. Each car model may have hundreds of different feature combinations, from the colour of the car to the engine size to whether or not it has a fitted sunroof.

First it was the 'e vehicles'. Ford's SUV range of vehicles contained brand names which began with the letter 'e', such as the Explorer, the Escape and the Excursion. Then came the F cars — the Ford Focus, Fiesta and Fusion. 'It's part of a strategy to establish some consistency in brand names ... that really ties back very well to a lot of the names that Ford used in the past that began with an F as well, such as Fairlane and [Galaxy] 500 and Focus and Futura' said Torrey Galida, vice-president of Ford Motor Co. of Canada Ltd. He also said that launching a new model 'can be a very difficult and time-consuming process, so putting a framework around it that makes sense and ties closely with your primary brand is something that we think will help us'. Some consultants argue that there are rules of naming which say that you cannot have nine different names starting with the same letter because it confuses customers. Other disagree. In the end, whether a vehicle succeeds or fails has little to do with its name, some argue. They suggest that it is the features, designs, quality, reliability and customer service that are important.

Source: adapted from www.metrostate.com.

1 Explain how (a) using a different name and (b) using different features might help to differentiate a motor vehicle for customers.
2 Explain TWO reasons why Ford introduced cars with brand names beginning with the same letter.
3 A breakfast manufacturer has a new range of products and wants to give them brand names all beginning with the letter 'a'. It currently has a successful brand with which begins with the letter 'c'. Discuss whether it should change the name of the successful brand.

McDonald's sells a variety of foods, from Big Macs to Chicken Nuggets to coffee. More expensive **up-market** products are likely to be better quality than a better selling but cheaper **mass market** product.

Name Different products have different names. The name of the product is important if it is to sell. Calling a coffee 'Cafe stink', for example, is likely to be a disaster in sales terms. Some products have names which are easy to remember and say something positive about the product. 'Gold Blend' coffee, for instance, links something valuable (gold) with a soft word (blend) which implies mellowness. Audio products often have abstract names designed to create a technical image, like the JVC Alneo range of MP3 players.

However, the name is only a small part of the marketing mix of the product. No marketing company would have advised a UK baked bean manufacturer to brand its product 'Heinz', and yet Heinz baked beans is one of the most successful brand names in the UK today.

Baked beans: brands vs own brands

Your task is to compare branded baked beans with own brands and write a report. Your aim is to find out whether branded products are worth the higher price usually charged for them. You may find it easier to do this working as part of a group.

In school
1 Make a list of the different brands of baked beans; then list the own brands you know.
2 Which do you think is the leading brand in the UK and why?
3 Decide which shops you will survey to find out about the prices of cans of baked beans. You should survey at least one supermarket and one local small shop. The more shops and supermarkets you can survey the better.
4 You need to buy different brands of baked beans for a tasting session. Decide who in your group is going to buy which brand.

In the shops
1 Note down the prices of the brands and own brands on your list. There will be different size of cans. You need to note down the weights and prices.
2 If there are any brands which you do not have on your list, record those too.
3 Buy the brands or own brands which you have agreed to use in the tasting.

Back in school
1 Organise a blind tasting with the rest of your group. One person needs to prepare the food and put it into bowls each with a number. The tasters need to record what they liked and disliked about each variety. For instance: 'too sweet', 'too chewy', 'just the right colour'. Give an overall mark out of 5 (5 = top mark) for each variety.
2 At the end of the tasting, the cans can be put by their bowls. Did you pick out as your favourite variety the one you thought you would?
3 Now look at the packaging on the cans. Comment on how effective it is.
4 Compare the ingredients by looking at the labelling.
5 Were branded baked beans better than own brands? In your report, compare price with taste, packaging and ingredients.

Database/Spreadsheet/Graphics
The results of the survey and the blind tasting can be recorded and analysed on a database. Results may also be recorded on a spreadsheet and graphs and charts produced from the data with a graphics program. The final report can be produced with agraphics package.

Packaging Packaging is used to deliver products safely to the consumer. For instance, JVC manufactured products are delivered in cardboard boxes with polystyrene padding and plastic wrapping inside. This keeps the products clean and secure before they are taken out to be used. Packaging can also prevent products from being scratched.

Packaging also gives information to the customer about the product. JVC packaging may contain information about where to place the product for best results and electrical information on the correct voltage to be used. It may give instructions on how to recycle packaging. It may contain details of any awards won by the product,

such as the EISA Best Product award 2006-2007 won by its EX-A10 compact music system. Food products contain nutritional information and cooking times are given, as well as how long the packet can safely be kept.

Packaging has other uses though. It is a way of promoting the product. Colours, designs and letters attract the customers' attention. For example, the JVC logo is placed on all product packaging. This can attract customers to the product.

Branding

Every business would like its products to be strong BRANDS. A branded product is a product which

in the eyes of customers is seen to be different from other, often similar products. Consumers, for example, might see JVC products as different from those of other electrical manufacturers.

The opposite of a branded product is a GENERIC PRODUCT. Potatoes are generic products. Consumers generally don't see any difference between the same type of potatoes produced on one farm compared with those of another farm. Coal, steel, milk and bananas are other examples of generic products.

Strong branding means that a business may be able charge a PREMIUM PRICE for the product. This is a price that is higher than those of competitors. There are two reasons why customers are willing to pay premium prices for branded products. First, the quality of the product is usually higher. For instance, the JVC brand statement is the 'The Perfect Experience'. It places emphasis on the quality of its products in all its operations. Consumers see might JVC products as higher quality than other audio products made by competitors as a result. Second, brands tend to be advertised heavily. Advertising and other forms of promotion mean that customers are more aware than they would otherwise be of the claimed advantages of the product.

Own brands

Maintaining the brand through promotion and improvement in the product is essential if the brand is to survive. Today, many brands are faced with strong competition from OWN BRANDS. These are products which carry the brand labels of retailers such as Sainsbury's or Woolworths. Nestlé, for example, faces competition from supermarket own brands of coffee, like those of Sainsbury's or Tescos. Own brands are usually

Staples stores has name brands, such as Duracell, Hewlett-Packard and 3M. But it has more than 1 000 products sold under its own brand, including Staples' yellow self-stick notes and stainless-steel shears. Staples started its private label business in the 1990s. In 2004 they were 17% of total sales. Unlike most private label operations, Staples is doing more than putting its name on products. It's getting into product development. It has filed patents for many new product lines. 'Our strategy is to develop the Staples brand, not just to offer consumers private label items,' said a spokesperson. 'We're putting the Staples logo and brand on products, infusing better quality than national brands, and offering the product at a discounted price.' Western Europe dominates the market for private labels. The UK had private label sales of around £8 billion in 2004.

www.informationweek.com, 18.5.2005.

1 What is the difference between a brand and an own brand?
2 Explain why the two Staples own brand products mentioned in the article might be similar to branded products.
3 Explain why (a) Staples is producing its own branded products and (b) other manufacturers might object to this.

cheaper than the branded products from manufacturers.

A danger for businesses like Nestlé is that customers might also see own brands as being of just as high quality as more expensive manufacturers' brands. If this happens, the customers could choose the own brands simply because they are cheaper.

Source: information from JVC.

key terms

Brand - a named product which customers see as being different from other products.
Generic product - a product made by a number of different businesses in which customers see no difference between the product of one business compared with the product of another business.
Own brand - a product which is sold under the brand name of a supermarket chain or other retailer rather than under the name of the business which manufactures the product.
Premium price - a price which is above the average for products of a particular type.
Product differentiation - making one product different from another, for instance through the quality of a product, its design, packaging or advertising.
Product mix - the combination of products that a business sells, like soap powders, cosmetics and medicines.
Range of products - a group of similar products made by a business, like a number of different soap powders.

SUMMARY CASE STUDY

IPOD

Apple's products include computers, software and iPod music players. On the horizon are iPhones and Internet devices. The iPod, introduced in 2001, has been an unqualified success. The first versions had unique features, including links with iTunes and 1000 song capacity, when most other players only held a few hours music. It was easy to use with a unique 'wheel' control. The iPod was seen as 'cool' and people were encouraged to use other Apple devices - the iPod 'halo' effect. Ipods were sold at high prices and could only be used on Macs. They were bought by few, but desired by many.

Over time iPods became PC accessible. Hard-drive models were launched with large memories at the high end of the market. Smaller devices were launched aimed at the middle of the market and small, featureless devices, such as shuffles, were aimed at the low end of the market. This allowed the Apple brand to move into new markets, keeping prices and profits high on the larger players. Apple's decision to allow third parties to produce accessories, such as cases and speakers, meant the success of others depended on Apple's iPod being a success:

The iPod Mini and the Nano produced in assorted colours have been criticised as silly. But Apple argue that the designs make them a reflection of the user's personality and are popular with women. There were other reasons for their success. The 1 000-song capacity is a 'sweet spot' of the market - not too many songs, but not too few. Products are also easy to use while exercising.

Source: adapted from hardware.silicon.com, www.macopinion.com and www.apple.com.

1 Using examples, describe the product mix of Apple.
2 Explain how Apple has differentiated (a) the products in its iPod range and (b) its iPod products from those of other similar branded products.
3 What are the advantages to Apple of using the 'i' brand across its range of products? Explain your answer referring to the effects on (a) sales; (b) costs and (c) profits.
4 A business consultant suggests that Apple should produce a soft drink and call it 'iCola' or a coffee machine called 'iCup'. Explain whether or not you think they would be a success for Apple.

Checklist ✓

1 Give THREE examples each of products in: (a) the Wall's ice cream range; (b) the Ford car range; (c) the Cadbury's range of chocolate.
2 Why do businesses usually sell ranges of products rather than just one single product?
3 How do the following businesses differentiate their products: (a) a multi-screen cinema; (b) a record company; (c) a manufacturer of crisps?
4 Why do you think the following brand names help sell their product: (a) Cadbury's Flake; (b) Kellogg's Frosties; (c) Bold, manufactured by Procter & Gamble?
5 Why do manufacturers use packaging?
6 What is the difference between a branded product and a generic product?
7 'Brands are sold at premium prices.' Explain what this means.
8 Why do own brands compete successfully against branded products?

Making decisions

Businesses sell products. The products they sell go through a life cycle. At each different point of the life cycle, the business needs to make decisions about how the product is to be priced, how it should be promoted and how it should be distributed. It also needs to consider how the product could be developed to extend the life of the product.

The original MINI came onto the market in 1959. It caused a revolution in car design. By the 1970s and 1980s sales had fallen. BMW bought Rover, the company which manufactured the Mini, in 1994. BMW saw that it was a great brand and set about designing a new car. Launched in 2001, the BMW MINI has been an outstanding success. In 2007, a new version of the BMW MINI was launched.

The product life cycle

The PRODUCT LIFE CYCLE shows the stages through which, it is argued, a product passes over time. A textbook product life cycle is illustrated in Figure 1. The product life cycle of the original mini, shown in Figure 2, is similar to this.

The development stage

Products start life at the **development stage**. The Mini, for instance, first started life in 1956 when Sir Leonard Lord, chairman of British Motor Cars (BMC),

ordered his designers to come up with a new small car. The **research and development** of the car took three years for the designer, Sir Alec Issigonis, and his team. This included the time needed to adapt two car plants to manufacture the Mini. Nowadays, any development of a car would also be heavily influenced by **market research**.

Launching the product

The product is then ready to be launched. Most products coming on the market will be backed up by some advertising and other forms of promotion. The Mini came onto

the market in August 1959. It was advertised in newspapers and specialist car magazines. BMC's car dealer network were given point

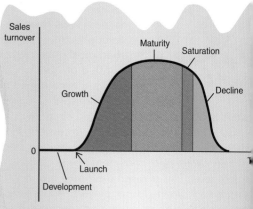

Figure 1 *The product life cycle*

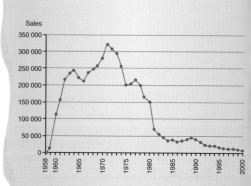

Figure 2 *The product life cycle of the original Mini.*
Source: adapted from information provided by Kevin Jones, Rover Group Ltd, Cambridge-MIT Institute.

In 2006 Sony was preparing for the launch of the Playstation 3. Jack Tretton, Sony Computer Entertainment of America's executive vice president, said 'The revenue ... being generated by PlayStation 2 is significant enough, we've sold 100 million systems worldwide. We're heading into the seventh year of what we believe is easily a 10-year product life cycle. While the launch of the PlayStation Portable last year was the most successful platform launch in the history of this industry, there's still a lot of work and a lot of education to be done there. On PlayStation 3, we're delivering a quantum leap in technology...'

Source: adapted from news.com.com, 8.5.2006.

1 What is meant by 'a ten year product life cycle'?
2 At what stage in the product life cycle would you say PlayStation was in 2006?
3 What evidence is there that Sony has been using extension strategies for its product?

of sale promotional material. Models were in the car showrooms so that customers could see the car.

The growth phase

In the **growth** phase of the cycle, sales and profits will be rising. In the first full year of production, in 1960, 116 677 Minis were produced. In 1961, this increased to 157 059.

Product maturity

In the **maturity** stage, the product reaches a peak in terms of sales. Research and development costs are likely to have been paid off. The product is profitable enough to be financing the development of new products. For the Mini, the maturity stage probably lasted for most of the 1960s and the early part of the 1970s.

Manufacturers are likely to try to extend the maturity stage of the product for as long as possible. Producing a completely new product would involve all the start up costs again. They usually do this through developing **extension strategies**. This involves slightly changing the product to give it fresh appeal to its target market. Extension strategies can also help a product appeal to a new **segment** of the market.

The original Mini constantly changed during its life. For instance, in 1961, a version called the Mini Cooper was launched with a more powerful engine. In 1964, a jeep-type version called the Mini Moke was first put on sale. 1967 saw a facelift of the Mini range with the new cars being called Mark II Minis. New variants of the Mini were launched in most years of its existence.

Saturation and decline

Towards the end of the maturity phase, the market becomes **saturated**. Competitors bring out products which take sales away. For the Mini, saturation occurred in the 1970s when other car manufactures began to bring out their own mini cars. These super-minis were larger than the Mini and took sales away from the Mini.

Eventually, a product is likely to go into **decline** and there are big falls in sales.

The new BMW MINI

In 1994, the German luxury car manufacturer, BMW, bought Rover, the UK company which produced the Mini. BMW decided to produce a completely new MINI, which was launched in 2001. Figure 3 shows that the car has been a great success. In 2007, BMW launched a new version of this car.

Source: information provided by Kevin Jones, Rover Group Ltd; Society of Motor Manufacturers and Traders.

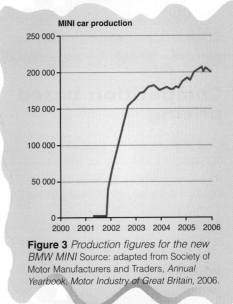

Figure 3 *Production figures for the new BMW MINI* Source: adapted from Society of Motor Manufacturers and Traders, *Annual Yearbook, Motor Industry of Great Britain*, 2006.

BISTO

Bisto gravy developed from an idea of two women for a product that would guarantee perfect gravy every time. It was first created in 1908. Nearly 100 years later the Bisto brand is still the strongest in the market with a 62% market share. There is a great heritage in the product, the result of investment and advertising. During this time there have been enormous changes in what people eat. Bisto has had to keep ahead of the game, benchmarking against competition and developing the product. Bisto granules were introduced in 1979. Bisto Best was introduced in the 1990s. It is a premium product sold in a glass jar to give it an air of quality as well as convenience.

The nearest branded competitor to Bisto is Oxo with a 7 per cent market share. The major threat, though, comes from supermarkets with their own-label products that have a quarter share of the gravy market.

Source: adapted from news.bbc.co.uk.

1 (a) Draw a product life cycle diagram.
  (b) Explain where Bisto was on the product life cycle in (i) 1908, (ii) the 1920s and (iii) 1979.
2 What types of extension strategy has Bisto used?
3 Discuss what you think might happen to the product life cycle of Bisto in future.

Table 1 *Bisto history*

1908	- Powder launched
1919	- Bisto Kids adverts born
1979	- Granules launched
1984	- Relaunched granules and new onion granules
1991	- 'Best' is launched
2000	- "Aah Bisto" slogan re-introduced after 13 years

Source: adapted from news.bbc.co.uk.

Checklist ✓

1 What happens during the development stage of a product's life?
2 Why is a product likely to need advertising and promotion when it is launched?
3 Profits for a product which is a market leader in its maturity stage tend to be very high. Why is this?
4 What is an extension strategy?
5 What happens to a product in the decline phase of its life cycle?

Making decisions

Price is one element of the marketing mix. A business must decide how to price its product. In making this decision it needs to consider:

- what are the prices charged by competitors;
- how price can be used to increase sales of the product;
- whether the price will cover costs of production.

The music industry is big business. Just over 154 million albums were sold in the UK in 2006. 66.9 million singles were sold, the highest total since 1999. Music DVD sales totalled 7.2 million. Record companies sell through retailers, but increasingly people are downloading music from the Internet. The growth in singles sales was mainly the result of growing sales of legal downloads. In 2006 digital downloads accounted for 79% of singles sales and in 2007 downloaded singles were included as part of the singles chart for the first time. Digital sales make up only 1.4 per cent of the album market.

Competition based pricing

One way in which music companies decide at what price to sell their CDs is to look at prices charged by other companies. This is known as COMPETITION BASED PRICING. Selling a CD to retailers for £12 when other CDs are around £6 is likely to lose sales. On the other hand, selling a new CD for £2 may give the message that the CD is not as good quality.

Setting the price at the market average avoids price competition and is a safe strategy. The music company can then compete using other strategies, like advertising or putting out CDs by new bands that it thinks will be popular.

Market orientated pricing

An alternative to competition based pricing is MARKET ORIENTATED PRICING. This is where the price charged is based upon an analysis of the market and its characteristics.

Penetration pricing Music businesses may sell certain CDs and singles at reduced prices. This is because the record companies want to maximise early sales so that they can get into the charts. Getting into the charts means that tracks will be played more often on radio and viewed in retailers, which will lead to further sales. Charging a lower price for a product at the start in order to gain

1 Suggest why the drinks shown in the photograph might all have a similar price.

Football ticket prices

Wigan Athletic, like most football clubs has a complicated pricing structure. Wigan has one of the lowest prices in the premiership, with match tickets varying depending where you are in the ground. Ticket prices also vary for important or 'Category A' matches. Earlier in the 2006/07 season prices were £35 for category A games and £30 and £25 for other matches. Table 1 shows the prices of season tickets at Wigan for the 2006/07 season.

Between 3 February 2007 and 5 May 2007 Wigan dropped its match day ticket prices even further. For example, the home match against West Ham United would cost fans £15, with concession prices costing just £10.

However, the pricing of tickets by some clubs has been criticised. For example, Manchester United fans visiting Fulham were charged £45 for a ticket. A senior executive from another of the Premiership's 'big four' clubs told *Observer Sport* that prices could not go any higher. 'Officially we are monitoring the situation,' he said. 'But privately we have realised that ticket prices have reached their maximum, at least in the immediate future.' High prices have also been cited as the reason for lower attendances at some clubs.

Source: adapted from news.bbc.co.uk, 4.1.2007, *The Observer*, 25.5.2007.

1 Explain how much it would have cost an adult Wigan fan to buy a season ticket in (a) the South Stand and (b) the East Stand Central.
2 How much would it cost a mother to buy Wigan tickets for her and her two children aged 14 and 12 for the home match against West Ham?
3 (a) Explain THREE factors that influence the different prices of tickets. (b) Why might football clubs charge different prices?
4 A football club has failed to sell all its tickets this season for most of its matches. It decides to reduce its prices next season. Should it cut the price of all types of tickets?

SEASON TICKET PRICES 2006/07	
WEST STAND	**PRICE**
Adult	£410
Senior Citizen/Amublant	£310
Student Concession	£310
Junior Under 16's	£310
Wheelchair Disabled/Carer	£310
SOUTH STAND	**PRICE**
Adult	£340
Senior Citizen/Amublant	£280
Student Concession	£280
Wheelchair Disabled/Carer	£280
JJ's Matchday Plus - U16's	£165
JJ's Matchday Plus - U11's	£83
JJ's Hi-Fives (Under 5's)	FOC
EAST STAND	**PRICE**
Adult - Central	£410
Adult - Wing	£340
Senior Citizen/Amublant: Central	£310
Senior Citizen/Amublant: Wing	£280
Student Concession - Central	£310
Student Concession - Wing	£280
Wheelchair Disabled/Carer	£280
Junior Eastender (5-16 Yrs)	£202
Under 5's JJ's World Members	Free

Table 1 *Wigan ticket prices 2006/07*

market share is known as PENETRATION PRICING. One problem with this strategy is that consumers may refuse to buy if a business attempts to raise the price later. They might see the initial price as a 'fair' price and the more expensive price as not representing value for money.

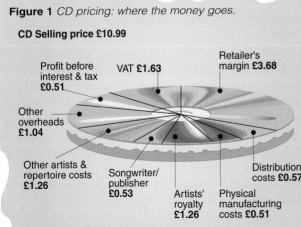

Figure 1 *CD pricing: where the money goes.*

CD Selling price £10.99

Profit before interest & tax £0.51
VAT £1.63
Retailer's margin £3.68
Other overheads £1.04
Other artists & repertoire costs £1.26
Songwriter/ publisher £0.53
Artists' royalty £1.26
Physical manufacturing costs £0.51
Distribution costs £0.57

Source: adapted from Media Research Publishings Ltd.

Creaming CREAMING (or SKIMMING) is the opposite of penetration pricing. It is setting a high price for a product initially and lowering it later on. It is used, for instance, with products such as MP3 players, CD and DVD players. In the early days, enthusiasts are often prepared to pay a high price to get a new product. However, to create a mass market, manufacturers have to lower their prices even though they put more features onto products.

Discounts, special offers and sales A music company may give retailers a special discount for a period on certain CDs to increase their sales. For example, in the Summer and in January, retailers often hold sales. They are a way of getting rid of stock that hasn't sold well at its usual price at other times in the year. Retailers may also offer loss leaders. These are products which are priced so cheaply that the retailer makes no profit or even a loss on every sale. But they attract customers into the store who then buy other, more expensive, products.

CDs may also be sold at a reduced price after a number of years. These may be albums that have sold very well and the business wants to get rid of large overstocks. Or they may be compilations of older artists. These CDs can appear in retailers' 'cheap charts'.

Price discrimination

Record companies sell CDs at different prices in different areas of the world. Selling the same product at different prices to different

Europe by Net

Consumers are often confident about buying books and CDs over the Internet. But ordering designer furniture online may make them think twice. The product is not standardised, there is a variety of finishes and shoppers often want to see samples. It also costs more to deliver bulky and fragile furniture than small items.

Julie Edwards, a former investment banker, has created a thriving Internet business selling upmarket Italian furniture. The reason, she says, is that 'rip-off Britain' allows her Europe by Net business to sell designer products online at prices consumers cannot resist. Her best offers are on furniture on sale in retailers. A mirror designed by Philippe Starck is priced at £1,051, just over half the UK retail price of £1,999. 'The mark-up in the UK is so high that we can pay for the transport costs and make a profit while undercutting shop prices by up to 40 per cent,' she says.

How has she persuaded consumers to buy online? A combination of unbeatable prices and high quality products, she says. 'We get very few returns'. Some customers know the model numbers and the fabric codes and just want the best price. Others value the convenience. Competitors are less happy. Europe by Net has come under attack from manufacturers and retailers concerned that Internet sales are undercutting their businesses. The European Commission is investigating a complaint by the company about 4 manufacturers it claims have tried to stop suppliers selling their products to Europe by Net. It is also alleged that glossy magazines have been threatened with lost advertising if they accept its adverts.

Source: adapted from the *Financial Times*, 22.12.2006.

1 What product is Europe by Net selling?
2 Suggest what might be (a) the fixed costs and (b) the variable costs ofEurope by Net.
3 'Rip-off Britain' has allowed Europe by Net to become successful. What does this suggest about the mark-up of Europe by Net's competitors.
4 Why might manufacturers and retailers be concerned about the pricing of Europe by Net?
5 How might Europe by Net's competitors react to its prices?

segments of the market is known as PRICE DISCRIMINATION. The record company may attempt to charge what the market will 'bear' in order to earn the highest profit possible in each market. For instance, it may charge more in the UK than in US markets if British buyers are prepared to pay higher prices than American buyers. A music business may also sell at different prices to different buyers. An Internet download is usually priced differently to a CD bought from a retailer, for example. It may be less expensive although downloading each track individually from a CD may be more expensive than buying the CD from a retailer.

Cost based pricing

Record companies are in business to make a profit. Charging a price similar to competitors is one way to set prices, but it might lead to losses. Another way would be to base price on costs of production.

A retailer selling CDs might use COST PLUS PRICING. It could calculate the cost of selling the CD and then add a MARK-UP or PROFIT MARGIN. The price of the CD would then be the cost plus a profit for the retailer.

The cost is the average cost and is made up of:
● the variable cost - mainly the cost of buying the CD from the record company;
● the fixed cost - such as the wages of staff, the rent of the

shop and heating and lighting. When the price covers both the average fixed and variable cost of the product, the business is said to be full-cost pricing.

Sometimes it is difficult to sell certain CDs. Some CDs take longer to sell than others. Some artists are only bought by a small number of people. Tastes may change and an artist may become unpopular. The retailer may have to cut the price to below the full cost price to sell these CDs. So long as the new price more than covers the variable cost, it will at least make some contribution towards the fixed costs of the business. In the long term, the retailer has to cover all its costs to survive. In the short term, charging a price above variable cost may make sense.

The Delicious Cake Company

The Delicious Cake Company is a mini-enterprise company. The board of directors has decided that its business will make cakes and gateaux and offer a free delivery service to the door of the customer.

The board is now meeting to decide what price the Company should charge for its cakes. The first cake on their list is a gateau with icing on top. Ingredients for one gateau cost £1.36. The box to put it in will cost 15p. The school is charging the company a flat £20 fee for the use of rooms etc. whilst the company is operating. Parents have agreed to lend baking tins and other equipment free. Parents have also agreed not to charge for the use of ovens to bake the cakes. It is estimated that a cake would take an hour to make. They haven't quite worked out how they will arrange the doorstep delivery.

1 What price do you think the Delicious Cake Company should charge for its gateaux? Explain your reasons carefully.
2 The company sends out a price list for its cakes to parents. It also advertises in local shops. It finds that its cakes aren't selling well, but it is making a substantial profit on each cake. Do you think that the company should reduce its prices? Consider as many arguments for and against as possible.

Checklist ✓

1 Explain, using teenage magazines as an example, what is meant by 'competitive pricing'.
2 Why do shops have sales?
3 How might a hairdresser price discriminate?
4 Why might penetration pricing be a good price strategy to use when launching a new brand of yogurts?
5 'Mobile phone networks have used price creaming strategies when setting prices.' Explain what this means.
6 Calculate the price of a product if its cost of production is: (a) £10 and the mark up is 50 per cent; (b) £100 and the mark-up is 10 per cent; (c) £5 and the mark-up is 100 per cent.
7 What is meant by a 'contribution' in pricing?

SUMMARY CASE STUDY

COMPUTER BIZ

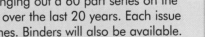

A magazine publisher is bringing out a 60 part series on the developments in computers over the last 20 years. Each issue will feature a DVD with games. Binders will also be available. The readers can place each edition in the ring binder so that the magazine can be built up into a comprehensive guide.

1 What pricing strategy might the publisher have used when fixing the price for the magazine? In your answer, give the advantages and disadvantages from the publisher's viewpoint.
2 Explain how you think the binders should be priced.
3 The final cost to the customer of buying 60 parts will be £179.40 plus the binders. Discuss why the publisher doesn't publish a set of books with all the material in it for £179 instead of publishing it as a 60 part series.

Making decisions

Businesses have to decide how best to promote the products they make and sell. Should they advertise, for instance, or should they use point of sale promotion? This decision involves weighing up the relative cost of each form of promotion and how best to target their potential customers. They also need to decide whether to organise the promotion themselves or use an outside organisation like an advertising agency.

innocent is a drinks manufacturer. It makes smoothies (100% pure crushed fruit and juices, never made from concentrate), thickies (yoghurt, fruit and spices) and natural thirst quenching water-based drinks, made with spring water and natural fruit juices. In 2006 it had a turnover of £76 million, 24 recipes, and sold 21 million smoothies a week in over 7,000 outlets.

Communication

Businesses need to communicate with customers. PROMOTION is about:
- making customers aware that the product is for sale;
- telling or explaining to customers what the product is;
- making customers aware of how the product will service their needs;
- persuading customers to buy a product for the first time or to buy it again.

Promotion is the most direct form of communication in the **marketing mix**. There is a number of techniques of promotion: advertising; direct mail; personal selling; public relations; sales promotion; sponsorship; and branding.

Media advertising

innocent, like other businesses, advertises through the **media**. The media includes;
- television, radio and cinema;
- the Internet;
- magazines;
- national and local newspapers;
- trade newspapers and journals – these are specialist publications aimed at businesses or workers in a particular industry;
- posters and transport, such as billboards at train stations or outside supermarkets and advertisements on buses, taxis and vans;
- directories – including Yellow Pages and local directories.

innocent wants to reach a large number of customers and has a budget to do this (£7m in 2006). It can afford to advertise on television - an expensive medium. It advertises in magazines and

Each of the photographs shows a different form of advertising medium.
1 Name each of these.
2 The following want to advertise their products. Explain which of the advertising media shown in the photographs would be suitable. In your answer, consider: (i) the cost of advertising; (ii) the target audience; (iii) the impact of the advertisement on the potential customer.
3 (a) Boots wants to advertise its Number 7 range of cosmetics.
   (b) Jill Hillier is a painter and decorator. She wants to advertise her business.
   (c) Redland's is a local concessionaire for Toyota cars. It wants to advertise its range of products, including servicing cars, body repairs, and the sale of new and second hand cars.

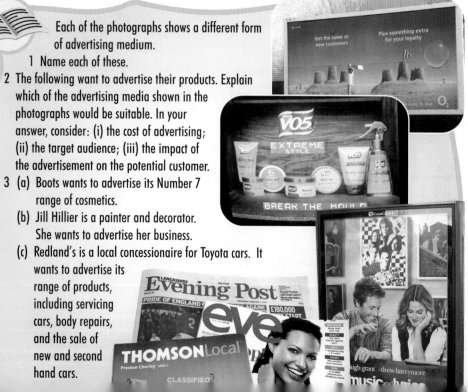

1996
Total spending £12,080m

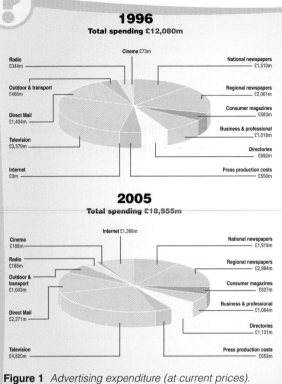

- Radio £344m
- Cinema £73m
- Outdoor & transport £466m
- Direct Mail £1,404m
- Television £3,379m
- Internet £0m
- National newspapers £1,510m
- Regional newspapers £2,061m
- Consumer magazines £583m
- Business & professional £1,018m
- Directories £692m
- Press production costs £550m

2005
Total spending £18,955m

- Internet £1,366m
- Cinema £188m
- Radio £188m
- Outdoor & transport £1,043m
- Direct Mail £2,371m
- Television £4,820m
- National newspapers £1,919m
- Regional newspapers £2,994m
- Consumer magazines £827m
- Business & professional £1,064m
- Directories £1,131m
- Press production costs £653m

Figure 1 *Advertising expenditure (at current prices).*
Source: adapted from The Advertising Association, *Advertising Statistics Yearbook* 1997.

1 Look at Figure 1. How much in 2005 was spent on advertising:
   (a) in national newspapers,
   (b) through directories,
   (c) on the Internet?
2 Between 1996 and 2005 the share of advertising spending on the Internet, outdoor & transport, radio and direct mail rose. At the same time the share of advertising spending on regional and national newspapers, consumer magazines and television fell. Suggest reasons why this occurred.
3 (a) What has happened to total advertising spending between 1996 and 2005? (b) Why do you think there has been this change?

innocent adverts

newspapers and on posters. It runs an Internet website which includes television adverts (which can also be found on YouTube) and posts blogs about its activities. It publishes books and booklets, such as the innocent Smoothie recipe book. Its vans are covered with artificial grass or have cow patterns. If innocent wanted to recruit employees it is unlikely to use television because of the cost. The style of advert would also be different from one selling innocent drinks to customers. innocent might make use of a jobs section in a national newspaper, such as the *Financial Times* or *The Guardian*. Or it might advertise in a trade journal, such as *Accountancy Age* or *The Grocer*. It will also place vacancies on its website under the 'jobs' section.

Media advertising is sometimes called ABOVE-THE-LINE promotion. BELOW-THE-LINE promotion is any other form of promotion. A small business, such as an electrician or local shop, would not be able to afford above-the-line promotion in a national newspaper or on television. It would want to use media which were affordable and reached target customers.

Advertising agencies

ADVERTISING AGENCIES are businesses which specialise in organising the advertising for other businesses. Within an advertising agency an account executive will be appointed to run a campaign. As shown in Figure 2, certain groups of people will then be involved.

- The market research department organises market research into the product. The information collected is then used to plan the advertising campaign.
- The creative department devises the advert, from the words to be used to the pictures and sound.
- The art buying department organises the making of film adverts, the taking of photographs etc.
- The media buying department buys slots on television, radio and newspapers and magazines.

An advertising agency can be crucial to the success of a campaign. Boring adverts will not attract attention. In 2005 innocent worked with a creative agency, Lowe, which produced the company's first TV advert, although the idea came from innocent. It was a low-key, low-budget commercial with a talking carton surrounded by a sea of juicy fresh fruit, which reflected the unpretentious style of the business.

Direct mail

DIRECT MAIL involves a business sending

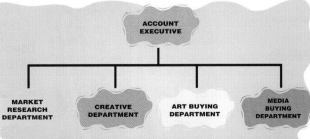

Figure 2 *An advertising agency.*

- ACCOUNT EXECUTIVE
  - MARKET RESEARCH DEPARTMENT
  - CREATIVE DEPARTMENT
  - ART BUYING DEPARTMENT
  - MEDIA BUYING DEPARTMENT

advertising leaflets directly to households or businesses through the post. To keep costs down the advertiser needs to make a list of potential customers. For instance, it may target households in a particular area, getting names and addresses from the electoral register. Or it might have a list of clients who have bought products in the past. This is often used by businesses such as banks, insurance companies and mail order firms. It might also buy in a list from a market research business. innocent makes use of direct mail to customers. It also makes use of email via a newsletter sent to customers.

Packaging

Packaging is an important means of advertising for many products. It needs to be instantly recognisable so that shoppers don't buy another brand by mistake or don't recognise it on shelves. The colour of the packaging and its design need to reflect the image of the product. It also needs to give any information required by law.

The design and packaging of innocent drinks include the company logo, a halo, information about what is included, only 100%

fruit, and what is not, and that bottles can be recycled. They reflect innocent's quirky, laid-back style, its ethical stance and its desire to promote healthy living.

Personal selling

Some products are sold door-to-door. A double glazing salesperson might arrange to call at a house. A sales representative (a sales 'rep') may call at a business trying to sell a product. These are examples of personal selling. The advantage is that the value of the product can be communicated directly to the customer. On the other hand, many people don't like feeling pressurised into buying a product and resent the time wasted by visiting sales reps. innocent does not use this method of sales.

Public relations

PUBLIC RELATIONS (PR) is another way in which businesses communicate with customers. The PR department tries to get good news about a product into the media. For instance, it might issue a press release about the launch of a new product. innocent has established the best form of public relations. It gets mentioned

favourably in many forms of media, including newspapers and on Internet sites. It mentions the awards it has won on its own website and also gives information that the media can use.

Sponsorship and product placement

This is where a business will provide financial support for an event or individual in exchange for its name being associated. An example might be a business associating with a football club in exchange for its name being printed on the shirt. Some business promote their products by arranging for them to be shown in films. In the past innocent has organised a free festival, Fruitstock, in Regent's Park.

Sales promotion

Sales promotion attempts to give a short term boost to sales. A number of methods can be used.
- Money off. A 'money off deal' is where a customer is charged a lower price or not charged at all if they buy a product. Examples include low priced mobile phones for customers signing up for a talk plan or free connection for signing to a broadband or Sky service.
- Better value offers. Businesses sometimes have offers for customers. For example, when a business first starts it may offer a cheaper price for a period until it gains customers.
- Competitions. Businesses sometimes offer prizes for competitions.
- Free gifts. A free gift may be given if a product is bought. innocent actually gives free screensavers which can be downloaded from its website.

Discount vouchers or loyalty cards These give money off future purchases. Examples might be a voucher reducing the price of the next meal at a restaurant or a free cup of coffee for every 10 bought.

Masterfoods

In February 2007 Masterfoods, the makers of confectionery products such as Mars and Snickers chocolate bars announced it would stop marketing confectionery to children under 12. This put pressure on rival food companies to follow its example. The self-imposed ban comes as pressure builds about the links between advertising and childhood obesity.

Masterfoods has also repackaged two of its Mars drinks - Mars Original Drink and Mars Drink Extra Choc. The designs are intended to stand out on shelves and differentiate the products from the soon to be launched Thick Shake. The bottles use Mars bar colours and the shape of the bottles is designed to look attractive to purchasers.

Source: adapted from www.brandrepublic.com, www.btl-europe.com

1 Suggest TWO reasons why Masterfoods changed the packaging of its Mars drinks.
2 Why might Masterfoods have made the decision to place a 'self-imposed ban' on marketing confectionery products to children under 12?
3 Discuss whether all confectionery companies should stop advertising to children under 12.

Collect information about promotions currently on offer. You could do this by:

- looking through local newspapers, including free newspapers, or using the Internet;
- noting down any promotions offered on television or radio commercials;
- checking through food, particularly tins and packets, which you have at home;
- visiting local shops, such as your nearest supermarket, and noting down products and promotions on offer.

1 Give TEN examples of different promotions you have found.
2 (a) For each one, explain why you think it could increase sales of the product.
   (b) Which do you think will be the most effective promotion and why?

PR promotions Businesses may donate an amount to charity for each product sold. In 2006, innocent knitted 220,000 small hats to put on drinks. For every bottle with a hat on it sold in an EAT café or Sainsbury's between the end of November and Christmas 2006, 50p went to Age Concern. innocent has also set up its own charity. The innocent Foundation is a grant giving charity that works with community projects in the countries where it buys fruit.

Another way to give a short term boost to sales is through POINT-OF-SALE MATERIAL. This is promotion that takes place where the product is sold. Manufacturers will supply posters and leaflets of products being sold by retailers, such as DVDs or CDs. Displays for windows may also be provided. In a supermarket, a product may be put into special **dump bins**, containers likely to be situated at the end of aisles. These attract customer attention.

Branding

The most important long term outcome of promotion for innocent is to build and maintain the innocent **brand**. innocent wants to see its name associated with providing healthy and quality products. Its promotion is designed to stress its ethical values, its straightforward approach to business and the service it provides to customers. For example, it only buys fruit from plantations that 'enhance human, social and environmental rights'. Its brand name, logo and catchline, 'little tasty drinks', support this. It has been successful in building its brand, with sales growing from 20 products a day in 1999 on its first trading day to over 2 million a week in 2007.

Source: information from innocent

key terms

Advertising agency - a business which specialises in organising the promotion for other businesses.
Above-the-line promotion - media advertising.
Below-the-line promotion - any form of promotion apart from media advertising, such as sales discounts.
Direct mail - advertising leaflets sent to potential customers, usually through the post.
Point-of-sale material - promotion of a product where it is sold. Examples include special displays or distribution of leaflets in shops.
Promotion - communication between business and customer, making the customer aware that the product is for sale, telling or explaining to them what is the product, making the customers aware of how the product will serve the customer's needs and persuading them to buy it for the first time or again.
Public relations - promotion of a positive image about a product or business through giving information about the product to the general public, other businesses or to the press.

SUMMARY CASE STUDY

EGGS

The British Egg Industry Council represents thousands of small farmers and a few larger businesses which supply eggs to supermarkets and other customers. The Council wants to conduct a promotion campaign for eggs. Egg consumption has been falling over the past 60 years as consumers have switched to other foods. In 2005, people on average ate 172 eggs per person per year. Ten years earlier, it had been 220.

Surveys show that some consumers have been worried about the high cholesterol content of eggs. However, high cholesterol in itself is not bad in food. It is when it is associated with high levels of saturated fat that it can be a cause of heart problems and eggs are low in saturated fat.

Surveys also show that some consumers are worried about animal welfare. They are also concerned about the chances of contracting salmonella.

Consumers are attracted to foods that they think are 'natural'. They also increasingly want fast food - food that can be eaten immediately or which takes little time to prepare.

DTP

1 Design a promotional campaign for eggs. You need to think about all aspects including designing an advert, sketching the script for a TV commercial and suggesting ideas for promotion. Think too about how public relations could be used because the Council's promotional funds are limited. You could use a desktop publishing package to present your ideas.

Checklist ✓

1 What is meant by 'media advertising'?
2 (a) What is a 'directory'? (b) Give TWO examples of sales directories used by businesses.
3 How can an advertising agency help a business?
4 How might a business make use of the Internet to promote its products?
5 How can direct mail increase sales of a product?
6 What can packaging communicate to customers about a product?
7 Give ONE advantage and ONE disadvantage of personal selling for a business.
8 Why are good public relations important for a business?
9 What point of sale material might there be in a large supermarket?
10 What are the advantages to a business of owning strongly branded products?

Making decisions

A product is unlikely to be successful if customers find it difficult to purchase. So 'place' is a vital part of the marketing mix. Producers must decide how to get their product to the customer. Channels of distribution need to be efficient and effective.

Nichols plc is the company which makes Vimto, a drink which was first marketed in 1908. As early as the 1920s, it was being exported to India, Burma and Ceylon and by 1930 was available in over thirty countries from Peru to Albania and Liberia. Today, Vimto is an established international brand name. Nichols has also developed a number of other brands of soft drinks including Sunkist, Panda Pops and Cabana.

Place in the marketing mix

For a product to sell, it must be in the right place at the right time for customers to buy. A village shop, miles from anywhere, is unlikely to sell many bottles, cans or Tetra Paks of Vimto a year.

This is true of services as well as goods. An electrician who won't travel more than two miles to a job won't get much work in a rural area. A hairdresser sited on the high street is likely to get more customers than one tucked away in a back alley.

So place is very important in the marketing mix. One reason why Vimto has such large sales in the Middle East, Far East and Africa, and sells into 65 countries worldwide, is because it works with licensees. They make Vimto concentrate into a variety of formats, such as carbonated, still and cordial drinks.

Channels of distribution

There is a CHANNEL OF DISTRIBUTION between the manufacturer of a product and the customer. This is the path taken to get products from producers to consumers.

Directly to retailers In the UK, Vimto is distributed to large supermarket chains for sale to customers. Companies like Asda and Tesco have large regional warehouses which take delivery of products from manufacturers. The goods are then distributed to individual supermarkets.

Through wholesalers A WHOLESALER is a type of business which specialises in selling to smaller shops and other traders. Small shops can't buy

Sandyknowe Drinking Yoghurt

A year ago in the Scottish borders near Kelso, farmer Alistair Stewart launched thick and creamy Sandyknowe Drinking Yoghurt made with whole milk and berries. Stewart was looking for ways to diversify the family dairy farm after a slump in milk prices. 'Too many people were making cheese and ice-cream, so I started thinking about smoothies,' he says. 'I thought there might be a market for yoghurt drinks. I wanted to make a completely natural, delicious product.' Farmers' markets have been a good launch pad and he now also supplies about 40 shops in Scotland. A farmers' market is where farmers take stalls and sell to consumers rather than selling trough supermarkets. 'It's going well but it's been a fast learning curve. We're still very small-scale, doing bottles in the hundreds not thousands and I drive the milk 100 miles every week to be processed and bottled.'

Initially, Stewart also distributed the yoghurt, but eventually he used the services of a wholesaler and distributor with a fast refrigerated service. He hopes, once the market builds, to set up a plant on the farm, 'but it will be a big investment, a big step'. There's little money for advertising, so he does promotion himself. 'I try to hold tastings at as many shops as possible, but I simply can't be everywhere at once. I'm still a farmer.'

Source: adapted from the *Financial Times*, 23.9.2006.

1 Explain why a farmers' market might be an example of selling directly to the customers.
2 Why do you think that Sandyknowe Drinking Yoghurt might have made use of a wholesaler?
3 Do you think that Alisatir should expand and sell his products through large supermarkets in the UK?

many goods directly from the manufacturer because their orders are too small. Nichols plc does not want the high cost of delivering only a few bottles at a time to a small shop. Instead, it sells large quantities to a wholesaler. The wholesaler then sells to the smaller retailer in small quantities.

The wholesaler acts then as a BREAK-OF-BULK POINT. This is a place where goods are delivered. They are then:

- either broken down into smaller quantities to be sold off as with a wholesaler;
- or possibly combined with other similar products and transported in a larger quantity elsewhere - an example of this would be grain being taken to a port in lorries and then loaded for export onto a ship.

Vimto bottles, cans and Tetra Paks are exported directly from the UK to some markets where they are sold to wholesalers and then to retailers.

Through agents Agents are people or businesses who bring buyers and sellers together. For example, Nichols plc might use an agent in Saudi Arabia to arrange sales to businesses in that country. Nichols plc supplies the products and receives money in payment. The agent receives a percentage of

Book distribution

How did this book get to you? Publishers use certain channels of distribution.

One method is through bookshops. Schools and colleges place orders for textbooks with a bookshop. It then orders the books from the publisher. Some bookshops give a discount to schools and colleges on orders for textbooks to encourage them to buy from them.

Bookshops may also choose to have a few copies of the most successful textbooks on their shelves. Customers will come into the bookshop to buy a single copy. Bookshops also increasingly sell books online, via websites.

Alternatively, schools and colleges may also place orders directly with the publisher. This cuts out the bookshop. Publishers sometimes give a discount on textbooks ordered directly from them.

1 What channels of distribution are used by publishers?
2 A book publisher could sell a single copy of a book either to a bookshop or to a school or college directly. Why do you think it much prefers to sell class sets of books?
3 Supermarkets sell some books and magazines. Do you think that a supermarket would be a good channel of distribution for this book, *GCSE Business Studies*, from the point of view of the publisher? Explain your answer.

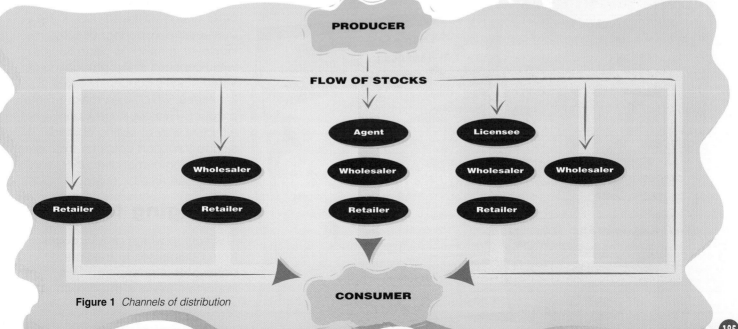

Figure 1 *Channels of distribution*

the value of every sale they make.

Agents can also be used to sell goods directly to consumers. In the UK, Avon selling cosmetics and Betterware selling household goods employ agents. They go from house to house collecting orders.

Through licensees Nichols plc licenses its products to manufacturers in other countries. For example, Vimto concentrate is exported to licensees who then make up the drinks in a variety of formats. The concentrate contains the secret recipe for Vimto that no one else can reproduce.

Directly to the consumer Some products are sold directly to the consumer. A farm might have a farm shop. A footwear company might have a factory store. An insurance company might send sales representatives to visit people in their own homes in order to sell them financial products. A manufacturer may sell by mail order. Many businesses now sell their products via their own websites through the Internet. Nichols plc has sold Vimto through vending machines.

Choosing the channel of distribution

Why does Nichols plc choose to distribute its products through certain channels of distribution and not others?

The product Vimto is not a perishable product like a lettuce. Perishable products need to be taken to the consumer quickly and so their channels of distribution need to be quick and efficient. Neither is Vimto a complex product like central heating or double glazing. Complex products are often sold directly because the manufacturer needs to be able to deal with any installation and running problems. Nor is Vimto a difficult product to transport. Products which are very heavy or are odd sizes are often sold directly to customers because

producers provide specialist transport for delivery.

Vimto is a low price high volume product. Its low price means that delivering a single can or bottle to a house would be enormously expensive. Large retailers like Tesco are very efficient at selling large amounts of low price products to consumers. So Nichols plc supplies in bulk either to large retailers like the major supermarkets or to wholesalers. They take large volumes and then perform the service of breaking bulk. This means that a consumer can afford to buy a single bottle at an affordable price.

The market Vimto is bought by millions of customers worldwide. Over 250 million litres of Vimto are consumed each year. With such a wide market Nichols plc has to make use of wholesalers, retailers and licensees to sell its products. On the other hand a business which sells relatively few products, like a building company, is likely to deal directly with customers.

Effectiveness Many businesses have little choice about the channels of distribution they use. Existing patterns of selling and buying determine what distribution channel is used. Nichols plc uses different channels of distribution in different markets. In the UK it makes use of retailers and wholesalers. In other countries it also uses these businesses, exporting directly. However, it also has partnerships with licensees in the production of Vimto. It sells concentrate to the licensees, which then make up the product. This could be a cost effective way of selling abroad, saving transport costs for example, The burden of manufacturing and selling can also be shared.

Changing trends

The way in which products get from businesses to the final consumer is changing. One important trend is the growth of supermarkets. One supermarket,

The advertisements shown here were displayed in *Grand Designs* and GQ magazines.
1 What channel of distribution are the businesses selling these products using?
2 Why do you think they are using this channel of distribution?
3 Do you think that a shop would be a suitable channel of distribution for the products sold in the advertisements?

Riviera Hot Tubs
Traditional Cedar Hot Tubs
www.riviera-hottubs.co.

www.hotsprings.co.uk
HotSpring Spas - celebrating 30 years of quality and innovation

HotSpring
Hot Tubs & Exercise Pools

30 ANNIVERSARY

For 30 years HotSpring Spas has led the way in quality and innovation in the spa industry.
And it doesn't end there. HotSpring Spas are determined that your experience with us will be one to remember. From initial purchase to your first plunge in your new HotSpring Spa and then throughout the life of your hot tub we are there for you. We are renowned just as much for our customer service as we are for our hot tubs!
HotSpring showrooms nationwide - for your nearest call 0800 085 8880 or go to www.hotspring.co.uk

Tesco, now sells £1 in every £8 spent in the UK on consumer goods. Small and medium sized retailers are being squeezed out of the market. This means that, over time, less is being bought at wholesalers. Manufacturers are able to sell directly to the supermarket chains.

A second trend has been the growth of Internet shopping. Most products will continue to be sold through traditionally channels because consumers like to be able to see what they are buying. They also like to be able to take the goods home immediately and not wait days for a delivery to be made.

However, Internet shopping could grow to 10 per cent of the total market over the next few years. The Internet allows manufacturers to sell directly to customers. It also allows small specialist retailers to remain competitive against much larger retailers.

Source: information from Nichols plc.

Ruffles

Ruffles is a mini-company whose business idea is to make and sell soft toys. It makes three designs - a rabbit, a teddy bear and a frog. It will sell the rabbit for £7, the teddy bear for £5 and the frog for £3.

EITHER write a report about the channels of distribution for your mini-enterprise OR answer the following questions.

1 State THREE different channels of distribution it could attempt to use to get its products to the consumer.

2 (a) What are the advantages and disadvantages of each of these channels of distribution for the mini-company?

(b) Which is the best channel of distribution for it to use and why?

key terms

Break-of-bulk point - place, such as a warehouse or a port, where goods are unloaded. They are usually then reloaded, often in smaller or larger quantities, and transported elsewhere for sale.

Channel of distribution - the path taken to get products from the manufacturer or service provider to the customer.

Wholesaler - a business which buys in bulk from a manufacturer and then sells the stock on in smaller quantities to retailers.

Checklist ✓

1 What is meant by 'place' in the marketing mix?
2 What is the difference between a wholesaler and a retailer?
3 'A retailer acts as a break-of-bulk point.' What does this mean?
4 How can agents help distribute products?
5 Why are new ships and aircraft sold directly to customers rather than through other channels of distribution?
6 Why do businesses like Kellogg's choose to distribute their products through wholesalers and retailers rather than direct to the customer?
7 When might a small business use an agent to distribute its products?

SUMMARY CASE STUDY

SELLING INSURANCE

Insurance companies use a variety of different channels to sell insurance.

- Some policies are sold directly to the customers through sales representatives. A potential customer would contact the company and enquire about insurance products. The sales representative would then visit the customer to explain the policies available and then make a sale.
- Some policies are sold through brokers. These are businesses which deal directly with customers, offering advice and support. They organise the buying and selling of insurance to customers from insurance companies. The broker is paid a commission by the insurance company for every policy sold.
- Some companies sell policies over the phone. Customers ring up a company and a telesales worker in a call centre would explain the policy and give a quote (a price) for taking out insurance.
- Insurance companies can sometimes sell through mail shots. They either have their own lists of existing customers or obtain lists of potential customers from other businesses. Advertising leaflets are sent out to everyone on the list, inviting people to buy the insurance on offer.
- Companies set up websites. Quotes can be given online Customers can also apply directly by filling in a secure online application form. Details of the policies appear on the website.

1 (a) List FIVE ways in which insurance companies sell insurance.
(b) Discuss TWO factors that an insurance company may feel are important when deciding which way to sell insurance.
2 A variety of other businesses including supermarkets such as Tesco now sell insurance. Discuss whether petrol stations should branch out to sell car insurance for oil companies.

Making decisions

Businesses have to decide how best to promote the products they make and sell. Should they advertise, for instance, or should they use point of sale promotion? This decision involves weighing up the relative cost of each form of promotion and how best to target their potential customers. They also need to decide whether to organise the promotion themselves or use an outside organisation like an advertising agency.

Food sales are increasing all the time. Today, the food industry is selling us £50 billion worth of food each year. With more people at work and rising earnings, we can afford to buy more food. There is also less time to spend at home preparing food. So we are eating more convenience foods. The result is that, on average, our diet is getting worse. More and more people are becoming obese. At the same time, there is a growing awareness that food might be affecting our health. The government is increasingly urging people to reduce their intake of sugar, salt and fat. Food companies are also cashing in on this message by launching ranges of more healthy products.

Ethical considerations

The supply of food is subject to rigorous hygiene standards. It is important that consumers can buy food that is not going to make them ill.

Generally, hygiene standards in the UK are very high. However, in recent years there has been a great deal of publicity about the amount of salt, sugar and fat that many of our foods contain. Food containing high levels of salt, sugar and fat has been linked to heart disease and obesity.

Some businesses have responded by offering products with reduced levels of salt, sugar and fat. For example, Walkers has reduced the amount of fat in its crisps. Heinz now offers baked beans with reduced levels of salt and sugar. McDonald's now offers a range of salads in addition to its 'normal' burger and fries ranges.

These food companies are facing up to an ethical problem. Ethics are the values and beliefs which influence how individuals, groups and societies behave. Some food companies are beginning to offer healthier food because they believe it is the right thing to do. All businesses face ethical problems. With some companies the ethical problem is obvious. Should a manufacturer of rifles be making arms which will kill people? Should asbestos companies around the world stop making asbestos

TV phone-in scandals

Television companies can raise revenue by organising phone-ins during programmes. Viewers phone-in and vote for a candidate in a competition or take part in a competition themselves by answering a question. The money from the phone calls, often premium rate, is shared between the broadcaster and the telephone company.

In 2007 it was found that thousands of votes cast by the public for the hit ITV show *Dancing on Ice* were not counted. Mobile phone company Vodafone said 11,500 votes were not registered on Saturday as they were 'not delivered on time'. Senders received a message the following morning saying their votes for the celebrity ice skaters had been cast too late. This was the latest in a string of scandals to hit phone voting on TV shows, including *Richard and Judy* and *Blue Peter*. Vodafone said it would be automatically refunding the cost of the votes.

Callers to Richard And Judy's *You Say, We Pay* competition were encouraged to ring in even though the contestants had already been selected. Broadcaster Five suspended all programming with premium rate telephone services, admitting some of its competition winners were faked. Premium-rate phone watchdog Icstis launched probes into a number of shows over potential phone-in scams involving quizzes and voting lines.

Even BBC flagship children's show *Blue Peter* was forced to apologise when it emerged that a member of the production team had asked a girl visiting the studio to pose as the winning contestant in a phone-in competition because of a 'technical problem'.

Source: adapted from the *Daily Mail* web site 21.03.2007

1 How do television companies generate revenue from phone-ins?
2 Describe the ethical problem in this case.
3 How does Icstis help protect consumers?
4 Do you think television companies deliberately 'trick' people into ringing as a means of raising revenue?

because it has been shown to be such a dangerous material? Should cigarette companies sell products which knowingly kill customers?

Other businesses face less obvious ethical problems. For instance, when advertising a product, should they use images which are known to offend some groups in society? Should they use images of beautiful women to sell products which are bought mainly by men? Should they use violent images in an advertisement when there is so much crime in society? Tobacco producers are not allowed to advertise their products by law in the UK and other countries.

Another ethical issue concerns information. For instance, does a drugs company, which has harmful evidence that one of its drugs has side effects, stop selling the drug? Should a washing powder manufacturer claim in an advert that its washing powder 'washes whiter' than other powders on the market when there is no scientific proof that it does? What should a tobacco company tell its customers?

Ethics and the market

Many businesses would argue that the market makes sure that they act correctly. If people really are shocked by an advertisement then they will stop buying that company's products. If a drug company knows that one of its drugs is causing harmful side effects, but carries on selling the drug, then it could lose its reputation, its future customers and could face being sued for damages. However, in the case of the food industry, some of the unhealthy food offered by firms is very popular. People like it even though they may be aware that it could harm them. Here the market is not working.

Critics argue that, in some cases, businesses only think about the short term. A new business might advertise 'high quality double glazing at incredibly low prices'. What is installed might be very poor quality windows. Having made a short term profit, the business might stop trading leaving plenty of dissatisfied customers.

Even more serious is when businesses are able to persuade customers over a long period of time that their products work when in fact they don't. In the past, for instance, adverts for drugs have claimed that they could cure everything from baldness to blindness, when they could not. For decades the world's tobacco companies denied that there was any link between smoking and cancer.

The law

Because the market can't always prevent businesses from misleading their customers or

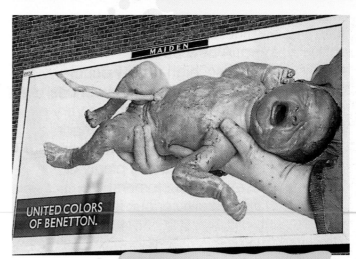

The ASA received complaints about this Benetton advertisement in the 1990s.

supplying inadequate goods, governments have stepped in to pass consumer protection laws. If a business breaks the following laws, it can be prosecuted and fined under criminal law.

The Food Safety Act 1990 This ensures that food is safe and does not mislead the consumer in the way it is presented. For example, it is an offence to sell food that does not comply with regulations, and is unfit to eat or contaminated.

Food Labelling Regulations 1996 This specifies exactly what information should be included on food labels. This is becoming an important area as firms are obliged to show consumers how much fat, salt and sugar food products contain.

The Trade Descriptions Act 1968 This states that it is illegal for products to be incorrectly described. If a sweater says that it is machine washable at 40 degrees, then the colours in the sweater mustn't run at that temperature.

The Weights and Measures Acts These acts make it illegal for a business to sell goods which are underweight or short measured.

The Food and Drugs Act 1955 This makes it illegal to sell food which is unfit for human consumption. It also lays down minimum standards for what must be contained in a food. For instance, a meat sausage must contain at least 30 per cent meat.

In 2004, new rules for genetically modified (GM) food labelling came into force in all EU Member States. The GM Food and Feed Regulation (EC) No. 1829/2003 lays down rules to cover all GM food and animal feed, regardless of the presence of any GM material in the final product. This means products such as flour, oils and glucose syrups will have to be labelled as GM if they are from a GM source.

Getting compensation

Fining the business doesn't help the consumer get his or her money back. To do this, consumers have to use civil law to sue businesses. The two main Acts under civil law are the Sale of Goods Act 1979 and the Supply of Goods and Services Act 1982. These acts allow consumers to sue a business if it sells them a product which is not of merchantable quality, isn't fit for the purpose or doesn't meet the description applied. For instance, a sweater sold with a hole in it is not of merchantable quality. A glue sold for glass which doesn't glue glass together is not fit for the purpose. Trousers labelled yellow in a presentation pack but which turn out to be blue do not meet the description applied.

In some cases, customers take action against businesses because they have been harmed by a product. They are not always successful. For example, in 2003 a US judge dismissed a lawsuit filed on behalf of New York children that claimed McDonald's food caused them health problems that included diabetes, high blood pressure and obesity. '…If consumers know (or reasonably should know) the potential ill health effects of eating at McDonald's, they cannot blame

McDonald's if they, nonetheless, choose to satiate their appetite with a surfeit of supersized McDonald's products,'… the judge said.

Codes of practice

The government has encouraged businesses to adopt codes of practice as an alternative to passing laws. Codes of practice are rules which businesses voluntarily agree to keep, but have no legal status. One important agency which enforces codes of practice is the Advertising Standards Authority (ASA). The British codes of advertising and sales promotion practice state that advertising must be legal, decent, honest and truthful and must not cause grave or widespread offence.

The ASA exists to make sure all advertising, wherever it appears, meets the standards laid down in the advertising codes. It is concerned with such things as the portrayal of women and children, and alcohol advertisements. Large companies will often ask the ASA to check that their advertising campaign complies with advertising codes of practice. Consumers and businesses have a right to complain to the ASA about any advertisement. The ASA received over 26 000 complaints in 2006. If the complaint is upheld, the ASA will ask the business to

Junk food

There has been a huge amount of publicity in recent years about the danger of eating too much junk which contains high levels of salt, sugar or fat. Figures released in 2007 show that 1-in-7 primary school children are clinically obese. This means they are dangerously overweight. Some of the blame for this has been put on the high levels of junk food people eat today.

It was also revealed in March 2007, that eating junk food raises women's risk of developing a range of cancers. Two studies demonstrated the dangers of a diet that includes high levels of fat and processed foods. A major European study shows that women with raised levels of blood sugar face significant extra risks of suffering cancers of the pancreas, skin, womb and urinary tract. And older women with the fattiest diets have a 15 per cent increase in their chances of developing breast cancer, according to a U.S. study. It found fat intake levels of 40 per cent in the diets of women most at risk. Levels rated as 'high' in the study were close to the British average of 38 per cent. High blood sugar levels are linked to unhealthy diets, including fatty and processed foods, and can lead to Type 2 diabetes.

Source: adapted from the *Daily Mail*, 21.03.2007.

1 What is junk food?
2 (a) Name four companies that it could be argued sell junk food.
   (b) Discuss whether these businesses are behaving ethically.
3 How might the government protect consumers from the effects of junk food?

stop the advertisement. The ASA can't force businesses to withdraw advertisements. However, it can make it uncomfortable for businesses to ignore its requests.

It can also discourage misleading advertisements appearing in the first place. The ASA does have the legal sanction of referring a business to the Office of Fair Trading, which may take out an injunction to prevent certain claims in future advertisements.

The food industry is monitored by the Food Standards Agency. This is an independent Government department set up by an Act of Parliament in 2000 to protect the public's health and consumer interests in relation to food. For example, it carries out a range of work to make sure food is safe to eat, including funding research on chemical, microbiological and radiological safety, as well as food hygiene and allergy.

Pressure groups

PRESSURE GROUPS are a further check on the activities of businesses. The Consumers' Association, for instance, is an organisation which defends consumers' rights by investigating and publishing reports on particular products. It also lobbies industry and government to promote consumers' interests.

There are also trade organisations. These are organisations of businesses which defend their rights. They might take action, for instance, to curb the power of large, powerful suppliers or customers.

One example of a pressure group which is involved in the food industry is Friends of the Earth. They oppose developments in GM food. For example, they believe that genetic engineering is imprecise and unpredictable, that most testing is carried out by the very biotech companies that have the most to gain from results that say GM food is safe. They say that growing GM crops also threatens wildlife and the production of GM free foods.

Source: adapted in part from Food Standards Agency, Friends of the Earth websites, www.food.gov.uk, www. foe.co.uk.

key terms

Pressure groups - groups which attempt to influence business, government and individuals.

Checklist ✓

1 List FIVE examples of areas which might give offence in advertising. For each one, give an example of an advertisement which you think might give offence to someone in this area.
2 Do you think that a manufacturer of weapons should continue to make and sell these products? Give arguments for and against.
3 How might a business be less than truthful when it deals with its customers?
4 Explain how the market can encourage businesses to act ethically when marketing their products.
5 How does the Trade Descriptions Act 1968 help protect consumers?
6 Describe the work of the Advertising Standards Authority.
7 How does the Consumer's Association work to protect consumer rights?

ADVERTISING STANDARDS AUTHORITY (ASA)

In 2007 Ford, the motor car company, launched a television advertisement for its Focus Zetec Climate model. The advertisement had footage from the new James Bond film, 'Casino Royale', mixed in with shots of a Ford car. Text on the screen stated 'Focus Zetec Climate licensed and loaded from just £12 999'. The advertisement ended with the text 'Casino Royale in cinemas November 16' followed by the Ford logo.

Two viewers complained to the ASA. They said the advertisement was misleading. Most of the shots in the advertisement showed a completely different car, the Ford Mondeo. It was only at the end of the advertisement that the Focus Zetec Climate model was shown. What is more, the Focus Zetec Climate model was never used in the film 'Casino Royale'. It was the Ford Mondeo that appeared in the film.

The ASA investigated the complaint. Ford argued that the advertisement was not misleading because it promoted the Ford Motor Company's link with the film 'Casino Royale'. However, the ASA upheld the complaint and said the advertisement could not be used again in its current form.

Source: adapted from www.asa.org.uk.

1 What is the role of the ASA?
2 Does the ASA have any real power?
3 Describe the complaint made by viewers in this case.
4 Explain how Ford has been subject to a constraint on marketing.

Making decisions

Every business has to decide how it will organise the production of the good or service it will sell. It has to plan:

* what inputs it needs to use and where it will purchase its supplies;
* how to organise production;
* what stocks it needs to keep;
* how it will sell the finished product to its customers.

Premier Foods is one of the UK's leading food companies. Some of the company's brands include Ambrosia custard and rice pudding, Branston pickle, Hartley's jams and marmalade and Sarsons vinegar. Every year, over three quarters of all UK households purchase at least one of their brands. The company has an annual group turnover over £800 million. Premier Foods also exports to over 70 countries in the world.

Planning

Any new product, whether it is a good or a service, goes through a planning stage before it can be produced and then sold. In the planning stage, someone has to decide:

* what is to be produced;
* how the product is to be made;
* where production is to take place;
* who will be the likely buyers of the product;
* how the product will be sold.

The development of a product will be influenced by a number of factors. These include the following.

The likely demand for the product The more that is likely to be sold, the more that business may consider investing in its research and development.

The product life cycle If a product has reached its maturity stage in the product life cycle, it may be possible to extend its life by slightly modifying the product. If it is in the decline stage, more money might be needed to develop a new product to replace the existing product.

Technological innovation
Changes in technology may allow products to be launched which have never been made before. Or new technology may allow products which are much more reliable, better quality or have more features. Or new technology may result in manufacturing to be much cheaper. To remain competitive, businesses must respond to technological innovation where it affects their products.

Changes in legislation Changes in legislation can mean that an existing product can no longer be sold. For example, it may contain ingredients which are now considered dangerous. Or the manufacturing process may now be judged to create too much pollution. So businesses have to respond by changing their products or the ways in which they make them.

Research and development

A manufacturer may have to carry out scientific or technological research. In 2005, Premier Foods spent £1.5 million on research and development into new products,

trying new recipes and new packaging. For example, they launched Branston relishes, beans and pasta, Loyd Grossman 'creamy' pasta sauces, pesto and chutneys and Ambrosia rice and custard with fruit sauce.

Any new product has to go through a process of development, where the original research idea is turned into a product which can be sold to the customer. How can a new type of chutney be manufactured in large quantities? In what sized jars should it be sold? What packaging will be needed to keep the chutney in perfect condition? How long can it be stored and in what conditions?

RESEARCH AND DEVELOPMENT (R&D) is potentially risky. Premier Foods is constantly coming up with ideas for new products or ways of improving existing products. In 2005, 26 new products were launched. Many products are rejected before they get to the stage where they are sold to customers. However, a few pass through the development process to become successful products like Quorn.

Purchasing

In a large business, the buying department is in charge of buying in goods and services needed for production. At Premier Foods, the buying department is responsible for buying raw materials such as sugar, salt, fruit, vegetables, rice, flavourings and many other ingredients that go into the manufacturing of their many food products. It is also responsible for buying the packaging - the jars, tins, plastic packaging, cardboard boxes - in which their brands are sold.

The buying department will look at a number of factors when deciding what to buy from the SUPPLIER.

Price The buying department will be looking for the best possible price given the quality required.

Quality The buyers will know the minimum quality standard. This may be laid down in a product specification, a written document which describes exactly what is required. Only suppliers able to supply to specification will be considered.

Service The buyer will be looking for suppliers who supply on time and can be flexible, accepting lower orders or higher orders if necessary. They want to make sure that the supplier is financially stable and will not go out of business before completing an order.

Production

In a large manufacturing business, the production manager is responsible for deciding how goods should be produced. At Premier Foods, production managers in charge of producing the many brands aim to:
• produce cost-effectively;
• ensure that the products meet the strict quality specifications, such as food agency standards, taste, colour and textures.

Stocks

Any business is likely to have STOCKS. Premier Foods had £89.8 million of stocks in 2005. This included stocks of raw materials used in the manufacture of its products. It also had stocks of finished products waiting for delivery to customers.

Purchasing · Planning · Stocks · Production · Stocks · Sales

Figure 1 *Organising production at a food manufacturer*

Simpsons Ltd

High Wycombe- based Simpsons Ltd manufacture sofas. It is an established company and has a reputation for high quality, speedy delivery and competitive prices. The company is about to manufacture a new line of sofas and needs a new style of fabric for covering. The purchasing manager has identified three possible suppliers. Details of their terms are shown in Table 1.

1 (a) Calculate the total cost of purchasing 800 metres from each supplier.
  (b) Using your answers in (a), which supplier would you choose if your aim was to minimise cost?
2 What other factors are likely to be taken into account by the purchaser before making a final decision?

Table 1 *Prices and terms of delivery for three fabric suppliers*

Supplier	Delivery time	Cost per metre	Delivery charge
Crawfords (Bradford)	1 week	£2.00	£100
Batemans (Oldham)	4 weeks	£1.80	£80
Jones (High Wycombe)	3 days	£2.10	Nil

British Polythene Industries (BPI)

BPI is the largest producer of polythene film and bags in Europe. They make a variety of plain, printed, converted and recycled products for a diverse range of markets. The company has a manufacturing capacity of 350 000 tonnes per year and employs nearly 3 000 staff in six countries.

BPI uses large quantities of oil, ethylene, polymer and electricity. BPI's stocks of raw materials as at 31 December 2005 were worth £15.2 million. Recently the company has been troubled by severe raw material shortages. These have been caused by a series of plant breakdowns at some of their European suppliers and by the impact of hurricanes in the Gulf of Mexico.

Source: adapted from British Polythene Industries, *Annual Report & Accounts*, 2005.

1 What is the most BPI could plan to produce per year?
2 (a) What has happened to the prices of key raw materials used by BPI?
   (b) What effect might the changes in raw material prices have on BPI's profits?
3 (a) What effect might shortages of raw materials have on BPI's production plans?
   (b) How might BPI deal with the shortages?
4 Discuss the costs of holding stock for BPI.

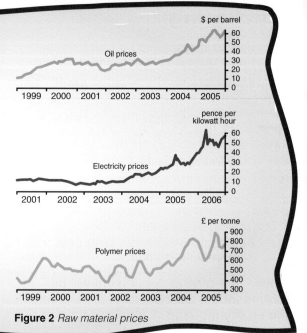

Figure 2 *Raw material prices*

Supermarkets which sell Premier Foods' brands will have stocks of Branston Pickle, for example, on their shelves and perhaps also in their store rooms. Stock management is very important to a business.

Cost Stocks cost money to hold. For example, assume that Premier Foods has to borrow the £89.8 million held in stocks. Then, at a yearly rate of interest of 7 per cent, it is costing the company £6.3 million per year or around £17 300 per day to keep that stock. What's more, the stock has to be kept in a warehouse and that costs money to build or rent, insure and run. Stock can also perish. Fruit and vegetables obviously deteriorate over time. For all these reasons, Premier Foods will want to keep its stock levels to a minimum to prevent overstocking.

Production needs Holding too little stock, understocking, could lead to loss of production and sales. If Premier Foods does not hold enough crucial stocks, then its production lines could be stopped because it doesn't have enough raw materials. Equally, Premier Foods wants to hold enough stocks of finished products to be able to supply customers immediately when orders come in.

Price Buying raw materials and components in large quantities may mean that Premier Foods can buy at competitive prices. Hence, holding more stock could reduce costs.

Sometimes, levels of stock are shown on a chart as in Figure 3 When stocks are received by the business, stock levels rise, shown by a vertical rise in the stock line. The maximum stock level on the chart shows the maximum amount of stock the business has decided to keep at any one time. The re-order level shows the level of stock at which the business orders new stock. Because there is delay between ordering and receiving new stock, stock levels carry on falling before suddenly rising when the stock is delivered. If stock levels go below the minimum shown on the chart, then the business may have difficulty carrying on production.

Many businesses now try to keep stocks to a minimum. They organise production so that stocks are

delivered only when they are needed. This is called 'Just-in-time' (JIT) production.

Sale

There is no point in producing if what is produced can't be sold. In the past, many businesses were product orientated. This meant that they made a product and hoped that it would sell. Today, an increasing number of businesses are market orientated. This means that they try to find out what their customers want to buy and then they make a product designed

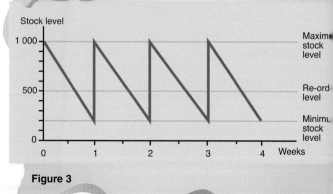

- 800 goods are used each week;
- Stock levels are not allowed to rise above 1 000 goods or fall below 200 goods;
- Stocks are re-ordered when they reach 500 goods;
- 800 goods are re-ordered and take around 3 days to arrive.

Figure 3

around the needs of the customer.
Production is important in sales. The product has to be of the right quality for the price to be charged. Costs of production have to be low enough for the business to set a price which will attract customers. Products must be available for sale when the customer wants to buy.

Source: adapted from Premier Foods, *Annual Report & Accounts*, 2005.

Jim is the stock manager of a small company which makes products from metal sheets. The metal sheets are purchased monthly from a steel wholesaler. Demand fluctuates during the year, and is greater in the winter months than in the summer months. The pattern of stock holding is shown in Figure 4.

1 Identify the: (a) maximum stock level; (b) minimum stock level; (c) re-order level; (d) re-order quantity.

2 On 1 June, Jim had 2 000 sheets of metal in stock. By the 31 July, this had fallen to 400 sheets. How many did he have in stock on: (a) 1st August; (b) 31 August; (c) 1st November?

3 (a) What happened to stock levels in June and July compared to September?
   (b) What does this indicate about sales in those months?

4 In late November, there was a sudden unexpected rush of orders. How can you tell this from the stock graph?

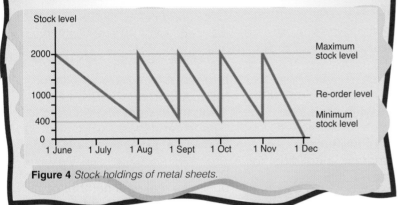

Figure 4 *Stock holdings of metal sheets.*

Research and development (R&D) - the process of scientific and technological research and then development of the findings of that research before a product is launched.
Stocks - materials that a business holds, either waiting to be used in the production process, or finished stock waiting to be delivered to its customers.
Supplier - a business which sells to or supplies products to another business.

Checklist ✓

1 What is the difference between research and development?
2 'R&D is a very risky activity for a business.' Why is this true?
3 What does a purchasing manager do in a business?
4 Why is a product specification important for a purchasing manager?
5 What does a production manager do in a business?
6 What is the difference between an input and an output of a business?
7 List FIVE raw materials or products which are needed by a car manufacturer to make a car.
8 What is the difference between overstocking and understocking?
9 Why is it important for a business not to carry excess stocks?
10 'Management stated that the company needed to be far more market orientated.' What does this mean?

SUMMARY CASE STUDY

ASTRAZENECA

AstraZeneca is one of the world's leading pharmaceutical companies. It manufactures a broad range of medicines designed to fight disease in important areas of healthcare. It focuses on six therapy areas drugs and cancer, cardiovascular, gastrointestinal, infection, neuroscience and respiratory & inflammation. AstraZeneca is active in over 100 countries with a growing presence in important emerging markets. It has a corporate office in London and major research and development (R&D) sites in Sweden, the UK and the US. Sales in 2006 totalled $26.5 billion, with an operating profit of $8.2 billion.

AstraZeneca spends over $16 million every working day on the research and development of new medicines that meet patient needs. The total R&D spending in 2006 was $3.9 billion. It employs around 12 000 people at 16 research and development centres in 8 countries and has 27 manufacturing sites in 19 countries.

Source: adapted from AstraZeneca, *Annual Reports & Accounts*, 2006.

1 What does AstraZeneca manufacture?
2 (a) How much money did AstraZeneca spend on R&D in the last three years?
   (b) Explain why R&D is risky.
3 To what extent is quality in production important to AstraZeneca?

R&D investment $m		Growth
2005	3 379	-4%
2004	3 467	+6%
2003	3 012	

Figure 5 *AstraZeneca R&D Investment $ million.*

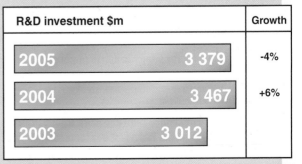

Making decisions

A business must decide how to organise production. There are three main choices:
- should each item be produced separately?
- should the product be made in batches?
- should the product be made continuously?

The decision is likely to be influenced by:
- cost - which is the cheapest method of production?
- quality - which method will ensure the right quality of product?
- quantity - how much needs to be made?

JVC is a global design, development and manufacturing company. In 1976 it invented the VHS video system and produced the first VHS home recorder. Today it manufactures a range of consumer electronic goods including LCD and projection televisions, video cameras and audio systems.

Job production

JVC has 13 manufacturing sites in 8 countries around the world, including Japan. It manufactures televisions in the UK for the European market, in Mexico for the US market and in Thailand and China for Asian markets. Audio devices are produced in Singapore, Malaysia, Indonesia and China. Each factory will have different features. For example, its factory at East Kilbride is 48 000 square metres, with production areas and warehousing space.

The method of production used to put up or improve a building, for example, is called JOB PRODUCTION. This is where a single item is produced from start to finish. Each item produced is likely to be unique. Other examples of job production include bridges, new motorways, taxi rides, a high quality restaurant meal and a work of art.

Batch production

BATCH PRODUCTION is where a business makes a number of products (a batch) and then changes production to make a batch of another component or product. It will remake the original product when it is needed again. For example, at JVC 's factory in East Kilbride, Scotland, printed circuit boards for televisions are made in batches. Printed circuit boards control the working of televisions. Many different models of television are made, each model needing a different circuit board. Machinery to make the circuit boards is expensive. So it is most cost-effective for the same machine to be use to make different circuit boards. A batch of one type of circuit board is made. Then the settings on the machinery is changed and another type of circuit board is made. Some circuit boards even have to go through the machines twice as they need components on each side.

Salisbury bookbinders

Salisbury bookbinders was set up in 1840. It has a long history of bookbinding, repair and conservation. One of the services it offers is one-off hand crafted bindings made to order. It uses skills and techniques built up over centuries and the highest quality leathers, papers and other materials. Most of its books are bound using traditional methods. They are then decorated in a traditional style or have a more modern design applied.

Costs vary greatly depending on the type of design and materials used, but start at around £300. The business offers a flexible and personal service, finding out exactly what the customer needs and meeting these requirements. One of its most popular items is wedding albums sold with guest books. It can use decorative papers it holds in stock for these, but often it works together with a nearby printer to design sets of pages which meet specific needs.

Source; adapted from www.salisburybookbinders.co.uk.

1 What type of production is used to make a hand crafted binding or a guest book?
2 Why do you think this is the best way for production to be organised?
3 Suggest why customers are prepared to pay over £300 for a book produced by the business.

Job production

Advantages The quality of work done is usually high. Employing skilled workers leads to higher quality. Also, workers tend to be relatively well motivated because the work they do is never quite the same, which again leads to higher quality work. Job production allows customers to order exactly what they want, rather than having to accept something which is mass produced.

Disadvantages Job production is a relatively expensive way of producing a good or service. High quality, high wage labour is usually needed to cope with producing a one-off product. British Aerospace workers in the aerospace division tend to be **skilled workers** for example. The work may also be **labour intensive**, with fewer opportunities for automating large parts of the process.

The JVC factory at East Kilbride, an example of job production.

Flow production

The second part of the television production process is the assembly of televisions on assembly lines. This is an example of CONTINUOUS FLOW PRODUCTION. It is a very efficient way of producing. Televisions pass down the line and components are added at different stages. Each job on the line takes the same time. Production is continuous, with the assembly line making the same product week after week. The television production lines operate on a day shift basis for 39 hours a week. 12 000 sets can be produced each week.

Flow production is often used when producing large numbers of standardised items, such as cars or fabrics. Lorries to transport

Batch production

Advantages Compared to job production, batch production allows workers to **specialise** and use specialist machinery more. Costs per unit produced should therefore be lower. It also means that different batches of slightly different products can be made, such as different sizes of ball bearings.

Disadvantages Batch production leads to goods having to be stored and this costs money. Body panels, for instance, or headlamp fittings have to be held in **stock** before final assembly on the car. Specialist machinery may have to be cleaned or reset to produce a different batch of products. This can take time. Specialisation of workers may result in some workers doing the same repetitive job all day which can be demotivating. The factory is also likely to be laid out in sections (called **layout by process**), with each section producing a particular batch of goods. In a car plant, one section might make the body panels for instance. This means that the parts have to be moved from one section to another, which takes time and therefore leads to higher costs.

Batch production of circuit boards at JVC.

Cadbury's chocolates

A chocolate manufacturer like Cadbury is constantly making decisions about what to make in its plants. Take, for instance, a plant which makes three different 'lines' - Cadbury's Dairy Milk, Cadbury's Whole Nut and Cadbury's Fruit and Nut, each in different sizes. Production is planned on a 12 week schedule. Cadbury's don't want to keep stocks for too long because stocks cost money to keep. On the other hand, changing production from one bar to another and from one size to another takes time.

Changing production from one type of bar to another type of bar of the same size loses Cadbury 8 hours of production time as ingredients are changed. For the next 8 hours, production averages only half full capacity as the machines settle in and any problems are sorted out.

Changing production from one size of bar to another size of bar of the same type is more costly. It takes 16 hours to change the moulds and the wrapping machines to cope with the new size. In addition, for the next 16 hours the production only averages half full capacity due to settling-in time.

If both size and recipe are changed, then it takes 24 hours to change the machines and another 24 hours settling-in time.

In a perfect world, Cadbury decides how to organise what to produce by comparing the cost of holding stock with the cost of changing the machines. In the real world, it also has to cope with what happens if:
• customers buy different quantities than forecast;
• there is a major breakdown at the plant;
• there is a delivery of faulty materials.

Source: adapted from Cadbury, *'Fact Card: Production'*.

1 'Cadbury's Dairy Milk is manufactured using batch production techniques.' Explain why this is so.
2 Explain ONE advantage of batch production for Cadbury.
3 What are the disadvantages of batch production for Cadbury?
4 What should be produced is planned 12 weeks in advance. How, if at all, should Cadbury react if:
(a) an advertising campaign for 100g bars of Cadbury's Whole Nut is far more successful than Cadbury expected;
(b) a long spell of hot weather in the summer reduces demand for all chocolate bars by 20 per cent and leads to a build up of stocks in the warehouse;
(c) a major breakdown in the plants leads to two days lost production of 54g Cadbury's Whole Nut bars;
(d) raisins delivered to Cadbury are found to be faulty and can't be used as anticipated in the production of Cadbury Fruit and Nut bars, and the suppliers have promised new deliveries 12 days after the next planned production date for the bars?

Flow production

Advantages The great advantage of flow production is that large numbers of products can roll off assembly lines at very low cost. This is mainly because so much capital machinery is used and so little time is lost in the assembly process. The cost of producing a new car on an assembly line, for instance, is a fraction of the cost of a garage putting a whole car together from a pile of components as a one off job. Also, what is produced can be extremely complex because it is the result of the work of so many different types of worker and machine.

Disadvantages Assembly lines require a large amount of capital equipment to start with. Once built, it is difficult, if not impossible, to adapt the assembly line to make other products. Much of the equipment is designed to be used by workers with few skills, cutting down the cost of labour. However, jobs on the assembly line tend to be very monotonous. A worker might perform the same operation several hundred times a day. This can demotivate workers and might result in poor workmanship. The product being assembled must be fairly standard because both workers and machinery have been trained or designed to cope with only one type of operation. There are likely to be stocks of products waiting to be used on the assembly line and stocks cost money to hold. A breakdown of the assembly line at any point can also lead to a complete shut down. For instance, a strike by workers on one part of the assembly line can bring the whole line to a halt.

Continuous flow production of television sets at JVC

Forging ahead

Mark Thorpe runs a business which makes up-market architectural ironmongery for designers, manufacturers and distributors throughout the world. For instance, it manufactures door fixings such as knobs and handles as well as fixings for furniture.

Growing sales has meant that the company's forge has been kept very busy in recent years. In fact, one of the key problems that has faced the company has been running out of stock of products. The forge might make 2 000 of a particular door handle in January, expecting the stock to last till June. But a large order can wipe out the stock and leave other customers frustrated. They have to wait for delivery until the forge has enough time to make more handles. With 500 different products being made, it is difficult to juggle the exact timing of when more of one item will be produced.

As recently as two years ago, the company also made one-off items. These were sold mainly to design clients who wanted a unique product to put into their latest house or office project. However, the company's designer and most skilled worker retired. The profit on these jobs was often almost zero. So the company decided not to replace him.

1 (a) Describe the method of production used by the company to make door fixings.
  (b) How does this method of production differ from that used to make one-off items?
2 Suggest why the profit made on the sale of one-off items was 'often almost zero'.
3 The company is thinking of increasing sales to retailers. It would buy in components for door and furniture fixings from other manufacturers. It would then package the fixings so that they could be displayed and sold in shops. Discuss what might be the best method of production for this.

supplies to JVC factories are made on assembly lines where windscreens and wheels are added to a chassis. Fabric for uniforms worn by workers at JVC passes through a series of processes, such as preparing (eg cutting), dyeing and finishing (eg preshrinking) before it is ready to make overalls.

Mass produced products are often made using repetitive flow production techniques. This is where large quantities of the same product are manufactured. Complicated machinery is needed to carry out the precise repetitive work. This machinery can sometimes run continuously for 24 hours. Plastic containers to hold milk or oil and chemical containers may be manufactured in this way.

Petrol to power JVC vehicles is made through PROCESS PRODUCTION methods, a form of flow production. At an oil refinery, crude oil is refined into petrol. An oil refinery is like a single huge machine (and hence is called a plant rather than a factory) with the oil flowing through pipes and tanks as it is chemically changed to turn it into petrol. Process production occurs where products like chemicals or liquids are fed through a plant on a continuous basis.

Source: information from JVC.

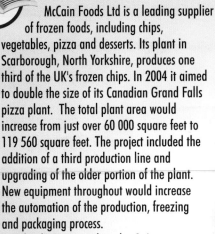

McCain Foods Ltd is a leading supplier of frozen foods, including chips, vegetables, pizza and desserts. Its plant in Scarborough, North Yorkshire, produces one third of the UK's frozen chips. In 2004 it aimed to double the size of its Canadian Grand Falls pizza plant. The total plant area would increase from just over 60 000 square feet to 119 560 square feet. The project included the addition of a third production line and upgrading of the older portion of the plant. New equipment throughout would increase the automation of the production, freezing and packaging process.

Cakes by Design is based is St Ives, Cornwall. The first step in the design process is a consultation with the client to establish exactly what is required. This may be a face-to-face consultation or ideas and pictures sent via e-mail or post. Designs can be traditional or novelty themed. A variety of cakes and fillings is offered. On a tiered cake, each tier can be a different flavour. Prices are quoted individually for each cake depending on size, design and flavour. The business recommends that orders are placed 6 months in advance. It can work to shorter time scales, but some designs may not always be possible.

Source: adapted from www.mccain.co.uk, www.cakes-bydesign.co.uk.

1 Identify the main methods of production at the Canadian Grand Falls pizza plant and at Cakes by Design.
2 What is the difference between the two methods of production?
3 Explain why the size and nature of the market has affected the production method chosen by these businesses.
4 Discuss whether Cakes by Design is likely to change its production method in future.

key terms

Batch production - method of production where a product is made in stages, with a particular operation being carried out on all products in a group or batch.
Flow production - method of production where a product is made continuously, often through the use of an assembly line. Mass produced goods are most suitable for this type of production.
Job production - method of production where a product is made individually from start to finish like a bridge or an aeroplane. Each product is likely to be different and unique.
Process production - method of production where a product is made continuously by being passed through a production plant rather than on an assembly line.

Checklist ✓

1 What is meant by job production?
2 Explain why: (a) building a bridge across a motorway; and (b) painting a house may be examples of job production.
3 What are: (a) the advantages; and (b) the disadvantages of job production?
4 What is the difference between job production and batch production?
5 What are: (a) the advantages and (b) the disadvantages of batch production?
6 What is the difference between batch production and flow production?
7 How are cars produced using a flow production method?
8 What are: (a) the advantages; and (b) the disadvantages of flow production?

PILKINGTON

Pilkington, founded in 1826, and a member of NSG group from June 2006, is one of the world's largest manufacturers of glass and glazing products. NSG/Pilkington has annual sales of around £4 billion and produces 6.4 million tonnes of float glass a year. The float process, invented by Sir Alastair Pilkington in 1952, is the world standard for high quality glass manufacture. Float glass is manufactured using a variety of processes. Raw materials that make glass are fed into a melting furnace. The molten glass is then formed and cooled. The glass is inspected, cut and stacked automatically using a computer controlled system.

A float plant is highly capital intensive rather then labour intensive. It is designed to operate continuously, 365 days per year, throughout its life of between 10 and 15 years. Float glass production requires a high capacity utilisation rate of around 70% (the amount that is used out of the maximum that could be used) before a plant becomes profitable. Standard float glass can be produced in large quantities. However, output can be lost, when changing the specifications from one order to another. This may involve cutting to different sizes.

Source: adapted from www.pilkington.com.

1 'Pilkington uses continuous flow production rather than job or batch production'. Explain the differences between the three methods.
2 Explain why float glass production requires a high capacity utilisation rate.
3 Explain THREE factors that might stop a furniture manufacturer from using this method of production.
4 Discuss whether a large scale chemicals company would use this method of production.

Making decisions

Businesses must decide how they will produce goods and services. Their choices will change over time because the business environment is changing. They need to consider:

- whether they can use techniques of mass production;
- how to minimise inputs to the production process in order to achieve lean production;
- if they are manufacturers, whether production should be organised in cells;
- how they can minimise holdings of stocks;
- how best they can involve the workforce in achieving their goals;
- whether they can check how competitive they are through benchmarking.

Welland Blades Ltd is a well established, privately owned business. It manufactures straight and formed knives for the packaging, food processing, graphics and other industries. With a turnover of £7.8million, the company is based in Sheffield, employs 129 people and exports a high proportion of its sales. The company had started to struggle towards the end of the 1990s and felt that radical changes to traditional production techniques were needed to save it from collapse. It employed a consultant to carry out a thorough examination of Welland's manufacturing practices and help implement completely new systems.

Mass production

Henry Ford founded the Ford motor car company in the USA in 1903. He revolutionised production with his Model T Ford motor car. This was the first complex product to be MASS PRODUCED. Before, cars were built individually. Workers came to each car in the factory and worked on the car. Ford built the first production line. On the **production line** the workers and machines stayed fixed. Cars were brought to the workers. Workers and machines could then **specialise**. Each worker only did one small operation. The tools used were specifically designed to help with that one operation. Workers had limited skills. They just needed to know how to complete one operation.

Mass production reduced costs and increased LABOUR PRODUCTIVITY - output per worker. This was because the same product was being made many times. Fifteen million Model T Fords were made in the USA in just one colour - black. But mass production

techniques had their problems.

- Production lines meant that the product was travelling long distances. This took time and meant that factory buildings had to be large.
- Large volumes of **stocks** were kept. If stocks of a particular part ran out, the production line could come to a halt.
- **Communication** between workers was poor. They were scattered along the production line. There were no systems to get workers to talk to each other about their work. They were seen more as robots than as people who could help improve production through their ideas.
- Workers had no responsibility for the **quality** of their work. It was someone else's responsibility to make sure that products were of the right standard. This often led to large numbers of faulty products that had to be rejected.
- Production was inflexible. With poorly skilled workers and a rigid production line, it was difficult to change in order to produce different products quickly.

Japanese industry found solutions to these problems. Toyota, the car manufacturer, helped bring about a second revolution in how products are manufactured. This system is called LEAN PRODUCTION. It is a system which reduces to a minimum all inputs to the production process - everything from workers to raw materials to factory space.

Welland Blades Ltd moved from traditional mass production techniques to lean production methods in 2002. It revolutionised its production and dramatically increased productivity.

Cell production

Up to the end of the 1990s, there were traditional straight production lines at Welland's Sheffield plant. This was changed in early 2002 to a system of CELL PRODUCTION. This is where production is broken down into a number of 'cells'. Each cell has similar tasks or processes which, together, complete a process or make a product. Cells

Harley Davidson

Harley Davidson, the famous motorcycle manufacturer, was minutes away from bankruptcy in 1985. Since then the company has been transformed. Senior management convinced lenders to accept a restructuring plan. Using management principles adopted from the Japanese, new marketing strategies and manufacturing techniques, Harley improved quality and began the long battle to regain its market share.

A wide range of lean production techniques were used. However, it was just-in-time (JIT) manufacturing that was the driving force behind Harley's quality-improvement programme. Suppliers of Harley had to implement JIT into their production process in order to compliment Harley's system. Previously, Harley utilised a complex, computerised stock control system, which was based on maintaining high levels of stock. High stocks meant that the assembly line would not come to a halt if there were problems. This system was inefficient because it did not solve the manufacturing process problems. It was like sweeping dirt under the carpet.

Harley recorded some impressive improvements as a result of introducing JIT:
- Stock turnover up from 5 to 20.
- Stock levels down 75 %.
- Percentage of motorcycles coming off the line completed up from 76 % to 99 %.
- Scrap and rework reduced by 68 %.
- Productivity up by 50 %.
- Space requirements down by 25 %.

It was also stated that without full employee participation in the planning and implementation stages, Harley's JIT would not have been effective.

Source: adapted from http://stroked.virtualave.net/.

1 What is meant by just-in-time (JIT) manufacturing?
2 What problems did Harley encounter before implementing JIT?
3 Why is holding large amounts of stock expensive?
4 Discuss the benefits to Harley Davidson of just-in-time manufacturing.

Just-in-time (JIT) production

JUST-IN-TIME (JIT) production is where stocks are delivered only when they are needed by the production system. This means that stocks are kept to a minimum. In a large factory, stocks will be delivered by the supplier straight to the right point on the production line. Welland Blades Ltd was forced by its overseas customers to offer just-in-time deliveries. This meant that customers could order knives from Welland and take delivery within 72 hours. But Welland has also moved to JIT production in its own Sheffield factory.

There are many advantages to JIT production.
- Holding stocks is costly. Money is tied up in stocks which could be used elsewhere. Stocks have to be held somewhere, like in a warehouse. This space costs the company money.
- Moving stock is costly. Stocks may be delivered to a warehouse and then taken out to go on the production line. This costs more than if the stock is delivered straight to the production line.
- Holding stock can lead to poor quality. If workers know that there are large stocks, they won't be worried if some of their work is poor. Good components can always be taken out of stock and the poor work thrown away. If there are no stocks, work must be accurate because faulty materials can stop production.

The workforce

The key to the changes at Welland have been changes to the workforce. Lean production is associated with KAIZEN. This is Japanese for 'continuous improvement'. Kaizen implies that production can always be improved. Quality can be better, production times can be reduced and costs can be lowered. In a traditional system, workers have no control over their work. It arrives on the production line which has been

may be 'U' shaped or horseshoe shaped similar to Figure 1. Materials are brought to a point at the start of the cell. They are then worked on at different machines around the cell. The finished product ends up near to where it started.

Cell production at Welland Blades Ltd involved organising production into two cells, each one focusing on the production of a particular family of products. This brought many benefits.
- Machines in cells were placed much closer together than on traditional production lines. Cell production took up less space on the factory floor as a result. This allowed Welland to move all production under one roof and sell off a part of its site to property developers
- Working more closely together, workers in the cell co-operated and sorted out problems together. Cells were given production targets. This helped increase productivity.
- Quality improved because of better co-operation between workers. It was also easier to see where faults in production were coming from. Worker morale also increased.

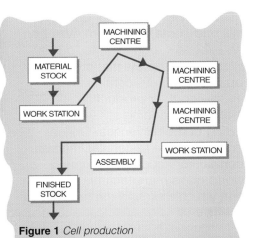

Figure 1 Cell production

designed by someone else. With Kaizen, workers have to be involved. In each cell, workers are typically part of a team. Problems faced by one worker in the cell become problems for all the workers in the cell. The cell cannot produce anything if there is a problem with one part of it.

At Welland Blades Ltd, there is a commitment to ongoing training of the workforce. If workers are to be able to work flexibly, then there has to be MULTI-SKILLING. This is where workers are trained to be able to do a variety of jobs because they have more than one skill.

Workers are also far more involved in problem solving. At Welland, for instance, weekly meetings are held for all staff to discuss problems that have arisen. The meetings are held in works time and are attended voluntarily. However, such is the culture now that everyone attends and sees the meeting as an opportunity to make their jobs easier. Problems are now solved more quickly and communication in the organisation has improved. These meetings are

very similar to **quality circles** which became popular in the 1980s. where workers met to discuss ways of improving work.

Another way of involving workers in problem solving is to run company **suggestion schemes**. Workers are invited to suggest ways in which the business could be improved. Most ideas are impractical. But a few can lead to important changes. Workers are rewarded financially if their schemes result in a reduction in costs or an improvement in productivity.

As a result of these changes productivity improvements have been made that range from 20 per cent to 100 per cent, with an 85 per cent reduction in the distance travelled by both product and operators. More significantly the project helped sales rise by over £1 million and more is expected as the programme continues. Motivation amongst the workforce was also greater. There was greater belief in the management team and workers felt that they were now trusted by management to work efficiently.

Benchmarking

Another technique used to achieve lean production is BENCHMARKING. This is where one business compares its performance with another. Welland Blades Ltd, for instance, knew that its performance had greatly improved after the changes made.

- In 2001 faults per million on components produced for overseas customers were measured in thousands per million parts. This was very high. In 2003, it fell to 815 per million and by 2005 it was just 75 per million.
- Between 2001 and 2005, output per worker nearly doubled.
- Stock turnover is the number of times per year an item of stock on average is moved in the production process. **Stock turnover** increased from 11 times to 20 times between 2001 and 2005. This resulted from much better stock control and the move toward just-in-time production.

However, when Welland Blades Ltd compared itself to other businesses, it could see that there was still room for improvement. Welland's management had contacts with other engineering companies in the Sheffield area. Although, they did not make the same products as Welland, they did use similar materials and almost identical production techniques. Comparisons were made between Welland and a company called AWA Engineering.

For instance, output per worker at Welland was still 20-30 per cent below AWA. In terms of quality, it still had some way to go. AWA had an excellent reputation for quality. Welland also knew that other businesses were continually improving their production methods. Standing still would mean losing competitiveness. Only by improving at a faster rate than its competitors could it become a world class manufacturing facility - one which matched the best in the world.

Crown Cork & Seal

Crown Bevcan Europe & Middle East (Bevcan), makes cans for companies like Coca-Cola, Pepsi, Heineken and Schweppes. In recent years Crown has been running an improvement programme called World Class Performance (WCP). In 1998, its Carlisle plant won an award for manufacturing excellence. The award recognises the achievement of results from continuous achievement programmes (Kaizen). Rob McIntyre was involved in this success and as a result was promoted to the role of world-class performance manager at another UK factory in Braunstone, Leicester.

One of Rob's first jobs was to restore worker morale at the factory and equip staff with the skills needed to adopt a new way of working. The plant invested in a programme of people development to 'unlock' the potential of the workforce. This involved:
- identifying the skills needed for each job;
- identifying training needs for all staff;
- redesigning staff appraisal to focus on their needs and skill recognition;
- providing special training manuals so training could be done on-the-job.

As a result of this programme Braunstone achieved the Investors In People Award. The plant used this to introduce changes to its organisational structure, including a new system of management. Instead of having one manager for each shift, it had one manager for each production line. These new line managers were then responsible for five shift teams. This made it easier to introduce improvements, since one manager would get to know all staff.

Source: adapted from www.crowncork.com.

1 What is meant by Kaizen?
2 Describe the purpose of the training programme introduced at Braunstone.
3 Why might communication between management and workers be improved as a result of the changes made to the organisational structure?
4 How important were the changes to the workforce to the Braunstone factory?

Toyota

Seventy years after it launched its first car, based on a Chrysler body and powered by a Chevrolet engine, Toyota is set to leapfrog America's General Motors to become the world's biggest auto manufacturer. It has already passed Ford, last year producing 8.1 million cars to the 6.8 million made by Ford. This year Toyota is aiming for 8.9 million. With GM producing 9.2 million in 2005 but cutting capacity, Toyota is expected to overtake it.

Toyota has 52 car factories all over the world. In Toyota City, the Tsutsumi plant turns out two cars a minute. It is one of the largest and most productive Japanese plants, employing 4 500 people. It is, says general manager Hiroshi Nakagawa, a demonstration of the Toyota Way and (another well-known Japanese buzzword) kaizen that have driven the company over the decades. Workers said picking up bolts was difficult wearing gloves. A contraption called the chameleon now does it for them.

Line 1 can produce a car in 57 seconds; line 2, 61 seconds. They turned out 432 800 last year. Tsutsumi is used as a benchmark for other plants, operating as advisory 'mother plant' to Burnaston in Derbyshire, as well as to factories in Kentucky, Turkey and Guangzhou, China.

Source: adapted from The Observer 2.4.2006.

1 Using examples from Toyota, explain what is meant by Kaizen.
2 What is benchmarking?
3 How does Toyota use benchmarking?
4 How have lean production techniques such as Kaizen and benchmarking helped Toyota?

Checklist ✓

1 Give THREE features of mass production.
2 Explain FOUR problems with mass production.
3 How is production organised in a cell?
4 What is meant by just-in-time production techniques?
5 How does JIT help reduce costs for a business?
6 New production techniques often require fewer but better trained workers. Why is this?
7 Why might greater efficiency in production lead to downsizing?
8 Why would a business want to benchmark its activities against world class companies?

Key terms

Benchmarking - comparing the performance of one business or one factory with another and, in particular, with the best in the world.
Cell production - a production system where a number of machines are grouped together, sometimes in a horse shoe shape, to perform a series of related operations.
Just-in-time - a production system where stocks are only delivered when they are needed by the production system. This minimises stock levels in a business.
Kaizen - a production system which is operated to generate continuous improvement in performance over a period of time.
Labour productivity - output per worker.
Lean production - a system which attempts to reduce to a minimum all inputs from workers to raw materials to factory space to the production process.
Mass production - the production of large quantities of identical products often on assembly lines.
Multi-skilling - where workers have more than one skill and are able to perform several tasks or jobs.

SUMMARY CASE STUDY

GOLD SEAL ENGINEERING

Gold Seal Engineering is an Indian company and employs over 150 people in 3 factories. It produces rubber components such as seals and body trimmings for cars and exports 15 per cent of turnover. The company employed a number of lean manufacturing techniques to improve its performance. Some of these are described briefly below.

• Production set-up time was reduced by 33 per cent using a lean production technique called single minute exchange of die (SMED). This involved taking measures to reduce the amount of time it took to reset machines when moving from one batch of products to another.

• Gold Seal engineers took part in a training program which focused on the standardisation of a number of procedures and processes in the factory. As a result about 50 per cent of the production processes performed on the company's shop floor were standardised. This led to a reduction of the lead time required for production and completion of goods by 25 per cent.

• Through training, workers were able to develop additional skills, which led to an increase in workforce flexibility. This meant that 57 per cent of the workforce at Gold Seal became multi-skilled.

• The 'culture of blame' was replaced by a more productive climate. A major contribution came from a female executive who showed a high level of motivation and ensured that the activities agreed upon were properly carried out.

• Quality circles (QCs) were established and they increasingly involved the workforce. A suggestion system was also introduced, with suggestions being reviewed twice a month.

Source: adapted from www.1000ventures.com.

1 Explain what is meant by lean production.
2 What evidence is there to suggest that more effort was made to listen to employees at Gold Seal Engineering?
3 Explain why a multi-skilled work force improves flexibility.
4 What evidence is there to suggest that Gold Seal Engineering has improved its performance since the introduction of lean manufacturing techniques?

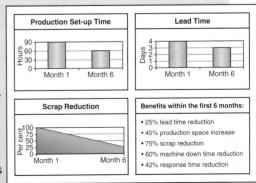

Figure 2 Improvements made at Gold Seal Engineering as a result of using lean production

Making decisions

Businesses must decide how they will produce goods and services. New technology has transformed the range of choices open to them. In manufacturing, businesses need to decide whether to invest in machines controlled by computers in the design and manufacturing processes. They also need to decide to what extent they wish to integrate different processes in a factory. In service industries, today's key technological decision is the extent to which IT applications can be used to make production more efficient.

Fitzgerald Lighting manufactures fluorescent lighting for domestic, commercial and industrial use, along with emergency and amenity lighting. Its customers are mainly electrical wholesalers and they are supplied from their regional depots. Production takes place at Bodmin, Cornwall. The main production processes include metal forming, paint spraying, electrical assembly, plastic injection extrusion and forming and Louvre production (plastic and metal). In-house design and product testing ensure its products are manufactured to a high quality.

Automation

Technology is constantly changing. However, the rate of change of technology has been particularly fast over the past 200 years and is still increasing.

- **Mechanisation**. There was widespread mechanisation during the UK Industrial Revolution in the late 18th century and 19th century. Machines driven by steam or water power replaced workers, but the workers still operated the machines.
- **Automation**. The process of automation in the late twentieth and early twenty first century has meant that some workers no longer have to operate machines. Now they supervise them as the machines work automatically. Automation has largely come about through the use of computers in the production process.

New technology in manufacturing

Prior to the 1980s most design work would have been done by hand. Designers would sketch ideas on paper. These would be developed into more detailed drawings. Then the drawings could be used to build prototypes or models. Prototypes could then be tested for strength and durability before the final product is made. The designer would have to work out, using mathematical equations, whether the proposed materials would be strong enough to do the job. Although some of this is still done today, increasingly computers are being used in designing and manufacturing. Fitzgerald Lighting uses new technology extensively.

Computer aided design (CAD)
Fitzgerald Lighting designs its products on computer using a COMPUTER AIDED DESIGN (CAD) package. CAD packages allow a designer to:

- produce drawings and prototypes so that the end product looks good and is aesthetically pleasing to the customer;

Design fabrics

Carrington Career & Workwear specialises in making high performance fabrics for both the 'workwear' and 'careerwear' market. For instance, it makes fabrics which are fire resistant. Clothes made from these fabrics are used in general heavy industry, including the oil industry in the North Sea where danger is ever present. It also makes careerwear or uniforms for companies, designed to express the ethos and tradition of the business.

Key to its success in the careerwear market is an in-house design facility utilising state-of-the-art CAD equipment. This allows new print or colour-woven designs to be made or existing designs recoloured to meet customers' precise requirements.

Source: adapted from IPT Group.

1 What is the difference between 'workwear' and 'careerwear'?
2 Explain in your own words how CAD technology helps the company.

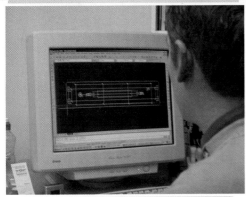

CAD at Fitzgerald Lighting

- put in details of the product and make sure that the product works effectively;
- make sure that the structure and the materials used are physically strong enough to do the job for which they are designed;
- produce two and three dimensional images of the product, as well as drawings of individual parts of the design. These can be rotated so that all aspects of the design can be seen.

CAD speeds up the design process considerably. It allows designs to be more sophisticated. Possibilities for alternative designs can be explored. Changes can be made easily, at little cost. The computer program will, in many parts of the design process, be able to show where there is a 'best' or optimal solution to a design problem. It also cuts out much of the need to build many physical models or prototypes because the computer pictures of the product are so good and because the programs can work out the most effective designs.

Computer Numerical Control (CNC) production
In many areas of manufacturing businesses use COMPUTER NUMERICAL CONTROLLED (CNC) machines. There is a number of different machines traditionally used in manufacturing. Some examples might be:
- milling machines to cut grooves, rebates and slits into materials;
- lathes to cut materials as they turn, to make cylinder shapes;
- routers to shape materials;
- spinning, cutting, sewing, knitting and printing machines used in the textile industry.

A modern CNC machine can be programmed to do a particular task. Instructions are inputted into the CNC machine by the operator. The machine then carries out the task automatically, controlled by the computer.

Businesses benefit from CNC machines. They are fast. This is because patterns or shapes can be cut quickly from stored and controlled information, compared with traditional machines that are controlled by hand. They are also highly accurate, cutting out human error in traditional manufacturing.

Some businesses also make use of probes and coordinate measuring machines (CMM). These check measurements accurately. MGA Developments, for example, a business that designs motor vehicle and aircraft bodies, uses surface measuring software to ensure that measurements of models are correct. Computer controlled temperature is used at McCain foods when making pizza.

Computer aided manufacturing (CAM)
Using computers in design and production means that the two processes can be linked. The computer data generated in design can then be fed into the manufacturing machines. This linkage of design and production is called COMPUTER AIDED MANUFACTURING (CAM) or CAD/CAM ENGINEERING. Businesses can link up many computer operated machines to carry out identical processes.

Fitzgerald Lighting uses computer aided manufacturing processes. Designs which are produced using CAD programs are transferred to plastic injection forming and extrusion, metal forming and electrical assembly machines which are computer controlled. These produce an extensive range of lighting applications.

Large businesses, such as car companies, make use of computerised assembly lines.

Robots
All large motor manufacturing companies like Ford or Rover now use robots on their production line. A ROBOT, like a CNC machine, is controlled by a

Treading carefully

After years of trying to make port, manufacturers found that they were able to make use of robotic technology. A robotic system that treads grapes perfectly, tirelessly and cleanly was designed in the late 1990s and was being introduced successfully in businesses in the early 2000s. Part of the port manufacturing process involves treading grapes, traditionally using feet. But the cost of labour was rising sharply and the number of workers willing to take on such exhausting work was dwindling.

The Symington Group, a family port wine company founded by a Scottish merchant in 1882, introduced robots in 1998. This proved so successful that it introduced robots into a number of wineries. Its robotic lagars look like nothing used in any other winery. A bank of stainless steel lagars, three or four at a time, each temperature controlled and built on a tipping mechanism to speed emptying, is worked by a gantry robot.

The advance of the robots does not mean an end to the age-old tradition of treading. 'The top vintage wines will continue to be trod by foot,' says Alistair Robertson, chairman of wine producer Taylor & Fonseca.

Source: adapted from www.portwinemagazine.com, the *Financial Times*.

1 How has the production of port changed?
2 Why has technology been introduced into the port production process?
3 Do you think that all port and wine manufacturers will change production methods?

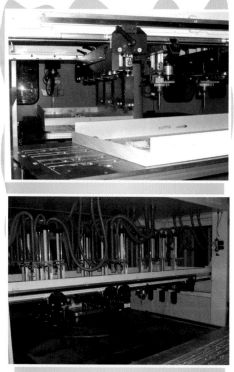

CAM at Fitzgerald Lighting

Computer integrated manufacturing (CIM) Some manufacturing plants have COMPUTER INTEGRATED MANUFACTURING (CIM) systems in place. CIM is where the whole of the production process is controlled by computer technology. Workers are in the factory to supervise and check that the systems are operating properly. They also do maintenance work. Parts can be ordered by computer for the production line as and when they are needed. An AGV may collect the parts from a store room. Or an outside supplier may be expected to deliver to the door of the factory from where it will be taken by an AGV to the production line. A robot may take the parts from the AGV and place them into components on

the production line. Larger CIM systems can be complex, relatively expensive and difficult to set up. They might also be inflexible if, say, a production line needs to be used to manufacture a different product.

New technology in service industries

Many service industries have seen radical changes in the way they work due to INFORMATION TECHNOLOGY. Banking and financial services have been transformed by the ability of computers to store information. Instead of holding paper records about a client, details are now held on computer. This has made it possible vastly to increase the amount of information held. It has

computer. The difference is that a robot has some form of arm which moves materials. For instance, a robot might take a component from a rack and install it into a car engine. Like CNC machines, robots can be programmed as part of a CAM package, linking CAD design with the manufacturing process.

Automatically Guided Vehicles (AGVs) Many motor manufacturing companies also use AUTOMATICALLY GUIDED VEHICLES (AGVs). These are carriages on which components or parts can be put. They are then taken to another part of the factory. The AGV is guided by inductive wires which are put into the floor or on the ceiling along the route that the AGV will travel. The AGV has sensors which prevent it from crashing into objects if there is something in its path. The sensors are linked to the programmable logic controller (plc). This is the microprocessor on board the AGV which has been programmed to control its movements in a particular way.

Internet shopping

Internet shopping came of age in 2006. Britain's online sales totalled £7.66bn in the 10 week run-up to Christmas according to the Interactive Media in Retail Group (IMRG). This was a 54% increase from Christmas 2005. Retailers backed up the findings. Home Retail Group said a fifth of Argos's sales were conducted online over Christmas. Tesco reported a 30% rise in sales over its Internet site. IMRG said online shopping figures over Christmas might have been higher if internet retailers had more capacity and stock. 'Websites struggled to cope with the soaring traffic levels, stocks sold out early, and delivery companies were at full stretch dispatching the 200m parcels ordered. Sales demand outstripped supply capacity by a significant margin,' it suggested.

The growth of online shopping has been fuelled by growing adoption of broadband. According to Ofcom, almost 40 per cent of households have a broadband connection in the UK. There has also been growing confidence in ordering higher value items over the Internet. The strongest growth was in pre-wrapped gift items sent directly to the recipient. The chief executive of the IMRG said companies had been wary of gift service and sent goods only to the address where the buyer's credit card was registered in order to minimise fraud. However, better fraud protection techniques were allowing online retailers to offer this option.

Source: adapted from the *Financial Times*, 18.1.2007.

1 What has happened to retailers' sales over the Internet over the Christmas period?
2 Why did this create a problem for retailers?
3 What factors might have led to the increased use of this technology at Christmas?

also speeded up the handling of information, like a withdrawal of money from the bank. This speed makes it possible, for instance, to use 'hole-in-the-wall' cash machines, which has reduced the need to have so many bank branches. People can manage money and savings using online accounts.

Communication has also been transformed. Computers have considerably increased the amount of information available to a worker. Email allows workers to communicate in written form to each other through their computers. The Internet has given businesses access to a wider range of information. It also allows a business to advertise and sell its products on its website.

In retailing, computer links between what is sold and what is in stock help to decide what needs to be re-ordered. This is called an EPOS (Electronic Point of Sale) system. Bar codes are used which can be scanned to give information about the product and its price. Some supermarkets allow customers to scan in the cost of products as they pick them up in the store. This saves queuing time. EFTPOS (Electronic Funds Transfer at Point of Sale) systems allow customers in a shop to pay by card. The EFTPOS system communicates between the card, the shop and the bank which will pay out the money.

IT is widely being used in administration. **Databases** are basically lists, for instance of customers or of stocks, which can be manipulated in certain ways. The database might be used to send a circular to every customer which has purchased a product over the past 12 months. **Spreadsheets** allow data to be manipulated. Spreadsheets are often used in accounts to help calculate cash flow or costs. **Desk top publishing** (DTP) packages allow graphics and text to be manipulated on screen. They can be used to produce promotional leaflets, internal memos or reports for instance.

Source: information from Fitzgerald Lighting.

Key terms

Automatically guided vehicle (AGV) - carriages on which materials can be carried round a factory guided by inductive wires and sensors.

Computer aided design (CAD) - the use of computers to design products.

Computer aided manufacturing (CAM) or CAD/CAM engineering - the use of computers to control production processes, for instance from design using CAD technology through to manufacture on CNC machines.

Computer integrated manufacturing (CIM) - the use of a computer or computer network to control production of a whole factory or part of a factory.

Computer numerical control (CNC) machines - machines in factories which receive instructions about what to do from a computer rather than directly from a worker.

Information technology - the use of computers to store, handle, produce and retrieve information.

Robot - a machine controlled by a computer which is able to move materials to achieve set tasks.

OLD TECHNIQUES AND NEW TECHNOLOGY

Steve Allen Originals (SAO) is a manufacturer of high quality carved and artistically designed pine furniture. The company designs the furniture itself. Ranges include the Gothic, Acorn and Mackintosh, as well as children's furniture. Its best-selling Princess Bed, is designed with safety in mind, featuring rounded edges and doors which prevent fingers from being trapped.

The company works with Blackburn CAD business Cad-Capture. They take its hand-drawn designs and create computer models that can be fed into SAO's CAM facility. A Computer Numerically Controlled (CNC) machine then mechanically carves out the intricate designs, increasing productivity of the furniture. This process allows SAO to be more flexible with its designs and respond quicker to market demands by improving the time to market. CAD designs are also helping to increase sales. 3D models are taken to customers, improving the effectiveness of sales presentations and reduce the reliance on expensive prototypes.

Design and manufacturing costs have been reduced by improving the time taken to create finished designs. The consistency and quality of the finished product has been improved by the mechanisation of these processes. SAO can also easily evolve existing designs and re-use complete or part designs in new designs. Steve Allen said, 'Cad-Capture has helped us to progress technologically within a traditionally slow-moving industry. Similar companies are still using traditional methods to produce their furniture; SAO has been able to adapt modern techniques to gain competitive advantage.'

Source: adapted from www.cadcap.co.uk.

1 (a) What is a CNC machine? (b) How does the link between a CNC machine and CAD operate?
2 How can CAD designs help when making a presentation?
3 Explain THREE benefits to SAO of using CAD/CAM production technology.
4 Do you think that all high quality carved furniture makers should use CAD/CAM technology?

Checklist ✓

1 What is the difference between mechanisation and automation?
2 A manufacturer wants to design a new bicycle. How could CAD help it to do so?
3 What are the advantages of a CNC lathe over a traditional manual lathe operated by a worker?
4 How might a manufacturer of train carriage components use CAM to speed up production of a new design?
5 What is the difference between a robot and a CNC machine?
6 (a) How does an AGV know where to move and (b) what prevents it from bumping into an object in its path?
7 Why is CIM more complex than CAM?
8 Give TWO examples of the use of information technology in service industries.

Making decisions

Businesses must decide how they will produce goods and services efficiently. Their choices will change over time because the business environment is changing. When considering whether to introduce new technology into the workplace, businesses must decide whether it will make them more competitive. Will it:
- reduce their costs of production;
- improve quality;
- improve working conditions and, in particular, health and safety;
- allow greater variety of products to be manufactured;
- lead to the manufacture of new products?

Toyota is a Japanese car manufacturer. It is a global business with factories on six continents around the world employing more than 250 000 people. Toyota has two production centres in the UK: a vehicle plant at Burnaston, near Derby, and an engine factory at Deeside, in North Wales. In 2005 it made record profits of $17 billion, while GM, one of its main competitors, made losses of $8.6 billion.

Competitiveness

Toyota operates in a very competitive market. It is about to become the world's largest motor car manufacturer. In 2007, it hoped to produce 8.9 million units. GM, the current market leader, produced 9.2 million in 2005 but it is cutting capacity. So Toyota is expected to overtake it.

Toyota has a sound business strategy.
- It uses the most up-to-date production techniques. It has pioneered many of the modern methods now used all over the world.
- It invests heavily in research and development, focusing on safety and environment-friendly hybrid vehicles to build 'the cars of the future'.
- It manufactures cars to a high technical standard which are safe, long lasting and aesthetically pleasing.
- It distributes its products to 160 markets worldwide.

Technology plays a key role in making Toyota a competitive company. Why is technology so important to Toyota?

Robots in manufacturing

Many robots have been built for manufacturing purposes and can be found in factories around the world. Japan and the United States lead the world in the development of these robots, generally called industrial robots. Robots in manufacturing can be divided into three categories:
- **material handling robots** are usually employed in the transport of goods, parts or cargo from one place to another, most often within the same factory or plant. Automated warehouses are examples of this.
- **processing operations robots** generally perform a specific task such as spot welding or spray painting. These robots are outfitted with specialised tools to perform the programmed tasks.
- **assembly line robots** are similar to process automatons in that they usually perform single tasks in the assembly line process such as fitting a cap on a bottle. Inspection robots are widely used to examine a finished part or product for defects or irregularities, for example, utilising any number of tools, such as lenses and scanners.

All manufacturing robots perform monotonous or repetitive and often dangerous work involving heavy machinery, industrial pollutants, poisonous chemicals or other hazardous materials. On the downside some staff may lose their jobs, robots can be expensive to introduce and products may have to become standardised.

Source: adapted from www.links999.net/robotics.

1 What is the difference between material handling robots and processing operations robots?
2 How can robots improve competitiveness in a business?
3 How have workers benefited from the introduction of robots in manufacturing?
4 Discuss the possible drawbacks of using robots in manufacturing.

Lowering costs

Toyota understand the importance of technology when it comes to lowering costs. For example, Toyota's Tsutsumi plant in Japan turns out two cars a minute. Its two heavily automated lines produce nine models of all colours. Robots weld a stream of different models, instructed by computers. Assembly workers work on car bodies, attaching wiring, dashboards and air-conditioning.

However, Toyota is working on a radically different approach to car design, development and manufacturing in an attempt to come up with an ultra-low-cost car. 'The focus is on low-cost technology,' Katsuaki Watanabe, Toyota president has said 'Everything from design to production methods will be radically changed and we are thinking of an ultra-low-cost way of designing, using ultra-low-cost materials, even developing new materials if necessary'.

Quality

Quality is vital to any business. It is vital to Toyota because one of the reasons why people buy Toyota cars is it has impressive reliability records. Technology allows businesses to produce to the necessary specifications. The introduction of CNC (Computer Numerical Controlled) machines, for instance, has allowed businesses to reduce the variance on work. Variance is the difference in size or weight between each component made. A 10mm bolt is unlikely to be exactly 10mm. It will be slightly longer or slightly shorter. CNC machines can reduce the differences between each bolt to nearly zero.

The cornerstone of Toyota's quality control system is the role of the team members in the production process. Toyota believes involving its workers by:

* encouraging an active role in quality control;
* utilising employee ideas and opinions in production processes;
* practising kaizen and striving for constant improvement.

Toyota team members treat the next person on the production line as their customer and will not pass a defective part on to that customer. If a team member finds a problem with a part or the automobile, the team member stops the line and corrects the problem before the vehicle goes any farther down the line. This is essential in a business environment where customers expect cars to have no defects (zero defects).

Health and safety

Working conditions today in factories are much better than even 30 years ago. New technology is a major reason for this. Many dangerous and unpleasant jobs which used to be done by workers are now done by machines.

Toyota makes use of AGVs (automatically guided vehicles) at its factories. These driverless trucks make it unnecessary for workers to handle work in progress round the factory. Components can be transported safely to wherever they are needed. This might prevent back injuries and injuries associated with dropping objects.

Painting and spraying of cars is another area where technology has transformed the workplace. Many coatings contain dangerous chemicals which, if breathed in or touched, can harm the worker. Use of fully automated spraying machines in sealed chambers means that workers do not need to be exposed to these dangers.

New technology also allows

Rail safety

There is a large number of automated systems for keeping trains apart and stopping them automatically in emergencies. In Europe each country has its own system for train signalling and safety. Operating systems have to be switched as trains cross from one country to another. Some trains have to be fitted with six different navigation systems. This adds to costs, takes up valuable on-board space and adds to the maintenance bill.

So a new unified system called the European Rail Traffic Management System (ERTMS) is being developed. It will have standardised train and trackside equipment. ERTMS provides all the functions needed to control and monitor rail operations. This includes receiving information about trains and tracks from a control room and passing them onto the train. It also includes selecting the safest speed for sections that trains have yet to reach.

Safety can be improved where human operations are replaced by automated systems. Automation gives constant supervision and control. It does not suffer any lack of concentration and it does not have to take time off. It also has automatic back-up systems that take over the running of trains or stop them safely if a problem arises.

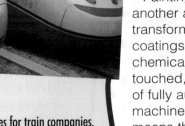

Source: adapted from www.engineerlive.com.

1 How is new technology being used to improve train safety?
2 Explain why new technology can improve safety on trains.
3 Explain why the new system might (a) reduce costs and (b) increase revenues for train companies.
4 Discuss whether all train driving systems should be automated.

products themselves to be much safer for consumers. For example, Toyota is always developing new technologies for improving preventive safety and pre-crash safety. Toyota must also ensure that its products meet international safety and production standards.

New products

Computers and information technology have been at the heart of the technological revolution of the past 30 years. They have created new machines and new ways of working. They have also created new products, including the personal computer, the internet, iPods and digital television.

Toyota has always been at the forefront of technological development in the car industry. For example, Toyota has invested heavily in environmental cars. It launched its Prius hybrid car, powered by battery motor and petrol engine in 1997, and now leads the market, along with Honda, selling 300 000 vehicles a year.

Toyota needs to stay at the forefront of change in order to survive. It spends 4-5 per cent of its sales revenue on research and development. Toyota has long been a heavy investor. For example, it is the only car company with its own semi-conductor plant. It believes that half of a car's value will eventually come in electronics.

Whenever Toyota creates new processes of production or new products it may decide to PATENT these. In 2004, Toyota patented a design for an emotion-displaying vehicle. The design has a shaped bonnet and headlights to represent eyebrows, eyelids and tears, along with an antennae and adjustable body height. It's meant to allow drivers to communicate with each other and make friendly gestures. Hopefully it might reduce aggression and road rage. A patent prevents other businesses or individuals from copying the process or product. Toyota has also

used COPYRIGHT to prevent people from copying some of its published materials, in manuals, for example.

Some companies LICENCE their name or trademark to other businesses, allowing them to use the trademark on products in return for a fee.

Mass customisation

One of the problems with mass production is that customers are forced to accept a standard product. Ford's Model T Ford, for instance, was only available in one colour, black. However, buyers often want mass-produced products which are customised to their own needs. New technologies reduce the cost of doing this. For instance, Toyota is now able to make each car on a production line to a different specification from each customer. This process of manufacturing a standard product in a large number of different variations to cater for the individual

needs of customers is called MASS CUSTOMISATION. Toyota can produce nine different models, of any colour, on one production line in its Tsutsumi plant in Japan.

Service industries

Toyota is a manufacturing company. Secondary or manufacturing industries possibly been more affected by changes in technology than service industries. Not only has technology created new products but it has also transformed the way in which those products are made.

However, many service industries have been changed too. Information technology has transformed banking and insurance. IT has allowed huge quantities of information about customers to be stored and accessed. Retailing too has been changed. Systems like EPOS and EFTPOS have changed the way in which goods are ordered and money is handled. The Internet has also had a huge impact. People can buy goods online at their own

Mass customisation

iPrint.com, a website that sells stationery, mugs, T-shirts, mousepads, brochures, business cards and more, allows customers to buy their own tailor-made designs. The site uses clickable graphics buttons on screen to steer the customer through the options and web forms to gather text and digital images or select combinations of pre-set designs. The programme shows the customer an impression of what the product will look like, including any uploaded images and customised text and graphics. 'The company has taken a traditionally cumbersome, time-consuming and potentially costly process and made it an easy, fast and inexpensive one,' claims iPrint.com's public relations associate Eric Atwood. The customer approves the final design and sends it straight for printing, without the human intervention that often causes re-work in traditional printing. Atwood claims the site has an error rate of less than 1 per cent compared to the 10-15 per cent rates traditional printers might encounter. The website technology alone costs over US$1 million to create, excluding the production technology.

Source: adapted from www.sean.co.uk.

1 What is mass customisation?
2 How does iPrint.com customise its products?
3 (a) How might mass customisation give iPrint.com a competitive edge?
   (b) What other benefits have iPrint.com enjoyed as a result of adopting a mass customisation approach?

convenience. Even, say, the restaurant trade has been affected. Much better refrigeration systems have allowed pubs and cafés to offer affordable meals to a mass market. Freezer food, together with the microwave oven, another new invention of the past 40 years, have cut costs.

On the other hand, service industries like education or tourism remain highly LABOUR INTENSIVE. This means that the number of workers relative to the amount produced is very high. It is the opposite of CAPITAL INTENSIVE, where the amount of capital, such as machines, factories and other buildings, is high relative to the amount produced. Toyota is a capital intensive producer. In labour intensive industries, relatively little capital is used. So the scope for changing production methods through technology is limited.

Source: adapted from Toyota website, www.toyota.com and *The Observer*, 2.4.2006.

Checklist ✓

1 Why is it important for a business to be competitive?
2 Explain THREE ways in which introducing new technology could lower costs of production.
3 How can new technology help businesses approach zero defect targets?
4 Why can new technologies improve health and safety in the workplace?
5 How can new technology lead to mass customisation in manufacturing?
6 Why are patents and copyrights important to businesses?
7 Give THREE new products that new technologies have created over the past forty years.
8 Give THREE ways in which new technology has affected service industries in recent years.

key terms

Capital and labour intensive production - in capital intensive industries, large amounts of capital are used relative to the amount produced; in labour intensive industries relatively large amounts of labour are used.
Copyrights and patents - legal protection to prevent inventions or new products being copied by other businesses for their own use.
Licence - the legal right to use the copyright or patent of another business, usually in return for a fee or a royalty.
Mass customisation - the process of manufacturing a standard product in a large number of different variations to cater for the individual needs of customers.

SUMMARY CASE STUDY

ROAD ANGEL

Road Angel uses global positioning satellite (GPS) technology to improve driver safety. It claims to reduce road accidents by up to 50 per cent. An independent one million mile fleet test has proved that business drivers using Road Angel have 50 per cent fewer accidents. They are 74 per cent less likely to get a speeding fine.

In its first three years Road Angel has become the UK's No.1 blackspot and camera alert device. Its key products are dashboard devices that tell drivers to speed cameras or accident blackspots. Sales have soared 160 per cent a year from £2.5 million in 2003 to £17.1 million in 2005.

The Compact Road Angel is one of Road Angel's stock products. It gives customers access to the UK's No.1 safety camera and accident blackspot database. The product provides visual, spoken and audible alerts for hazards such as:
• fixed, mobile and average speed safety cameras;
• accident blackspot warnings;
• primary school locations;
• congestion charging zones;
• mobile van locations;
• unprotected railway crossings;
• advisory speed limits displayed during camera alerts.

Source: adapted from Road Angel website, www.roadangel.co.uk and www.fasttrack.co.uk.

1 What new technology is Road Angel making use of?
2 How is the new product contributing to health and safety?
3 How might patents help Road Angel?
4 What evidence is there to suggest that Road Angel has exploited new technology successfully?

Making decisions

Every business needs to ensure quality. Poor quality products are likely to lead to low sales and possible insolvency. A business must decide:
- what is the minimum acceptable quality level to customers;
- who in the business is responsible for making sure that quality is maintained;
- how the business can be organised to ensure quality at least cost.

The GSM Group employs over 300 people in five self-contained companies in the UK and a wholly owned subsidiary based in Germany. Examples of some of the products supplied by the group include metal, plastic and digitally printed labels, fascias and overlays; treadplates, interior trims and labels for the motor industry and industry; and label printing software, barcode scanners and portable data capture systems. The group has a reputation for providing a friendly helpful service at competitive prices.

What is quality?

The GSM Group is committed to producing quality products. In business, QUALITY has a special meaning. It is not about whether one product is better than another. It is about whether a product meets the standards that have been set for the product. For example, a Rolls Royce car is more luxurious than a Volkswagen Polo. But if Rolls Royce and Volkswagen set themselves a quality standard that there should be zero faults on the tyres they supply with their cars, then both are of equal quality when they achieve this zero fault rate.

GSM has high profile car manufacturing customers like Nissan, Ford and General Motors. These car companies set GSM quality standards for all the products they supply. GSM works closely with these customers to make sure it always meets these quality standards.

Product recall at B&Q

On 27.2.2007 the following notice appeared in the press.

Performance Power 1050W Rotary Hammer Drill
Bar code - 05075294 or 05096510
Model Number - NLH1050SDS
Despite rigorous quality control procedures it has been brought to B&Q's attention that in some instances the clutch on these units fails to operate as expected, which could result in serious injury to the user. Any potentially faulty product cannot be identified visually - the only means of identification is from the bar code numbers shown on the product rating label. If you have purchased this product between 1st July 2005 and 6th February 2007 with the following EAN Numbers - 05075294 or 05096510

PLEASE STOP USING IT IMMEDIATELY

and urgently contact the helpline...
The helpline staff will validate that you have the correct model and give you an authorisation number so that you can return the product to any B&Q store for an exchange to the value of the original purchase or full refund.

Source: adapted from the Trading Standards website, www.tradingstandards.gov.uk.

1 Using this case as an example, explain what is meant by a product recall.
2 Why is a quality standard so important for products like the one in the case?
3 How might B&Q be affected by this product recall (a) in the short term (b) in the long term?

Traditional quality control

The approach to quality has changed in the last thirty years. The traditional approach saw quality control as part of the chain of production. A product would be designed and the materials to be used would be chosen. The design would be handed over to the production department. It would decide how the product should be made and set about making it. The product would be tested for quality at the end of the production process by quality controllers or inspectors, whose responsibility it was to check for quality. If the product didn't meet the quality standard, it would have to be altered or made again. In some factories, goods which didn't meet quality standards might be thrown away or sold as 'seconds'. Quality inspectors would also test materials bought in from suppliers. There was no guarantee that they would be of the right standard.

Total quality management (TQM)

At the end of the 1980s, many companies took on a new approach to quality control. The traditional method was dropped and a move over to TOTAL QUALITY MANAGEMENT (TQM) was made. This brought about a complete change in the way in which quality was dealt with.

Quality as part of every process TQM makes quality part of every process. So quality is not tested just at certain stages of the production process. It is built into production. For example, quality is important at the design stage. GSM appreciate this and takes the trouble to visit customers when they are designing future products.

Quality is everyone's job Before, quality was the responsibility of the quality inspector. With TQM, every worker is responsible for quality. This may mean that a worker or group of workers does the job that a quality inspector did before. It may mean that quality is being tested at a stage of the production process where it wasn't being tested before. If products are not of the right quality, then it is important that the problem can be identified quickly so that it can be put right. When implementing TQM training and teamwork is very important. At GSM every employee signs a contract to say that they are a member of a team. At each site there are six teams and team leaders have to demonstrate good quality communication skills. Training in communication is also given. GSM spend 1.4 per cent of revenue on training and every employee has a personal development plan.

Customers and suppliers To help build quality into the production process, workers need to recognise the needs of customers. Suppliers must take into account the requirements of businesses, their customers. Workers in sales must take into account the needs of the public or other businesses buying their products or services. By recognising that their work affects customers, workers become more responsible for what they do. They see their importance in the overall work of the business. GSM found that in the electronics market, customers wanted one supplier for all non-electronic parts. GSM is now making everything that customers were buying from lots of different suppliers. Continuing down the supply chain, GSM itself has cut down the number of suppliers it has, searching for single source arrangements wherever possible.

Kaizen Kaizen or continuous improvement provides ideal support for TQM. To achieve the highest possible quality standards continuous improvements are necessary. Kaizen is very active throughout GSM. At GSM's Thirsk site, more than 4 000 suggestions for improvements were made over a four year period alone. And these were the ones that were implemented. One example of Kaizen was the elimination of the wrapping process at GSM. This saved money in wrapping materials and made it easier for the customer when receiving orders.

Zero defects The ultimate aim of a business using TQM techniques like GSM is to have zero defects. This means that all its work meets the required quality standards at every stage of the production process. To reach this, the business may set itself intermediate targets where it aims to reduce defects to a certain level within, say, the next year.

The role of management Although every worker is

Quality control at Iglo Ola

Iglo Ola, the Dutch-based manufacturer of ice creams, lollies and frozen yoghurts has installed metal detection and check-weighing equipment at its factories in Hellendoorn and Wilp. Part of the multi-national Unilever Group, Iglo Ola has installed the new quality inspection equipment as part of a group-wide upgrade in quality control procedures. Nine metal detectors and one check-weigher have been installed at the factories in Hellendoorn and Wilp which manufacture products under the Ola, Caraco and Davino brand names including ice creams such as Calipso, Roombeker, Split and Rocket lollies.

Source: adapted from BNET website, www.bnet.com.

1 Describe the quality inspection equipment that Iglo Ola has installed.
2 Why do you think metal detection equipment is needed in the Iglo Ola factories?
3 What are the advantages of using technology in quality control?

responsible for quality, it is the responsibility of management to set up systems which will ensure this quality. For instance, if a worker or group of workers is producing faulty goods, then there must be a system for identifying the nature of the problem. It could be they are working with inadequate machinery. It could be that they haven't been trained sufficiently to do the job. It could be that there is inadequate lighting where they work or that machines are poorly spaced out on the factory floor. Then the system must put the problem right. At GSM management is very involved in TQM. For example, there is a team leaders' conference every six months where objectives are reviewed and ideas discussed. Although decision making is not democratic, there is a feeling at GSM that the views of workers are heard.

Quality assurance When products or services are sold to customers a business gives its assurance that certain standards have been met. It will guarantee that legal requirements have been observed and that quality has been maintained in the production process, for example. It is impossible for every customer to check this, so codes of practice tell a customer that standards of quality have been achieved. Examples are ISO, an international standard, and EN, a European standard.

Quality standards

Many products are made to standards which are laid down by quality assurance bodies. The British Standards Institution (BSI), for example, is an organisation which draws up standards for a wide range of products from beds to nails. Some consumer products like kettles are sold with kite marks on them. This shows that they have been made to a standard drawn up by the British Standards Institution. Other examples are the British Electrotechnical Approvals Board (BEAB), which tests and approves

ISO 9001 requirements

Procedures are required for the following
- Management responsibility, eg for creating a quality policy and quality systems, and appointing quality representatives.
- To review incoming orders.
- To control design planning, inputs, outputs, changes etc.
- To control documents and data, eg drawings, specifications.
- To control purchasing, eg lists and performance of suppliers.
- To control customer-supplied products, eg verify, store, handle.
- To identify and trace products.
- Controlling and planning of production, eg use of equipment, work instructions, monitoring and control of processes.
- Inspection and testing of a product at all stages of production.
- The control of inspection, measuring and test equipment.
- To check a product has or has not been tested.
- To identify products that do not meet standards.
- To take corrective or preventative action.
- Handling, storage, packaging, preservation and delivery.
- Control of quality records.
- Internal quality audits.
- Training.
- Servicing, eg site regulations.
- The use of statistical techniques, eg for sampling or testing.

Forticrete

Forticrete is one of the UK's most important manufacturers of quality concrete products, with 14 manufacturing plants, offices and depots throughout the country. It is a leader in the field of Architectural Masonry, Cast Stone, Walling Stone and an innovator in Concrete Roofing products and Retaining Wall systems.

Forticrete was originally registered to ISO 9000 in 1986 but has recently switched to the newer version, ISO 9000:2000. Before the switch, Forticrete's quality management system (QMS), was an old paper-based system consisting of 8 quality manuals. Switching to the newer version provided Forticrete with an opportunity to:

- radically review the current system;
- move to an electronic system based on flow charts;
- increase the focus on customer needs.

Adopting the new ISO 9000:2000 has allowed Forticrete to streamline its QMS and integrate it with other business functions. As a result, a customer satisfaction survey revealed:

- 18% improvement in product quality;
- 18% increase in Customer Satisfaction Rating;
- 21% rise in Performance Against Competitors.

In addition, there has been a 42 per cent decrease in product complaints and a number of accolades have been picked up. These include the Queens Award for Enterprise (Innovation) 2001, Contract Journal Construction Product Manufacturer of the year 2002 and Construction News Quality in Construction: Innovation 2003.

Source: adapted from the BSI website, www.bsi-global.com.

1 What is ISO 9000:2000?
2 How might the switch from a paper-based QMS to an electronic system help Forticrete?
3 Explain the benefits to Forticrete of registering with ISO 9000:2000.

electrical products, and the British Toy and Hobby Association which grants a Lion Mark for approved toys.

Product standards are very helpful in measuring quality. However, they don't say anything about how that quality was achieved. A business might, for instance, have a defect rate of 50 per cent on what it produces. So there are also standards for the quality of production systems. One standard is ISO 9000. GSM believes that an effective quality system leads to a more efficient business overall. They currently work to QS9000 and are preparing to adopt others.

Other standards include ISO 9001, a quality system standard for manufacturing and service businesses with design. ISO 9002 is for manufacturing and service businesses, without design, and ISO 9003 is for suppliers only.

To get ISO 9000, GSM registered with the British Standards Institution. It had to show the BSI, through its documentation and through factory visits, that its operating processes met the required standard. Where they didn't, it had to modify its processes to comply with the standard.

There are two main advantages in meeting ISO 9000 standards. First, GSM was forced to review its quality procedures and make improvements to them. Second, because ISO 9000 is an international standard, it is widely recognised by GSM's overseas customers such as Ford, Nissan and GM. By buying from GSM, they know that the company is committed to and able to deliver quality products. This helps GSM to sell its products.

The ISO 9000 family of standards were revised in December 2000 and are now sometimes referred to as ISO 9000:2000.

Source: adapted from GSM website, www.gsmgroup.co.uk, and dti: *from quality to excellence.*

Checklist ✓

1 What is meant by 'quality' of a product?
2 How was quality maintained in a traditional business?
3 Why does everyone need to be involved in quality control issues in a business?
4 Who are a worker's customers?
5 What is meant by 'zero defect' production?
6 Explain the role of management in TQM.
7 What does the British Standards Institution do?
8 How can ISO 9000 help a business achieve quality?

key terms

Quality - achieving a standard for a product or service, or a production process, which meets customers' needs.
Total quality management (TQM) - a method for a business to focus on quality by making it an important aim of every department and worker.

SUMMARY CASE STUDY

CREALY ADVENTURE PARK

Crealy Adventure Park started as an open farm with an outdoor playground and restaurant. It is now a full scale adventure park offering rides and other attractions on two sites in Devon and Cornwall. The business was set up by Angela Wright in 1989 and is now a multi-million pound operation. Angela believes that the success of the park has a lot to do with the staff. 'Our staff are our greatest asset ... they are the ones who ensure our clients are happy and receiving the best service possible.' The mission of the business is 'Maximum Fun Guaranteed'. Customer satisfaction is measured through guest comments, surveys, exit surveys, mystery shoppers and internal brand audits.

Another key contribution to the success of the business was the introduction in 1989 of Total Quality Management methodology. According to Angela Wright, 'TQM is designed to create a culture of constant improvement and we have implemented it whereby each job has a TQM method statement and staff are encouraged to contribute to improving and updating these pro-active documents. TQM is introduced at induction training, operational training and monitored by line managers'.

In recent years Crealy Adventure Park has won a number of awards. These include South West Tourism's Attraction of the Year Award, Best Website and Best Brochure awards from IAPPA, 'Parents at Work' – Best Boss Award, Business Challenge Award and the Investors in People award.

Source: adapted from Crealy Adventure Park website, www.crealy.co.uk, and www.beaconsw.org.

1 How is quality assessed at Crealy Adventure Park?
2 Explain the role of TQM at Crealy Adventure Park.
3 Discuss whether quality standards can lead to higher profits for a business like Crealy Adventure Park.

Making decisions

Businesses can operate at different scales. Large businesses can often enjoy lower average costs of production than small businesses. So a business has to make a decision about what size it should be for most efficient production. If it is too small and its average costs of production are higher than large competitors, it must find other ways of competiting in the market than simply on price. Equally, large businesses must decide whether they are too large and their average costs of production are too high because their size makes them inefficient. Businesses can also take decisions about where to locate because in some places, concentration of the industry in that location gives all businesses lower costs.

Young's Bluecrest is one of Europe's leading specialist seafood businesses. Its products are made from over 60 species of fish and used to create a wide variety of frozen and chilled seafood products. It has sales turnover of over £500 million a year making it one of the largest food companies in the UK. It employs over 4 800 people at sites around the UK. Large scale production gives Young's Bluecrest a competitive advantage in its markets.

Average costs of production

Young's is a large company in an industry where there are many smaller producers. Large scale production at Youngs gives its a competitive advantage because it can exploit INTERNAL ECONOMIES OF SCALE. As businesses expand in size, they can cut their average costs of production in a variety of ways. The larger the business, the lower the average costs of production.

This is shown in Figure 1. Assume this is a car manufacturing business from which Young's buys vehicles. If the car company makes 500 000 cars a year, the average cost of production per car is £7 000. But if it can make 2 million cars a year, the average cost of production per car falls to £5 000. Economies of scale then occur between an output of 0 and 2 million cars. However, sometimes businesses are too large and become inefficient. Large scale production becomes a problem. This is because their average costs of production rise. They then

experience DISECONOMIES OF SCALE. Looking at Figure 1 again, the average cost of producing a car rises to £6 000 when 3 million cars are produced. The business experiences diseconomies of scale between production of 2 million and 3 million cars.

Sources of internal economies of scale

There is a number of reasons why larger businesses may have lower average costs of production than smaller businesses.

Technical economies of scale Technical economies of scale occur because of what happens in the production process. A large business like Youngs can buy plant and machinery which is cheaper to buy and run than a small

business per unit of output. For example, the average cost of storing frozen food in a large freezer store is lower than in a small freezer store. The average cost of transporting frozen food in a 40 tonne lorry is lower than in a 32 tonne lorry. So Young's can gain a competitive cost advantage because of its high volumes of production.

Purchasing economies of scale Shoppers in a supermarket expect

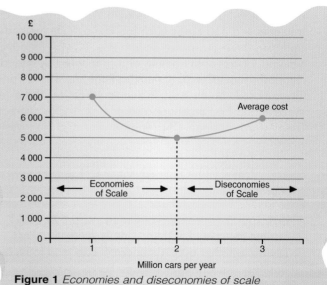

Figure 1 *Economies and diseconomies of scale*

to pay lower average prices if they buy Young's products in larger sizes or in multipacks. Similarly, businesses like Young's can pay lower average prices for materials if they buy in bulk. So bulk buying gives rise to purchasing economies of scale.

Marketing economies of scale The cost of buying advertising space in a magazine is the same for Young's as a smaller rival company. The same is true for sending out a sales representative to a potential customer. Larger companies like Young's can spread out the costs of marketing over a much larger sales volume than a smaller company. Hence, the average cost of marketing per unit sold can be lower. This is known as marketing economies of scale.

Financial economies of scale A large company like Young's has access to a wide range of sources of finance, from bank loans to

leasing to new equity. Smaller rival companies have less choice and therefore might have to pay more to borrow money or get investment money. Borrowing large sums of money is also often cheaper than borrowing small amounts because banks charge lower interest rates and arrangement fees. So the cost of finance for a large company like Young's is often lower per unit of output than for a smaller business. This is known as financial economies of scale.

Managerial economies of scale Managerial economies of scale occur because it can be cheaper per unit of output to manage a large business than a small business. A large business like Young's will employ specialist managers, from production managers to financial managers to human resource managers. In a small business, one person might have to do several of these jobs. That person may have

little expertise in any of these jobs.

Sometimes, purchasing and marketing economies of scale are known as COMMERCIAL or TRADING ECONOMIES OF SCALE.

Diseconomies of scale

Large businesses face the risk that they become inefficient. Their average costs of production can be higher than smaller businesses. When this occurs, there are diseconomies of scale. There is a number of reasons why diseconomies of scale can occur.

Bureaucracy Sometimes, a business can employ too many managers for the amount of work to be done. The business becomes too bureaucratic. This raises average costs. Smaller firms with far fewer managers can then gain a cost advantage.

Channels of communication In a large business, the channels of communication from the top to the bottom can be very long. Senior managers can find it difficult to get orders followed in the way they want. So the business becomes far more difficult to manage than a small business.

Employee empathy In a large business, employees can feel very unimportant. They can also feel that they don't care whether the business is successful or not. What is important to them is the size of their wage package and whether they are enjoying their job. So employees don't empathise with or feel for what is best for the business. This is likely to make the business less efficient and so average costs will rise.

Labour relations In a large business, labour (or industrial) relations can be poor because of lack of employee empathy. Workers and management can clash over issues such as pay or conditions of work. Workers may go on strike or find other ways to put pressure on management. If labour relations are

PowerGym plc

PowerGym plc manufactures equipment for gyms and fitness centres. Its main product is a multi-gym. Last year, operating at full capacity, it produced 5 400 units. The market is growing and PowerGym wants to become a big player. It has taken the decision to move to bigger premises where more modern machinery and a better factory layout will improve efficiency. At the moment the total cost of producing the 5 400 units was £2.7 million. It is estimated that when the move is made to the new factory the total cost of producing 10 000 units (which PowerGym thinks it can eventually sell) will be £3.1 million.

1 (a) Calculate the average cost of producing 5 400 units in the old factory.
  (b) Calculate the average cost of producing 10 000 units in the new factory.
2 Explain what has happened to average cost in question 1 and explain the reason for this.
3 How will PowerGym benefit from the move to the new factory?

Grocery retailing

The local corner grocery store has had a hard time over the past twenty years. As the large supermarket chains have expanded, local corner shops have closed. One of the main reasons why supermarkets have won the grocery battle is because of price. They can sell groceries at lower prices than the corner shop due to economies of scale.

- They enjoy substantial purchasing and marketing economies. Purchasing economies mean that the supermarkets can buy in large quantities and so get bulk purchase low prices. Marketing economies mean that the average cost of promotion is very low when supermarket chains are selling such large volumes.

- They are able to gain managerial economies. The cost of managing a large supermarket per item sold can be very low. Supermarket chains can afford to employ specialist workers, such as checkout assistants, store managers, accountants and lawyers. Small corner shop owners may do these tasks themselves, or perhaps hire expensive expertise to do those they cannot.

- Financial economies are important. A large supermarket chain can borrow very cheaply from the banks. It can also get up to three months' free credit from its suppliers. The local corner shop will have to pay much higher interest rates on borrowed money. It also often has to pay immediately for its supplies.

- Supermarkets can obtain technical economies of scale. They can buy equipment, like a meat slicer, which is used all the time and not just some of the time as in a small grocer's shop. Large supermarkets also have a much larger rate of turnover than a small shop. This means they sell goods much faster, cutting back on the time they have to hold expensive stock.

1 What has happened to the number of small grocery shops in recent years?
2 Explain why large supermarkets can sell products at lower prices than the small corner shop.

DTP

3 A new supermarket opens half a mile from your corner grocery store. Design a poster to put in the window of your shop telling your customers why they should still shop with you. You could use a desktop publishing package for this.

---

poor, this is likely to lead to higher average costs.

Young's works very hard to ensure that diseconomies of scale don't occur in its business. It has an efficient management structure and good relations with its workers.

External economies of scale

Internal economies of scale are gained when a business grows in size. EXTERNAL ECONOMIES OF SCALE are gained when an industry grows in size in a particular area. Young's benefits from external economies of scale in its operations in the North East Lincolnshire area of the UK. This is because this area of England has a large concentration of food processing firms. The fishing port of Grimsby has been branded by its local council as 'Food Town'. 15 000 out of 68 000 employees in North East Lincolnshire work in the food processing industry directly, with many more working indirectly in cold stores, transport and engineering related to the food industry. External economies of scale give a business lower costs because of the size of the industry in an area.

Young's benefits from external economies in the North East Lincolnshire area in a number of ways.

Availability of skilled labour When one industry dominates a local area, workers over time acquire skills to work in that industry. Local colleges provide courses for jobs in the industry, for example. Workers build up long periods of service in the industry. Young's benefits from this because it is able to recruit the right sort of worker for its plants in North East Lincolnshire more easily.

Infrastructure Infrastructure is the buildings, roads, ports, railways and airports of an area. North East Lincolnshire has developed a particularly strong network of infrastructure to serve the food industry. For example, property developers have built factories, offices and industrial estates designed for occupation by firms in the food industry. Local councils have developed roads, ports and airports to help transport food products. Young's benefits from all this spending.

Suppliers Young's benefits from being among other food producers in North East Lincolnshire because there are a large number of specialist suppliers also located in the area. Suppliers concentrate in this area because they know they can pick up business more easily than if they were in, say, Northumberland.

Source: adapted from www.youngsbluecrest.co.uk.

George Wimpey and Taylor Woodrow merger

It was announced in March 2007 that George Wimpey and Taylor Woodrow are merging to create the UK's largest housebuilder, a move that will lead to significant job losses. The deal will create a new company called Taylor Wimpey and will have annual revenues of £6.7 billion. The two companies said the deal should lead to increased profits, and economies of scale in the UK where they will pool a total of 92 000 housing plots for future development. They believe it will also create a more powerful competitor in the US market, where sales of new houses have declined.

The two companies said that they expect to generate cost savings of at least £70 million in the first year following the merger, but there are fears this could mean the loss of at least 1 000 jobs.

Source: adapted from the *Guardian* 26.3.2007.

1 What do George Wimpey and Taylor Woodrow both produce?
2 'Taylor Wimpey is likely to enjoy purchasing and marketing economies after the merger.' Explain what this means.
4 Discuss whether Taylor Wimpey could exploit external economies of scale. Explain your answer.

Checklist ✓

1 What is meant by 'large scale production'?
2 Explain the link between economies of scale and average costs of production.
3 What is the difference between economies of scale and diseconomies of scale?
4 Why might a car manufacturer enjoy technical economies of scale?
5 What might Tesco, the supermarket, chain enjoy marketing economies of scale?
6 Why might bureaucracy in a company lead to diseconomies of scale?
7 What is the difference between internal and external economies of scale?
8 How might suppliers lead to external economies of scale for a business?

key terms

Commercial or trading economies of scale - the fall in average cost of production per unit as output increases that occurs as a result of the purchasing or marketing activities of the business.
Diseconomies of scale – the rise in average costs of production as a business grows in size, usually caused by inefficiency resulting from the increased size.
External economies of scale – the fall in average cost of production per unit for a business as the size of the industry in which it operates increases.
Internal economies of scale - the fall in average cost of production per unit as output increases that occurs as a business expands in size.

SUMMARY CASE STUDY

COGIR PLC

Cogir plc is a large international printing corporation. It prints magazines, brochures and labels for drinks manufacturers. It has grown rapidly in recent years and enjoyed significant cost savings – particularly through the merger and consolidation of administrative operations such as head office functions. Its growth strategy has been driven by the acquisition of smaller printing companies in the EU.

In 2004 Cogir bought companies in Eastern Europe for the first time. It was hoped that the cost savings in the past would continue. However, there were a number of problems. Communications were becoming difficult due to language and cultural differences. There were also problems with some of the workers. There seemed to be a lack of employee empathy. Many didn't seem to care whether the business was successful or not. As a result the senior management ordered a review of the strategy.

1 State two financial economies of scale a large international company like Cogir might enjoy.
2 How might Cogir plc enjoy technical economies of scale?
3 Explain how merging the head office of two companies reduces average costs.
4 What evidence is there that Cogir might be experiencing diseconomies of scale?

Making decisions

Starting up a business is difficult and risky. Anyone setting up needs to consider:
- whether they have the right experience and skills to make the business a success;
- how they are going to produce and market their product or service;
- where they are going to get finance for the business;
- how they can get help and advice that is available to them from outside the business;
- what will happen if the business is not a success.

Enamore

n the countryside outside Bath, Canadian Jenny Ambrose runs the organic fashion business Enamore. It manufactures clothing using either organic products or reusing materials from old clothing.

Identifying the opportunity

John is a plumber working for a building company. He decides to set up his own business. Sashuma works as a manager in a plastics factory. She decides to set up a business selling chairs from recycled plastic. John and Sashuma both have a lot of experience working for others. They know a lot already about their businesses.

Tim is 18. He has just left school. He wants to set up his own business but he doesn't really know what to do. People can find it difficult to make a success of new businesses if they have no experience. That is why people who set up their own business often have had some experience of working in that industry or from hobbies where they have developed skills and knowledge.

Jenny Ambrose is no exception. She trained at college where she first made use of organic fabrics in her designs such as hemp. She also developed skills in drawing and art.

Identifying a business opportunity is the first thing a person wanting to set up their own business must do. Business ideas often come from what they have been doing in work

and the contacts they have made or their own hobbies. They then have to find out whether the idea will work. Jenny first became interested in fashion when shopping for fabrics with her mother. She also grew up wearing hand-made clothing. These experiences influenced her designs

and gave her the idea of a potential business opportunity.

Researching the market

Businesses only survive if they can attract customers and at least make

Identifying the opportunity

You need to find a business opportunity for your mini-company.
1 Start off by listing any experiences you may have had which could be useful in a business. For instance, have you had or do you have a part-time job? Have you any hobbies which could be turned into a business idea? Have you helped to do anything at home, like sewing or gardening which could be seen as a job? Have you helped anyone with their job or business? Have you done anything at school or college which could be turned into something which could be sold, like helping in the school tuck shop or making a product in a Technology lesson?
2 List any contacts which you personally know who could be useful to your business. Also write down how they might be useful. For instance, your uncle might work in a wholesalers and be able to help you buy goods for resale. Your neighbour might work in sales and be able to advise you on sales strategies for your business.
3 List any resources which you would easily be able to use for your business. For instance, if you need transport, could you get hold of a car and a driver? If you need a room to store materials, could you arrange that?
4 Pool your answers to questions 1-3 amongst all the members of your mini-enterprise. Are there any similarities? Does one person have a skill or talent which the rest of the members could support? Do the results show that you want to make/manufacture a good rather than sell a service?
5 Most mini-enterprises find it very difficult to come up with a business idea. Why does lack of experience partly explain why this is so?

Sears Studios

Yolanda Sears studied music at university. She was particularly keen on the engineering and mixing side. She worked in a recording studio for three years but wanted to start her own business. In the 1990s many people were making home recordings using computers and keyboards. Some still did this, but the growth of many young people playing guitars in the 2000s led her to believe that she could set up a studio that offered recording and mastering facilities. Bands could have their music recorded as a CD or MP3 for sale or as downloads on their own websites.

Yolanda realised she would need equipment and had saved money for a desk, mikes and other recording equipment. She could make use of her own computer which had the capacity to handle the tasks involved. She found a small room in an industrial site that she could rent. Very quickly local bands started to make use of her facilities. And also very quickly she faced problems. Her computer was not nearly powerful enough to handle the amount of data she was working with. The rent went up soon after she moved in and she was having problems finding enough cash to order materials she needed. She also realised that the soundproofing was not adequate. Yolanda felt that she clearly had underestimated the money she would need at the start and to run the business.

1 What business is Yolanda running?
2 Explain how the recording market has changed.
3 Explain why Yolanda might be said to be undercapitalised.

---

enough money to cover their costs. So it is important to find out whether there are likely to be enough customers. There are two ways of researching the market.

- Desk research involves finding existing information about the market. For instance, a person wanting to set up a hairdressing salon might look in *Yellow Pages* at all the salons in the area to find the location. This information can be used to assess the likely competition.
- Field research involves finding information which is not available in books etc. For example, a person wanting to set up a hairdressing salon might interview customers at local salons to find out if they are happy with the service and how it could be improved. They may be asked to fill in a questionnaire about the new business and whether they would use its services.

Researching the product

Some people who set up their own business know exactly what they are going to sell and how they are going to sell it. Others, though, have to research their product. Jenny Ambrose knew that she would make her products from organic or reused materials. She had already used these materials in her college designs. For example, she made dresses from 100 per cent Indian cotton, hemp, and tencel, a form of wood pulp. Businesses also have to decide how the product will be produced. Jenny employed outworkers to manufacture her designs.

Finance

No business can be set up without finance. Jenny Ambrose received £2 000 in 2004 from the Fredericks

Foundation to start the business. The foundation also provided three expansion loans as the business developed. It also helped to find an investor to put £5 000 into the business. Jenny has also tried to keep costs down. There is no budget for advertising and she has been helped as models have been prepared to work in promotions for expenses and the exposure they give.

Jenny Ambrose has been very careful with finance. However, some people who start their own businesses underestimate the amount of money they will need to set up. They are often UNDER CAPITALISED and this causes problems as the business expands. Some businesses have the potential to be highly profitable but fail because they run out of cash at a crucial early stage in the life of the business. So it is important to work out how much money is needed to

Lara Nichols

Mike Nichols was made redundant. But today his cleaning business, Lara Nichols, is making £2 million a year. Set up in 2004, his wife had identified a problem about business cleaning when she was working part time. Mike thought that the problems of reliability of service might exist in many businesses. He phoned around local businesses and found this was the case. He also looked nationally at the problem and identified that many businesses faced difficulties in organising an efficient cleaning service.

Certain aspects of Mike's business are fairly unique. First, Mike hires students who are graduates as part time cleaners. After working for the firm he then employs them as managers. Many are in their early 20s and bring in new ideas to the business. Second, Mike has no formal contracts with customers. Businesses often have an arrangement that ties in the customers and business for a period of time. Third, Mike also has no franchise operations as many cleaning services do.

Source: adapted from BBC Working Lunch, 12.2.2007.

1 (a) Where did the idea for the business develop? (b) What research did Mike carry out before setting up the business?
2 Suggest THREE reasons why it is important that businesses stay clean.
3 For each of the 3 unique features of Mike's business explain ONE advantage and ONE disadvantage of running the business in this way.

start the business and identify where the money will come from.

Businesses can finance expansion by putting the profits they make back into the business. If there is not enough retained profit then they may have to take out a bank loan to expand the business further.

Identifying sources of help

Many new businesses don't survive for more than three years of trading. However, their chance of success is much greater if those setting up the business have received help from expert, either before the launch or in the early stages. Jenny Ambrose received help from the Princes Trust. This is an organisation which helps new businesses to set up and often provides grants or loans.

Many new small businesses turn to the local business link for help when first setting up or expanding. It can identify any grants, loans or other benefits that are available from government or bodies such as the Princes Trust. It can also organise training in setting up small businesses that is so vital to the survival of the business.

The business plan

Drawing up a business plan is very important. The business plan sets out how the business is to be set up and run. It contains projections of future sales, revenues and costs. It will include how the product is to be made or bought and how it is to be marketed.

Drawing up the business plan make sure that all aspects of the business have been researched and considered. It helps people to be more realistic about the problems they are likely to face when the business is to start trading. What is more, any applications for loans or grants will usually be supported by a business plan. So a business plan is crucial for financing the business.

Operating the business

Jenny Ambrose first set up Enamore while working in temporary jobs. She then began to work on her own, but employed outworkers to manufacture her designs. Initially, her designs were sold in shops. But as the business developed and the

designs became more popular she set up a website, enamore.co.uk, to expand her sales. Sales through the website are more profitable for the business. Although the budget for advertising is very limited she has been helped by models prepared to work for expenses. Her designs have also been shown at London fashion week which has helped to promote them to a wider audience.

All the time Jenny is having to think about designing new ranges, how the clothes will be made, financing the business and marketing her products. The environment in which businesses work is constantly changing. Businesses like Enamore need to adapt by changing themselves. For instance, Jenny Ambrose would like to expand her range in future. She would also like to be involved in manufacturing, perhaps in Fair Trade in countries like India.

Unless businesses change they will die. If however, they are constantly adapting to changing conditions they are likely to survive and prosper.

Source: adapted from BBC Working Lunch, 2.3.2007.

Checklist ✓

1 'Businesses are most likely to succeed when they are started by people who have experience and training in the business area already.' Why is this true?
2 How can someone research a market?
3 Suggest and explain TWO ways in which someone wanting to set up a health and fitness club might research the market.
4 How might a new business research the product it is going to sell?
5 Give TWO ways in which a business might find the money to set itself up in business.
6 What help is available to businesses setting up?
7 (a) What is a business plan? (b) How does a business plan help a business setting up?

key terms

Undercapitalised - lacking the necessary financial resources to allow a business to trade without getting into constant financial difficulties.

SUMMARY CASE STUDY

BUG BUSINESS

In early 2004 Ian Batten first got an interest in reptiles when he was at school. He received a present of a gecko for his birthday. Then he got two more and had the idea to breed them. Branching out, he looked around to find what other exotic animals people kept. The idea of breeding insects and selling them resulted even though he had no previous business experience. He started by selling some to pet shops. Then he moved on to selling insects online. A new business was starting to take shape in a niche market. It soon was doing well.

Ian sells a variety of bugs, including a Baby Chinese Mantis for 12p for beginners, a Giant Spiny Stick Insect originally from New Guinea £2.50 for small children and a Devils Flower Mantis for a more expensive £15. His website Insectstore.com is linked to Google. Ian sells insects from the site and gives advice on keeping them. Ian also has his own forum, Insectchat.com, where people can discuss insect matters. Other promotion comes in the form of emails to people about the website and also through word of mouth. Ian invests all profits back into the business buying computer equipment and more stock of insects.

Source: adapted from BBC Working Lunch, 16.2.2007.

1 'Ian is operating in a niche market'. What does this mean?
2 What research did Ian carry out when setting up his business?
3 Identify THREE factors that might influence the success of the business.
4 Discuss whether Ian's business is likely to be successful in the next few years.

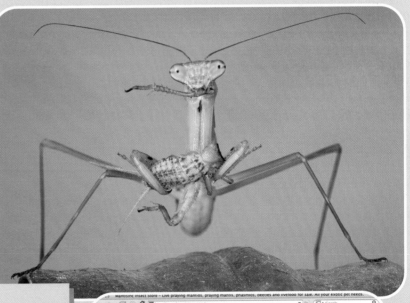

Table 1 *Ian Batten's turnover*

2004	£200
2005	£4 000
2006	£6 000
2007 target	£8 000

Making decisions

Businesses face constant pressures both internally and externally. To survive and prosper, they have to adapt to changing conditions. They have to decide how to change their business strategy in order to cope with changes such as new laws, new technology, increased competition or different foreign exchange rates.

HMV Group is one of the world's leading retailers of music and video. It is also the largest retailer of books in the UK. The company was created through a series of mergers. In 1998, HMV, the music and video business, Dillons the book store and Waterstones, also a book store, came together to form one company. The Dillons book stores were rebranded to become Waterstones stores. In 2006, HMV Media bought Ottakar's, another large chain of 143 book stores. In 2007, HMV operated over 730 stores worldwide including around 400 stores in the UK.

Internal pressures

HMV Group, like all businesses, faces **internal pressures**. An internal pressure is one which comes from within the business. For example, from 2006 HMV faced the challenge of how to integrate the Ottakar's book business with Waterstones. The company was looking for ways of cutting costs. It could do this, for example, by combining the buying power of Ottakar's and Waterstones. It could also make staff redundant where there was overlap of jobs.

HMV Group also faces other internal pressures. For example, HMV staff may expect a pay rise each year. How much will this be and where will HMV Group get the funds to pay for it? Will it come from lower profits, higher prices to customers or efficiency gains within the company?

External pressures

External pressures are pressures which come from outside the business. In 2007, HMV faced a number of serious external pressures on its business.

Competition The music, film and book retailing market is very competitive. Consumers have plenty of choice about where to buy their next CD, DVD or favourite book. Competition for HMV, though, has been growing recently. Supermarket chains like Tesco are selling increasing numbers of CDs, DVDs and books. Even more seriously, the Internet has directly hit sales at HMV stores. The book

and entertainment Internet seller, Amazon, has taken away market share from HMV. Apple's iTunes, which allows single tracks to be downloaded onto devices like the Apple iPod, has hit worldwide sales of physical CDs. Television companies like Sky are also hoping to eat into DVD sales by offering film download services. A 2006 forecast suggests that total world sales of CDs would be down 26 per

BA

British Airways (BA) is facing a crisis today. Talks with unions represent 11 000 flight attendants have collapsed. As a result, the flight attendants have gone on strike. BA has been forced to cancel all its 1 300 fights out Heathrow and Gatwick airports for two days. 154 000 passengers can no longer fly BA and will have to make alternative travel arrangements. The cost to BA in lost sales revenues could rise to up to £100 million.

The dispute mainly centres around two issues. One issue is about sick leave policy. BA's management and trade unions can't agree on the terms for allowing workers to take sick leave. The other issue is about a two-tier pay structure which now exists. Flight attendants who have worked for BA for a long time are being paid substantially more than those who joined recently the airline. BA wants to sort out this problem when pay is next negotiated with the trade unions. The trade unions want to agree a deal on this issue now.

Source: adapted from the *Guardian* 25.1.2007.

1 Using this case as an example, explain what is meant by internal pressures.
2 What might be the possible costs of the dispute to BA in: (a) the short term; (b) the long term?

cent by 2010 and DVD sales would be down 17 per cent. In 2006, HMV was already under pressure with falling sales and falling profits.

New technology The Internet is a new technology. It poses a major threat to HMV with its wordwide chain of stores. Equally, it is an opportunity. HMV has set up its own website where it sells products online. The problem is that HMV has a much smaller market share of online sales than the market share of CDs, DVDs and books sold from stores in the UK. If more and more CDs, DVDs and books are sold online and fewer bought from stores, then it is likely to see falling sales overall in the future.

New products Rival businesses like Amazon are offering a one-stop shop to buy a variety of products including CDs, DVDs and electronic games. Electronic games for games consoles like PlayStation 3, Nintendo's Wii and Microsoft Xbox are sold in packages very similar to those of CDs and DVDs. So moving into the electronic games market is a natural extension of its more

Figure 1 *Financial Statistics, HMV Media Group.*

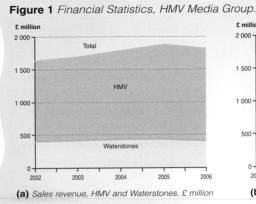
(a) *Sales revenue, HMV and Waterstones, £ million*

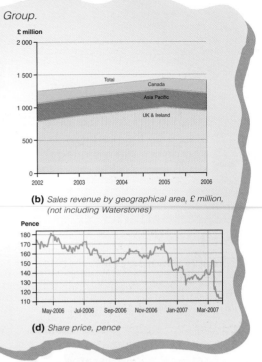
(b) *Sales revenue by geographical area, £ million, (not including Waterstones)*

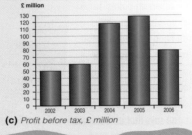
(c) *Profit before tax, £ million*

(d) *Share price, pence*

traditional range of products for HMV. Competitive pressure is forcing HMV to increase sales in this area as its more traditional CD and DVD markets decline.

New sites The major supermarket chains are taking market share away from HMV. New supermarket sites

are opened each year. One way for HMV to respond to this external pressure is also to increase the number of its stores. If there is an HMV store in your local shopping centre, you are less likely to buy a CD, DVD or game from the supermarket. HMV has been expanding its number of stores in the UK particularly in medium-sized towns where previously there had been no HMV store.

Stakeholders

HMV, like any large company, has a number of stakeholders - groups who have an interest in the business. There are the managers, under pressure to increase sales and cut costs. Workers want to see their working conditions improved. They might be worried that the difficulties in their company could put their job at risk. Governments of the countries where HMV has stores will want the company to grow, creating prosperity for its citizens and contributing taxes. Governments, along with environmental groups, will also monitor new store locations. Customers want high quality books, DVDs, CDs and games at competitive prices. Suppliers are reliant on HMV for orders.

Jessops

Jessops, the camera retailer, announced a third profits warning in as many months in March 2007. It has suffered severely at the hands of the camera-equipped mobile phone. The announcement suggests the future of the company is in question. The shares fell 70 per cent. Jessops was floated at 155p in October 2004 when the company was worth £160 million.

The photography retailer says it is conducting a 'strategic review'. But given tough market conditions, it is not clear who might want to buy Jessops out of its problems. A statement said prices have collapsed, leading in February to a 16 per cent fall by value in sales of digital cameras and a 22 per cent fall in camcorders.

Jessops said: 'Market conditions have continued to deteriorate since the group's last trading statement.' Its strategic review is being led by chief executive Chris Langley, while chairman Gavin Simonds is quitting the board.

Source: adapted from www.thisismoney.co.uk.

1 How has Jessops been affected by external pressures?

2 What might happen to Jessops in the future?

The owners of the company, the shareholders, are also very important. The directors of HMV are answerable to the shareholders to protect their interests. The company's performance in 2005 and 2006 was disappointing. This can be seen in Figure 1. So there was pressure on the management team to come up with a strategy which would improve the returns to shareholders.

Restructuring the company

The management at HMV needed to make changes in 2007 to deal with its problems. In March 2007, it announced a restructuring programme. It planned to make a number of changes to the way in which the company operated.

- Up to 30 less well performing Waterstones book shops would be closed.
- More space in Waterstones book shops would be given to products which had high profit margins. In contrast, some low profit margin books would be taken off the shelves to make space. Out would go some academic books. In would come more novels, cookery and children's books.
- The distribution systems for HMV and Waterstones would be merged giving one centralised system. The distribution system is how products get from the book publishers and record companies into HMV and Waterstones stores. A single system should save money.
- Loyalty cards would be issued for customers, giving them money off every time they made a purchase. This would encourage customers to shop at HMV and Waterstones rather than at rival stores.
- HMV would stock a wider range of digital music products such as iPods and there would be instore booths to burn CDs.
- A new type of HMV store with a different layout, carrying slightly different products would be piloted to see if a new format could raise sales.
- Money would be spent on advertising the two online stores, HMV.co.uk and Waterstones.com. This would be crucial to combating the threat from online stores like Amazon.
- A new social networking site on the Internet is planned.

All these measures are aimed at increasing sales revenues, cutting costs and increasing profit. HMV Media Group recognised that, to survive, it had to change. Whether the changes are big enough remains to be seen.

Source: adapted from the HMV website, www.hmv.co.uk and the *Guardian*, 14.3.2007.

Battery recycling

In 2006, the EU agreed the wording to a future directive to make recycling of batteries compulsory from 2008. The directive will ban most batteries with more than a trace of the toxic chemicals cadmium or mercury. It says a quarter of all used batteries must be collected by 2012, rising to 45% by 2016 and that at least half of them must be recycled. It also says all batteries must be clearly labelled to show how long they will last, from 2009 onwards. EU Environment Commissioner Stavros Dimas said 'The faster we start to collect and recycle batteries, the better for the environment'.

The directive called for 'collection points' to be set up where consumers can hand in used batteries from toys, computers or mobile phones. Shops must collect used batteries from consumers at no extra cost. It also says that all batteries must be removable, and that all producers of batteries must be registered. The cost of implementing the new rules will be paid for by industry.

Only six EU countries had systems to collect all types of used portable batteries in 2006. In 2002 the collection rates were 59% in Belgium, 55% in Sweden, 44% in Austria, 39% in Germany, 32% in the Netherlands, and 16% in France'.

Source: adapted from news.bbc.co.uk, 3.5.2006.

1 Explain whether the battery recycling directive is an internal or external pressure for shops and battery manufacturers.
2 Discuss how legislation to make recycling compulsory could affect (a) consumers; (b) shops; (c) local communities; (d) recycling businesses; (e) battery manufacturers; (f) toy manufacturers.
3 Discuss whether legislation should be passed to make all batteries recyclable.

Checklist ✓

1 Explain THREE examples of internal pressures facing a business.
2 What is the difference between internal and external pressures on a business?
3 Why might an increase in the numbers of people aged 75 plus in the population affect drugs companies?
4 Explain TWO ways in which a company might cope with a change from a boom economy into a slump.
5 A company is performing well and last year made record profits. How might the different stakeholders in a company want to see the company change now?
6 A company is in difficulties. (a) How could rationalisation of the company help it out of those difficulties? (b) Who do you think would stand to lose most from any rationalisation?
7 How might a merger improve the performance of a company?

SUMMARY CASE STUDY

GREGGS RESTRUCTURING

Greggs, the UK's biggest bakery chain, announced in March 2007 that pre-tax profits for 2006 fell 19.8 per cent to £40.2 million. This included a £3.5 million cost of restructuring its Bakers Oven chain, which operates in Scotland and the north of England. Rising energy prices also put pressure on profits.

In 2006, Greggs announced the restructuring of Bakers Oven in the North and Scotland, involving the closure of these two divisions and the transfer of 49 of their shops either to the Greggs brand or to the successful Bakers Oven Midlands operation. A further 14 poorly performing shops were closed. These changes have been made and profits are expected to rise by £1.25 million per annum from 2007.

48 new shops were opened during the year and 31 were closed, giving a net increase of 17 units to a total of 1,336. There were a larger number of closures than usual as a result of the restructuring. Also, Greggs completed 29 comprehensive shop refurbishments and 24 minor refits during the year. The company is also testing other products, including hot breakfasts and a range of sandwiches aimed at health-conscious shoppers. It is also planning to increase its marketing spend, and looking to open more outlets to push its reach beyond the high street.

Sir Michael Darrington, Greggs' managing director, said that 2006 had been a 'challenging year'. 'We are taking clear steps to address the difficulties we encountered in 2006, and have initiated a programme of change that will build on the enormous fundamental strengths of the group. This will help us to develop an even more responsive and cost-effective business that can satisfy the needs of customers, employees and shareholders alike,' he said.

Source: adapted from the *Guardian* 12.3.2007 and www.ir.greggs.plc.uk

1 What is meant by restructuring?
2 Describe the restructuring that took place at Greggs.
3 State two external pressures that Greggs is responding to.
4 What effect did the restructuring have on the profits of Greggs?
5 Do you think Greggs' stakeholders will benefit from the changes at Greggs?

Index

Page references which appear in colour are defined in the Key Terms sections in each unit.